W9-BKY-214

Use These Tabs to Navigate This Book

All the forms found in this book along with many others are available for download from the website that supports this book. Go to **www.entrepreneur.com/formnet** to learn more.

ULTIMATE BOOK OF BUSINESS AND LEGAL FORMS FOR STARTUPS

200+ Downloadable Forms and Spreadsheets

KAREN THOMAS

Entrepreneur Press

Publisher: Jere Calmes
Cover Design: Beth Hanson-Winter
Composition: CWL Publishing Enterprises, Inc., Madison, Wisconsin, www.cwlpub.com

This publication is designed to provide accurate and authoritative information in regard to the subject matter
covered. It is sold with the understanding that the publisher is not engaged in rendering legal, accounting, or
other professional services. If legal advice or other expert assistance is required, the services of a competent
professional person should be sought.

> −From a Declaration of Principles jointly adopted by a
> Committee of the American Bar Association and
> a Committee of Publishers and Associations

ISBN 13: 978-1-59918-389-3
        10: 1-59918-389-7

Library of Congress Cataloging-in-Publication Data

Thomas, Karen (Karen M.), 1979-
    Ultimate book of business and legal forms for startups / by Karen Thomas.
        p. cm.
    Rev. ed. of: Ultimate book of business forms.
    ISBN-13: 978-1-59918-389-3 (alk. paper)
    ISBN-10: 1-59918-389-7
    1. New business enterprises—Law and legislation—United States—Forms.
    I. Thomas, Karen (Karen M.), 1979—Ultimate book of business forms. II. Title. III. Series.
    KF1355.A65T48 2010b
    346.73'0650269--dc22

                                                                        2010016454

Printed in the U.S.A.

14 13 12 11   10 9 8 7 6 5 4 3 2 1

Contents

Preface

The Ultimate Book of Business and Legal Forms for Startups is a compilation of essential legal forms for small business owners, both new and veteran, as well as their employees whose responsibilities include the handling and/or enforcement of legal documents. Unlike any other small business legal reference guide, this book includes many custom legal forms created by practicing business attorneys who specialize in business structures, business law, legal contracts, partnerships, franchising, estate planning, and more. Each chapter addresses specific legal issues that a business owner may not see coming that can cause them problems down the road. While this book encompasses several legal topics, it is not meant to replace professional advice—but it is designed to help you identify when you will need such advice.

The legal landscape small business owners and their employees face is not the easiest to navigate, and when revenue generation is the priority, maintaining legal compliance can unintentionally fall by the wayside. Structuring and enforcing legal compliance is not an easy task. Business owners must keep up on changes in individual state laws, human resource-related policy, internet legalities, and that's just assuming the business already exists. A number of laws mandate how a business is started and operated, and compliance is mandatory. This book was researched and organized to enable a small business to be operated not only legally—but proactively.

The scope of the book covers legal issues every business owner should know from legally filing the structure of the business to establishing a culture of business ethics to protecting it should you be sued or summoned to court. The chapters include legal forms, legal worksheets, and legal reference guides that are to be used for reference and in a preventive manner. In addition, you can download and customize these forms to adhere to your specific business purposes at the website that supports this book.

Supporting Website

Every small business is unique. Therefore it's essential to have business forms that are customizable depending on your business's needs. The forms included in this book can be found online at **www.entrepreneur.com/formnet**. Forms will be available in the following formats: Word, Excel, and PDF, and can be completely customized to match your business's brand, processes, and culture.

This book can be used as your reference guide as you work with each customizable form. Refer to the book to understand when and how to use the forms. There are hundreds of forms at your disposal, and each one serves a specific purpose that will help streamline business processes and maximize time.

Finding the forms online is easy. Simply visit the site, **www.entrepreneur.com/formnet**, select the appropriate forms category, and download as many forms as you need from each. There's no cost or special code required to access and customize these forms for your business.

About the Author

Karen Thomas is an accomplished writer who has much experience in business and technical writing. Thomas reported for the *Orange County Register*, published business and startup books with Entrepreneur Press, and continues to produce technical and consumer-friendly articles for several online properties. In addition to authoring business books, Thomas is the creative director at Affnet, Inc., an Orange County-based marketing and technological firm.

Acknowledgments

I would like to thank Jere Calmes and the team at Entrepreneur Press for allowing me this opportunity to put together the *Ultimate Book of Business and Legal Forms for Startups*. Their innate understanding of a small business owner's needs is proven in each Entrepreneur Press publication including the *Ultimate Book of Business and Legal Forms for Startups*, which strives to be the go-to legal reference for small business owners who don't have time to sift through irrelevant online search results, or fund daily calls with legal counsel. This is the book to help the small business owner operate legally and still have the time to focus on the bottom line.

CHAPTER 1

Legal Forms to Establish a Sole Proprietorship

THE GOOD NEWS ABOUT STARTING A BUSIness solo is that there are only a few forms you need to file to get started. The sole proprietorship is essentially the simplest form of business. The definition of a *sole proprietorship* is that it's an operation of one person in business for profit. The distinction between the sole proprietor and the business itself is that there is no distinction. This means that the sole proprietor's personal assets are at risk for the debts, obligations, and judgments of the business.

To get your sole proprietorship off and running, the first thing to do is name your business and file a *Fictitious Business Name Statement* by registering the name of your business in the county where you do business.

This chapter provides a sample form *SS-4*, which provides a sole proprietor with an Employer Identification Number (EIN). Regardless of the number of businesses operated, a sole proprietor should file only one Form SS-4 and needs only one EIN. Once you receive your EIN, you can put it to use immediately. As a sole proprietor, an EIN enables you to open a bank account, apply for business licenses, and file your tax return.

When it comes time to pay taxes, sole proprietors use form 1040 just as one would to file personal income taxes. Refer to the *Sample Form 1040* to view the information required by this form. In addition to Form 1040, we included *Sample Form 1040 Schedule C*, which must be filed to report income or loss from a business operated by a sole proprietor.

1. IRS Form SS-4, Application for Employer Identification Number

Form **SS-4** (Rev. January 2010) Department of the Treasury Internal Revenue Service	**Application for Employer Identification Number** (For use by employers, corporations, partnerships, trusts, estates, churches, government agencies, Indian tribal entities, certain individuals, and others.) ▶ See separate instructions for each line. ▶ Keep a copy for your records.	OMB No. 1545-0003 EIN

Type or print clearly.

1	Legal name of entity (or individual) for whom the EIN is being requested

2	Trade name of business (if different from name on line 1)	3	Executor, administrator, trustee, "care of" name

4a	Mailing address (room, apt., suite no. and street, or P.O. box)	5a	Street address (if different) (Do not enter a P.O. box.)

4b	City, state, and ZIP code (if foreign, see instructions)	5b	City, state, and ZIP code (if foreign, see instructions)

6	County and state where principal business is located

7a	Name of responsible party	7b	SSN, ITIN, or EIN

8a	Is this application for a limited liability company (LLC) (or a foreign equivalent)? . . . . ☐ Yes ☐ No	8b	If 8a is "Yes," enter the number of LLC members . . . . ▶

8c	If 8a is "Yes," was the LLC organized in the United States? . . . . ☐ Yes ☐ No

9a Type of entity (check only one box). **Caution.** If 8a is "Yes," see the instructions for the correct box to check.

☐ Sole proprietor (SSN) _____
☐ Partnership
☐ Corporation (enter form number to be filed) ▶ _____
☐ Personal service corporation
☐ Church or church-controlled organization
☐ Other nonprofit organization (specify) ▶ _____
☐ Other (specify) ▶

☐ Estate (SSN of decedent) _____
☐ Plan administrator (TIN) _____
☐ Trust (TIN of grantor) _____
☐ National Guard   ☐ State/local government
☐ Farmers' cooperative   ☐ Federal government/military
☐ REMIC   ☐ Indian tribal governments/enterprises
Group Exemption Number (GEN) if any ▶

9b	If a corporation, name the state or foreign country (if applicable) where incorporated	State	Foreign country

10 Reason for applying (check only one box)

☐ Started new business (specify type) ▶ _____
☐ Hired employees (Check the box and see line 13.)
☐ Compliance with IRS withholding regulations
☐ Other (specify) ▶

☐ Banking purpose (specify purpose) ▶ _____
☐ Changed type of organization (specify new type) ▶ _____
☐ Purchased going business
☐ Created a trust (specify type) ▶ _____
☐ Created a pension plan (specify type) ▶ _____

11	Date business started or acquired (month, day, year). See instructions.	12	Closing month of accounting year

13	Highest number of employees expected in the next 12 months (enter -0- if none). If no employees expected, skip line 14.	14	If you expect your employment tax liability to be $1,000 or less in a full calendar year **and** want to file Form 944 annually instead of Forms 941 quarterly, check here. (Your employment tax liability generally will be $1,000 or less if you expect to pay $4,000 or less in total wages.) If you do not check this box, you must file Form 941 for every quarter. ☐

Agricultural	Household	Other

15	First date wages or annuities were paid (month, day, year). **Note.** If applicant is a withholding agent, enter date income will first be paid to nonresident alien (month, day, year) . . . . ▶

16 Check **one** box that best describes the principal activity of your business.

☐ Construction   ☐ Rental & leasing   ☐ Transportation & warehousing
☐ Real estate   ☐ Manufacturing   ☐ Finance & insurance

☐ Health care & social assistance   ☐ Wholesale-agent/broker
☐ Accommodation & food service   ☐ Wholesale-other   ☐ Retail
☐ Other (specify)

17	Indicate principal line of merchandise sold, specific construction work done, products produced, or services provided.

18	Has the applicant entity shown on line 1 ever applied for and received an EIN? ☐ Yes ☐ No If "Yes," write previous EIN here ▶

Third Party Designee	Complete this section **only** if you want to authorize the named individual to receive the entity's EIN and answer questions about the completion of this form.	
	Designee's name	Designee's telephone number (include area code) ( )
	Address and ZIP code	Designee's fax number (include area code) ( )

Under penalties of perjury, I declare that I have examined this application, and to the best of my knowledge and belief, it is true, correct, and complete.

Name and title (type or print clearly) ▶ _____ | Applicant's telephone number (include area code)
( )

Signature ▶ _____ Date ▶ _____ | Applicant's fax number (include area code)
( )

For Privacy Act and Paperwork Reduction Act Notice, see separate instructions.   Cat. No. 16055N   Form **SS-4** (Rev. 1-2010)

2. IRS Form 1040 Schedule C, Profit or Loss from Business

SCHEDULE C
(Form 1040)

Department of the Treasury
Internal Revenue Service (99)

Profit or Loss From Business
(Sole Proprietorship)

▶ Partnerships, joint ventures, etc., generally must file Form 1065 or 1065-B.

▶ **Attach to Form 1040, 1040NR, or 1041.**   ▶ See Instructions for Schedule C (Form 1040).

OMB No. 1545-0074

20**09**

Attachment
Sequence No. **09**

Name of proprietor | Social security number (SSN)

A Principal business or profession, including product or service (see page C-2 of the instructions) | **B** Enter code from pages C-9, 10, & 11 ▶

C Business name. If no separate business name, leave blank. | **D** Employer ID number (EIN), if any

E Business address (including suite or room no.) ▶ ‑‑‑
City, town or post office, state, and ZIP code

F Accounting method: **(1)** ☐ Cash   **(2)** ☐ Accrual   **(3)** ☐ Other (specify) ▶ ‑‑‑‑‑‑‑‑‑‑‑‑‑‑‑‑‑‑‑‑‑‑‑‑‑‑‑‑‑‑‑

G Did you "materially participate" in the operation of this business during 2009? If "No," see page C-3 for limit on losses   ☐ Yes   ☐ No

H If you started or acquired this business during 2009, check here . . . . ▶ ☐

Part I   Income

1	Gross receipts or sales. **Caution.** See page C-4 and check the box if:		
	• This income was reported to you on Form W-2 and the "Statutory employee" box on that form was checked, or		
	• You are a member of a qualified joint venture reporting only rental real estate income not subject to self-employment tax. Also see page C-3 for limit on losses.	. . ▶ ☐	**1**
2	Returns and allowances		**2**
3	Subtract line 2 from line 1		**3**
4	Cost of goods sold (from line 42 on page 2)		**4**
5	**Gross profit.** Subtract line 4 from line 3		**5**
6	Other income, including federal and state gasoline or fuel tax credit or refund (see page C-4)		**6**
7	**Gross income.** Add lines 5 and 6 . . . . ▶		**7**

Part II   Expenses.   Enter expenses for business use of your home **only** on line 30.

8	Advertising	**8**		18	Office expense	**18**	
9	Car and truck expenses (see page C-4)	**9**		19	Pension and profit-sharing plans .	**19**	
				20	Rent or lease (see page C-6):		
10	Commissions and fees .	**10**		**a**	Vehicles, machinery, and equipment	**20a**	
11	Contract labor (see page C-4)	**11**		**b**	Other business property . . .	**20b**	
12	Depletion	**12**		21	Repairs and maintenance . . .	**21**	
13	Depreciation and section 179 expense deduction (not included in Part III) (see page C-5)	**13**		22	Supplies (not included in Part III) .	**22**	
				23	Taxes and licenses	**23**	
				24	Travel, meals, and entertainment:		
				a	Travel	**24a**	
14	Employee benefit programs (other than on line 19) . .	**14**		**b**	Deductible meals and entertainment (see page C-6) . .	**24b**	
15	Insurance (other than health)	**15**		25	Utilities	**25**	
16	Interest:			26	Wages (less employment credits) .	**26**	
a	Mortgage (paid to banks, etc.)	**16a**		27	Other expenses (from line 48 on page 2)	**27**	
b	Other	**16b**					
17	Legal and professional services	**17**					

28	**Total expenses** before expenses for business use of home. Add lines 8 through 27 . . . . . ▶	**28**	
29	Tentative profit or (loss). Subtract line 28 from line 7	**29**	
30	Expenses for business use of your home. Attach **Form 8829**	**30**	
31	Net profit or (loss). Subtract line 30 from line 29.		
	• If a profit, enter on both **Form 1040, line 12,** and **Schedule SE, line 2,** or on **Form 1040NR, line 13** (if you checked the box on line 1, see page C-7). Estates and trusts, enter on **Form 1041, line 3.**	**31**	
	• If a loss, you **must** go to line 32.		
32	If you have a loss, check the box that describes your investment in this activity (see page C-7).		
	• If you checked 32a, enter the loss on both **Form 1040, line 12,** and **Schedule SE, line 2,** or on **Form 1040NR, line 13** (if you checked the box on line 1, see the line 31 instructions on page C-7). Estates and trusts, enter on **Form 1041, line 3.**	**32a** ☐ All investment is at risk.	
	• If you checked 32b, you **must** attach **Form 6198.** Your loss may be limited.	**32b** ☐ Some investment is not at risk.	

For Paperwork Reduction Act Notice, see page C-9 of the instructions.   Cat. No. 11334P   Schedule C (Form 1040) 2009

Schedule C (Form 1040) 2009   Page **2**

Part III   **Cost of Goods Sold** (see page C-8)

33   Method(s) used to value closing inventory: **a** ☐ Cost   **b** ☐ Lower of cost or market   **c** ☐ Other (attach explanation)

34   Was there any change in determining quantities, costs, or valuations between opening and closing inventory?
If "Yes," attach explanation . . . .   ☐ **Yes**   ☐ **No**

35 Inventory at beginning of year. If different from last year's closing inventory, attach explanation . . .	**35**	
36 Purchases less cost of items withdrawn for personal use	**36**	
37 Cost of labor. Do not include any amounts paid to yourself	**37**	
38 Materials and supplies	**38**	
39 Other costs	**39**	
40 Add lines 35 through 39	**40**	
41 Inventory at end of year	**41**	
42 **Cost of goods sold.** Subtract line 41 from line 40. Enter the result here and on page 1, line 4 . . .	**42**	

Part IV   **Information on Your Vehicle.** Complete this part **only** if you are claiming car or truck expenses on line 9 and are not required to file Form 4562 for this business. See the instructions for line 13 on page C-5 to find out if you must file Form 4562.

43   When did you place your vehicle in service for business purposes? (month, day, year)   ▶   ___/___/___

44   Of the total number of miles you drove your vehicle during 2009, enter the number of miles you used your vehicle for:

   a Business _____   **b** Commuting (see instructions) _____   **c** Other _____

45   Was your vehicle available for personal use during off-duty hours? . . . . ☐ **Yes**   ☐ **No**

46   Do you (or your spouse) have another vehicle available for personal use?. . . . . ☐ **Yes**   ☐ **No**

47a   Do you have evidence to support your deduction? . . . . ☐ **Yes**   ☐ **No**

   b If "Yes," is the evidence written? . . . . ☐ **Yes**   ☐ **No**

Part V   **Other Expenses.** List below business expenses not included on lines 8–26 or line 30.

_____		
_____		
_____		
_____		
_____		
_____		
_____		
_____		
48 **Total other expenses.** Enter here and on page 1, line 27	**48**	

Schedule C (Form 1040) 2009

3. IRS Form 1040, U.S. Individual Tax Return

Form 1040

Department of the Treasury—Internal Revenue Service

U.S. Individual Income Tax Return **2009** (99) IRS Use Only—Do not write or staple in this space.

For the year Jan. 1–Dec. 31, 2009, or other tax year beginning , 2009, ending , 20 | OMB No. 1545-0074

Label

(See instructions on page 14.)

Use the IRS label.

Otherwise, please print or type.

L A B E L H E R E		
Your first name and initial	Last name	Your social security number
If a joint return, spouse's first name and initial	Last name	Spouse's social security number
Home address (number and street). If you have a P.O. box, see page 14.	Apt. no.	You **must** enter your SSN(s) above. ▲
City, town or post office, state, and ZIP code. If you have a foreign address, see page 14.		Checking a box below will not change your tax or refund.

Presidential Election Campaign ▶ Check here if you, or your spouse if filing jointly, want $3 to go to this fund (see page 14) ▶ ☐ You ☐ Spouse

Filing Status

Check only one box.

1 ☐ Single
2 ☐ Married filing jointly (even if only one had income)
3 ☐ Married filing separately. Enter spouse's SSN above and full name here. ▶
4 ☐ Head of household (with qualifying person). (See page 15.) If the qualifying person is a child but not your dependent, enter this child's name here. ▶
5 ☐ Qualifying widow(er) with dependent child (see page 16)

Exemptions

6a ☐ **Yourself.** If someone can claim you as a dependent, **do not** check box 6a . . . . .
b ☐ **Spouse** . . . .
c **Dependents:**

(1) First name Last name	(2) Dependent's social security number	(3) Dependent's relationship to you	(4) ✓ if qualifying child for child tax credit (see page 17)
			☐
			☐
			☐
			☐

If more than four dependents, see page 17 and check here ▶ ☐

Boxes checked on 6a and 6b

No. of children on 6c who:
• lived with you
• did not live with you due to divorce or separation (see page 18)

Dependents on 6c not entered above

Add numbers on lines above ▶

d Total number of exemptions claimed . . . .

Income

Attach Form(s) W-2 here. Also attach Forms W-2G and 1099-R if tax was withheld.

If you did not get a W-2, see page 22.

Enclose, but do not attach, any payment. Also, please use Form 1040-V.

7	Wages, salaries, tips, etc. Attach Form(s) W-2	7
8a	**Taxable** interest. Attach Schedule B if required	8a
b	**Tax-exempt** interest. **Do not** include on line 8a . . . 8b	
9a	Ordinary dividends. Attach Schedule B if required	9a
b	Qualified dividends (see page 22) 9b	
10	Taxable refunds, credits, or offsets of state and local income taxes (see page 23) . .	10
11	Alimony received	11
12	Business income or (loss). Attach Schedule C or C-EZ	12
13	Capital gain or (loss). Attach Schedule D if required. If not required, check here ▶ ☐	13
14	Other gains or (losses). Attach Form 4797	14
15a	IRA distributions . 15a b Taxable amount (see page 24)	15b
16a	Pensions and annuities 16a b Taxable amount (see page 25)	16b
17	Rental real estate, royalties, partnerships, S corporations, trusts, etc. Attach Schedule E	17
18	Farm income or (loss). Attach Schedule F	18
19	Unemployment compensation in excess of $2,400 per recipient (see page 27) . . .	19
20a	Social security benefits 20a b Taxable amount (see page 27)	20b
21	Other income. List type and amount (see page 29)	21
22	Add the amounts in the far right column for lines 7 through 21. This is your **total income** ▶	22

Adjusted Gross Income

23	Educator expenses (see page 29) 23	
24	Certain business expenses of reservists, performing artists, and fee-basis government officials. Attach Form 2106 or 2106-EZ 24	
25	Health savings account deduction. Attach Form 8889 . 25	
26	Moving expenses. Attach Form 3903 26	
27	One-half of self-employment tax. Attach Schedule SE . 27	
28	Self-employed SEP, SIMPLE, and qualified plans . 28	
29	Self-employed health insurance deduction (see page 30) 29	
30	Penalty on early withdrawal of savings 30	
31a	Alimony paid b Recipient's SSN ▶ 31a	
32	IRA deduction (see page 31) 32	
33	Student loan interest deduction (see page 34) . . . 33	
34	Tuition and fees deduction. Attach Form 8917 . . . 34	
35	Domestic production activities deduction. Attach Form 8903 35	
36	Add lines 23 through 31a and 32 through 35	36
37	Subtract line 36 from line 22. This is your **adjusted gross income** . . . . . ▶	37

For Disclosure, Privacy Act, and Paperwork Reduction Act Notice, see page 97. Cat. No. 11320B Form **1040** (2009)

Form 1040 (2009)   Page **2**

Tax and Credits	38	Amount from line 37 (adjusted gross income)	38	
	39a	Check if: ☐ **You** were born before January 2, 1945, ☐ Blind. / ☐ **Spouse** was born before January 2, 1945, ☐ Blind. } **Total boxes checked ▶ 39a**		
Standard Deduction for—	b	If your spouse itemizes on a separate return or you were a dual-status alien, see page 35 and check here ▶ 39b ☐		
	40a	**Itemized deductions** (from Schedule A) **or** your **standard deduction** (see left margin)	40a	
• People who check any box on line 39a, 39b, or 40b **or** who can be claimed as a dependent, see page 35.	b	If you are increasing your standard deduction by certain real estate taxes, new motor vehicle taxes, or a net disaster loss, attach Schedule L and check here (see page 35) . ▶ 40b☐		
	41	Subtract line 40a from line 38	41	
	42	**Exemptions.** If line 38 is $125,100 or less and you did not provide housing to a Midwestern displaced individual, multiply $3,650 by the number on line 6d. Otherwise, see page 37	42	
	43	**Taxable income.** Subtract line 42 from line 41. If line 42 is more than line 41, enter -0-	43	
• All others:	44	**Tax** (see page 37). Check if any tax is from: a ☐ Form(s) 8814 b ☐ Form 4972	44	
Single or Married filing separately, $5,700	45	**Alternative minimum tax** (see page 40). Attach Form 6251	45	
	46	Add lines 44 and 45 . ▶	46	
Married filing jointly or Qualifying widow(er), $11,400	47	Foreign tax credit. Attach Form 1116 if required	47	
	48	Credit for child and dependent care expenses. Attach Form 2441	48	
	49	Education credits from Form 8863, line 29	49	
Head of household, $8,350	50	Retirement savings contributions credit. Attach Form 8880	50	
	51	Child tax credit (see page 42)	51	
	52	Credits from Form: a ☐ 8396 b ☐ 8839 c ☐ 5695	52	
	53	Other credits from Form: a ☐ 3800 b ☐ 8801 c ☐	53	
	54	Add lines 47 through 53. These are your **total credits**	54	
	55	Subtract line 54 from line 46. If line 54 is more than line 46, enter -0- ▶	55	
Other Taxes	56	Self-employment tax. Attach Schedule SE	56	
	57	Unreported social security and Medicare tax from Form: a ☐ 4137 b ☐ 8919	57	
	58	Additional tax on IRAs, other qualified retirement plans, etc. Attach Form 5329 if required	58	
	59	Additional taxes: a ☐ AEIC payments b ☐ Household employment taxes. Attach Schedule H	59	
	60	Add lines 55 through 59. This is your **total tax** ▶	60	
Payments	61	Federal income tax withheld from Forms W-2 and 1099	61	
	62	2009 estimated tax payments and amount applied from 2008 return	62	
	63	Making work pay and government retiree credits. Attach Schedule M	63	
If you have a qualifying child, attach Schedule EIC.	64a	**Earned income credit (EIC)**	64a	
	b	Nontaxable combat pay election 64b		
	65	Additional child tax credit. Attach Form 8812	65	
	66	Refundable education credit from Form 8863, line 16	66	
	67	First-time homebuyer credit. Attach Form 5405	67	
	68	Amount paid with request for extension to file (see page 72)	68	
	69	Excess social security and tier 1 RRTA tax withheld (see page 72)	69	
	70	Credits from Form: a ☐ 2439 b ☐ 4136 c ☐ 8801 d ☐ 8885 70		
	71	Add lines 61, 62, 63, 64a, and 65 through 70. These are your **total payments** . ▶	71	
Refund	72	If line 71 is more than line 60, subtract line 60 from line 71. This is the amount you **overpaid**	72	
Direct deposit? See page 73 and fill in 73b, 73c, and 73d, or Form 8888.	73a	Amount of line 72 you want **refunded to you.** If Form 8888 is attached, check here . ▶ ☐	73a	
	▶ b	Routing number ▶ c Type: ☐ Checking ☐ Savings		
	▶ d	Account number		
	74	Amount of line 72 you want **applied to your 2010 estimated tax** ▶ 74		
Amount You Owe	75	**Amount you owe.** Subtract line 71 from line 60. For details on how to pay, see page 74 . ▶	75	
	76	Estimated tax penalty (see page 74) 76		

Third Party Designee

Do you want to allow another person to discuss this return with the IRS (see page 75)? ☐ **Yes.** Complete the following. ☐ **No**

Designee's name ▶   Phone no. ▶   Personal identification number (PIN) ▶

Sign Here

Under penalties of perjury, I declare that I have examined this return and accompanying schedules and statements, and to the best of my knowledge and belief, they are true, correct, and complete. Declaration of preparer (other than taxpayer) is based on all information of which preparer has any knowledge.

Joint return? See page 15. Keep a copy for your records.

Your signature	Date	Your occupation	Daytime phone number
Spouse's signature. If a joint return, **both** must sign.	Date	Spouse's occupation	

Paid Preparer's Use Only

Preparer's signature ▶	Date	Check if self-employed ☐	Preparer's SSN or PTIN
Firm's name (or yours if self-employed), address, and ZIP code ▶		EIN	
		Phone no.	

Form **1040** (2009)

CHAPTER 2

Legal Forms to Establish an LLC

THE *LLC-1, CALIFORNIA LLC ARTICLES OF Organization* is the form required in the State of California to organize and register a limited liability company. Each state requires a different form. The *Sample Letter to Secretary of State Accompanying Articles of Organization* is a simple cover letter that you should include when submitting LLC papers to the Secretary of State.

A *registered agent* is a person or entity authorized and obligated to receive legal papers on behalf of an LLC. *The Sample Letter to Registered Agent Accompanying Articles of Organization* is a simple cover letter that you should deliver to your registered agent upon the organization of your LLC.

LLCs are managed in one of two ways, either "member-managed" or "manager-managed." Member-managed LLCs are governed by the LLC's owners (members) equally, like a standard partnership. Manager-managed LLCs are governed by one or more appointed managers who often need not be members of the LLC. This manner of management by appointment is called "representative management." Manager-managed LLCs are managed much like corporations—with an appointed body of persons other than the company's ownership. The body of managers that undertakes governing responsibilities can come in the form of a board of managers or a committee of managers. Thus, the *Short-Form Operating Agreement for Member-Managed LLC* and the *Long-Form Agreement for Member-Managed LLC* are the short and long versions of operating agreements for member-managed LLCs.

The *Membership Ledger* is a written table showing the owners of an LLC. The ledger must also indicate the percentage held by each owner. As members are added to the LLC through the sale of membership interests, their ownership is recorded on the ledger. The membership ledger should also show transfers of members' ownership interest, as when a member dies and transfers his or her interest through his or her will.

Each member admitted to the LLC should execute the *Investment Representation Letter*. The investment representation letter offers some measure of protection to the entity because the member being admitted to the LLC makes certain representations regarding his qualifications and fitness to serve as a member of the LLC.

The *Appointment of Proxy for Member's Meeting* is an authorization by one member giving another person the right to vote the owner's shares in a company, in this case an LLC. The term *proxy* also refers to the document granting such authority.

The *Call for Meeting of Members* is an instruction by LLC members to the managers that the members want to call a meeting of members.

The *Notice of Meeting of LLC Members* is an LLC's announcement to its members that a meeting of members has been called.

While LLC members and managers enjoy far fewer corporate formalities than corporation owners, an LLC must still maintain records of its meetings. When an LLC's members meet to formally vote on any matter, the results of that vote should be committed to written minutes called the *Minutes of Meeting of LLC Members*.

In the real world, most LLC votes are taken by written consent in a document called an *Action by Written Consent of LLC Members* rather than by notice and meeting and an in-person vote. Use the written consent form when you wish to take a company action in writing, rather than by a noticed meeting.

The *Written Consent of Members Approving a Certificate of Amendment of Articles of Organization Changing an LLC's Name* is a specific example of a written consent. In this case, the written consent authorizes a change to the LLC's charter to change the LLC's legal name.

4. LLC-1, California LLC Articles of Organization

 Secretary of State
Business Programs Division

1500 11th Street, 3rd Floor
Sacramento, CA 95814

Business Entities
(916) 657-5448

LIMITED LIABILITY COMPANIES

California Tax Information

Registration of a limited liability company (LLC) with the California Secretary of State (SOS) will obligate an LLC that is not taxed as a corporation to pay to the Franchise Tax Board (FTB) an annual minimum tax of $800.00 and a fee based on the annual total income of the entity. The tax and fee are required to be paid for the taxable year of registration and each taxable year, or part thereof, until a Certificate of Cancellation is filed with the SOS. (Rev. and Tax. Code §§ 17941 and 17942.) An LLC is not subject to the taxes and fees imposed by Revenue and Taxation Code sections 17941 and 17942 if the LLC did no business in California during the taxable year and the taxable year was 15 days or less. (Rev. and Tax. Code § 17946.)

An LLC that is taxed as a corporation generally determines its California income under the Corporation Tax Law commencing with Revenue and Taxation Code section 23001.

PLEASE NOTE: A domestic nonprofit LLC is a taxable entity and subject to the tax requirements stated above unless the LLC has applied for tax-exempt status and the FTB determines the LLC qualifies for tax-exempt status. Therefore, until such a determination is made, a nonprofit LLC must file a return and pay the associated tax (and, if applicable, the fee) every year until the LLC is formally cancelled. If the LLC intends to seek tax exempt status:

- At the time of filing its Articles of Organization with the SOS, the LLC must include, in an attachment to that document, additional statements as required by the law under which the LLC is seeking exemption. Please refer to the FTB's Exemption Application Booklet (FTB 3500 Booklet) for information regarding the required statements and for suggested language.

- After filing its Articles of Organization with the SOS, the LLC may apply for tax-exempt status by mailing an Exemption Application (Form FTB 3500), along with an endorsed copy of the Articles of Organization and all other required supporting documentation, to the FTB, P.O. Box 942857, Sacramento, California 94257-4041.

- The FTB 3500 Booklet and Form FTB 3500 can be accessed from the FTB's website at www.ftb.ca.gov or can be requested by calling the FTB at 1-800-338-0505. For further information regarding franchise tax exemption, refer to the FTB's website or call the FTB at (916) 845-4171.

For further information regarding franchise tax requirements, please contact the FTB at:

From within the United States (toll free) ....(800) 852-5711
From outside the United States (not toll free) ....(916) 845-6500
Automated Toll Free Phone Service..(800) 338-0505

Professional Services Information

A domestic or foreign LLC may not render professional services. (Corp. Code § 17375.) "Professional services" are defined in California Corporations Code sections 13401(a) and 13401.3 as:

> Any type of professional services that may be lawfully rendered only pursuant to a license, certification, or registration authorized by the Business and Professions Code, the Chiropractic Act, the Osteopathic Act or the Yacht and Ship Brokers Act.

If your business is required to be licensed, registered or certified, it is recommended that you contact the appropriate licensing authority before filing with the SOS's office in order to determine whether your services are considered professional.

LLC Info (REV 04/2007)

INSTRUCTIONS FOR COMPLETING THE ARTICLES OF ORGANIZATION (FORM LLC-1)

For easier completion, this form is available on the Secretary of State's website at http://www.sos.ca.gov/business/ and can be viewed, filled in and printed from your computer. The completed form along with the applicable fees can be mailed to Secretary of State, Document Filing Support Unit, P.O. Box 944228, Sacramento, CA 94244-2280 or delivered in person to the Sacramento office, 1500 11th Street, 3rd Floor, Sacramento, CA 95814. If you are not completing this form online, please type or legibly print in black or blue ink. This form is filed only in the Sacramento office.

Statutory filing requirements are found in California Corporations Code sections 17051 and 17052. All statutory references are to the California Corporations Code, unless otherwise stated.

FEES: The fee for filing Form LLC-1 is $70.00. There is an additional $15.00 special handling fee for processing a document delivered in person to the Sacramento office. The special handling fee must be remitted by separate check for each submittal and will be retained whether the document is filed or rejected. The preclearance and/or expedited filing of a document within a guaranteed time frame can be requested for an additional fee (in lieu of the special handling fee). Please refer to the Secretary of State's website at http://www.sos.ca.gov/business/precexp.htm for detailed information regarding preclearance and expedited filing services. The special handling fee or preclearance and expedited filing services are not applicable to documents submitted by mail. Check(s) should be made payable to the Secretary of State.

COPIES: The Secretary of State will certify two copies of the filed document(s) without charge, provided that the copies are submitted to the Secretary of State with the document(s) to be filed. Any additional copies submitted will be certified upon request and payment of the $8.00 per copy certification fee.

Pursuant to Section 17375, a domestic limited liability company may not render professional services, as defined in Sections 13401(a) and 13401.3. Professional services are defined as any type of professional services that may be lawfully rendered only pursuant to a license, certification, or registration authorized by the Business and Professions Code, the Chiropractic Act, the Osteopathic Act or the Yacht and Ship Brokers Act. If your business is required to be licensed, certified or registered, it is recommended that you contact the appropriate licensing authority before filing with the Secretary of State's office in order to determine whether your services are considered professional.

Filing this document shall obligate most limited liability companies to pay an annual minimum tax of $800.00 to the Franchise Tax Board pursuant to Revenue and Taxation Code section 17941.

Complete the Articles of Organization (Form LLC-1) as follows:

Item 1. Enter the name of the limited liability company. The name must end with the words "Limited Liability Company," or the abbreviations "LLC" or "L.L.C." The words "Limited" and "Company" may be abbreviated to "Ltd." and "Co.," respectively. The name of the limited liability company may not contain the words "bank," "trust," "trustee," "incorporated," "inc.," "corporation," or "corp.," and must not contain the words "insurer" or "insurance company" or any other words suggesting that it is in the business of issuing policies of insurance and assuming insurance risks.

Item 2. This statement is required by statute and should not be altered. Provisions limiting or restricting the business of the limited liability company may be included as an attachment.

Items 3 & 4 Enter the name of the agent for service of process in California. An agent is an individual, whether or not affiliated with the limited liability company, who resides in California or a corporation designated to accept service of process if the company is sued. The agent should agree to accept service of process on behalf of the limited liability company prior to designation.

If a corporation is designated as agent, that corporation must have previously filed with the Secretary of State, a certificate pursuant to Corporations Code section 1505. Note, **a limited liability company cannot act as its own agent** and no domestic or foreign corporation may file pursuant to Section 1505 unless the corporation is currently authorized to engage in business in California and is in good standing on the records of the Secretary of State.

If an individual is designated as agent, complete Items 3 and 4. If a corporation is designated as agent, complete Item 3 and proceed to Item 5 (do not complete Item 4).

Item 5. Check the appropriate provision indicating whether the limited liability company is to be managed by one manager, more than one manager or all limited liability company members. Only one box may be checked.

Item 6. Attach any other information to be included in Form LLC-1, provided that the information is not inconsistent with law.

Item 7. Form LLC-1 must be signed by the organizer. The person signing Form LLC-1 need not be a member or manager of the limited liability company.

- If Form LLC-1 is signed by an attorney-in-fact, the signature should be followed by the words "Attorney-in-fact for (name of person)."

- If Form LLC-1 is signed by an entity, the person who signs on behalf of the entity should note their name and position/title and the entity name. Example: If a limited liability company ("Smith LLC") is the organizer, the signature of the person signing on behalf of the Smith LLC should be reflected as Joe Smith, Manager of Smith LLC, Organizer.

- If Form LLC-1 is signed by a trust, the trustee should sign as follows:_____, trustee for _____ trust (including the date of the trust, if applicable). Example: Mary Todd, trustee of the Lincoln Family Trust (U/T 5-1-94).

Any attachments to Form LLC-1 are incorporated by reference. All attachments should be 8 ½" x 11", one-sided and legible.

State of California
Secretary of State

| | LLC-1 | File # _____ |

LIMITED LIABILITY COMPANY
ARTICLES OF ORGANIZATION

A $70.00 filing fee must accompany this form.

IMPORTANT – Read instructions before completing this form.

This Space For Filing Use Only

ENTITY NAME (End the name with the words "Limited Liability Company," or the abbreviations "LLC" or "L.L.C." The words "Limited" and "Company" may be abbreviated to "Ltd." and "Co.," respectively.)

1. NAME OF LIMITED LIABILITY COMPANY

PURPOSE (The following statement is required by statute and should not be altered.)

2. THE PURPOSE OF THE LIMITED LIABILITY COMPANY IS TO ENGAGE IN ANY LAWFUL ACT OR ACTIVITY FOR WHICH A LIMITED LIABILITY COMPANY MAY BE ORGANIZED UNDER THE BEVERLY-KILLEA LIMITED LIABILITY COMPANY ACT.

INITIAL AGENT FOR SERVICE OF PROCESS (If the agent is an individual, the agent must reside in California and both Items 3 and 4 must be completed. If the agent is a corporation, the agent must have on file with the California Secretary of State a certificate pursuant to Corporations Code section 1505 and Item 3 must be completed (leave Item 4 blank).

3. NAME OF INITIAL AGENT FOR SERVICE OF PROCESS

4. IF AN INDIVIDUAL, ADDRESS OF INITIAL AGENT FOR SERVICE OF PROCESS IN CALIFORNIA   CITY   STATE   ZIP CODE

CA

MANAGEMENT (Check only one)

5. THE LIMITED LIABILITY COMPANY WILL BE MANAGED BY:

☐ ONE MANAGER

☐ MORE THAN ONE MANAGER

☐ ALL LIMITED LIABILITY COMPANY MEMBER(S)

ADDITIONAL INFORMATION

6. ADDITIONAL INFORMATION SET FORTH ON THE ATTACHED PAGES, IF ANY, IS INCORPORATED HEREIN BY THIS REFERENCE AND MADE A PART OF THIS CERTIFICATE.

EXECUTION

7. I DECLARE I AM THE PERSON WHO EXECUTED THIS INSTRUMENT, WHICH EXECUTION IS MY ACT AND DEED.

_____
DATE

_____
SIGNATURE OF ORGANIZER

_____
TYPE OR PRINT NAME OF ORGANIZER

LLC-1 (REV 04/2007)   APPROVED BY SECRETARY OF STATE

5. Sample Letter to Secretary of State
Accompanying Articles of Organization

Note: This letter is a version appropriate for use in Delaware, but can be modified for use in any state.

Michael Spadaccini
123 Elm Street
San Francisco, CA 94107
415-555-1212

(Date) _____

State of Delaware
Division of Corporations
401 Federal Street, Suite 4
Dover, DE 19901

To whom it may concern:

Enclosed you will find articles of organization for 17 Reasons, LLC. Please file the enclosed articles.

I have enclosed five copies of the filing and a check for $_____ to cover filing fees. Please return any necessary papers in the envelope that I have provided.

Yours truly,

Michael Spadaccini

6. Sample Letter to Registered Agent Accompanying Articles of Organization

Michael Spadaccini
123 Elm Street
San Francisco, CA 94107
415-555-1212

(Date) _____

Harvard Business Services, Inc.
25 Greystone Manor
Lewes, DE 19958

To whom it may concern:

I have enclosed a copy of articles of incorporation I am filing today. As you can see, I have used you as our registered agents in the state of Delaware.

Please use the following contact information:

17 Reasons, LLC
c/o Michael Spadaccini
123 Elm Street
San Francisco, CA 94107

I have enclosed a check for $50.00 to cover the first year's services.

Yours truly,

Michael Spadaccini

7. Long-Form Operating Agreement for Member-Managed LLC

OPERATING AGREEMENT OF (Insert full name of LLC)

THIS OPERATING AGREEMENT (the "Agreement") is made and entered into on _____, 20__, and those persons whose names, addresses, and signatures are set forth below, being the Members of (Insert Name), LLC (the "Company"), represent and agree that they have caused or will cause to be filed, on behalf of the Company, Articles of Organization, and that they desire to enter into an operating agreement.

The Members agree as follows:

ARTICLE I. DEFINITIONS

1.1. "Act" means the Limited Liability Company Law of the State in which the Company is organized or chartered, including any amendments or the corresponding provision(s) of any succeeding law.

1.2. "Affiliate" or "Affiliate of a Member" means any Person under the control of, in common control with, or in control of a Member, whether that control is direct or indirect. The term "control," as used herein, means, with respect to a corporation or limited liability company, the ability to exercise more than fifty percent (50%) of the voting rights of the controlled entity, and with respect to an individual, partnership, trust, or other entity or association, the ability, directly or indirectly, to direct the management of policies of the controlled entity or individual.

1.3. "Agreement" means this Operating Agreement, in its original form and as amended from time to time.

1.4. "Articles" means the Articles of Organization or other charter document filed with the Secretary of State in the state of organization forming this limited liability company, as initially filed and as they may be amended from time to time.

1.5. "Capital Account" means the amount of the capital interest of a Member in the Company, consisting of the amount of money and the fair market value, net of liabilities, of any property initially contributed by the Member, as (1) increased by any additional contributions and the Member's share of the Company's profits; and (2) decreased by any distribution to that Member as well as that Member's share of Company losses.

1.6. "Code" means the Internal Revenue Code of 1986, as amended from time to time, the regulations promulgated thereunder, and any corresponding provision of any succeeding revenue law.

1.7. "Company Minimum Gain" shall have the same meaning as set forth for the term "Partnership Minimum Gain" in the Regulations section 1.704-2(d) (26 CFR Section1.704-2(d)).

1.8. "Departing Member" means any Member whose conduct results in a Dissolution Event or who withdraws from or is expelled from the Company in accordance with Section 4.3, where such withdrawal does not result in dissolution of the Company.

1.9. "Dissolution Event" means, with respect to any Member, one or more of the following: the death, resignation, retirement, expulsion, bankruptcy, or dissolution of any Member.

1.10. "Distribution" means the transfer of money or property by the Company to the Members without consideration.

1.11. "Member" means each Person who has been admitted into membership in the Company, executes this Agreement and any subsequent amendments, and has not engaged in conduct resulting in a Dissolution Event or terminated membership for any other reason.

1.12. "Member Nonrecourse Debt" shall have the same meaning as set forth for the term "Partnership Nonrecourse Debt" in the Code.

1.13. "Member Nonrecourse Deductions" means items of Company loss, deduction, or Code Section 705(a)(2)(B) expenditures which are attributable to Member Nonrecourse Debt.

1.14. "Membership Interest" means a Member's rights in the Company, collectively, including the Member's economic interest, right to vote and participate in management, and right to information concerning the business and affairs of the Company provided in this Agreement or under the Act.

1.15. "Net Profits" and "Net Losses" mean the Company's income, loss, and deductions computed at the close of each fiscal year in accordance with the accounting methods used to prepare the Company's information tax return filed for federal income tax purposes.

1.16. "Nonrecourse Liability" has the meaning provided in the Code.

1.17. "Percentage Interest" means the percentage ownership of the Company of each Member as set forth in the column entitled "Member's Percentage Interest" contained in Table A as recalculated from time to time pursuant to this Agreement.

1.18. "Person" means an individual, partnership, limited partnership, corporation, limited liability company, registered limited liability partnership, trust, association, estate, or any other entity.

1.19. "Remaining Members" means, upon the occurrence of a Dissolution Event, those members of the Company whose conduct did not cause its occurrence.

ARTICLE II. FORMATION AND ORGANIZATION

2.1. Initial Date and Initial Parties. This Agreement is deemed entered into upon the date of the filing of the Company's Articles.

2.2. Subsequent Parties. No Person may become a Member of the Company without agreeing to and without becoming a signatory of this Agreement, and any offer or assignment of a Membership Interest is contingent upon the fulfillment of this condition.

2.3. Term. The Company shall commence upon the filing of its Articles and it shall continue in existence until December 31, 2050, unless terminated earlier under the provisions of this Agreement.

2.4. Principal Place of Business. The Company will have its principal place of business at (insert address of principal place of business), or at any other address upon which the Members agree. The Company shall maintain its principal executive offices at its principal place of business, as well as all required records and documents.

2.5. Authorization and Purpose. The purpose of the Company is to engage in any lawful business activity that is permitted by the Act.

ARTICLE III. CAPITAL CONTRIBUTIONS AND ACCOUNTS

3.1. Initial Capital Contributions. The initial capital contribution of each Member is listed in Table A attached hereto. Table A shall be revised to reflect and additional contributions pursuant to Section 3.2.

3.2. Additional Contributions. No Member shall be required to make any additional contributions to the Company. However, upon agreement by the Members that additional capital is desirable or necessary, any Member may, but shall not be required to, contribute additional capital to the Company on a pro rata basis consistent with the Percentage Interest of each of the Members.

3.3. Interest Payments. No Member shall be entitled to receive interest payments in connection with any contribution of capital to the Company, except as expressly provided herein.

3.4. Right to Return of Contributions. No Member shall be entitled to a return of any capital contributed to the Company, except as expressly provided in the Agreement.

3.5. Capital Accounts. A Capital Account shall be created and maintained by the Company for each Member, in conformance with the Code, which shall reflect all Capital Contributions to the Company. Should any Member transfer or assign all or any part of his or her membership interest in accordance with this Agreement, the successor shall receive that portion of the Member's Capital Account attributable to the interest assigned or transferred.

ARTICLE IV. MEMBERS

4.1. Limitation of Liability. No Member shall be personally liable for the debts, obligations, liabilities, or judgments of the Company solely by virtue of his or her Membership in the Company, except as expressly set forth in this Agreement or required by law.

4.2. Additional Members. The Members may admit additional Members to the Company only if approved by a two-thirds majority in interest of the Company Membership. Additional Members shall be permitted to participate in management at the discretion of the existing Members. Likewise, the existing Members shall agree upon an Additional Member's participation in Net Profits, Net Losses, and Distributions, as those terms are defined in this Agreement. Table A shall be amended to include the name, present mailing address, and percentage ownership of any Additional Members.

4.3. Withdrawal or Expulsion from Membership. Any Member may withdraw at any time after sixty (60) days' written notice to the company, without prejudice to the rights of the Company or any Member under any contract to which the withdrawing Member is a party. Such withdrawing Member shall have the rights of a transferee under this Agreement and the remaining Members shall be entitled to purchase the withdrawing Member's Membership Interest in accordance with this Agreement. Any Member may be expelled from the Company upon a vote of two-thirds majority in interest of the Company Membership. Such expelled Member shall have the rights of a transferee under this Agreement and the remaining Members shall be entitled to purchase the expelled Member's Membership Interest in accordance with this Agreement.

4.4. Competing Activities. The Members and their officers, directors, shareholders, partners, managers, agents, employees, and Affiliates are permitted to participate in other business activities which may be in competition, direct or indirect, with those of the Company. The Members further acknowledge that they are under no obligation to present to the Company any business or investment opportunities, even if the opportunities are of such a character as to be appropriate for the Company's undertaking. Each Member hereby waives the right to any claim against any other Member or Affiliate on account of such competing activities.

4.5. Compensation of Members. No Member or Affiliate shall be entitled to compensation for services rendered to the Company, absent agreement by the Members. However, Members and Affiliates shall be entitled to reimbursement for the actual cost of goods and services provided to the Company, including, without limitation, reimbursement for any professional services required to form the Company.

4.6. Transaction with the Company. The Members may permit a Member to lend money to and transact business with the Company, subject to any limitations contained in this Agreement or in the Act. To the extent permitted by applicable laws, such a Member shall be treated like any other Person with respect to transactions with the Company.

4.7. Meetings.

(a) There will be no regular or annual meeting of the Members. However, any Member(s) with an aggregate Percentage Interest of ten percent (10%) or more may call a meeting of the Members at any time. Such meeting shall be held at a place to be agreed upon by the Members.

(b) Minutes of the meeting shall be made and maintained along with the books and records of the Company.

(c) If any action on the part of the Members is to be proposed at the meeting, then written notice of the meeting must be provided to each Member entitled to vote not less than ten (10) days or more than sixty (60) days prior to the meeting. Notice may be given in person, by fax, by first class mail, or by any other written communication, charges prepaid, at the Members' address listed in Table A. The notice shall contain the date, time, and place of the meeting and a statement of the general nature of this business to be transacted there.

4.8. Actions at Meetings.

(a) No action may be taken at a meeting that was not proposed in the notice of the meeting, unless there is unanimous consent among all Members entitled to vote.

(b) No action may be taken at a meeting unless a quorum of Members is present, either in person or by proxy. A quorum of Members shall consist of Members holding a majority of the Percentage Interest in the Company.

(c) A Member may participate in, and is deemed present at, any meeting by clearly audible conference telephone or other similar means of communication.

(d) Any meeting may be adjourned upon the vote of the majority of the Membership Interests represented at the meeting.

(e) Actions taken at any meeting of the Members have full force and effect if each Member who was not present, in person or by proxy, signs a written waiver of notice and consent to the holding of the meeting or approval of the minutes of the meeting. All such waivers and consents shall become Company records.

(f) Presence at a meeting constitutes a waiver of the right to object to notice of a meeting, unless the Member expresses such an objection at the start of the meeting.

4.9. Actions Without Meetings. Any action that may be taken at a meeting of the Members may be taken without a meeting and without prior notice, if written consents to the action are submitted to the Company within sixty (60) days of the record date for the taking of the action, executed by Members holding a sufficient number of votes to authorize the taking of the action at a meeting at which all Members entitled to vote thereon are present and vote. All such consents shall be maintained as Company records.

4.10. Record Date. For the purposes of voting, notices of meetings, distributions, or any other rights under this Agreement, the Articles, or the Act, the Members representing in excess of ten percent (10%) of the Percentage Interests in the Company may fix, in advance, a record date that is not more than sixty (60) or less than ten (10) days prior to the date of such meeting or sixty (60) days prior to any other action. If no record date is fixed, the record date shall be determined in accordance with the Act.

4.11. Voting Rights. Except as expressly set forth in this Agreement, all actions requiring the vote, approval, or consent of the Members may be authorized upon the vote, approval, or consent of those Members holding a majority of the Percentage Interests in the Company. The following actions require the unanimous vote, approval, or consent of all Members who are neither the subjects of a dissolution event nor the transferors of a Membership Interest:

(a) Approval of the purchase by the Company or its nominee of the Membership Interest of a transferor Member;

(b) Approval of the sale, transfer, exchange, assignment, or other disposition of a Member's interest in the Company and admission of the transferee as a Member;

(c) A decision to make any amendment to the Articles or to this Agreement; and

(d) A decision to compromise the obligation of any Member to make a Capital Contribution or return money or property distributed in violation of the Act.

ARTICLE V. MANAGEMENT

5.1. Management by Members. The Company shall be managed by the Members. Each Member has the authority to manage and control the Company and to act on its behalf, except as limited by the Act, the Articles, or this Agreement.

5.2. Limitation on Exposing Members to Personal Liability. Neither the Company nor any Member may take any action that will have the effect of exposing any Member of the Company to personal liability for the obligations of the Company, without first obtaining the consent of the affected Member.

5.3. Limitation on Powers of Members. The Members shall not be authorized to permit the Company to perform the following acts or to engage in the following transactions without first obtaining the affirmative vote or written consent of the Members holding a majority Interest or such greater Percentage Interest as may be indicated below:

(a) The sale or other disposition of all or a substantial part of the Company's assets, whether occurring as a single transaction or a series of transactions over a 12-month period, except if the same is part of the orderly liquidation and winding up of the Company's affairs upon dissolution;

(b) The merger of the Company with any other business entity without the affirmative vote or written consent of all members;

(c) Any alteration of the primary purpose or business of the Company shall require the affirmative vote or written consent of Members holding at least sixty-six percent (66%) of the Percentage Interest in the Company;

(d) The establishment of different classes of Members;

(e) Transactions between the Company and one or more Members or one or more of any Member's Affiliates, or transactions in which one or more Members or Affiliates thereof have a material financial interest;

(f) Without limiting subsection (e) of this section, the lending of money to any Member or Affiliate of the Company;

(g) Any act which would prevent the Company from conducting its duly authorized business;

(h) The confession of a judgment against the Company.

Notwithstanding any other provisions of this Agreement, the written consent of all of the Members is required to permit the Company to incur an indebtedness or obligation greater than one hundred thousand dollars ($100,000.00). All checks, drafts, or other instruments requiring the Company to make payment of an amount less than fifty thousand dollars ($50,000.00) may be signed by any Member, acting alone. Any check, draft, or other instrument requiring the Company to make payment in the amount of fifty thousand dollars ($50,000.00) or more shall require the signature of two (2) Members acting together.

5.4. Fiduciary Duties. The fiduciary duties a Member owes to the Company and to the other Members of the Company are those of a partner to a partnership and to the partners of a partnership.

5.5. Liability for Acts and Omissions. As long as a Member acts in accordance with Section 5.4, no Member shall incur liability to any other Member or to the Company for any act or omission which occurs while in the performance of services for the Company.

ARTICLE VI. ALLOCATION OF PROFIT AND LOSS

6.1. Compliance with the Code. The Company intends to comply with the Code and all applicable Regulations, including without limitation the minimum gain chargeback requirements, and intends that the provisions of this Article be interpreted consistently with that intent.

6.2. Net Profits. Except as specifically provided elsewhere in this Agreement, Distributions of Net Profit shall be made to Members in proportion to their Percentage Interest in the Company.

6.3. Net Losses. Except as specifically provided elsewhere in this Agreement, Net Losses shall be allocated to the Members in proportion to their Percentage Interest in the Company. However, the foregoing will not apply to the extent that it would result in a Negative Capital Account balance for any Member equal to the Company Minimum Gain which would be realized by that Member in the event of a foreclosure of the Company's assets. Any Net Loss which is not allocated in accordance with the foregoing provision shall be allocated to other Members who are unaffected by that provision. When subsequent allocations of profit and loss are calculated, the losses reallocated pursuant to this provision shall be taken into account such that the net amount of the allocation shall be as close as possible to that which would have been allocated to each Member if the reallocation pursuant to this section had not taken place.

6.4. Regulatory Allocations. Notwithstanding the provisions of Section 6.3, the following applies:

(a) Should there be a net decrease in Company Minimum Gain in any taxable year, the Members shall specially allocate to each Member items of income and gain for that year (and, if necessary, for subsequent years) as required by the Code governing minimum gain chargeback requirements.

(b) Should there be a net decrease in Company Minimum Gain based on a Member Nonrecourse Debt in any taxable year, the Members shall first determine the extent of each Member's share of the Company Minimum Gain attributable to Member Nonrecourse Debt in accordance with the Code. The Members shall then specially allocate items of income and gain for that year (and, if necessary, for subsequent years) in accordance with the Code to each Member who has a share of the Company Nonrecourse Debt Minimum Gain.

(c) The Members shall allocate Nonrecourse Deductions for any taxable year to each Member in proportion to his or her Percentage Interest.

(d) The Members shall allocate Member Nonrecourse Deductions for any taxable year to the Member who bears the risk of loss with respect to the Nonrecourse Debt to which the Member Nonrecourse Deduction is attributable, as provided in the Code.

(e) If a Member unexpectedly receives any allocation of loss or deduction, or item thereof, or distributions which result in the Member's having a Negative Capital Account balance at the end of the taxable year greater than the Member's share of Company Minimum Gain, the Company shall specially allocate items of income and gain to that Member in a manner designed to eliminate the excess Negative Capital Account balance as rapidly as possible. Any allocations made in accordance with this provision shall taken into consideration in determining subsequent allocations under Article VI, so that, to the extent possible, the total amount allocated in this and subsequent allocations equals that which would have been allocated had there been no unexpected adjustments, allocations, and distributions and no allocation pursuant to Section 6.4(e).

(f) In accordance with Code Section 704(c) and the Regulations promulgated pursuant thereto, and notwithstanding any other provision in this Article, income, gain, loss, and deductions with respect to any property contributed to the Company shall, solely for tax purposes, be allocated among Members, taking into account any variation between the adjusted basis of the property to the Company for federal income tax purposes and its fair market value on the date of contribution. Allocations pursuant to this subsection are made solely for federal, state, and local taxes and shall not be taken into consideration in determining a Member's Capital Account or share of Net Profits or Net Losses or any other items subject to Distribution under this agreement.

6.5. Distributions. The Members may elect, by unanimous vote, to make a Distribution of assets at any time that would not be prohibited under the Act or under this Agreement. Such a Distribution shall be made in proportion to the unreturned capital contributions of each Member until all contributions have been paid, and thereafter in proportion to each Member's Percentage Interest in the Company. All such Distributions shall be made to those Persons who, according to the books and records of the Company, were the holders of record of Membership Interests on the date of the Distribution. Subject to Section 6.6, neither the Company nor any Members shall be liable for the making of any Distributions in accordance with the provisions of this section.

6.6. Limitations on Distributions.

(a) The Members shall not make any Distribution if, after giving effect to the Distribution, (1) the Company would not be able to pay its debts as they become due in the usual course of business, or (2) the Company's total assets would be less than the sum of its total liabilities plus, unless this Agreement provides otherwise, the amount that would be needed, if the Company were to be dissolved at the time of Distribution, to satisfy the preferential rights of other Members upon dissolution that are superior to the rights of the Member receiving the Distribution.

(b) The Members may base a determination that a Distribution is not prohibited under this section on any of the following: (1) financial statements prepared on the basis of accounting practices and principles that are reasonable under the circumstances, (2) a fair valuation, or (3) any other method that is reasonable under the circumstances.

6.7. Return of Distributions. Members shall return to the Company any Distributions received which are in violation of this Agreement or the Act. Such Distributions shall be returned to the account or accounts of the Company from which they were taken in order to make the Distribution. If a Distribution is made in compliance with the Act and this Agreement, a Member is under no obligation to return it to the Company or to pay the amount of the Distribution for the account of the Company or to any creditor of the Company.

6.8. Members Bound by These Provisions. The Members understand and acknowledge the tax implications of the provisions of this Article of the Agreement and agree to be bound by these provisions in reporting items of income and loss relating to the Company on their federal and state income tax returns.

ARTICLE VII. TRANSFERS AND TERMINATIONS OF MEMBERSHIP INTERESTS

7.1. Restriction on Transferability of Membership Interests. A Member may not transfer, assign, encumber, or convey all or any part of his or her Membership Interest in the Company, except as provided herein. In entering into this Agreement, each of the Members acknowledges the reasonableness of this restriction, which is intended to further the purposes of the Company and the relationships among the Members.

7.2. Permitted Transfers. In order to be permitted, a transfer or assignment of all or any part of a Membership Interest must have the approval of a two-thirds majority of the Members of the Company. Each Member, in his or her sole discretion, may proffer or withhold approval. In addition, the following conditions must be met:

(a) The transferee must provide a written agreement, satisfactory to the Members, to be bound by all of the provisions of this Agreement;

(b) The transferee must provide the Company with his or her taxpayer identification number and initial tax basis in the transferred interest;

(c) The transferee must pay the reasonable expenses incurred in connection with his or her admission to Membership;

(d) The transfer must be in compliance with all federal and state securities laws;

(e) The transfer must not result in the termination of the Company pursuant to Code Section 708.

(f) The transfer must not render the Company subject to the Investment Company Act of 1940, as amended; and

(g) The transferor must comply with the provisions of this Agreement.

7.3. Company's Right to Purchase Transferor's Interest and Valuation of Transferor's Interest. Any Member who wishes to transfer all or any part of his or her interest in the Company shall immediately provide the Company with written notice of his or her intention. The notice shall fully describe the nature of the interest to be transferred. Thereafter, the Company, or its nominee, shall have the option to purchase the transferor's interest at the Repurchase Price (as defined below).

(a) The "Repurchase Price" shall be determined as of the date of the event causing the transfer or dissolution event (the "Effective Date"). The date that the Company receives notice of a Member's intention to transfer his or her interest pursuant to this paragraph shall be deemed to be the Effective Date. The Repurchase Price shall be determined as follows:

i. The Repurchase Price of a Member's Percentage Interest shall be computed by the independent certified public accountant (CPA) regularly used by the Company or, if the Company has no CPA or if the CPA is unavailable, then by a qualified appraiser selected by the Company for this purpose. The Repurchase Price of a Member's Percentage Interest shall be the sum of the Company's total Repurchase Price multiplied by the Transferor's Percentage Interest as of the Effective Date.

ii. The Repurchase Price shall be determined by the book value method, as more further described herein. The book value of the interests shall be determined in accordance with the regular financial statements prepared by the Company and in accordance with generally accepted accounting principles, applied consistently with the accounting principles previously applied by the Company, adjusted to reflect the following:

(1) All inventory, valued at cost.

(2) All real property, leasehold improvements, equipment, and furnishings and fixtures valued at their fair market value.

(3) The face amount of any accounts payable.

(4) Any accrued taxes or assessments, deducted as liabilities.

(5) All usual fiscal year-end accruals and deferrals (including depreciation), prorated over the fiscal year.

(6) The reasonable fair market value of any good will or other intangible assets.

(b) The cost of the assessment shall be borne by the Company.

(c) The option provided to the Company shall be irrevocable and shall remain open for thirty (30) days from the Effective Date, except that if notice is given by regular mail, the option shall remain open for thirty-five (35) days from the Effective Date.

(d) At any time while the option remains open, the Company (or its nominee) may elect to exercise the option and purchase the transferor's interest in the Company. The transferor Member shall not vote on the question of whether the Company should exercise its option.

(e) If the Company chooses to exercise its option to purchase the transferor Member's interest, it shall provide written notice to the transferor within the option period. The notice shall specify a "Closing Date" for the purchase, which shall occur within thirty (30) days of the expiration of the option period.

(f) If the Company declines to exercise its option to purchase the transferor Member's interest, the transferor Member may then transfer his or her interest in accordance with Section 7.2. Any transfer not in compliance with the provisions of Section 7.2 shall be null and void and have no force or effect.

(g) In the event that the Company chooses to exercise its option to purchase the transferor Member's interest, the Company may elect to purchase the Member's interest on the following terms:

i. The Company may elect to pay the Repurchase Price in cash, by making such cash payment to the transferor Member upon the Closing Date.

ii. The Company may elect to pay any portion of the Repurchase Price by delivering to the transferor Member, upon the Closing Date, all of the following:

(1) An amount equal to at least 10% of the Repurchase Price in cash or in an immediately negotiable draft, and

(2) A Promissory Note for the remaining amount of the Repurchase Price, to be paid in 12 successive monthly installments, with such installments beginning 30 days following the Closing Date, and ending one year from the Closing Date, and

(3) A security agreement guaranteeing the payment of the Promissory Note by offering the Transferor's former membership interest as security for the payment of the Promissory Note.

7.4. Occurrence of Dissolution Event. Upon the death, withdrawal, resignation, retirement, expulsion, insanity, bankruptcy, or dissolution of any Member (a Dissolution Event), the Company shall be dissolved, unless all of the Remaining Members elect by a majority in interest within 90 days thereafter to continue the operation of the business. In the event that the Remaining Members to agree, the Company and the Remaining Members shall have the right to purchase the interest of the Member whose actions caused the occurrence of the Dissolution Event. The interest shall be sold in the manner described in Section 7.6.

7.5. Withdrawal from Membership. Notwithstanding Section 7.4, in the event that a Member withdraws in accordance with Section 4.3 and such withdrawal does not result in the dissolution of the Company, the Company and the Remaining Members shall have the right to purchase the interest of the withdrawing Member in the manner described in Section 7.6.

7.6. Purchase of Interest of Departing Member. The purchase price of a Departing Member's interest shall be determined in accordance with the procedure provided in Section 7.3.

(a) Once a value has been determined, each Remaining Member shall be entitled to purchase that portion of the Departing Member's interest that corresponds to his or her percentage ownership of the Percentage Interests of those Members electing to purchase a portion of the Departing Member's interest in the Company.

(b) Each Remaining Member desiring to purchase a share of the Departing Member's interest shall have thirty (30) days to provide written notice to the Company of his or her intention to do so. The failure to provide notice shall be deemed a rejection of the opportunity to purchase the Departing Member's interest.

(c) If any Member elects not to purchase all of the Departing Member's interest to which he or she is entitled, the other Members may purchase that portion of the Departing Member's interest. Any interest which is not purchased by the Remaining Members may be purchased by the Company.

(d) The Members shall assign a closing date within 60 days after the Members' election to purchase is completed. At that time, the Departing Member shall deliver to the Remaining Members an instrument of title, free of any encumbrances and containing warranties of title, duly conveying his or her interest in the Company and, in return, he or she shall be paid the purchase price for his or her interest in cash. The Departing Member and the Remaining Members shall perform all acts reasonably necessary to consummate the transaction in accordance with this agreement.

7.7. No Release of Liability. Any Member or Departing Member whose interest in the Company is sold pursuant to Article VII is not relieved thereby of any liability he or she may owe the Company.

ARTICLE VIII. BOOKS, RECORDS, AND REPORTING

8.1. Books and Records. The Members shall maintain at the Company's principal place of business the following books and records: a current list of the full name and last known business or residence address of each Member together with the Capital Contribution, Capital Account, and Membership Interest of each Member; a copy of the Articles and all amendments thereto; copies of the Company's federal, state; and local income tax or information returns and reports, if any; for the six (6) most recent taxable years; a copy of this Agreement and any amendments to it; copies of the Company's financial statements, if any; the books and records of the Company as they relate to its internal affairs for at least the current and past four (4) fiscal years; and true and correct copies of all relevant documents and records indicating the amount, cost, and value of all the property and assets of the Company.

8.2. Accounting Methods. The books and records of the Company shall be maintained in accordance with the accounting methods utilized for federal income tax purposes.

8.3. Reports. The Members shall cause to be prepared and filed in a timely manner all reports and documents required by any governmental agency. The Members shall cause to be prepared at least annually all information concerning the Company's operations that is required by the Members for the preparation of their federal and state tax returns.

8.4. Inspection Rights. For purposes reasonably related to their interests in the Company, all Members shall have the right to inspect and copy the books and records of the Company during normal business hours, upon reasonable request.

8.5. Bank Accounts. The Members shall maintain all of the funds of the Company in a bank account or accounts in the name of the Company, at a depository institution or institutions to be determined by a majority of the Members. The Members shall not permit the funds of the Company to be commingled in any manner with the funds or accounts of any other Person. The Members shall have the powers enumerated in Section 5.3 with respect to endorsing, signing, and negotiating checks, drafts, or other evidence of indebtedness to the Company or obligating the Company money to a third party.

ARTICLE IX. DISSOLUTION, LIQUIDATION, AND WINDING UP

9.1. Conditions Under Which Dissolution Shall Occur. The Company shall dissolve and its affairs shall be wound up upon the happening of the first of the following: at the time specified in the Articles; upon the happening of a Dissolution Event; and the failure of the Remaining Members to elect to continue, in accordance with Section 7.4; upon the vote of all of the Members to dissolve; upon the entry of a decree of judicial dissolution pursuant to the Act; upon the happening of any event specified in the Articles as causing or requiring dissolution; or upon the sale of all or substantially all of the Company's assets.

9.2. Winding Up and Dissolution. If the Company is dissolved, the Members shall wind up its affairs, including the selling of all of the Company's assets and the provision of written notification to all of the Company's creditors of the commencement of dissolution proceedings.

9.3. Order of Payment. After determining that all known debts and liabilities of the Company in the process of winding up have been paid or provided for, including, without limitation, debts and liabilities to Members who are creditors of the Company, the Members shall distribute the remaining assets among the Members in accordance with their Positive Capital Account balances, after taking into consideration the profit and loss allocations made pursuant to Section 6.4. Members shall not be required to restore Negative Capital Account Balances.

ARTICLE X. INDEMNIFICATION

10.1. Indemnification. The Company shall indemnify any Member and may indemnify any Person to the fullest extent permitted by law on the date such indemnification is requested for any judgments, settlements, penalties, fines, or expenses of any kind incurred as a result of the Person's performance in the capacity of Member, officer, employee, or agent of the Company, as long as the Member or Person did not behave in violation of the Act or this Agreement.

ARTICLE XI. MISCELLANEOUS PROVISIONS

11.1. Assurances. Each Member shall execute all documents and certificates and perform all acts deemed appropriate by the Members and the Company or required by this Agreement or the Act in connection with the formation and operation of the Company and the acquisition, holding, or operation of any property by the Company.

11.2. Complete Agreement. This Agreement and the Articles constitute the complete and exclusive statement of the agreement among the Members with respect to the matters discussed herein and therein and they supersede all prior written or oral statements among the Members, including any prior statement, warranty, or representation.

11.3. Section Headings. The section headings which appear throughout this Agreement are provided for convenience only and are not intended to define or limit the scope of this Agreement or the intent of subject matter of its provisions.

11.4. Binding Effect. Subject to the provisions of this Agreement relating to the transferability of Membership Interests, this Agreement is binding upon and shall inure to the benefit of the parties hereto and their respective heirs, administrators, executors, successors, and assigns.

11.5. Interpretation. All pronouns and common nouns shall be deemed to refer to the masculine, feminine, neuter, singular, and plural, as the context may require. In the event that any claim is made by any Member relating to the drafting and interpretation of this Agreement, no presumption, inference, or burden of proof or persuasion shall be created or implied solely by virtue of the fact that this Agreement was drafted by or at the behest of a particular Member or his or her counsel.

11.6. Applicable Law. Each Member agrees that all disputes arising under or in connection with this Agreement and any transactions contemplated by this Agreement shall be governed by the internal law, and not the law of conflicts, of the state of organization.

11.7. Specific Performance. The Members acknowledge and agree that irreparable injury shall result from a breach of this Agreement and that money damages will not adequately compensate the injured party. Accordingly, in the event of a breach or a threatened breach of this Agreement, any party who may be injured shall be entitled, in addition to any other remedy which may be available, to injunctive relief to prevent or to correct the breach.

11.8. Remedies Cumulative. The remedies described in this Agreement are cumulative and shall not eliminate any other remedy to which a Person may be lawfully entitled.

11.9. Notice. Any notice or other writing to be served upon the Company or any Member thereof in connection with this Agreement shall be in writing and shall be deemed completed when delivered to the address specified in Table A, if to a Member, and to the resident agent, if to the Company. Any Member shall have the right to change the address at which notices shall be served upon ten (10) days' written notice to the Company and the other Members.

11.10. Amendments. Any amendments, modifications, or alterations to this Agreement or the Articles must be in writing and signed by all of the Members.

11.11. Severability. Each provision of this Agreement is severable from the other provisions. If, for any reason, any provision of this Agreement is declared invalid or contrary to existing law, the inoperability of that provision shall have no effect on the remaining provisions of the Agreement, which shall continue in full force and effect.

11.12. Counterparts. This Agreement may be executed in counterparts, each of which shall be deemed an original and all of which shall, when taken together, constitute a single document.

_____ (Member)

_____ (Member)

_____ (Member)

Table A: Name, Address and Initial Capital Contribution of the Members			
Name and Address of Member	Value of Initial Capital Contribution	Nature of Member's Initial Capital Contribution (i.e., cash, services, property)	Percentage Interest of Member

8. Short-Form Operating Agreement for Member-Managed LLC

OPERATING AGREEMENT OF (insert full name of LLC)

THIS OPERATING AGREEMENT (the "Agreement") is hereby entered into by the undersigned, who are owners and shall be referred to as Member or Members.

RECITALS

The Members desire to form (insert full name of LLC), a limited liability company (the "Company"), for the purposes set forth herein, and, accordingly, desire to enter into this Agreement in order to set forth the terms and conditions of the business and affairs of the Company and to determine the rights and obligations of its Members.

NOW, THEREFORE, the Members, intending to be legally bound by this Agreement, hereby agree that the limited liability company operating agreement of the Company shall be as follows:

ARTICLE I. DEFINITIONS

When used in this Agreement, the following terms shall have the meanings set forth below.

1.1 "Act" means the Limited Liability Company Law of the State in which the Company is organized or chartered, including any amendments or the corresponding provision(s) of any succeeding law.

1.2 "Capital Contribution(s)" means the amount of cash and the agreed value of property, services rendered, or a promissory note or other obligation to contribute cash or property or to perform services contributed by the Members for such Members' Interest in the Company, equal to the sum of the Members' initial Capital Contributions plus the Members' additional Capital Contributions, if any, made pursuant to Sections 4.1 and 4.2, respectively, less payments or distributions made pursuant to Section 5.1.

1.3 "Code" means the Internal Revenue Code of 1986 and the regulations promulgated thereunder, as amended from time to time (or any corresponding provision or provisions of succeeding law).

1.4 "Interest" or "Interests" means the ownership Interest, expressed as a number, percentage, or fraction, set forth in Table A, of a Member in the Company.

1.5 "Person" means any natural individual, partnership, firm, corporation, limited liability company, joint-stock company, trust, or other entity.

1.6 "Secretary of State" means the Office of the Secretary of State or the office charged with accepting articles of organization in the Company's state of organization.

ARTICLE II. FORMATION

2.1 Organization. The Members hereby organize the Company as a limited liability company pursuant to the provisions of the Act.

2.2 Effective Date. The Company shall come into being on, and this Agreement shall take effect from, the date the Articles of Organization of the Company are filed with the Secretary of State in the state of organization or charter.

2.3 Agreement: Invalid Provisions and Saving Clause. The Members, by executing this Agreement, hereby agree to the terms and conditions of this Agreement. To the extent any provision of this Agreement is prohibited or ineffective under the Act, this Agreement shall be deemed to be amended to the least extent necessary in order to make this Agreement effective under the Act. In the event the Act is subsequently amended or interpreted in such a way to validate any provision of this Agreement that was formerly invalid, such provision shall be considered to be valid from the effective date of such amendment or interpretation.

ARTICLE III. PURPOSE; NATURE OF BUSINESS

3.1 Purpose; Nature of Business. The purpose of the Company shall be to engage in any lawful business that may be engaged in by a limited liability company organized under the Act, as such business activities may be determined by the Member or Members from time to time.

3.2 Powers. The Company shall have all powers of a limited liability company under the Act and the power to do all things necessary or convenient to accomplish its purpose and operate its business as described in Section 3.1 here.

ARTICLE IV. MEMBERS AND CAPITAL CONTRIBUTIONS

4.1 Members and Initial Capital Contribution. The name, address, Interest, and value of the initial Capital Contribution of the Members shall be set forth on Table A attached hereto.

4.2 Additional Capital Contributions. The Members shall have no obligation to make any additional Capital Contributions to the Company. The Members may make additional Capital Contributions to the Company as the Members unanimously determine are necessary, appropriate, or desirable.

ARTICLE V. DISTRIBUTIONS AND ALLOCATIONS

5.1 Distributions and Allocations. All distributions of cash or other assets of the Company shall be made and paid to the Members at such time and in such amounts as the majority of the Members may determine. All items of income, gain, loss, deduction, and credit shall be allocated to the Members in proportion to their Interests.

ARTICLE VI. TAXATION

6.1 Income Tax Reporting. Each Member is aware of the income tax consequences of the allocations made by Article V here and agrees to be bound by the provisions of Article V here in reporting each Member's share of Company income and loss for federal and state income tax purposes.

6.2 Tax Treatment. Notwithstanding anything contained herein to the contrary and only for purposes of federal and, if applicable, state income tax purposes, the Company shall be classified as a partnership for such federal and state income tax purposes unless and until the Members unanimously determine to cause the Company to file an election under the Code to be classified as an association taxable as a corporation.

ARTICLE VII. MANAGEMENT BY MEMBERS

7.1 Management by Members. The Company shall be managed by its Members, who shall have full and exclusive right, power, and authority to manage the affairs of the Company and to bind the Company to contracts and obligations, to make all decisions with respect thereto, and to do or cause to be done any and all acts or things deemed by the Members to be necessary, appropriate, or desirable to carry out or further the business of the Company.

7.2 Voting Power in Proportion to Interest. The Members shall enjoy voting power and authority in proportion to their Interests. Unless expressly provided otherwise in this Agreement or the Articles of Organization, Company decisions shall be made by majority vote.

7.3 Duties of Members. The Members shall manage and administer the day-to-day operations and business of the Company and shall execute any and all reports, forms, instruments, documents, papers, writings, agreements, and contracts, including but not limited to deeds, bills of sale, assignments, leases, promissory notes, mortgages, and security agreements and any other type or form of document by which property or property rights of the Company are transferred or encumbered, or by which debts and obligations of the Company are created, incurred, or evidenced.

ARTICLE VIII. BOOKS AND RECORDS

8.1 Books and Records. The Members shall keep, or cause to be kept, at the principal place of business of the Company true and correct books of account, in which shall be entered fully and accurately each and every transaction of the Company. The Company's taxable and fiscal years shall end on December 31. All Members shall have the right to inspect the Company's books and records at any time, for any reason.

ARTICLE IX. LIMITATION OF LIABILITY; INDEMNIFICATION

9.1 Limited Liability. Except as otherwise required by law, the debts, obligations, and liabilities of the Company, whether arising in contract, tort, or otherwise, shall be solely the debts, obligations, and liabilities of the Company, and the Members shall not be obligated personally for any such debt, obligation, or liability of the Company solely by reason of being Members. The failure of the Company to observe any formalities or requirements relating to the exercise of its powers or the management of its business or affairs under this Agreement or by law shall not be grounds for imposing personal liability on the Members for any debts, liabilities, or obligations of the Company. Except as otherwise expressly required by law, the Members, in such Members' capacity as such, shall have no liability in excess of (a) the amount of such Members' Capital Contributions, (b) such Members' share of any assets and undistributed profits of the Company, and (c) the amount of any distributions required to be returned according to law.

9.2 Indemnification. The Company shall, to the fullest extent provided or allowed by law, indemnify, save harmless, and pay all judgments and claims against the Members, and each of the Company's or Members' agents, affiliates, heirs, legal representatives, successors, and assigns (each, an "Indemnified Party") from, against, and in respect of any and all liability, loss, damage, and expense incurred or sustained by the Indemnified Party in connection with the business of the Company or by reason of any act performed or omitted to be performed in connection with the activities of the Company or in dealing with third parties on behalf of the Company, including costs and attorneys' fees before and at trial and at all appellate levels, whether or not suit is instituted (which attorneys' fees may be paid as incurred), and any amounts expended in the settlement of any claims of liability, loss, or damage, to the fullest extent allowed by law.

9.3. Insurance. The Company shall not pay for any insurance covering liability of the Members or the Company's or Members' agents, affiliates, heirs, legal representatives, successors, and assigns for actions or omissions for which indemnification is not permitted hereunder; provided, however, that nothing contained here shall preclude the Company from purchasing and paying for such types of insurance, including extended coverage liability and casualty and worker's compensation, as would be customary for any Person owning, managing, and/or operating comparable property and engaged in a similar business, or from naming the Members and any of the Company's or Members, agents, affiliates, heirs, legal representatives, successors, or assigns or any Indemnified Party as additional insured parties thereunder.

9.4 Non-Exclusive Right. The provisions of this Article IX shall be in addition to and not in limitation of any other rights of indemnification and reimbursement or limitations of liability to which an Indemnified Party may be entitled under the Act, common law, or otherwise.

ARTICLE X. AMENDMENT

10.1 Amendment. This Agreement may not be altered or modified except by the unanimous written consent or agreement of the Members as evidenced by an amendment hereto whereby this Agreement is amended or amended and restated.

ARTICLE XI. WITHDRAWAL

11.1 Withdrawal of a Member. No Member may withdraw from the Company except by written request of the Member given to each of the other Members and with the unanimous written consent of the other Members (the effective date of withdrawal being the date on which the unanimous written consent of all of the other Members is given) or upon the effective date of any of the following events:

(a) the Member makes an assignment of his or her property for the benefit of creditors;

(b) the Member files a voluntary petition of bankruptcy;

(c) the Member is adjudged bankrupt or insolvent or there is entered against the Member an order for relief in any bankruptcy or insolvency proceeding;

(d) the Member seeks, consents to, or acquiesces in the appointment of a trustee or receiver for, or liquidation of the Member or of all or any substantial part of the Member's property;

(e) the Member files an answer or other pleading admitting or failing to contest the material allegations of a petition filed against the Member in any proceeding described in Subsections 11.1 (a) through (d);

(f) if the Member is a corporation, the dissolution of the corporation or the revocation of its articles of incorporation or charter;

(g) if the Member is an estate, the distribution by the fiduciary of the estate's Interest in the Company;

(h) if the Member is an employee of the Company and he or she resigns, retires, or for any reason ceases to be employed by the Company in any capacity; or

(i) if the other Members owning more than fifty percent (50%) of the Interests vote or request in writing that a Member withdraw and such request is given to the Member (the effective date of withdrawal being the date on which the vote or written request of the other Members is given to the Member).

11.2 Valuation of Interest. The value of the withdrawing Member's Interest in all events shall be equal to the greater of the following: (a) the amount of the Member's Capital Contribution or (b) the amount of the

Member's share of the Members' equity in the Company, plus the amount of any unpaid and outstanding loans or advances made by the Member to the Company (plus any due and unpaid interest thereon, if interest on the loan or advance has been agreed to between the Company and the Member), calculated as of the end of the fiscal quarter immediately preceding the effective date of the Member's withdrawal.

11.3 Payment of Value. The value shall be payable as follows: (a) If the value is equal to or less than $500, at closing, and (b) If the value is greater than $500, at the option of the Company, $500 at closing with the balance of the purchase price paid by delivering a promissory note of the Company dated as of the closing date and bearing interest at the prime rate published in The Wall Street Journal as of the effective date of withdrawal, with the principal amount being payable in five (5) equal annual installments beginning one (1) year from closing and with the interest on the accrued and unpaid balance being payable at the time of payment of each principal installment.

11.4 Closing. Payment of the value of the departing Member's Interest shall be made at a mutually agreeable time and date on or before thirty (30) days from the effective date of withdrawal. Upon payment of the value of the Interest as calculated in Section 11.3 above: (a) the Member's right to receive any and all further payments or distributions on account of the Member's ownership of the Interest in the Company shall cease; (b) the Member's loans or advances to the Company shall be paid and satisfied in full; and (c) the Member shall no longer be a Member or creditor of the Company on account of the Capital Contribution or the loans or advances.

11.5 Limitation on Payment of Value. If payment of the value of the Interest would be prohibited by any statute or law prohibiting distributions that would

(a) render the Company insolvent; or

(b) be made at a time that the total Company liabilities (other than liabilities to Members on account of their Interests) exceed the value of the Company's total assets;

then the value of the withdrawing Member's Interest in all events shall be $1.00.

ARTICLE XII. MISCELLANEOUS PROVISIONS

12.1 Assignment of Interest and New Members. No Member may assign such person's Interest in the Company in whole or in part except by the vote or written consent of the other Members owning more than fifty percent (50%) of the Interests. No additional Person may be admitted as a Member except by the vote or written consent of the Members owning more than fifty percent (50%) of the Interests.

12.2 Determinations by Members: Except as required by the express provisions of this Agreement or of the Act:

(a) Any transaction, action, or decision which requires or permits the Members to consent to, approve, elect, appoint, adopt, or authorize or to make a determination or decision with respect thereto under this Agreement, the Act, the Code, or otherwise shall be made by the Members owning more than fifty percent (50%) of the Interests.

(b) The Members shall act at a meeting of Members or by consent in writing of the Members. Members may vote or give their consent in person or by proxy.

(c) Meetings of the Members may be held at any time, upon call of any Member or Members owning, in the aggregate, at least ten percent (10%) of the Interests.

(d) Unless waived in writing by the Members owning more than fifty percent (50%) of the Interests (before or after a meeting), at least two (2) business days, prior notice of any meeting shall be given to each Member. Such notice shall state the purpose for which such meeting has been called. No business may be conducted or action taken at such meeting that is not provided for in such notice.

(e) Members may participate in a meeting of Members by means of conference telephone or similar communications equipment by means of which all Persons participating in the meeting can hear each other, and such participation shall constitute presence in person at such meeting.

(f) The Members shall cause to be kept a book of minutes of all meetings of the Members in which there shall be recorded the time and place of such meeting, by whom such meeting was called, the notice thereof given, the names of those present, and the proceedings thereof. Copies of any consents in writing shall also be filed in such minute book.

12.3 Binding Effect. This Agreement shall be binding upon and inure to the benefit of the undersigned Members, their legal representatives, heirs, successors, and assigns. This Agreement and the rights and duties of the Members hereunder shall be governed by, and interpreted and construed in accordance with, the laws of the Company's state of organization or charter, without regard to principles of choice of law.

12.5 Headings. The article and section headings in this Agreement are inserted as a matter of convenience and are for reference only and shall not be construed to define, limit, extend, or describe the scope of this Agreement or the intent of any provision.

12.6 Number and Gender. Whenever required by the context here, the singular shall include the plural, and vice versa, and the masculine gender shall include the feminine and neuter genders, and vice versa.

12.7 Entire Agreement and Binding Effect. This Agreement constitutes the sole operating agreement among the Members and supersedes and cancels any prior agreements, representations, warranties, or communications, whether oral or written, between the Members relating to the affairs of the Company and the conduct of the Company's business. No amendment or modification of this Agreement shall be effective unless approved in writing as provided in Section 10.1. The Articles of Organization and this Agreement are binding upon and shall inure to the benefit of the Members and Agent(s) and shall be binding upon their successors, assigns, affiliates, subsidiaries, heirs, beneficiaries, personal representatives, executors, administrators, and guardians, as applicable and appropriate.

IN WITNESS WHEREOF, this Agreement has been made and executed by the Members effective as of the date first written above.

_____ (Member)

_____ (Member)

_____ (Member)

Table A: Name, Address, and Initial Capital Contribution of the Members

Name and Address of Member	Value of Initial Capital Contribution	Nature of Member's Initial Capital Contribution (i.e., cash, services, property)	Percentage Interest of Member

9. Long-Form Operating Agreement for Manager-Managed LLC

OPERATING AGREEMENT OF (insert full name), LLC

THIS OPERATING AGREEMENT (the "Agreement") is made and entered into on _____, 20__, and those persons whose names, addresses and signatures are set forth below, being the Members of (insert name) LLC (the "Company"), represent and agree that they have caused or will cause to be filed, on behalf of the Company, Articles of Organization, and that they desire to enter into an operating agreement.

The Members agree as follows:

ARTICLE I. DEFINITIONS

1.1. "Act" means the Limited Liability Company Law of the State in which the Company is organized or chartered, including any amendments or the corresponding provision(s) of any succeeding law.

1.2. "Affiliate" or "Affiliate of a Member" means any Person under the control of, in common control with, or in control of a Member, whether that control is direct or indirect. The term "control," as used herein, means, with respect to a corporation or limited liability company, the ability to exercise more than fifty percent (50%) of the voting rights of the controlled entity, and with respect to an individual, partnership, trust, or other entity or association, the ability, directly or indirectly, to direct the management of policies of the controlled entity or individual.

1.3. "Agreement" means this Operating Agreement, in its original form and as amended from time to time.

1.4. "Articles" means the Articles of Organization or other charter document filed with the Secretary of State in the state of organization forming this limited liability company, as initially filed and as they may be amended from time to time.

1.5. "Capital Account" means the amount of the capital interest of a Member in the Company, consisting of the amount of money and the fair market value, net of liabilities, of any property initially contributed by the Member, as (1) increased by any additional contributions and the Member's share of the Company's profits; and (2) decreased by any distribution to that Member as well as that Member's share of Company losses.

1.6. "Code" means the Internal Revenue Code of 1986, as amended from time to time, the regulations promulgated thereunder, and any corresponding provision of any succeeding revenue law.

1.7. "Company Minimum Gain" shall have the same meaning as set forth for the term "Partnership Minimum Gain" in the Regulations section 1.704-2(d) (26 CFR Section 1.704-2(d)).

1.8. "Departing Member" means any Member whose conduct results in a Dissolution Event or who withdraws from or is expelled from the Company in accordance with Section 4.3, where such withdrawal does not result in dissolution of the Company.

1.9. "Dissolution Event" means, with respect to any Member, one or more of the following: the death, resignation, retirement, expulsion, bankruptcy, or dissolution of any Member.

1.10. "Distribution" means the transfer of money or property by the Company to the Members without consideration.

1.11 "Manager" means each Person who has been appointed to serve as a Manager of the Company in accordance with the Act, the Articles, and this Agreement.

1.12. "Member" means each Person who has been admitted into membership in the Company, executes this Agreement and any subsequent amendments, and has not engaged in conduct resulting in a Dissolution Event or terminated membership for any other reason.

1.13. "Member Nonrecourse Debt" shall have the same meaning as set forth for the term "Partnership Nonrecourse Debt" in the Code.

1.14. "Member Nonrecourse Deductions" means items of Company loss, deduction, or Code Section 705(a)(2)(B) expenditures which are attributable to Member Nonrecourse Debt.

1.15. "Membership Interest" means a Member's rights in the Company, collectively, including the Member's economic interest, right to vote and participate in management, and right to information concerning the business and affairs of the Company provided in this Agreement or under the Act.

1.16. "Net Profits" and "Net Losses" mean the Company's income, loss, and deductions computed at the close of each fiscal year in accordance with the accounting methods used to prepare the Company's information tax return filed for federal income tax purposes.

1.17. "Nonrecourse Liability" has the meaning provided in the Code.

1.18. "Percentage Interest" means the percentage ownership of the Company of each Member as set forth in the column entitled "Member's Percentage Interest" contained in Table A as recalculated from time to time pursuant to this Agreement.

1.19. "Person" means an individual, partnership, limited partnership, corporation, limited liability company, registered limited liability partnership, trust, association, estate, or any other entity.

1.20. "Remaining Members" means, upon the occurrence of a Dissolution Event, those members of the Company whose conduct did not cause its occurrence.

ARTICLE II. FORMATION AND ORGANIZATION

2.1. Initial Date and Initial Parties. This Agreement is deemed entered into upon the date of the filing of the Company's Articles.

2.2. Subsequent Parties. No Person may become a Member of the Company without agreeing to and without becoming a signatory of this Agreement, and any offer or assignment of a Membership Interest is contingent upon the fulfillment of this condition.

2.3. Term. The Company shall commence upon the filing of its Articles and it shall continue in existence until December 31, 2050, unless terminated earlier under the provisions of this Agreement.

2.4. Principal Place of Business. The Company will have its principal place of business at (insert address) or at any other address upon which the Members agree. The Company shall maintain its principal executive offices at its principal place of business, as well as all required records and documents.

2.5. Authorization and Purpose. The purpose of the Company is to engage in any lawful business activity that is permitted by the Act.

ARTICLE III. CAPITAL CONTRIBUTIONS AND ACCOUNTS

3.1. Initial Capital Contributions. The initial capital contribution of each Member is listed in Table A attached hereto. Table A shall be revised to reflect and additional contributions pursuant to Section 3.2.

3.2. Additional Contributions. No Member shall be required to make any additional contributions to the Company. However, upon agreement by the Members that additional capital is desirable or necessary, any Member may, but shall not be required to, contribute additional capital to the Company on a pro rata basis consistent with the Percentage Interest of each of the Members.

3.3. Interest Payments. No Member shall be entitled to receive interest payments in connection with any contribution of capital to the Company, except as expressly provided herein.

3.4. Right to Return of Contributions. No Member shall be entitled to a return of any capital contributed to the Company, except as expressly provided in the Agreement.

3.5. Capital Accounts. A Capital Account shall be created and maintained by the Company for each Member, in conformance with the Code, which shall reflect all Capital Contributions to the Company. Should any Member transfer or assign all or any part of his or her membership interest in accordance with this Agreement, the successor shall receive that portion of the Member's Capital Account attributable to the interest assigned or transferred.

ARTICLE IV. MEMBERS

4.1. Limitation of Liability. No Member shall be personally liable for the debts, obligations, liabilities, or judgments of the Company solely by virtue of his or her Membership in the Company, except as expressly set forth in this Agreement or required by law.

4.2. Additional Members. The Members may admit additional Members to the Company only if approved by a two-thirds majority in interest of the Company Membership. Additional Members shall be permitted to participate in management at the discretion of the existing Members. Likewise, the existing Members shall agree upon an Additional Member's participation in Net Profits, Net Losses, and Distributions, as those terms are defined in this Agreement. Table A shall be amended to include the name, present mailing address, and percentage ownership of any Additional Members.

4.3. Withdrawal or Expulsion from Membership. Any Member may withdraw at any time after sixty (60) days' written notice to the company, without prejudice to the rights of the Company or any Member under any contract to which the withdrawing Member is a party. Such withdrawing Member shall have the rights of a transferee under this Agreement and the remaining Members shall be entitled to purchase the withdrawing Member's Membership Interest in accordance with this Agreement. Any Member may be expelled from the Company upon a vote of two-thirds majority in interest of the Company Membership. Such expelled Member shall have the rights of a transferee under this Agreement and the remaining Members shall be entitled to purchase the expelled Member's Membership Interest in accordance with this Agreement.

4.4. Competing Activities. The Members and their officers, directors, shareholders, partners, managers, agents, employees, and Affiliates are permitted to participate in other business activities which may be in competition, direct or indirect, with those of the Company. The Members further acknowledge that they are under no obligation to present to the Company any business or investment opportunities, even if the opportunities are of such a character as to be appropriate for the Company's undertaking. Each Member hereby waives the right to any claim against any other Member or Affiliate on account of such competing activities.

4.5. Compensation of Members. No Member or Affiliate shall be entitled to compensation for services rendered to the Company, absent agreement by the Members. However, Members and Affiliates shall be entitled to reimbursement for the actual cost of goods and services provided to the Company, including, without limitation, reimbursement for any professional services required to form the Company.

4.6. Transaction with the Company. The Members may permit a Member to lend money to and transact business with the Company, subject to any limitations contained in this Agreement or in the Act. To the extent permitted by applicable laws, such a Member shall be treated like any other Person with respect to transactions with the Company.

4.7. Meetings.

(a) There will be no regular or annual meeting of the Members. However, any Member(s) with an aggregate Percentage Interest of ten percent (10%) or more may call a meeting of the Members at any time. Such meeting shall be held at a place to be agreed upon by the Members.

(b) Minutes of the meeting shall be made and maintained along with the books and records of the Company.

(c) If any action on the part of the Members is to be proposed at the meeting, then written notice of the meeting must be provided to each Member entitled to vote not less than ten (10) days or more than sixty (60) days prior to the meeting. Notice may be given in person, by fax, by first class mail, or by any other written communication, charges prepaid, at the Members' address listed in Table A. The notice shall contain the date, time, and place of the meeting and a statement of the general nature of this business to be transacted there.

4.8. Actions at Meetings.

(a) No action may be taken at a meeting that was not proposed in the notice of the meeting, unless there is unanimous consent among all Members entitled to vote.

(b) No action may be taken at a meeting unless a quorum of Members is present, either in person or by proxy. A quorum of Members shall consist of Members holding a majority of the Percentage Interest in the Company.

(c) A Member may participate in, and is deemed present at, any meeting by clearly audible conference telephone or other similar means of communication.

(d) Any meeting may be adjourned upon the vote of the majority of the Membership Interests represented at the meeting.

(e) Actions taken at any meeting of the Members have full force and effect if each Member who was not present in person or by proxy, signs a written waiver of notice and consent to the holding of the meeting or approval of the minutes of the meeting. All such waivers and consents shall become Company records.

(f) Presence at a meeting constitutes a waiver of the right to object to notice of a meeting, unless the Member expresses such an objection at the start of the meeting.

4.9. Actions Without Meetings. Any action that may be taken at a meeting of the Members may be taken without a meeting and without prior notice, if written consents to the action are submitted to the Company within sixty (60) days of the record date for the taking of the action, executed by Members holding a sufficient number of votes to authorize the taking of the action at a meeting at which all Members entitled to vote thereon are present and vote. All such consents shall be maintained as Company records.

4.10. Record Date. For the purposes of voting, notices of meetings, distributions, or any other rights under this Agreement, the Articles, or the Act, the Members representing in excess of ten percent (10%) of the Percentage Interests in the Company may fix, in advance, a record date that is not more than sixty (60) or less than ten (10) days prior to the date of such meeting or sixty (60) days prior to any other action. If no record date is fixed, the record date shall be determined in accordance with the Act.

4.11. Voting Rights. Except as expressly set forth in this Agreement, all actions requiring the vote, approval, or consent of the Members may be authorized upon the vote, approval, or consent of those Members holding a majority of the Percentage Interests in the Company. The following actions require the unanimous vote, approval, or consent of all Members who are neither the subjects of a dissolution event nor the transferors of a Membership Interest:

(a) Approval of the purchase by the Company or its nominee of the Membership Interest of a transferor Member;

(b) Approval of the sale, transfer, exchange, assignment, or other disposition of a Member's interest in the Company, and admission of the transferee as a Member;

(c) A decision to make any amendment to the Articles or to this Agreement; and

(d) A decision to compromise the obligation to any Member to make a Capital Contribution or return money or property distributed in violation of the Act.

ARTICLE V. MANAGEMENT

5.1. Management by Appointed Managers. The Company shall be managed by one or more appointed Managers. The number of Managers and the identity of each Manager are set forth in Table B, below. The Members shall elect and appoint the Managers (and also determine the number of managers), who shall have the full and exclusive right, power, and authority to manage the affairs of the Company and to bind the Company to contracts and obligations, to make all decisions with respect thereto, and to do or cause to be done any and all acts or things deemed by the Members to be necessary, appropriate, or desirable to carry out or further the business of the Company. All decisions and actions of the Managers shall be made by majority vote of the Managers as provided in this Agreement. There shall be no annual meetings of the Members or Managers; Managers shall serve at the pleasure of the Members and until their successors and are duly elected and appointed by the Members.

5.2. Limitation on Powers of Managers; Member Vote Required for Some Actions. The Mangers shall not be authorized to permit the Company to perform the following acts or to engage in the following transactions without first obtaining the affirmative vote or written consent of the Members holding a majority Interest or such greater Percentage Interest as may be indicated below:

(a) The sale or other disposition of all or a substantial part of the Company's assets, whether occurring as a single transaction or a series of transactions over a 12-month period, except if the same is part of the orderly liquidation and winding up of the Company's affairs upon dissolution;

(b) The merger of the Company with any other business entity without the affirmative vote or written consent of all members;

(c) Any alteration of the primary purpose or business of the Company shall require the affirmative vote or written consent of Members holding at least sixty-six percent (66%) of the Percentage Interest in the Company;

(d) The establishment of different classes of Members;

(e) Transactions between the Company and one or more Members or one or more of any Member's Affiliates, or transactions in which one or more Members or Affiliates thereof have a material financial interest;

(f) Without limiting subsection (e) of this section, the lending of money to any Member or Affiliate of the Company;

(g) Any act which would prevent the Company from conducting its duly authorized business;

(h) The confession of a judgment against the Company.

Notwithstanding any other provisions of this Agreement, the written consent of all of the Members is required to permit the Company to incur an indebtedness or obligation greater than one hundred thousand dollars ($100,000.00). All checks, drafts, or other instruments requiring the Company to make payment of an amount less than fifty thousand dollars ($50,000.00) may be signed by any Member, acting alone. Any check, draft, or other instrument requiring the Company to make payment in the amount of fifty thousand dollars ($50,000.00) or more shall require the signature of two (2) Members acting together.

5.3. Fiduciary Duties. The fiduciary duties a Member owes to the Company and to the other Members of the Company are those of a partner to a partnership and to the partners of a partnership.

5.4. Liability for Acts and Omissions. As long as a Member acts in accordance with Section 5.3, no Member shall incur liability to any other Member or to the Company for any act or omission which occurs while in the performance of services for the Company.

ARTICLE VI. ALLOCATION OF PROFIT AND LOSS

6.1. Compliance with the Code. The Company intends to comply with the Code and all applicable Regulations, including without limitation the minimum gain chargeback requirements, and intends that the provisions of this Article be interpreted consistently with that intent.

6.2. Net Profits. Except as specifically provided elsewhere in this Agreement, Distributions of Net Profit shall be made to Members in proportion to their Percentage Interest in the Company.

6.3. Net Losses. Except as specifically provided elsewhere in this Agreement, Net Losses shall be allocated to the Members in proportion to their Percentage Interest in the Company. However, the foregoing will not apply to the extent that it would result in a Negative Capital Account balance for any Member equal to the Company Minimum Gain which would be realized by that Member in the event of a foreclosure of the

Company's assets. Any Net Loss which is not allocated in accordance with the foregoing provision shall be allocated to other Members who are unaffected by that provision. When subsequent allocations of profit and loss are calculated, the losses reallocated pursuant to this provision shall be taken into account such that the net amount of the allocation shall be as close as possible to that which would have been allocated to each Member if the reallocation pursuant to this section had not taken place.

6.4. Regulatory Allocations. Notwithstanding the provisions of Section 6.3, the following applies:

(a) Should there be a net decrease in Company Minimum Gain in any taxable year, the Members shall specially allocate to each Member items of income and gain for that year (and, if necessary, for subsequent years) as required by the Code governing minimum gain chargeback requirements.

(b) Should there be a net decrease in Company Minimum Gain based on a Member Nonrecourse Debt in any taxable year, the Members shall first determine the extent of each Member's share of the Company Minimum Gain attributable to Member Nonrecourse Debt in accordance with the Code. The Members shall then specially allocate items of income and gain for that year (and, if necessary, for subsequent years) in accordance with the Code to each Member who has a share of the Company Nonrecourse Debt Minimum Gain.

(c) The Members shall allocate Nonrecourse Deductions for any taxable year to each Member in proportion to his or her Percentage Interest.

(d) The Members shall allocate Member Nonrecourse Deductions for any taxable year to the Member who bears the risk of loss with respect to the Nonrecourse Debt to which the Member Nonrecourse Deduction is attributable, as provided in the Code.

(e) If a Member unexpectedly receives any allocation of loss or deduction, or item thereof, or distributions which result in the Member's having a Negative Capital Account balance at the end of the taxable year greater than the Member's share of Company Minimum Gain, the Company shall specially allocate items of income and gain to that Member in a manner designed to eliminate the excess Negative Capital Account balance as rapidly as possible. Any allocations made in accordance with this provision shall taken into consideration in determining subsequent allocations under Article VI, so that, to the extent possible, the total amount allocated in this and subsequent allocations equals that which would have been allocated had there been no unexpected adjustments, allocations, and distributions and no allocation pursuant to Section 6.4(e).

(f) In accordance with Code Section 704(c) and the Regulations promulgated pursuant thereto, and notwithstanding any other provision in this Article, income, gain, loss, and deductions with respect to any property contributed to the Company shall, solely for tax purposes, be allocated among Members, taking into account any variation between the adjusted basis of the property to the Company for federal income tax purposes and its fair market value on the date of contribution. Allocations pursuant to this subsection are made solely for federal, state, and local taxes and shall not be taken into consideration in determining a Member's Capital Account or share of Net Profits or Net Losses or any other items subject to Distribution under this agreement.

6.5. Distributions. The Members may elect, by unanimous vote, to make a Distribution of assets at any time that would not be prohibited under the Act or under this Agreement. Such a Distribution shall be made in proportion to the unreturned capital contributions of each Member until all contributions have been paid, and thereafter in proportion to each Member's Percentage Interest in the Company. All such Distributions shall be made to those Persons who, according to the books and records of the Company, were the holders of record of Membership Interests on the date of the Distribution. Subject to Section 6.6, neither the Company nor any Members shall be liable for the making of any Distributions in accordance with the provisions of this section.

6.6. Limitations on Distributions.

(a) The Members shall not make any Distribution if, after giving effect to the distribution, (1) the Company would not be able to pay its debts as they become due in the usual course of business, or (2) the Company's total assets would be less than the sum of its total liabilities plus, unless this Agreement provides otherwise, the amount that would be needed, if the Company were to be dissolved at the time of Distribution, to satisfy the preferential rights of other Members upon dissolution that are superior to the rights of the Member receiving the Distribution.

(b) The Members may base a determination that a Distribution is not prohibited under this section on any of the following: (1) financial statements prepared on the basis of accounting practices and principles that are reasonable under the circumstances, (2) a fair valuation, or (3) any other method that is reasonable under the circumstances.

6.7. Return of Distributions. Members shall return to the Company any Distributions received which are in violation of this Agreement or the Act. Such Distributions shall be returned to the account or accounts of the Company from which they were taken in order to make the Distribution. If a Distribution is made in compliance with the Act and this Agreement, a Member is under no obligation to return it to the Company or to pay the amount of the Distribution for the account of the Company or to any creditor of the Company.

6.8. Members Bound by These Provisions. The Members understand and acknowledge the tax implications of the provisions of this Article of the Agreement and agree to be bound by these provisions in reporting items of income and loss relating to the Company on their federal and state income tax returns.

ARTICLE VII. TRANSFERS AND TERMINATIONS OF MEMBERSHIP INTERESTS

7.1. Restriction on Transferability of Membership Interests. A Member may not transfer, assign, encumber, or convey all or any part of his or her Membership Interest in the Company, except as provided herein. In entering into this Agreement, each of the Members acknowledges the reasonableness of this restriction, which is intended to further the purposes of the Company and the relationships among the Members.

7.2. Permitted Transfers. In order to be permitted, a transfer or assignment of all or any part of a Membership interest must have the approval of a two-thirds majority of the Members of the Company. Each Member, in his or her sole discretion, may proffer or withhold approval. In addition, the following conditions must be met:

(a) The transferee must provide a written agreement, satisfactory to the Members, to be bound by all of the provisions of this Agreement;

(b) The transferee must provide the Company with his or her taxpayer identification number and initial tax basis in the transferred interest;

(c) The transferee must pay the reasonable expenses incurred in connection with his or her admission to Membership;

(d) The transfer must be in compliance with all federal and state securities laws;

(e) The transfer must not result in the termination of the Company pursuant to Code Section 708.

(f) The transfer must not render the Company subject to the Investment Company Act of 1940, as amended; and

(g) The transferor must comply with the provisions of this Agreement.

7.3. Company's Right to Purchase Transferor's Interest and Valuation of Transferor's Interest. Any Member who wishes to transfer all or any part of his or her interest in the Company shall immediately provide the Company with written notice of his or her intention. The notice shall fully describe the nature of the interest to be transferred. Thereafter, the Company, or its nominee, shall have the option to purchase the transferor's interest at the Repurchase Price (as defined below).

(a) The "Repurchase Price" shall be determined as of the date of the event causing the transfer or dissolution event (the "Effective Date"). The date that the Company receives notice of a Member's intention to transfer his or her interest pursuant to this paragraph shall be deemed to be the Effective Date. The Repurchase Price shall be determined as follows:

i. The Repurchase Price of a Member's Percentage Interest shall be computed by the independent certified public accountant (CPA) regularly used by the Company or, if the Company has no CPA or if the CPA is unavailable, then by a qualified appraiser selected by the Company for this purpose. The Repurchase Price of a Member's Percentage Interest shall be the sum of the Company's total Repurchase Price multiplied by the Transferor's Percentage Interest as of the Effective Date.

ii. The Repurchase Price shall be determined by the book value method, as more further described herein. The book value of the interests shall be determined in accordance with the regular financial statements prepared by the Company and in accordance with generally accepted accounting principles, applied consistently with the accounting principles previously applied by the Company, adjusted to reflect the following:

(1) All inventory, valued at cost.

(2) All real property, leasehold improvements, equipment, and furnishings and fixtures valued at their fair market value.

(3) The face amount of any accounts payable.

(4) Any accrued taxes or assessments, deducted as liabilities.

(5) All usual fiscal year-end accruals and deferrals (including depreciation), prorated over the fiscal year.

(6) The reasonable fair market value of any good will or other intangible assets.

The cost of the assessment shall be borne by the Company.

(b) The option provided to the Company shall be irrevocable and shall remain open for thirty (30) days from the Effective Date, except that if notice is given by regular mail, the option shall remain open for thirty-five (35) days from the Effective Date.

(c) At any time while the option remains open, the Company (or its nominee) may elect to exercise the option and purchase the transferor's interest in the Company. The transferor Member shall not vote on the question of whether the Company should exercise its option.

(d) If the Company chooses to exercise its option to purchase the transferor Member's interest, it shall provide written notice to the transferor within the option period. The notice shall specify a "Closing Date" for the purchase, which shall occur within thirty (30) days of the expiration of the option period.

(e) If the Company declines to exercise its option to purchase the transferor Member's interest, the transferor Member may then transfer his or her interest in accordance with Section 7.2. Any transfer not in compliance with the provisions of Section 7.2 shall be null and void and have no force or effect.

(f) In the event that the Company chooses to exercise its option to purchase the transferor Member's interest, the Company may elect to purchase the Member's interest on the following terms:

i. The Company may elect to pay the Repurchase Price in cash, by making such cash payment to the transferor Member upon the Closing Date.

ii. The Company may elect to pay any portion of the Repurchase Price by delivering to the transferor Member, upon the Closing Date, all of the following:

(1) An amount equal to at least 10% of the Repurchase Price in cash or in an immediately negotiable draft, and

(2) A Promissory Note for the remaining amount of the Repurchase Price, to be paid in 12 successive monthly installments, with such installments beginning 30 days following the Closing Date, and ending one year from the Closing Date, and

(3) A security agreement guaranteeing the payment of the Promissory Note by offering the Transferor's former membership interest as security for the payment of the Promissory Note.

7.4. Occurrence of Dissolution Event. Upon the death, withdrawal, resignation, retirement, expulsion, insanity, bankruptcy, or dissolution of any Member (a Dissolution Event), the Company shall be dissolved, unless all of the Remaining Members elect by a majority in interest within 90 days thereafter to continue the operation of the business. In the event that the Remaining Members to agree, the Company and the Remaining Members shall have the right to purchase the interest of the Member whose actions caused the occurrence of the Dissolution Event. The interest shall be sold in the manner described in Section 7.6.

7.5. Withdrawal from Membership. Notwithstanding Section 7.4, in the event that a Member withdraws in accordance with Section 4.3 and such withdrawal does not result in the dissolution of the Company, the Company and the Remaining Members shall have the right to purchase the interest of the withdrawing Member in the manner described in Section 7.6.

7.6. Purchase of Interest of Departing Member. The purchase price of a Departing Member's interest shall be determined in accordance with the procedure provided in Section 7.3.

(a) Once a value has been determined, each Remaining Member shall be entitled to purchase that portion of the Departing Member's interest that corresponds to his or her percentage ownership of the Percentage Interests of those Members electing to purchase a portion of the Departing Member's interest in the Company.

(b) Each Remaining Member desiring to purchase a share of the Departing Member's interest shall have thirty (30) days to provide written notice to the Company of his or her intention to do so. The failure to provide notice shall be deemed a rejection of the opportunity to purchase the Departing Member's interest.

(c) If any Member elects not to purchase all of the Departing Member's interest to which he or she is entitled, the other Members may purchase that portion of the Departing Member's interest. Any interest which is not purchased by the Remaining Members may be purchased by the Company.

(d) The Members shall assign a closing date within 60 days after the Members' election to purchase is completed. At that time, the Departing Member shall deliver to the Remaining Members an instrument of title, free of any encumbrances and containing warranties of title, duly conveying his or her interest in the Company and, in return, he or she shall be paid the purchase price for his or her interest in cash. The Departing Member and the Remaining Members shall perform all acts reasonably necessary to consummate the transaction in accordance with this agreement.

7.7. No Release of Liability. Any Member or Departing Member whose interest in the Company is sold pursuant to Article VII is not relieved thereby of any liability he or she may owe the Company.

ARTICLE VIII. BOOKS, RECORDS, AND REPORTING

8.1. Books and Records. The Members shall maintain at the Company's principal place of business the following books and records: a current list of the full name and last known business or residence address of each Member, together with the Capital Contribution, Capital Account, and Membership Interest of each Member; a copy of the Articles and all amendments thereto; copies of the Company's federal, state, and local income tax or information returns and reports, if any, for the six (6) most recent taxable years; a copy of this Agreement and any amendments to it; copies of the Company's financial statements, if any; the books and records of the Company as they relate to its internal affairs for at least the current and past four (4) fiscal years; and true and correct copies of all relevant documents and records indicating the amount, cost, and value of all the property and assets of the Company.

8.2. Accounting Methods. The books and records of the Company shall be maintained in accordance with the accounting methods utilized for federal income tax purposes.

8.3. Reports. The Members shall cause to be prepared and filed in a timely manner all reports and documents required by any governmental agency. The Members shall cause to be prepared at least annually all information concerning the Company's operations that is required by the Members for the preparation of their federal and state tax returns.

8.4. Inspection Rights. For purposes reasonably related to their interests in the Company, all Members shall have the right to inspect and copy the books and records of the Company during normal business hours, upon reasonable request.

8.5. Bank Accounts. The Managers shall maintain all of the funds of the Company in a bank account or accounts in the name of the Company, at a depository institution or institutions to be determined by a majority of the Members. The Managers shall not permit the funds of the Company to be commingled in any manner with the funds or accounts of any other Person. The Managers shall have the powers enumerated in Section 5.2 with respect to endorsing, signing, and negotiating checks, drafts, or other evidence of indebtedness to the Company or obligating the Company money to a third party.

ARTICLE IX. DISSOLUTION, LIQUIDATION, AND WINDING UP

9.1. Conditions Under Which Dissolution Shall Occur. The Company shall dissolve and its affairs shall be wound up upon the happening the first of the following: at the time specified in the Articles; upon the happening of a Dissolution Event; and the failure of the Remaining Members to elect to continue, in accordance with Section 7.4; upon the vote of all of the Members to dissolve; upon the entry of a decree of judicial dissolution pursuant to the Act; upon the happening of any event specified in the Articles as causing or requiring dissolution; or upon the sale of all or substantially all of the Company's assets.

9.2. Winding Up and Dissolution. If the Company is dissolved, the Members shall wind up its affairs, including the selling of all of the Company's assets and the provision of written notification to all of the Company's creditors of the commencement of dissolution proceedings.

9.3. Order of Payment. After determining that all known debts and liabilities of the Company in the process of winding up have been paid or provided for, including, without limitation, debts and liabilities to Members who are creditors of the Company, the Members shall distribute the remaining assets among the Members in accordance with their Positive Capital Account balances, after taking into consideration the profit and loss allocations made pursuant to Section 6.4. Members shall not be required to restore Negative Capital Account Balances.

ARTICLE X. INDEMNIFICATION

10.1. Indemnification. The Company shall indemnify any Member and may indemnify any Person to the fullest extent permitted by law on the date such indemnification is requested for any judgments, settlements, penalties, fines, or expenses of any kind incurred as a result of the Person's performance in the capacity of Member, officer, employee, or agent of the Company, as long as the Member, or Person did not behave in violation of the Act or this Agreement.

ARTICLE XI. MISCELLANEOUS PROVISIONS

11.1. Assurances. Each Member shall execute all documents and certificates and perform all acts deemed appropriate by the Members and the Company or required by this Agreement or the Act in connection with the formation and operation of the Company and the acquisition, holding, or operation of any property by the Company.

11.2. Complete Agreement. This Agreement and the Articles constitute the complete and exclusive statement of the agreement among the Members with respect to the matters discussed herein and therein and they supersede all prior written or oral statements among the Members, including any prior statement, warranty, or representation.

11.3. Section Headings. The section headings which appear throughout this Agreement are provided for convenience only and are not intended to define or limit the scope of this Agreement or the intent of subject matter of its provisions.

11.4. Binding Effect. Subject to the provisions of this Agreement relating to the transferability of Membership Interests, this Agreement is binding upon and shall inure to the benefit of the parties hereto and their respective heirs, administrators, executors, successors, and assigns.

11.5. Interpretation. All pronouns and common nouns shall be deemed to refer to the masculine, feminine, neuter, singular, and plural, as the context may require. In the event that any claim is made by any Member relating to the drafting and interpretation of this Agreement, no presumption, inference, or burden of proof or persuasion shall be created or implied solely by virtue of the fact that this Agreement was drafted by or at the behest of a particular Member or his or her counsel.

11.6. Applicable Law. Each Member agrees that all disputes arising under or in connection with this Agreement and any transactions contemplated by this Agreement shall be governed by the internal law, and not the law of conflicts, of the state of organization.

11.7. Specific Performance. The Members acknowledge and agree that irreparable injury shall result from a breach of this Agreement and that money damages will not adequately compensate the injured party. Accordingly, in the event of a breach or a threatened breach of this Agreement, any party who may be injured shall be entitled, in addition to any other remedy which may be available, to injunctive relief to prevent or to correct the breach.

11.8. Remedies Cumulative. The remedies described in this Agreement are cumulative and shall not eliminate any other remedy to which a Person may be lawfully entitled.

11.9. Notice. Any notice or other writing to be served upon the Company or any Member thereof in connection with this Agreement shall be in writing and shall be deemed completed when delivered to the address specified in Table A, if to a Member, and to the resident agent, if to the Company. Any Member shall have the right to change the address at which notices shall be served upon ten (10) days' written notice to the Company and the other Members.

11.10. Amendments. Any amendments, modifications, or alterations to this Agreement or the Articles must be in writing and signed by all of the Members.

11.11. Severability. Each provision of this Agreement is severable from the other provisions. If, for any reason, any provision of this Agreement is declared invalid or contrary to existing law, the inoperability of that provision shall have no effect on the remaining provisions of the Agreement, which shall continue in full force and effect.

11.12. Counterparts. This Agreement may be executed in counterparts, each of which shall be deemed an original and all of which shall, when taken together, constitute a single document.

IN WITNESS WHEREOF, this Agreement has been made and executed by the Members effective as of the date first written above.

_____ (Member)

_____ (Member)

_____ (Member)

Table A. Name, Address, and Initial Capital Contribution of the Members

Name and Address of Member	Value of Initial Capital Contribution	Nature of Member's Initial Capital Contribution (i.e., cash, services, property)	Percentage Interest of Member

Table B. Managers

Name of Manager	Address of Manager

10. Short Form Operating Agreement For Manager-Managed LLC

OPERATING AGREEMENT OF [insert full name of LLC]

THIS OPERATING AGREEMENT (the "Agreement") is hereby entered into by the undersigned, who are owners and shall be referred to as Member or Members.

RECITALS

The Members desire to form [insert full name of LLC], a limited liability company (the "Company"), for the purposes set forth herein, and, accordingly, desire to enter into this Agreement in order to set forth the terms and conditions of the business and affairs of the Company and to determine the rights and obligations of its Members.

NOW, THEREFORE, the Members, intending to be legally bound by this Agreement, hereby agree that the limited liability company operating agreement of the Company shall be as follows:

ARTICLE I. DEFINITIONS

When used in this Agreement, the following terms shall have the meanings set forth below.

1.1 "Act" means the Limited Liability Company Law of the State in which the Company is organized or chartered, including any amendments or the corresponding provision(s) of any succeeding law.

1.2 "Capital Contribution(s)" means the amount of cash and the agreed value of property, services rendered, or a promissory note or other obligation to contribute cash or property or to perform services contributed by the Members for such Members' Interest in the Company, equal to the sum of the Members' initial Capital Contributions plus the Members' additional Capital Contributions, if any, made pursuant to Sections 4.1 and 4.2, respectively, less payments or distributions made pursuant to Section 5.1.

1.3 "Code" means the Internal Revenue Code of 1986 and the regulations promulgated thereunder, as amended from time to time (or any corresponding provision or provisions of succeeding law).

1.4 "Interest" or "Interests" means the ownership Interest, expressed as a number, percentage, or fraction, set forth in Table A, of a Member in the Company.

1.5 "Manager" or "Managers" means the natural person or persons who have authority to govern the Company according to the terms of this Agreement.

1.6 "Person" means any natural individual, partnership, firm, corporation, limited liability company, joint-stock company, trust or other entity.

1.7 "Secretary of State" means the Office of the Secretary of State or the office charged with accepting articles of organization in the Company's state of organization.

ARTICLE II. FORMATION

2.1 Organization. The Members hereby organize the Company as a limited liability company pursuant to the provisions of the Act.

2.2 Effective Date. The Company shall come into being on, and this Agreement shall take effect from, the date the Articles of Organization of the Company are filed with the Secretary of State in the state of organization or charter.

2.3 Agreement: Invalid Provisions and Saving Clause. The Members, by executing this Agreement, hereby agree to the terms and conditions of this Agreement. To the extent any provision of this Agreement is prohibited or ineffective under the Act, this Agreement shall be deemed to be amended to the least extent necessary in order to make this Agreement effective under the Act. In the event the Act is subsequently amended or interpreted in such a way to validate any provision of this Agreement that was formerly invalid, such provision shall be considered to be valid from the effective date of such amendment or interpretation.

ARTICLE III. PURPOSE; NATURE OF BUSINESS

3.1 Purpose; Nature of Business. The purpose of the Company shall be to engage in any lawful business that may be engaged in by a limited liability company organized under the Act, as such business activities may be determined by the Manager or Managers from time to time.

3.2 Powers. The Company shall have all powers of a limited liability company under the Act and the power to do all things necessary or convenient to accomplish its purpose and operate its business as described in Section 3.1 here.

ARTICLE IV. MEMBERS AND CAPITAL CONTRIBUTIONS

4.1 Members and Initial Capital Contribution. The name, address, Interest, type of property, and value of the initial Capital Contribution of the Members shall be set forth on Table A attached hereto.

4.2 Additional Capital Contributions. The Members shall have no obligation to make any additional Capital Contributions to the Company. The Members may make additional Capital Contributions to the Company as the Members unanimously determine are necessary, appropriate or desirable.

ARTICLE V. DISTRIBUTIONS AND ALLOCATIONS

5.1 Distributions and Allocations. All distributions of cash or other assets of the Company shall be made and paid to the Members at such time and in such amounts as a majority of the Managers may determine. All items of income, gain, loss, deduction and credit shall be allocated to the Members in proportion to their Interests.

ARTICLE VI. TAXATION

6.1 Income Tax Reporting. Each Member is aware of the income tax consequences of the allocations made by Article V here and agrees to be bound by the provisions of Article V here in reporting each Members' share of Company income and loss for federal and state income tax purposes.

6.2 Tax Treatment. Notwithstanding anything contained herein to the contrary and only for purposes of federal and, if applicable, state income tax purposes, the Company shall be classified as a partnership for such federal and state income tax purposes unless and until the Members determine to cause the Company to file an election under the Code to be classified as an association taxable as a corporation.

ARTICLE VII. MANAGERS AND AGENTS

7.1 Management by Manager(s). The Members shall elect and appoint the Manager(s) who shall have the full and exclusive right, power and authority to manage the affairs of the Company and to bind the Company, to make all decisions with respect thereto and to do or cause to be done any and all acts or things deemed by the Members to be necessary, appropriate or desirable to carry out or further the business of the Company. All decisions and actions of the Manager(s) shall be made by majority vote of the Manager(s) as provided in Section 12.3. No annual meeting shall be required to reappoint Manager(s). Such Person(s) shall serve in such office(s) at the pleasure of the Members and until his, her or their successors and are duly elected and appointed by the Members. Until further action of the Members as provided herein, the Manager(s) whose names appear on Table B below are the Manager(s) of the Company.

7.2 Agents. Without limiting the rights of the Members or the Manager(s), or the Company, the Manager(s) shall appoint the Person(s) who is (are) to act as the agent(s) of the Company to carry out and further the decisions and actions of the Members or the Manager(s), to manage and the administer the day-to-day operations and business of the Company and to execute any and all reports, forms, instruments, documents, papers, writings, agreements and contracts, including but not limited to deeds, bills of sale, assignments, leases, promissory notes, mortgages, and security agreements and any other type or form of document by which property or property rights of the Company are transferred or encumbered, or by which debts and obligations of the Company are created, incurred or evidenced, which are necessary, appropriate or beneficial to carry out or further such decisions or actions and to manage and administer the day-to-day operations and business.

ARTICLE VIII. BOOKS AND RECORDS

8.1 Books and Records. The Managers shall keep, or cause to be kept, at the principal place of business of the Company true and correct books of account, in which shall be entered fully and accurately each and every transaction of the Company. The Company's taxable and fiscal years shall end on December 31. All Members shall have the right to inspect the Company's books and records at any time, for any reason.

ARTICLE IX. LIMITATION OF LIABILITY; INDEMNIFICATION

9.1 Limited Liability. Except as otherwise required by law, the debts, obligations, and liabilities of the Company, whether arising in contract, tort or otherwise, shall be solely the debts, obligations, and liabilities of the Company, and the Members shall not be obligated personally for any such debt, obligation or liability of the Company solely by reason of being Members. The failure of the Company to observe any formalities or requirements relating to the exercise of its powers or the management of its business or affairs under this Agreement or by law shall not be grounds for imposing personal liability on the Members for any debts, liabilities or obligations of the Company. Except as otherwise expressly required by law, the Members, in such Members' capacity as such, shall have no liability in excess of (a) the amount of such Members' Capital Contributions, (b) such Members' share of any assets and undistributed profits of the Company, and (c) the amount of any distributions required to be returned according to law.

9.2 Indemnification. The Company shall, to the fullest extent provided or allowed by law, indemnify, save harmless, and pay all judgments and claims against the Members or Manager(s), and each of the Company's, Members', or Manager(s)' agents, affiliates, heirs, legal representatives, successors and assigns (each, an "Indemnified Party") from, against and in respect of any and all liability, loss, damage and expense incurred or sustained by the Indemnified Party in connection with the business of the Company or by reason of any act performed or omitted to be performed in connection with the activities of the Company or in dealing with third parties on behalf of the Company, including costs and attorneys' fees before and at trial and at all appellate levels, whether or not suit is instituted (which attorneys' fees may be paid as incurred), and any amounts expended in the settlement of any claims of liability, loss or damage, to the fullest extent allowed by law.

9.3. Insurance. The Company shall not pay for any insurance covering liability of the Members or the Manager(s) or the Company's, Members' or Manager(s)' agents, affiliates, heirs, legal representatives, successors and assigns for actions or omissions for which indemnification is not permitted hereunder; provided, however, that nothing contained here shall preclude the Company from purchasing and paying for such types of insurance, including extended coverage liability and casualty and worker's compensation, as would be customary for any Person owning, managing and/or operating comparable property and engaged in a similar business, or from naming the Members or the Manager(s) and any of the Company's, Members' or Manager(s)' agents, affiliates, heirs, legal representatives, successors or assigns or any Indemnified Party as additional insured parties thereunder.

9.4 Non-Exclusive Right. The provisions of this Article IX shall be in addition to and not in limitation of any other rights of indemnification and reimbursement or limitations of liability to which an Indemnified Party may be entitled under the Act, common law, or otherwise.

ARTICLE X. AMENDMENT

10.1 Amendment. This Agreement may not be altered or modified except by the unanimous written consent or agreement of the Members as evidenced by an amendment hereto whereby this Agreement is amended or amended and restated.

ARTICLE XI. WITHDRAWAL

11.1 Withdrawal of a Member. No Member may withdraw from the Company except by written request of the Member given to each of the other Members and with the unanimous written consent of the other Members (the effective date of withdrawal being the date on which the unanimous written consent of all of the other Members is given), or upon the effective date of any of the following events:

(a) the Member makes an assignment of his or her property for the benefit of creditors;

(b) the Member files a voluntary petition of bankruptcy;

(c) the Member is adjudged bankrupt or insolvent or there is entered against the Member an order for relief in any bankruptcy or insolvency proceeding;

(d) the Member seeks, consents to, or acquiesces in the appointment of a trustee or receiver for, or liquidation of the Member or of all or any substantial part of the Member's property;

(e) the Member files an answer or other pleading admitting or failing to contest the material allegations of a petition filed against the Member in any proceeding described in Subsections 11.1 (a) through (d);

(f) if the Member is a corporation, the dissolution of the corporation or the revocation of its articles of incorporation or charter;

(g) if the Member is an estate, the distribution by the fiduciary of the estate's Interest in the Company;

(h) if the Member is an employee of the Company and he or she resigns, retires or for any reason ceases to be employed by the Company in any capacity; or

(i) if the other Members owning more than fifty percent (50%) of the Interests vote or request in writing that a Member withdraw and such request is given to the Member (the effective date of withdrawal being the date on which the vote or written request of the other Members is given to the Member).

11.2 Valuation of Interest. The value of the withdrawing Member's Interest in all events shall be equal to the greater of the following: (a) the amount of the Member's Capital Contribution or (b) the amount of the Member's share of the Members' equity in the Company, plus the amount of any unpaid and outstanding loans or advances made by the Member to the Company (plus any due and unpaid interest thereon, if interest on the loan or advance has been agreed to between the Company and the Member), calculated as of the end of the fiscal quarter immediately preceding the effective date of the Member's withdrawal.

11.3 Payment of Value. The value shall be payable as follows: (i) If the value is equal to or less than $500, at closing, and (ii) If the value is greater than $500, at the option of the Company, $500 at closing with the balance of the purchase price paid by delivering a promissory note of the Company dated as of the closing date and bearing interest at the prime rate published in the Wall Street Journal as of the effective date of withdrawal with the principal amount being payable in five (5) equal annual installments beginning one (1) year from closing and with the interest on the accrued and unpaid balance being payable at the time of payment of each principal installment.

11.4 Closing. Payment of the value of the departing Member's Interest shall be made at a mutually agreeable time and date on or before thirty (30) days from the effective date of withdrawal. Upon payment of the value of the Interest as calculated in Section 11.3 above: (a) the Member's right to receive any and all further payments or distributions on account of the Member's ownership of the Interest in the Company shall cease; (b) the Member's loans or advances to the Company shall be paid and satisfied in full; and (c) the Member shall no longer be a Member or creditor of the Company on account of the Capital Contribution or the loans or advances.

11.5 Limitation on Payment of Value. If payment of the value of the Interest would be prohibited by any statute or law prohibiting distributions that would

(a) render the Company insolvent; or

(b) be made at a time that the total Company liabilities (other than liabilities to Members on account of their Interests) exceed the value of the Company's total assets;

then the value of the withdrawing Member's Interest in all events shall be $1.00.

ARTICLE XII. MISCELLANEOUS PROVISIONS

12.1 Assignment of Interest and New Members. No Member may assign such person's Interest in the Company in whole or in part except by the vote or written consent of the other Members owning more than fifty percent (50%) of the Interests. No additional Person may be admitted as a Member except by the vote or written consent of the Members owning more than fifty percent (50%) of the Interests.

12.2 Determinations by Members: Except as required by the express provisions of this Agreement or of the Act:

(a) Any transaction, action or decision which requires or permits the Members to consent to, approve, elect, appoint, adopt or authorize or to make a determination or decision with respect thereto under this Agreement, the Act, the Code or otherwise shall be made by the Members owning more than fifty percent (50%) of the Interests.

(b) The Members shall act at a meeting of Members or by consent in writing of the Members. Members may vote or give their consent in person or by proxy.

(c) Meetings of the Members may be held at any time, upon call of any Manager or a Member or Members owning, in the aggregate, at least ten percent (10 %) of the Interests.

(d) Unless waived in writing by the Members owning more than fifty percent (50%) of the Interests (before or after a meeting), at least two (2) business days' prior notice of any meeting shall be given to each Member. Such notice shall state the purpose for which such meeting has been called. No business may be conducted or action taken at such meeting that is not provided for in such notice.

(e) Members may participate in a meeting of Members by means of conference telephone or similar communications equipment by means of which all Persons participating in the meeting can hear each other, and such participation shall constitute presence in person at such meeting.

(f) The Managers shall cause to be kept a book of minutes of all meetings of the Members in which there shall be recorded the time and place of such meeting, by whom such meeting was called, the notice thereof given, the names of those present, and the proceedings thereof. Copies of any consents in writing shall also be filed in such minute book.

12.3 Determinations by Managers. Except as required by the express provisions of this Agreement or of the Act and if there shall be more than one Manager:

(a) Any transaction, action or decision which requires or permits the Mangers to consent to, approve, elect, appoint, adopt or authorize or to make a determination or decision with respect thereto under this Agreement, the Act, the Code or otherwise shall be made by a majority of the Managers.

(b) The Managers shall act at a meeting of the Managers or by consent in writing of the Managers. Managers may vote or give their consent in person only and not by proxy.

(c) Meetings of the Managers may be held at any time, upon call of any agent of the Company appointed pursuant to Section 7.2 of this Agreement or any Manager.

(d) Notice of any meeting shall be given to a majority of the Managers at any time prior to the meeting, in writing or by verbal communication. Such notice need not state the purpose for which such meeting has been called.

(e) The Managers may participate in a meeting of the Managers by means of conference telephone or similar communications equipment by means of which all Persons participating in the meeting can hear each other, and such participation shall constitute presence in person at such meeting.

(f) The Managers may cause to be kept a book of minutes of all meetings of the Managers in which there shall be recorded the time and place of such meeting, by whom such meeting was called, the notice thereof given, the names of those present, and the proceedings thereof. Copies of any consents in writing shall also be filed in such minute book.

12.4 Binding Effect. This Agreement shall be binding upon and inure to the benefit of the undersigned, their legal representatives, heirs, successors and assigns. This Agreement and the rights and duties of the Members hereunder shall be governed by, and interpreted and construed in accordance with, the laws of the State of Florida, without regard to principles of choice of law.

12.5 Headings. The article and section headings in this Agreement are inserted as a matter of convenience and are for reference only and shall not be construed to define, limit, extend or describe the scope of this Agreement or the intent of any provision.

12.6 Number and Gender. Whenever required by the context here, the singular shall include the plural, and vice versa, and the masculine gender shall include the feminine and neuter genders, and vice versa.

12.7 Entire Agreement and Binding Effect. This Agreement constitutes the sole operating agreement among the Members and supersedes and cancels any prior agreements, representations, warranties or communications, whether oral or written, between the Members relating to the affairs of the Company and the conduct of the Company's business. No amendment or modification of this Agreement shall be effective unless approved in writing as provided in Section 10.1. The Articles of Organization and this Agreement are binding upon and shall inure to the benefit the Members and Agent(s) and shall be binding upon their successors, assigns, affiliates, subsidiaries, heirs, beneficiaries, personal representatives, executors, administrators and guardians, as applicable and appropriate.

IN WITNESS WHEREOF, this Agreement has been made and executed by the Members effective as of the date first written above.

_____[MEMBER]

_____[MEMBER]

_____[MEMBER]

Table A. Name, Address, and Initial Capital Contribution of the Members

Name and Address of Member	Value of Initial Capital Contribution	Nature of Member's Initial Capital Contribution (i.e., cash, services, property)	Percentage Interest of Member

Table B. Managers

Name of Manager	Address of Manager

11. Membership Ledger

Date of Original Issue	Member Name	Percentage Interest	Disposition of Shares (transferred or surrendered stock certificate)

12. Investment Representation Letter

Note: The following Investment Representation Letter should be executed by each LLC member and delivered to the company. The Representation Letter seeks to ensure company compliance with securities laws, by asking owners to certify that they are joining the LLC as an investment, and not to trade shares in the LLC.

(insert date)

To whom it may concern,

I am delivering this letter to Olde Craft, LLC in connection with my purchase of a 25% interest in Olde Craft, Inc. for a total sum of $75,000.00. I represent the following:

I am purchasing the shares in my own name and for my own account, for investment and not with an intent to sell or for sale in connection with any distribution of such stock; and no other person has any interest in or right with respect to the shares; nor have I agreed to give any person any such interest or right in the future.

I recognize that the shares have not been registered under the Federal Securities Act of 1933, as amended, or qualified under any state securities law, and that any sale or transfer of the shares is subject to restrictions imposed by federal and state law.

I also recognize that I cannot dispose of the shares absent registration and qualification or an available exemption from registration and qualification. I understand that no federal or state securities commission or other government body has approved of the fairness of the shares offered by the corporation and that the Commissioner has not and will not recommend or endorse the shares.

I have not seen or received any advertisement or general solicitation with respect to the sale of the shares.

I have a preexisting personal or business relationship with the Company or one or more of its officers, directors, or controlling persons and I am aware of its character and general financial and business circumstances.

I acknowledge that during the course of this transaction and before purchasing the shares I have been provided with financial and other written information about the Company. I have been given the opportunity by the Company to obtain any information and ask questions concerning the Company, the shares, and my investment that I felt necessary; and to the extent I availed myself of that opportunity, I have received satisfactory information and answers.

In reaching the decision to invest in the shares, I have carefully evaluated my financial resources and investment position and the risks associated with this investment, and I acknowledge that I am able to bear the economic risks of this investment.

_____

John Miller

13. Appointment of Proxy for Members' Meeting

Note: Use the following form when a Member wants to give his or her vote to another person at a meeting of an LLC's membership.

APPOINTMENT OF PROXY FOR (Annual/Special) MEETING

MadHatter, LLC

SHAREHOLDER: John Miller

PERCENTAGE INTEREST HELD BY SHAREHOLDER: 32%

I, the undersigned, as record holder of a 32% interest in MadHatter, LLC, revoke any previous proxies and appoint the person whose name appears just below this paragraph as my proxy to attend the member's meeting on _____ and any adjournment of that meeting.

The person I want to appoint as my proxy is _____

The proxy holder is entitled to cast a total number of votes equal to, but not exceeding the number of shares which I would be entitled to cast if I were personally present.

I authorize my proxy holder to vote and otherwise represent me with regard to any business that may come before this meeting in the same manner and with the same effect as if I were personally present.

I may revoke this proxy at any time. This proxy will lapse three months after the date of its execution.

If you are signing for a business entity, state your title:

Date (*important*):_____

_____
Name

_____
Title

Note: All proxies must be signed. Sign exactly as your name appears on your stock certificate. Joint shareholders must each sign this proxy. If signed by an attorney in fact, the Power of Attorney must be attached.

14. Call for Meeting of Members

Note: This "call" is an instruction by LLC members to the managers that the members want to call a meeting of members. This serves as official notice. This call is required only in manager-managed LLCs; if a member in a member-managed LLC wants to call a meeting of members, he or she would skip the call and simply send a notice of meeting of members to all other members. The next form is a notice of meeting of members.

CALL FOR MEETING OF LLC MEMBERS

TO: The Managers of MadHatter, LLC

(insert date)

The party or parties whose name appears below are members of MadHatter, LLC, and own percentage interests entitled to cast not less than 10 percent of MadHatter's votes. We hereby call a meeting of the members of MadHatter to be held _____ (date), at _____ (time), for the purpose of considering and acting upon the following matters:

(Insert matters to be considered, such as "A proposal that John Jones be removed as a manager of MadHatter.")

You are directed to give notice of this meeting of the members, in the manner prescribed by MadHatter's operating agreement and by law, to all members entitled to receive notice of the meeting.

Date _____

_____

_____

_____

15. Notice of Meeting of LLC Members

Note: This form is an LLC's announcement to its members that a meeting of members has been called.

NOTICE OF MEETING OF MEMBERS OF OLDECRAFT, LLC

Certain members of OldeCraft, LLC, have called a meeting of the members of OldeCraft pursuant to OldeCraft's operating agreement.

Therefore, this is your official notice as an OldeCraft member that a meeting of members of OldeCraft, LLC, will be held on _____ (date), at _____ (time), at _____ (address), to consider and act on the following matters:

(insert matters to be considered, such as "A proposal that John Jones be removed from the board of directors.")

If you do not expect to be present at the meeting and wish your shares to be voted, you may complete the attached form of proxy and mail it in the enclosed addressed envelope.

Date _____

_____
John Wilson, Manager

16. Minutes of Meeting of LLC Members

Note: While LLC members and managers enjoy far fewer corporate formalities than corporation owners, an LLC must still maintain records of its meetings. When an LLC's members meet to formally vote on any matter, the results of that vote should be committed to written minutes.

MINUTES OF MEETING OF MEMBERS OF OLDECRAFT, LLC

The members of OLDECRAFT, LLC, held a meeting on _____ (date), at _____ (time), at _____ (place). The meeting was called by John Miller and the company managers mailed notice to all members that the meeting would take place.

The following members were present at the meeting, in person or by proxy, representing membership interests as indicated:

> John Jones, 50%
> John Smith, 30%
> John Miller, 20%

Also present were Michael Spadaccini, attorney to the company, and Lisa Jones, wife of John Jones, and the company's president and sole manager.

The company's president called the meeting to order and announced that she would chair the meeting, that a quorum was present, and that the meeting was held pursuant to a written notice of meeting given to all members of the company. A copy of the notice was ordered inserted in the minute book immediately preceding the minutes of this meeting.

The minutes of the previous meeting of shareholders were then read and approved.

The chairperson then announced that the election of a manager was in order. Lisa Jones stated that she could no longer serve as manager of the company. John Smith was then elected to serve until the next meeting of members, and until the manager's successor was duly elected and qualified, as follows:

(Include agreement for selecting new manager here.)

There being no further business to come before the meeting, on motion duly made, seconded, and adopted, the meeting was adjourned.

_____
John Smith, Manager

17. Action by Written Consent of LLC Members

Note: Most company votes are taken by written consent rather than by notice and meeting and an in-person vote. Use the following form when you wish to take a company action in writing, rather than by a noticed meeting. Keep in mind, however, that your operating agreement and articles may require more than a simple majority to pass certain actions. Written consents are important company records and should be maintained in the record books.

ACTION BY WRITTEN CONSENT OF SHAREHOLDERS OF OLDECRAFT, LLC

The undersigned members of OldeCraft, LLC, owning of record the number of shares entitled to vote as set forth, hereby consent to the following company actions. The vote was unanimous. (For actions where a unanimous vote is not required: "A vote of 66% was required to take the actions listed below, and 80% of the membership interest in the company have given their consent."):

1. Pete Wilson is hereby removed as manager of the company.

2. The number of managers of the company is increased from one to two.

John Smith and John Miller, both also members, are hereby elected to serve as company managers until the next meeting of members.

DATED: _____

_____
John Smith

Percentage Owned: _____

DATED: _____

_____
John Miller

Percentage Owned:_____

18. Written Consent of Members Approving a Certificate of Amendment of Articles of Organization Changing an LLC's Name

ACTION OF MEMBERS BY WRITTEN CONSENT TO APPROVE AN AMENDMENT TO ARTICLES OF ORGANIZATION CHANGING LLC NAME

The undersigned, who comprise all the members of PLASTICWORLD, LLC, agree unanimously to the following:

RESOLVED, that the Certificate of Amendment of Articles of Organization presented to the undersigned members, specifically changing the name of the company to PLASTICUNIVERSE, LLC is approved.

Date _____

_____
Scott Bess

_____
Brian Bess

CHAPTER 3

Legal Forms to Establish a Corporation

THE *SAMPLE CALIFORNIA ARTICLES OF Incorporation* are suitable articles of incorporation for a basic California corporation. Similarly, the *Sample Delaware Certificate of Incorporation* is a suitable certificate of incorporation for a basic Delaware corporation. The *Sample Nevada Articles of Incorporation (Long Form, with Full Indemnity Provisions)* are suitable articles of incorporation for a Nevada corporation; this sample is a long form, with provisions that indemnify officers and directors from lawsuits and claims made against them as a result of their duties to the corporation.

The *Optional Provisions for Inclusion in Articles of Incorporation* are a set of optional provisions that one can include in articles of incorporation that authorize two separate classes of stock. The *Sample Letter to Secretary of State Accompanying Articles of Incorporation* is a sample letter that one can include when presenting corporation paperwork for filing with a Secretary of State.

A *registered agent* is a person or entity authorized and obligated to receive legal papers on behalf of a corporation. The *Sample Letter to Registered Agent* (which is intended to accompany articles of incorporation) is a simple cover letter that you should deliver to your registered agent on the organization of your corporation. Keep in mind that your state of organization may use a different term than "registered agent." Typical equivalents include "agent for service of process" and "local agent."

An *incorporator* is the person or entity that organizes a corporation and files its articles of incorporation. The incorporator enjoys certain powers: he or she can take corporate actions before directors and officers are appointed. For example, an incorporator can amend the articles of incorporation, approve bylaws, and appoint directors. Typically, an incorporator's power is quite broad. The *Sample Action by Incorporator Appointing Directors and Approving Bylaws* is a written resolution undertaken by the incorporator that appoints directors and approves bylaws for governance of the corporation.

Bylaws cover such matters as holding meetings, voting, quorums, elections, and the powers of directors and officers. The *Sample Corporate Bylaws* are simple, universal bylaws usable in any state. Consider, however, that these simple bylaws may not take advantage of favorable laws in your particular state of incorporation.

If and when you want to issue stock as a corporation, refer to the *Blank Stock Certificate* on the website supporting this book.

To finalize your incorporation, you must have an organizational meeting of the board of directors. You must also prepare minutes of this meeting. Because the format of the meeting is relatively standard, the minutes are nearly always drafted beforehand, and followed like a script. The *Sample Minutes of Organizational Meeting of the Board of Directors* is such a document.

The *Shareholder's Agreement* (on the Web) is an agreement among the shareholders of a corporation that covers various matters such as a commitment to vote particular persons as directors and allow other shareholders to have a right of first refusal to purchase the shares of departing shareholders. Shareholders' agreements are complex documents best handled by an attorney, but this sample should give you some insight into the devices available in such a document.

The *Share Transfer Ledger* is a ledger indicating the owners of a corporation and their proportion of ownership, as well as transfers of such ownership. All corporations should begin the ledger upon the formation of the corporation and should diligently update the ledger when shares are transferred, gifted, sold, repurchased by the corporation, or when new shares are issued. Each member admitted to the corporation should execute the *Investment Representation Letter*. The investment representation letter offers some measure of protection to the entity because the member being admitted to the corporation makes certain representations regarding his or her qualifications and fitness to serve as a member of the corporation. Also, in the investment representation letter, the member makes certain representations regarding his or her investment objectives, which are necessary to comply with state and federal securities laws.

A *proxy* is an authorization by one member giving another person the right to vote the member's shares. Proxy also refers to the document granting such authority. We have included several proxy forms here: The *Appointment of Proxy for Annual or Special Shareholders' Meeting*, a simple proxy form in which shareholder's grant their proxy for a shareholder's meeting, and the *Long-Form Appointment of Proxy for Annual or Special Shareholders' Meeting*, which serves the same purpose but is a more thorough and complex document.

A *call* is an instruction by a corporation's shareholders to the corporation's officers and managers that the shareholders want to call a meeting of shareholders. This *Call for Special Meeting of Shareholders* (on the Web) serves as official notice to the managers that the members wish to call a meeting. The *Notice of Special Meeting of Shareholders* is a notice to shareholders that a meeting has been called.

Annual and special meetings of shareholders and of directors must be recorded. The written record of the actions taken at such meetings are called *minutes*. Minutes are simple to prepare and are often short. We have included several sample minutes here. The *Minutes of Annual or Special Meeting of Shareholders* is appropriate for documenting a shareholder meeting. As an alternative to a formally called meeting, subject to certain restrictions, shareholders or directors may take an action without a meeting if their action is memorialized in a written consent. A *written consent* is a formal written document that sets forth a corporate action or resolution to be taken or made, and is signed by the shareholders or directors consenting to the action. The *Action by Written Consent of Shareholder(s)* is such a document.

The *Call for Special Meeting of Directors* serves as official notice to the directors that either an officer or director wishes to call a meeting of a corporation's board of directors. The *Minutes of Annual Meeting of Directors* is a sample document memorializing the actions taken at an annual meeting of directors. The *Minutes of Special Meeting of Directors* (on the Web) memorializes the actions taken at a special meeting of directors.

A corporation's directors, like shareholders, can vote by written consent in lieu of a formally noticed and held meeting. The *Action of Directors by Written Consent to Approve Stock* allows directors to take such action. Note, however, that most bylaws require the unanimous vote of directors to use a written consent. A more specific use of the written consent form is the *Written Consent of Directors Approving a Certificate of Amendment of Articles of Incorporation Changing Corporation's Name* in which the directors unanimously vote to amend the corporation's charter to change the corporation's name.

The *Certificate of Amendment of Articles of Incorporation Changing Corporation's Name* is the formal and official document that a corporation would file with a Secretary of State in its state of incorporation that formally amends its articles of incorporation to change its name, while the *Certificate of Amendment of Articles of Incorporation Electing Close Corporation Status* formally effects a change to the corporation's status from regular corporation to close corporation. A *close corporation*, generally speaking, is a smaller corporation that elects close corporation status and is therefore entitled to operate without the strict formalities normally required in the operation of standard corporations. Many small business owners find this benefit invaluable. In essence, a *close corporation* is a corporation whose shareholders and directors are entitled to operate much like a partnership.

IRS Tax Form SS-4 is the form by which a business entity obtains its Federal Tax ID Number (included in Chapter 1). The *IRS Tax Form 2553* is the tax form under which a corporation elects "S" corporation status. Subchapter S of the IRS Code permits eligible smaller corporations to avoid double taxation and be taxed as partnerships. Corporations that make such an election are known as "S" corporations. An S corporation differs from a standard C corporation solely with respect to its taxation.

A corporation must meet certain conditions to be eligible for a subchapter S election. First, the corporation must have no more than 75 shareholders. In calculating the 75-shareholder limit, a husband and wife count as one shareholder. Also, only the following entities may be shareholders: individuals, estates, certain trusts, certain partnerships, tax-exempt charitable organizations, and other S corporations (but only if the other S corporation is the sole shareholder). S corporations may only have one class of stock. A corporation must make the subchapter S election no later than two months and 15 days after the first day of the taxable year—it cannot wait until the end of the taxable year to elect. Subchapter S election requires the consent of all shareholders.

The states treat S corporations differently. Some states disregard subchapter S status entirely, offering no tax break. Other states honor the federal election automatically. Finally, some states require the filing of a state-specific form to complete subchapter S election.

19. Sample California Articles of Incorporation

ARTICLES OF INCORPORATION
OF
(CORPORATION NAME)

1. The name of this corporation is (Corporation Name).

2. The purpose of the corporation is to engage in any lawful act or activity for which a corporation may be organized under the General Corporation Law of California other than the banking business, the trust company business, or the practice of a profession permitted to be incorporated by the California Corporations Code.

3. The name and address in the State of California of this corporation's initial agent for service of process is (insert name and address of initial agent for service of process).

4. This corporation is authorized to issue only one class of shares of stock; and the total number of shares which this corporation is authorized to issue is one million (1,000,000) shares.

5. The liability of the directors of the corporation for monetary damages shall be eliminated to the fullest extent permissible under California law.

Dated:

_____
Donald Leland, Incorporator

20. Sample Articles of Incorporation: Delaware Long Form

The following sample is long-form articles suitable for use in Delaware. Note that in Delaware articles of incorporation are called a certificate of incorporation, but the meaning is exactly the same. The articles contain the required provisions: the name of the corporation, the corporate purpose, the resident agent, and the number of authorized shares.

CERTIFICATE OF INCORPORATION OF TONOSILVER RESOURCES, INC.

ARTICLE ONE. The name of this corporation is TONOSILVER RESOURCES, INC. (the "Corporation").

ARTICLE TWO. The address of the Corporation's registered office in the State of Delaware is 874 Walker Road, Suite C, City of Dover, ZIP Code: 19904, County of Kent. The name of its registered agent is United Corporate Services, Inc.

ARTICLE THREE. The nature of the business or purposes to be conducted or promoted by the Corporation is to engage in any lawful act or activity for which corporations may be organized under the General Corporation Law of Delaware.

ARTICLE FOUR. This Corporation is authorized to issue Common Stock and Preferred Stock. The total number of shares this Corporation shall have the authority to issue is one hundred forty million (140,000,000) shares. One hundred million (100,000,000) shares shall be designated Common Stock and shall have a par value of $0.001 per share. Forty million (40,000,000) shares shall be Preferred Stock and shall have a par value of $0.001 per share.

The Preferred Stock may be issued from time to time in one or more series. The Board of Directors is hereby authorized, subject to limitations prescribed by law, to fix by resolution or resolutions the designations, powers, preferences, and rights and the qualifications, limitations, or restrictions thereof, of each such series of Preferred Stock, including without limitation authority to fix by resolution or resolutions the dividend rights, dividend rate, conversion rights, voting rights, rights and terms of redemption (including sinking fund provisions), redemption price or prices, and liquidation preferences of any wholly unissued series of Preferred Stock, and the number of shares constituting any such series and the designation thereof, or any of the foregoing. The Board of Directors is further authorized to increase (but not above the total number of authorized shares of the class) or decrease (but not below the number of shares of any such series then outstanding) the number of shares of any series, the number of which was fixed by it, subsequent to the issue of shares of such series then outstanding, subject to the powers, preferences, and rights and the qualifications, limitations, and restrictions thereof stated in the resolution of the Board of Directors originally fixing the number of shares of such series. If the number of shares of any series is so decreased, then the shares constituting such decrease shall resume the status which they had prior to the adoption of the resolution originally fixing the number of shares of such series.

ARTICLE FIVE. The Corporation is to have perpetual existence.

ARTICLE SIX. The number of Directors which constitute the whole Board of Directors of the Corporation and the manner of their election shall be designated in the Bylaws of the Corporation.

ARTICLE SEVEN. In furtherance and not in limitation of the powers conferred by statute, the Board of Directors is expressly authorized to make, alter, amend, or repeal the Bylaws of the Corporation.

ARTICLE EIGHT.

(a) To the fullest extent permitted by the Delaware General Corporation Law as the same exists or as may hereafter be amended, a Director of the Corporation shall not be personally liable to the Corporation or its stockholders for monetary damages for breach of fiduciary duty as a Director; provided, however, that this provision shall not eliminate or limit the liability of a Director:

(i) for any breach of the Director's duty of loyalty to the corporation or its stockholders;
(ii) for acts or omissions not in good faith or which involve material misconduct or a knowing violation of law;
(iii) under the Delaware General Corporation Law; or
(iv) for any transaction from which the Director derived an improper personal benefit.

(b) The Corporation may indemnify to the fullest extent permitted by law any person made or threatened to be made a party to an action or proceeding, whether criminal, civil, administrative, or investigative, by reason of the fact that he or his testator or intestate is or was a director, officer, employee, or agent of the Corporation or any predecessor of the Corporation or serves or served at any other enterprise as a director, officer, employee, or agent at the request of the Corporation or any predecessor to the Corporation.

(c) Neither any amendment nor repeal of this Article Eight, nor the adoption of any provision of this Corporation's Certificate of Incorporation inconsistent with this Article Eight, shall eliminate or reduce the effect of this Article Eight, in respect of any matter occurring, or any action or proceeding accruing or arising or that, but for this Article Eight, would accrue or arise, prior to such amendment, repeal, or adoption of an inconsistent provision.

ARTICLE NINE. Vacancies created by newly created directorships, created in accordance with the Bylaws of this Corporation, may be filled by the vote of a majority, although less than a quorum, of the Directors then in office or by a sole remaining Director.

ARTICLE TEN. Advance notice of new business and stockholder nominations for the election of Directors shall be given in the manner and to the extent provided in the Bylaws of the Corporation.

ARTICLE ELEVEN. The Corporation reserves the right to amend, alter, change, or repeal any provision contained in this Certificate of Incorporation, in the manner now or hereafter prescribed by statute, and all rights conferred upon stockholders herein are granted subject to this reservation.

Date:_____

_____
Donald Leland
Incorporator

21. Nevada Long Form with Optional Provisions and Continuation Sheet

The following sample is long-form articles suitable for use only in Nevada. In some states, the use of fill-in forms is optional. In Nevada, it is now mandatory. So, if you want long-form articles in Nevada, you have to build them in two parts. The first part is the standard Nevada form and the second part is your continuation page. Note that the Article numbers appear out of order. This is because the article numbers for "shares of stock" and "directors" must correspond to the Article numbers on the fill-in form. Thereafter, the Article numbers continue where the fill-in form leaves off.

CONTINUATION OF ARTICLES OF INCORPORATION OF TONOSILVER, INC.,
a Nevada Corporation

ARTICLE THREE. SHARES OF STOCK

Section 3.01. Number of Shares and Classes. The Corporation shall have two classes of stock. One class shall be Class A Common Stock, par value $0.001, of which 70,000,000 shares shall be authorized. The holders of the Class A Common Stock are entitled to one vote per share and are entitled to receive the net assets of the Corporation upon dissolution. The second class shall be Class B Common Stock, par value $0.001, of which 5,000,000 shares shall be authorized. The holders of the Class B Common Stock are entitled to ten votes per share and are not entitled to receive the net assets of the Corporation upon dissolution.

ARTICLE FOUR. DIRECTORS

Section 4.01. Board of Directors. The Board of Directors shall consist of not less than one (1) and not more than five (5) members.
Section 4.02. Change in Number of Directors. The number of Directors may be increased or decreased by a duly adopted amendment to the Bylaws of the Corporation.

ARTICLE EIGHT. DIRECTORS' AND OFFICERS' LIABILITY

A Director or Officer of the Corporation shall not be personally liable to this Corporation or its Stockholders for damages for breach of fiduciary duty as a Director or Officer, but this Article shall not eliminate or limit the liability of a Director or Officer for (i) acts or omissions which involve intentional misconduct, fraud, or a knowing violation of law or (ii) the unlawful payment of distributions. Any repeal or modification of this Article by the Stockholders of the Corporation shall be prospective only and shall not adversely affect any limitation on the personal liability of a Director or Officer of the Corporation for acts or omissions prior to such repeal or modification.

ARTICLE NINE. INDEMNITY

Every person who was or is a party to, or is threatened to be made a party to, or is involved in any action, suit, or proceeding, whether civil, criminal, administrative, or investigative, by reason of the fact that he, or a person of whom he is the legal representative, is or was a Director or Officer of the Corporation, or is or was serving at the request of the Corporation as a Director or Officer of another Corporation, or as its representative in a partnership, joint venture, trust, or other enterprise, shall be indemnified and held harmless to the fullest extent legally permissible under the laws of the State of Nevada from time to time against all expenses, liability, and loss (including attorneys' fees judgments, fines, and amounts paid or to be paid in settlement) reasonably incurred or suffered by him in connection therewith. Such right of indemnification shall be a contract right which may be enforced in any manner desired by such person. The expenses of Officers and Directors incurred in defending a civil or criminal action, suit, or proceeding must be paid by the Corporation as they are incurred and in advance of the final disposition of the action, suit, or proceeding, upon receipt of an undertaking by or on behalf of the Director or Officer to repay the amount if it is ultimately determined by a court of competent jurisdiction that he is not entitled to be indemnified by the Corporation. Such right of indemnification shall not be exclusive of any other right which such Directors, Officers, or representatives may have or hereafter acquire, and, without limiting the generality of such statement, they shall be entitled to their respective rights of indemnification under any bylaw, agreement, vote of Stockholders, provision of law, or otherwise, as well as their rights under this Article. Without limiting the application of the foregoing, the Stockholders or Board of Directors may adopt bylaws from time to time with respect to indemnification, to provide at all times the fullest indemnification permitted by the laws of the State of Nevada, and may cause the Corporation to purchase and maintain insurance on behalf of any person who is or was a Director or Officer of the Corporation, or is or was serving at the request of the Corporation as a Director or Officer of another Corporation, or as its representative in a partnership, joint venture, trust, or other enterprise against any liability asserted against such person and incurred in any such capacity or arising out of such status, whether or not the Corporation would have the power to indemnify such person. The indemnification provided in this Article shall continue as to a person who has ceased to be a Director, Officer, Employee, or Agent, and shall inure to the benefit of the heirs, executors and administrators of such person.

ARTICLE TEN. AMENDMENTS

This Corporation reserves the right to amend, alter, change, or repeal any provision contained in these Articles of Incorporation or its Bylaws, in the manner now or hereafter prescribed by statute or by these Articles of Incorporation or said Bylaws, and all rights conferred upon the Stockholders are granted subject to this reservation.

ARTICLE ELEVEN. POWERS OF DIRECTORS

In furtherance and not in limitation of the powers conferred by statute the Board of Directors is expressly authorized: (1) Subject to the Bylaws, if any, adopted by the Stockholders, to make, alter, or repeal the Bylaws of the Corporation; (2) To authorize and cause to be executed mortgages and liens, with or without limit as to amount, upon the real and personal property of the Corporation; (3) To authorize the guaranty by the Corporation of securities, evidences of indebtedness, and obligations of other persons, corporations, and business entities; (4) To set apart out of any of the funds of the Corporation available for distributions a reserve or reserves for any proper purpose and to abolish any such reserve; (5) By resolution, to designate one or more committees, each committee to consist of at least one Director of the Corporation, which to the extent provided in the resolution or in the Bylaws of the Corporation, shall have and may exercise the powers of the Board of Directors in the management of the business and affairs of the Corporation, and may authorize the seal of the Corporation to be affixed to all papers which may require it. Such committee or committees shall have such name or names as may be stated in the Bylaws of the Corporation or as may be determined from time to time by resolution adopted by the Board of Directors; and (6) To authorize the Corporation by its Officers or agents to exercise all such powers and to do all such acts and things as may be exercised or done by the Corporation, except and to the extent that any such statute shall require action by the Stockholders of the Corporation with regard to the exercising of any such power or the doing of any such act or thing.

In addition to the powers and authorities hereinbefore or by statute expressly conferred upon them, the Board of Directors may exercise all such powers and do all such acts and things as may be exercised or done by the Corporation, except as otherwise provided herein and by law.

22. Sample Articles of Incorporation: Short Form

The following sample is as brief as articles can be. This document covers only the bare minimum: the name of the corporation, the corporate purpose, the resident agent, and the number of authorized shares.

ARTICLES OF INCORPORATION
OF
[CORPORATION NAME]

1. The name of this corporation is [CORPORATION NAME]

2. The purpose of the corporation is to engage in any lawful act or activity for which a corporation may be organized.

3. The name and address in the State of [STATE] of this Corporation's initial agent for service of process is [NAME AND ADDRESS OF INITIAL AGENT].

4. This corporation is authorized to issue only one class of shares of stock; and the total number of shares which this corporation is authorized to issue is one million (1,000,000) shares.

Date: _____

_____
Donald Leland
Incorporator

23. Nevada Articles of Incorporation, Long Form

DEAN HELLER
Secretary of State
206 North Carson Street
Carson City, Nevada 89701-4299
(775) 684 5708
Website: secretaryofstate.biz

Articles of Incorporation
(PURSUANT TO NRS 78)

Important. Read attached instructions before completing form.

ABOVE SPACE IS FOR OFFICE USE ONLY

1. **Name of Corporation:**	
2. **Resident Agent Name and Street Address:** (must be a Nevada address where process may be served)	Name
	Street Address — City — **NEVADA** — Zip Code
	Optional Mailing Address — City — State — Zip Code
3. **Shares:** (number of shares corporation authorized to issue)	Number of shares with par value: ___ Par value: $ ___ Number of shares without par value: ___
4. **Names & Addresses, of Board of Directors/Trustees:** (attach additional page there is more than 3 directors/trustees)	1. Name — Street Address — City — State — Zip Code
	2. Name — Street Address — City — State — Zip Code
	3. Name — Street Address — City — State — Zip Code
5. **Purpose:** (optional-see instructions)	The purpose of this Corporation shall be:
6. **Names, Address and Signature of Incorporator.** (attach additional page there is more than 1 incorporator)	Name — Signature
	Address — City — State — Zip Code
7. **Certificate of Acceptance of Appointment of Resident Agent:**	I hereby accept appointment as Resident Agent for the above named corporation.
	Authorized Signature of R. A. or On Behalf of R. A. Company — Date

This form must be accompanied by appropriate fees. See attached fee schedule.

24. Optional Provisions for Inclusion in Articles of Incorporation

a. Clause establishing a class of voting common stock and a class of non-voting common stock:

This corporation is authorized to issue two classes of shares: "Class A Common Stock" and "Class B Common Stock." This corporation may issue 1,000,000 shares of Class A Common Stock and 500,000 shares of Class B Common Stock. The Class B Common Stock has no voting rights. The Class A Common Stock has exclusive voting rights except as otherwise provided by law.

b. Clause establishing a class of voting common stock and a class of preferred stock:

This corporation is authorized to issue two classes of shares: "Common Stock" and "Preferred Stock." This corporation may issue 1,000,000 shares of Common Stock and 500,000 shares of Preferred Stock. The Common Stock has voting rights. The Preferred Stock has no voting rights except as otherwise provided by law.

The Preferred Stock has a liquidation preference. Upon the liquidation or dissolution of the corporation, holders of the Preferred Stock are entitled to receive out of the assets available for distribution to shareholders, before any payment to the holders of the Common Stock, the sum of $_____ per share. If the assets of the corporation are insufficient to pay this liquidation preference to the Preferred Stock, all of the entire remaining assets shall be paid to holders of the Preferred Stock and holders of the Common Stock shall receive nothing. After the liquidation preference has been paid or set apart for holders of the Preferred Stock, the remaining assets shall be paid to holders of the Common Stock.

The Preferred Stock has a dividend preference. Holders of the Preferred Stock are entitled to receive dividends on a noncumulative basis at the rate of $_____ per share, as and when declared by the board of directors from funds legally available for dividends and distributions. The holders of the Common Stock may not receive dividends or other distributions during any fiscal year of the corporation until dividends on the Preferred Stock in the total amount of $_____ per share during that fiscal year have been declared and paid or set apart for payment. The payment of such dividends is discretionary, and the holders of the Preferred Stock shall not enjoy a right to dividends if such dividends are not declared, even if the corporation has sufficient funds to lawfully pay such dividends.

25. Sample Letter to Secretary of State Accompanying Articles of Incorporation

Note: This letter is a version appropriate for use in Delaware, but can be modified for use in any state.

Michael Spadaccini
123 Elm Street
San Francisco, CA 94107
415-555-1212

September 28, 2004

State of Delaware
Division of Corporations
401 Federal Street, Suite 4
Dover, DE 19901

To whom it may concern:

Enclosed you will find articles of incorporation for Banquo Acquisition Corporation, a corporation that I wish to file in Delaware.

I have enclosed a filing fee of $74.00. Please return any necessary papers in the envelope that I have provided.

Yours truly,

Michael Spadaccini

26. Sample Letter to Registered Agent

Michael Spadaccini
123 Elm Street
San Francisco, CA 94107
415-555-1212

September 28, 2004

Harvard Business Services, Inc.
25 Greystone Manor
Lewes, DE 19958

To whom it may concern:

I have enclosed a copy of articles of incorporation I am filing today. As you can see, I have used you as our registered agents in the state of Delaware.

Please use the following contact information:

Banquo Acquisition Corporation
c/o Michael Spadaccini
801 Minnesota Street, Suite 7
San Francisco, CA 94107
Phone: (415) 282-7901

I have enclosed a check for $50.00 to cover the first year's services.

Yours truly,

Michael Spadaccini

27. Sample Action by Incorporator
Appointing Directors and Approving Bylaws

MINUTES OF ACTION OF INCORPORATOR TAKEN WITHOUT A MEETING BY WRITTEN CONSENT

The following action is taken by the incorporator of OLDE CRAFT, INC., by written consent, without a meeting on the date specified below.

The following resolution approving a form of bylaws for the governance of this corporation is adopted:

RESOLVED, that the bylaws presented to the incorporator be adopted as the bylaws of this corporation, and that a copy of those bylaws shall be inserted in the minute book of this corporation.

The following resolution electing the directors of the corporation is adopted:

RESOLVED, that pursuant to the foregoing bylaws, authorizing *three* directors, the following persons are hereby appointed as directors of this corporation for the ensuing year and until their successor(s) have been elected and qualified.

John Jones
John Smith
John Miller

The undersigned, the incorporator of this corporation, consents to the foregoing action.

Dated: _____

_____
Michael Spadaccini, Incorporator

28. Share Transfer Ledger

Stock Certificate Number	Date of Original Issue	Stockholder Name	Number of Shares	Disposition of Shares (transferred or surrendered stock certificate)

29. IRS Form 2553 Election by a Small Business Corporation

Form **2553** (Rev. December 2007) Department of the Treasury Internal Revenue Service	**Election by a Small Business Corporation** (Under section 1362 of the Internal Revenue Code) ▶ See Parts II and III on page 3 and the separate instructions. ▶ The corporation can fax this form to the IRS (see separate instructions).	OMB No. 1545-0146

Note. This election to be an S corporation can be accepted only if all the tests are met under   Who May Elect   on page 1 of the instructions; all shareholders have signed the consent statement; an officer has signed below; and the exact name and address of the corporation and other required form information are provided.

Part I	**Election Information**	
Type or Print	Name (see instructions)	**A** Employer identification number
	Number, street, and room or suite no. (If a P.O. box, see instructions.)	**B** Date incorporated
	City or town, state, and ZIP code	**C** State of incorporation

D Check the applicable box(es) if the corporation, after applying for the EIN shown in   A above, changed its ☐ name or ☐ address

E Election is to be effective for tax year beginning (month, day, year) (see instructions) . . . . . ▶ ___ / ___ / ___

Caution.   A corporation (entity) making the election for its first tax year in existence will usually enter the beginning date of a short tax year that begins on a date other than January 1.

F Selected tax year:

(1) ☐ Calendar year

(2) ☐ Fiscal year ending (month and day)   ▶ _____

(3) ☐ 52-53-week year ending with reference to the month of December

(4) ☐ 52-53-week year ending with reference to the month of   ▶ _____

If box (2) or (4) is checked, complete Part II

G If more than 100 shareholders are listed for item J (see page 2), check this box if treating members of a family as one shareholder results in no more than 100 shareholders (see test 2 under   Who May Elect   in the instructions) ▶ ☐

H Name and title of officer or legal representative who the IRS may call for more information	**I** Telephone number of officer or legal representative ( )

If this S corporation election is being filed with Form 1120S, I declare that I had reasonable cause for not filing Form 2553 timely, and if this election is made by an entity eligible to elect to be treated as a corporation, I declare that I also had reasonable cause for not filing an entity classification election timely. See below for my explanation of the reasons the election or elections were not made on time (see instructions).

Sign Here ▶

Under penalties of perjury, I declare that I have examined this election, including accompanying schedules and statements, and to the best of my knowledge and belief, it is true, correct, and complete.

_____ Signature of officer	_____ Title	_____ Date

For Paperwork Reduction Act Notice, see separate instructions.   Cat. No. 18629R   Form **2553** (Rev. 12-2007)

Form 2553 (Rev. 12-2007) — Page **2**

Par t I   Election Information   (continued)

J Name and address of each shareholder or former shareholder required to consent to the election. (See the instructions for column K.)	K Shareholders' Consent Statement. Under penalties of perjury, we declare that we consent to the election of the above-named corporation to be an S corporation under section 1362(a) and that we have examined this consent statement, including accompanying schedules and statements, and to the best of our knowledge and belief, it is true, correct, and complete. We understand our consent is binding and may not be withdrawn after the corporation has made a valid election. (Sign and date below.)		L Stock owned or percentage of ownership (see instructions)		M Social security number or employer identification number (see instructions)	N Shareholder's tax year ends (month and day)
	Signature	Date	Number of shares or percentage of ownership	Date(s) acquired		

Form **2553** (Rev. 12-2007)

Form 2553 (Rev. 12-2007)   Page **3**

Part II	**Selection of Fiscal Tax Year**	(see instructions)

Note. All corporations using this part must complete item O and item P, Q, or R.

O   Check the applicable box to indicate whether the corporation is:

   1. ☐ A new corporation   adopting   the tax year entered in item F, Part I.

   2. ☐ An existing corporation   retaining   the tax year entered in item F, Part I.

   3. ☐ An existing corporation   changing   to the tax year entered in item F, Part I.

P   Complete item P if the corporation is using the automatic approval provisions of Rev. Proc. 2006-46, 2006-45 I.R.B. 859, to request (1) a natural business year (as defined in section 5.07 of Rev. Proc. 2006-46) or (2) a year that satisfies the ownership tax year test (as defined in section 5.08 of Rev. Proc. 2006-46). Check the applicable box below to indicate the representation statement the corporation is making.

   1. **Natural Business Year** ▶ ☐ I represent that the corporation is adopting, retaining, or changing to a tax year that qualifies as its natural business year (as defined in section 5.07 of Rev. Proc. 2006-46) and has attached a statement showing separately for each month the gross receipts for the most recent 47 months (see instructions). I also represent that the corporation is not precluded by section 4.02 of Rev. Proc. 2006-46 from obtaining automatic approval of such adoption, retention, or change in tax year.

   2. **Ownership Tax Year** ▶ ☐ I represent that shareholders (as described in section 5.08 of Rev. Proc. 2006-46) holding more than half of the shares of the stock (as of the first day of the tax year to which the request relates) of the corporation have the same tax year or are concurrently changing to the tax year that the corporation adopts, retains, or changes to per item F, Part I, and that such tax year satisfies the requirement of section 4.01(3) of Rev. Proc. 2006-46. I also represent that the corporation is not precluded by section 4.02 of Rev. Proc. 2006-46 from obtaining automatic approval of such adoption, retention, or change in tax year.

Note. If you do not use item P and the corporation wants a fiscal tax year, complete either item Q or R below. Item Q is used to request a fiscal tax year based on a business purpose and to make a back-up section 444 election. Item R is used to make a regular section 444 election.

Q   Business Purpose—To request a fiscal tax year based on a business purpose, check box Q1. See instructions for details including payment of a user fee. You may also check box Q2 and/or box Q3.

   1. Check here ▶ ☐ if the fiscal year entered in item F, Part I, is requested under the prior approval provisions of Rev. Proc. 2002-39, 2002-22 I.R.B. 1046. Attach to Form 2553 a statement describing the relevant facts and circumstances and, if applicable, the gross receipts from sales and services necessary to establish a business purpose. See the instructions for details regarding the gross receipts from sales and services. If the IRS proposes to disapprove the requested fiscal year, do you want a conference with the IRS National Office?

   ☐ Yes ☐ No

   2. Check here ▶ ☐ to show that the corporation intends to make a back-up section 444 election in the event the corporation's business purpose request is not approved by the IRS. (See instructions for more information.)

   3. Check here ▶ ☐ to show that the corporation agrees to adopt or change to a tax year ending December 31 if necessary for the IRS to accept this election for S corporation status in the event (1) the corporation's business purpose request is not approved and the corporation makes a back-up section 444 election, but is ultimately not qualified to make a section 444 election, or (2) the corporation's business purpose request is not approved and the corporation did not make a back-up section 444 election.

R   Section 444 Election—To make a section 444 election, check box R1. You may also check box R2.

   1. Check here ▶ ☐ to show that the corporation will make, if qualified, a section 444 election to have the fiscal tax year shown in item F, Part I. To make the election, you must complete Form 8716, Election To Have a Tax Year Other Than a Required Tax Year, and either attach it to Form 2553 or file it separately.

   2. Check here ▶ ☐ to show that the corporation agrees to adopt or change to a tax year ending December 31 if necessary for the IRS to accept this election for S corporation status in the event the corporation is ultimately not qualified to make a section 444 election.

Part III	**Qualified Subchapter S Trust (QSST) Election Under Section 1361(d)(2)***

Income beneficiary's name and address	Social security number
Trust's name and address	Employer identification number

Date on which stock of the corporation was transferred to the trust (month, day, year) . . . . ▶   /   /

In order for the trust named above to be a QSST and thus a qualifying shareholder of the S corporation for which this Form 2553 is filed, I hereby make the election under section 1361(d)(2). Under penalties of perjury, I certify that the trust meets the definitional requirements of section 1361(d)(3) and that all other information provided in Part III is true, correct, and complete.

Signature of income beneficiary or signature and title of legal representative or other qualified person making the election	Date

*Use Part III to make the QSST election only if stock of the corporation has been transferred to the trust on or before the date on which the corporation makes its election to be an S corporation. The QSST election must be made and filed separately if stock of the corporation is transferred to the trust   after   the date on which the corporation makes the S election.

✸ Printed on recycled paper   Form **2553** (Rev. 12-2007)

30. Investment Representation Letter

July 31, 2004

To whom it may concern,

I am delivering this letter to Olde Craft, Inc. in connection with my purchase of 100,000 shares of Olde Craft, Inc. for a total sum of $75,000.00. I represent the following:

I am purchasing the shares in my own name and for my own account, for investment and not with an intent to sell or for sale in connection with any distribution of such stock; and no other person has any interest in or right with respect to the shares; nor have I agreed to give any person any such interest or right in the future.

I recognize that the shares have not been registered under the Federal Securities Act of 1933, as amended, or qualified under any state securities law, and that any sale or transfer of the shares is subject to restrictions imposed by federal and state law.

I also recognize that I cannot dispose of the shares absent registration and qualification or an available exemption from registration and qualification. I understand that no federal or state securities commission or other government body has approved of the fairness of the shares offered by the corporation and that the Commissioner has not and will not recommend or endorse the shares.

I have not seen or received any advertisement or general solicitation with respect to the sale of the shares.

I have a preexisting personal or business relationship with the Company or one or more of its officers, directors, or controlling persons and I am aware of its character and general financial and business circumstances.

I acknowledge that during the course of this transaction and before purchasing the shares I have been provided with financial and other written information about the Company. I have been given the opportunity by the Company to obtain any information and ask questions concerning the Company, the shares, and my investment that I felt necessary; and to the extent I availed myself of that opportunity, I have received satisfactory information and answers.

In reaching the decision to invest in the shares, I have carefully evaluated my financial resources and investment position and the risks associated with this investment, and I acknowledge that I am able to bear the economic risks of this investment.

John Miller

31. Appointment of Proxy for Annual or Special Shareholders' Meeting

APPOINTMENT OF PROXY FOR (ANNUAL/SPECIAL) MEETING

SuperCorp, Inc.

SHAREHOLDER: John Miller

NUMBER OF SHARES HELD: 100,000

I, the undersigned, as record holder of the shares of stock of SuperCorp, Inc. described above, revoke any previous proxies and appoint the person whose name appears just below this paragraph in the box to the right (**Note:** on a regular proxy form, this would appear) as my proxy to attend the (annual/special) share-holders' meeting on _____ and any adjournment of that meeting.

THE BOARD STRONGLY RECOMMENDS THAT YOU RETURN THIS PROXY IF YOU DO NOT INTEND TO APPEAR PERSONALLY AT THE (ANNUAL/SPECIAL) SHAREHOLDERS' MEETING.

The person I want to appoint as my proxy is _____

The proxy holder is entitled to cast a total number of votes equal to but not exceeding the number of shares which I would be entitled to cast if I were personally present.

I authorize my proxy holder to vote and otherwise represent me with regard to any business that may come before this meeting in the same manner and with the same effect as if I were personally present.

I may revoke this proxy at any time. This proxy will lapse three months after the date of its execution.

Please sign your name below and, if you are signing for a business entity, please state your title.

Date (*important*): _____

_____
Name

_____
Title

ALL PROXIES MUST BE SIGNED. PLEASE SIGN EXACTLY AS YOUR NAME APPEARS ON YOUR STOCK CER-TIFICATE. JOINT SHAREHOLDERS MUST EACH SIGN THIS PROXY. IF SIGNED BY AN ATTORNEY IN FACT, THE POWER OF ATTORNEY MUST BE ATTACHED.

IF YOU REQUIRE ASSISTANCE WITH THIS PROXY, PLEASE CONTACT THE CORPORATE SECRETARY, _____, AT 415-555-1212.

32. Long-Form Appointment of Proxy for Annual or Special Meeting of Shareholders

APPOINTMENT OF PROXY FOR (ANNUAL/SPECIAL) MEETING

SuperCorp, Inc.

SHAREHOLDER: John Miller

NUMBER OF SHARES HELD: 100,000

I, the undersigned, as record holder of the shares of stock of SuperCorp, Inc. described above, revoke any previous proxies and appoint the person whose name appears just below this paragraph in the box to the right (**Note:** on a regular proxy form, this would appear) as my proxy to attend the (annual/special) shareholders' meeting on _____ and any adjournment of that meeting.

THE BOARD STRONGLY RECOMMENDS THAT YOU RETURN THIS PROXY IF YOU DO NOT INTEND TO APPEAR PERSONALLY AT THE (ANNUAL/SPECIAL) SHAREHOLDERS' MEETING.

The person I want to appoint as my proxy is _____

The proxy holder is entitled to cast a total number of votes equal to but not exceeding the number of shares which I would be entitled to cast if I were personally present.

The shares represented by this proxy shall be voted in the following manner:

ACTIONS PROPOSED TO BE TAKEN

1. Shareholder John Miller has proposed a shareholder vote to remove John Jones from the board of directors.

❑ I want my proxy to vote FOR this proposal.
❑ I want my proxy to vote AGAINST this proposal.
❑ I withhold my proxy with respect to this specific vote.

2. Shareholder John Miller has proposed a shareholder vote to elect to make the corporation a close corporation.

❑ I want my proxy to vote FOR this proposal.
❑ I want my proxy to vote AGAINST this proposal.
❑ I withhold my proxy with respect to this specific vote.

3. Shareholder John Miller has proposed, in the event that John Jones is removed from the board of directors, that he, John Miller, be elected to serve on the board of directors.

❑ I want my proxy to vote FOR this proposal.
❑ I want my proxy to vote AGAINST this proposal.
❑ I withhold my proxy with respect to this specific vote.

IF YOU DO NOT INDICATE HOW YOU DESIRE YOUR SHARES TO BE VOTED, THE PROXY HOLDER WILL HAVE COMPLETE DISCRETION IN VOTING THE SHARES ON ANY MATTER VOTED AT THE MEETING.

I may revoke this proxy at any time. This proxy will lapse three months after the date of its execution.

Please sign your name below and, if you are signing for a business entity, please state your title.

Date (*important*):_____

_____
Name

_____
Title

ALL PROXIES MUST BE SIGNED. PLEASE SIGN EXACTLY AS YOUR NAME APPEARS ON YOUR STOCK CER-TIFICATE. JOINT SHAREHOLDERS MUST EACH SIGN THIS PROXY. IF SIGNED BY AN ATTORNEY IN FACT, THE POWER OF ATTORNEY MUST BE ATTACHED.

IF YOU REQUIRE ASSISTANCE WITH THIS PROXY, PLEASE CONTACT THE CORPORATE SECRETARY: _____, AT 415-555-1212.

33. Minutes of Annual Meeting of Shareholders, Alternate Form

BALL PLAY INTERNATIONAL, INC. ANNUAL MEETING OF STOCKHOLDERS, CERTIFICATE OF SECRETARY AND MINUTES

Bob Emmett, as duly elected Secretary of BALL PLAY INTERNATIONAL, INC. (the "Company"), and acting as Secretary and Inspector of Election of the Annual Meeting of Stockholders of the Company (the "Meeting") held on July 18, 2010, hereby certify as follows:

1. The Meeting was held at the Holiday Inn in DeLand, FL on July 18, 2010 at 1:05 p.m. EST. The Meeting was called and noticed pursuant to the Bylaws of the Company.

2. Based upon the stockholders list prepared by the Company's transfer agent, Interwest Transfer Company, there were 31,760,823 shares of the Company's common stock issued and outstanding and entitled to one vote per share at the Meeting. Of the shares available for voting, 28,807,136 shares of common stock were present in person or represented by proxy at the beginning of the Meeting.

3. At the Meeting we received, counted, and ascertained ballots cast by the shareholders of the Company entitled to vote thereat.

4. The following items were voted at the Meeting:

a. The election of Larry Emmett to the board of directors, to serve for a term of one year or until a successor is qualified and elected.

FOR: 28,806,948
Against: 188
Abstentions: 0
Based on the foregoing, this item PASSED.

b. The election of Bob Emmett to the board of directors, to serve for a term of one year or until a successor is qualified and elected.

FOR: 28,806,948
Against: 188
Abstentions: 0
Based on the foregoing, this item PASSED.

c. The change of the name of the corporation from Allergy Immuno Technologies to Ball Play International, Inc.

FOR: 28,807,136
Against: 0
Abstentions: 0
Based on the foregoing, this item PASSED.

d. Ratification of the selection of Parks, Tschopp & Whitcomb, P.A. as the independent public accountants to the Company.

FOR: 28,807,136
Against: 0
Abstentions: 0
Based on the foregoing, this item PASSED.

I have made and subscribed this Certificate this 21st of July, 2010

Bob Emmett

34. Minutes of Annual Meeting of Directors

MINUTES OF ANNUAL MEETING OF THE DIRECTORS OF SUPERCORP, INC.

The directors of Supercorp, Inc. held an annual meeting on _____ (date), at _____ (time), at _____ (place).

The following directors were present at the meeting:

John Jones
John Smith
John Miller

Also present were Michael Spadaccini, attorney to the corporation, and Lisa Jones.

The chairman called the meeting to order and announced that the meeting was held pursuant to the bylaws of the corporation and was held without notice.

It was then moved, seconded, and resolved to dispense with the reading of the minutes of the last meeting.

The directors considered the election of officers to serve until the next annual meeting of directors. The directors unanimously voted to elect the following persons to the corresponding positions:

John Jones, President and CEO
John Smith, Treasurer and CFO
John Miller, Corporate Secretary

There being no further business to come before the meeting, the meeting was duly adjourned.

_____
Corporate Secretary

35. Action by Written Consent of Shareholder(s)

ACTION BY WRITTEN CONSENT OF SHAREHOLDER(S) OF SUPERCORP, INC.

The undersigned shareholder(s) of SuperCorp, Inc., owning of record the number of shares entitled to vote as set forth, hereby consent(s) to the following corporate actions:

1. John Smith is hereby elected to serve on the board of directors and to occupy the vacancy left by the resignation of John Jones. He shall serve until the next annual meeting of shareholders.

2. The corporation hereby elects to be a close corporation.

3. The Articles of Incorporation shall be amended to include language sufficient to make the close corporation election under state law.

Date _____

_____
John Smith

_____
Number of Shares Owned

Date _____

_____
John Miller

_____
Number of Shares Owned

36. Call for Special Meeting of Directors

CALL FOR SPECIAL MEETING OF DIRECTORS

TO: The Secretary of SuperCorp, Inc.

The party whose name appears below, the (director/CEO/president), by this notice hereby calls a special meeting of directors, which shall be held on _____(date), at _____ (time), at _____ (place), to consider and act on the following proposals and such other business as may properly come before the board.

1. Acceptance of resignation of John Jones as corporate secretary.

2. Appointment of John Miller to position of corporate secretary.

3. Consideration of acquisition of Newcorp, Inc. by Supercorp, Inc.

You are directed to give notice of this special meeting, in the manner prescribed by the corporation's bylaws and by law, to all shareholders entitled to receive notice of the meeting.

Date: _____

_____
Name

_____
Position (i.e., director, CEO, president)

37. Action of Directors by Written Consent to Approve Stock Option Plan and to Issue Shares of Stock

The undersigned, the director(s) of Evolution Water Company, Inc., agree unanimously to the following:

RESOLVED, that the undersigned directors waive notice of a special meeting of directors pursuant to the corporation's bylaws and hereby agree that the following actions and resolutions be taken by this written consent.

RESOLVED, that the "Evolution Water Company Stock Option Plan" presented to the undersigned directors and attached to this written consent as an exhibit is hereby adopted by the corporation.

RESOLVED FURTHER: That the officers of this corporation be, and they hereby are, authorized to sell and issue to the following persons the number of shares of capital stock of this corporation and for the consideration indicated opposite each name:

NAME	NUMBER OF SHARES	$ PER SHARE	TYPE AND AMOUNT OF CONSIDERATION
John Jones	100,000	$0.75	$75,000 in cash

Date _____

_____
Scott Bess, Director

_____
Brian Bess, Director

38. Action of Directors by Written Consent
Approving Purchase of Another Corporation

RESOLUTION OF THE BOARD OF DIRECTORS OF BALL PLAY INTERNATIONAL, INC.

The undersigned, who constitute the entire Board of Directors of Ball Play International, Inc., a Delaware corporation (the "Corporation"), acting pursuant to Article III of the Bylaws of the Corporation, and pursuant to Section 141(f) of the General Corporation Law of the State of Delaware, hereby adopt and approve the recitals and resolutions set forth below, which shall have the same force and effect as if adopted and approved at a duly held meeting.

The purpose of this resolution is to approve the purchase of a majority interest in the Telas Olefinas, a Mexico corporation.

WHEREAS, the Corporation and Telas Olefinas, a Mexico corporation affiliated with the Corporation, desire to engage in a private stock transaction whereby Telas Olefinas issues new and unissued securities of Telas Olefinas totaling 540 shares, which shall immediately following issuance represent 80% of the total outstanding securities of Telas Olefinas, to the Corporation for consideration; further, that the Purchase Price to be paid by the Corporation for the shares shall be the following: the Corporation shall forgive debt for which Telas Olefinas is obliged to the Corporation in the amount of $US 1,041,552.

RESOLVED, that the board of directors hereby approve the transaction on the preceding terms, and the Corporation, through and by the further action of any officer, is authorized to enter the transaction and to execute a Share Purchase and Subscription Agreement memorializing the transaction.

Witness our Signatures to be effective the 31st day of May, 2010.

_____   _____
Bob Emmett   Wolf D.H. Koch

_____
Larry Emmett

39. Action of Directors by Written Consent
Appointing Directors to Fill Vacant Board Seats

RESOLUTION OF THE BOARD OF DIRECTORS OF BALL PLAY INTERNATIONAL, INC.

The undersigned, who constitute the entire Board of Directors of Ball Play International, Inc., a Delaware corporation (the "Corporation"), acting pursuant to Article III of the Bylaws of the Corporation, and pursuant to Section 141(f) of the General Corporation Law of the State of Delaware, hereby adopt and approve the recitals and resolutions set forth below, which shall have the same force and effect as if adopted and approved at a duly held meeting.

WHEREAS, available seats on the board of directors are five and only one seat is occupied, leaving four vacancies;

RESOLVED, that the sitting board of directors, consisting of one director, hereby avails himself of the power of appointment of vacant seats as outlined in the Bylaws and the General Corporation Law of the State of Delaware and appoints the following persons to serve as directors of the Corporation:

Dean Martin

Frank Sinatra

Harry Connick

Witness our Signatures to be effective the 18th day of December, 2010.

_____

Bill DeLander

40. Written Consent of Directors Approving a Certificate of Amendment of Articles of Incorporation Changing Corporation's Name

ACTION OF DIRECTOR(S) BY WRITTEN CONSENT TO APPROVE AN AMENDMENT TO ARTICLES OF INCORPORATION CHANGING CORPORATE NAME

The undersigned, the director(s) of Plasticworld.com, Inc., a California corporation, agree unanimously to the following:

RESOLVED, that the undersigned directors waive notice of a special meeting of directors pursuant to the corporation's bylaws and hereby agree that the following actions and resolutions be taken by this written consent.

RESOLVED, that the Certificate of Amendment of Articles of Incorporation presented to the undersigned directors, specifically changing the name of the corporation to PlasticUniverse, Inc., be approved by the directors.

Date _____

_____
Scott Bess, Director

_____
Brian Bess, Director

41. Certificate of Amendment of Articles of Incorporation Changing Corporation's Name

CERTIFICATE OF AMENDMENT OF
ARTICLES OF INCORPORATION

The undersigned certify that:

1. They are the president and secretary, respectively, of PlasticWorld.com, Inc., corporation number 10134944.

2. Article I of the Articles of Incorporation of this corporation is hereby amended to read as follows:

The name of this Corporation is hereby changed to PlasticUnverse, Inc.

3. The foregoing Amendment of Articles of Incorporation has been duly approved by the board of directors.

4. The foregoing Amendment of Articles of Incorporation has been duly approved by the required vote of shareholders in accordance with state law. The total number of outstanding shares of the corporation is 10,000,000. The number of shares voting in favor of the amendment equaled or exceeded the vote required. The percentage vote required was more than 50%.

We further declare, under penalty of perjury under the laws of the State of California, that the matters set forth in this certificate are true and correct of our own knowledge.

Dated _____

_____
Scott Bess, President

_____
Brian Bess, Secretary

42. Certificate of Amendment of Articles of Incorporation Electing Close Corporation Status

CERTIFICATE OF AMENDMENT OF
ARTICLES OF INCORPORATION

The undersigned certify that:

1. They are the president and secretary, respectively, of Evolution Water Company, Inc., corporation number 1059964.

2. Article V of the Articles of Incorporation of this corporation is hereby added, and the Articles of Incorporation are hereby amended to read as follows:

All of this Corporation's issued shares of all classes shall be held of record by not more than 35 persons, and this Corporation is a close corporation.

3. The foregoing Amendment of Articles of Incorporation has been duly approved by the board of directors.

4. The foregoing Amendment of Articles of Incorporation has been duly approved by the required vote of shareholders. The total number of outstanding shares of the corporation is 98,333. The vote with respect to this amendment was unanimous.

We further declare, under penalty of perjury under the laws of the State of California, that the matters set forth in this certificate are true and correct of our own knowledge.

Dated _____

_____
Donald Leland, President

_____
Alexandra Leland, Secretary

43. Sample Delaware Certificate of Dissolution

CERTIFICATE OF DISSOLUTION

The corporation organized and existing under the General Corporation Law of the State of Delaware DOES HEREBY CERTIFY AS FOLLOWS: The dissolution of said DEF Corporation has been duly authorized by all the stockholders of the Corporation entitled to vote on a dissolution in accordance with subsection (c) of Section 275 of the General Corporation Law of the State of Delaware. The date the dissolution was authorized is December 11, 2010. The following is a list of the names and addresses of the directors of the said corporation:

[Enter names and addresses of directors here]

The following is a list of the names and addresses of the officers of the said corporation:

[Enter names and addresses of officers here]

By: _____
   Signature of Authorized Officer

Name: _____
   Print or Type

Title: _____

44. Written Consent of Shareholders Approving a Conversion from a California Corporation to a Delaware Limited Liability Company

ACTION OF SHAREHOLDERS BY WRITTEN CONSENT TO APPROVE A CONVERSION OF CORPORATION TO LIMITED LIABILITY COMPANY

The undersigned, being all the shareholders of PLASTICWORLD, Inc., agree unanimously to the following:

RESOLVED, that the shareholders, following consultation, have agreed that it is in the best interests of PLASTICWORLD, Inc. to convert the legal status of the entity from a California Corporation to a Limited Liability Company chartered in Delaware, to be entitled PLASTICWORLD LLC.

To facilitate the tax reporting of the LLC, it is agreed that the conversion shall be filed so that it takes place on January 1, 2011. The officers of PLASTICWORLD, Inc. are authorized and directed to file the appropriate Certificate of Conversion with the Secretary of State of California and to file a Certificate of Conversion from a Delaware or Non-Delaware Corporation to a Delaware Limited Liability Company with the State of Delaware and to file a Certificate of Formation with the State of Delaware simultaneously with the Certificate of Conversion to accomplish the conversion.

Date: _____

_____
Scott Bess

_____
Brian Bess

45. Sample Certificate/Articles of Conversion from a California Corporation to a Delaware Limited Liability Company

Notes: The following document is a simple certificate of conversion document that converts a California corporation to a Delaware LLC. This document illustrates fairly clearly how conversion is accomplished. The states offer slightly different procedures for conversion, so we recommend that you use form specific to your state if attempting a conversion.

STATE OF DELAWARE CERTIFICATE OF CONVERSION FROM A CORPORATION TO A LIMITED LIABILITY COMPANY PURSUANT TO SECTION 18-214 OF THE LIMITED LIABILITY ACT

1. The jurisdiction where the Corporation first formed is California.
2. The jurisdiction immediately prior to filing this Certificate is California.
3. The date the corporation first formed is September 1, 2001.
4. The name of the Corporation immediately prior to filing this Certificate is Plasticworld, Inc.
5. The name of the Limited Liability Company as set forth in the Certificate of Formation is Plasticworld, LLC.
6. IN WITNESS WHEREOF, the undersigned being duly authorized to sign on behalf of the converting Limited

  Liability Company have executed this Certificate on the 12th day of November, 2010

By: _____ Scott Bess President

46. Notice to Remaining Members by a Member Desiring to Withdraw from a Corporation

Joan Donner
123 Elm Street
San Francisco, CA 94107
415-555-1212

September 28, 2010

Dear Brian, This is my formal notice that I will be withdrawing from my ownership in Tonosilver, Inc.

The shareholder's agreement states that:

Section 5.1. Voluntary Termination; Resignation. In the event any Shareholder voluntarily terminates his or her employment with the Corporation for any reason whatsoever, other than as provided in Section 4.2, the terminating Shareholder shall sell to the Corporation and the Corporation shall purchase from the Shareholder all of the terminating Shareholder's shares in the Corporation now owned or hereafter acquired and which are owned by the terminating Shareholder as of the date of termination for the purchase price determined in the manner provide in Article VI and upon the terms provided in Article VII.

We must next discuss the valuation of my interest. I suggest that we speak informally first. If we can't come to some resolution, we can then trigger the appraisal rights under the operating agreement. I'll await your response.

Yours,

Joan Donner

CHAPTER 4

You're Free to Franchise

MAKING THE DECISION TO FRANCHISE your business or become a franchisee opens doors to many opportunities as well as many legal questions. The legal touch points for the franchise industry are different from those of corporations, LLCs, and the like. This chapter provides legal forms for franchisors and franchisees to help them achieve their entrepreneurial goals while remaining in compliance with the unique requirements that govern franchise law.

FORMS FOR THE FRANCHISOR

Use the self-assessment questionnaire, *Are You Ready to Be a Franchisor*, to evaluate yourself, your family, and your lifestyle to determine if being a franchisor is right for you. The *Franchise Feasibility Test* will help you assess whether to franchise your business.

Franchisors uniformly reserve the right to approve an assignment of the franchise agreement by a franchisee to a third party, or a sale of the franchisee's assets to a third party, and to prohibit such transfers and sales that the franchisor does not ultimately approve of. The *Assignment of Franchise Agreement* spells this out.

The *Compliance Guide* is intended to help franchisors comply with the Federal Trade Commission's amended Franchise Rule. The original Franchise Rule went into effect on October 21, 1979. The Federal Trade Commission (FTC) approved amendments to the Franchise Rule on January 22, 2007.

The Franchise Rule requires franchise and business opportunity sellers to provide prospective purchasers with the *Franchise Disclosure Document*.

Starting a franchise can be a daunting proposition, which is why franchisors provide an operations manual, providing franchisees with a guidebook that often includes 500-plus pages of operational information. Refer to the *Operations Manual Outline* to structure your own document.

In addition to rules mandated by the FTC,

several states have implemented franchise rules. Refer to the *State Franchise Guidelines* list for franchise information specific to a franchise's locale.

FORMS FOR THE FRANCHISEE

Use the checklist for evaluating your suitability as a franchisee or small business buyer to get a better understanding of the financial, personal, and business commitments involved.

In the trade, the *Franchise Agreement* or contract is sometimes referred to as "money in the bank" because a good agreement that protects the best interests of the franchisee and franchisor will be a major factor in ensuring future revenues from the franchise business for both parties.

Similar to the UFOC, the Franchise Agreement is a lengthy document so we've included a sample table of contents that outlines the necessary components of the agreement.

The *Franchise Area Development Agreement* will enable a franchise to develop a particular area of land oftentimes if the performance targets and schedules are identified.

When assessing what franchise to go with (out of the hundreds of options) it helps to organize your choices. Use the *Franchise Comparison Worksheet* to help you determine the potential of each franchise you're considering.

Whether you're the acting franchisor or franchisee, use the necessary legal forms to see you through your franchise endeavor.

47. Are You Ready to Be a Franchisor?

Before you even see a franchisor, you should evaluate your readiness, asking yourself such questions as:

- Will your franchise be taking a considerable amount of your time away from your family? If so, how do you feel about that?

- Is your family enthused about the franchise? Will you enjoy working with them if they will be employees?

- Do you enjoy working with others?

- Do you have the background or character traits necessary to succeed in owning a business?

- Do you have the necessary capital resources? Can you make the financial sacrifices?

- Are you emotionally prepared for working long, hard hours?

48. Franchise Feasibility Test

Use this form to help you determine the feasibility of your business as a franchisable concept. Answer each question along the left side of the form assigning a rating of 1-5 for each question, with 5 being the strongest. Total each column after you've finished, then add all five columns together for a grand total. The higher the score, the more potential the concept has of becoming a successful franchise.

	1	2	3	4	4
1. Does your business have an established track record of more than 5 years?					
2. Do you and/or any of your partners have experience in the business greater than the period of time your business has been in operation?					
3. Does your business have 10 or more locations?					
4. During the time your business has been in operation, has it maintained average net profits in each location of more than $200,000?					
5. Does the business generate repeat customers on a frequency greater than two times per month?					
6. Does the business attract customers from a 5-mile radius or greater?					
7. Do you have more than $250,000 to invest in the development of your franchise concept?					
8. Do you and/or any of your partners have business management experience greater than 10 years?					
9. Will the start-up requirements for franchisees be less than $25,000?					
10. Are training requirements less than three months?					
11. Does your business have international adaptability?					
12. Rate the competitiveness of your industry.					
13. Have you received more than 10 franchising inquiries in the last year?					
Total for Each Column					
Total Score					

49. Typical Franchise Agreement Table of Contents

I. LICENSES, SERVICE MARKS, TRADE PRACTICES, AND CLAIMS OF INFRINGEMENT
   A. License
   B. Trade Practices
   C. Service Marks
   D. Exclusive Territory and Minimum Average Gross Sales
   E. Modification or Discontinuance of Service Mark Use

II. FRANCHISOR ASSISTANCE
   A. Pre-Opening
      1. Operating Manuals and Vehicle Specifications
      2. Franchise Training
      3. Initial Supplies
      4. Initial Training
      5. Territorial Assistance

III. FRANCHISE FEE, TERM, AND RENEWAL FEE
   A. Initial Franchise Fee
   B. Term
   C. Renewal Fee

IV. SERVICE FEES, ADVERTISING AND PROMOTIONAL FUND FEES, AND TRANSFER FEES
   A. Service Fees
   B. Advertising and Promotional Fund Fees
   C. Transfer Fees

V. BUSINESS OPERATION
   A. Employees; Inability to Conduct Business; Products and Services Sold
   B. Business Records and Books of Account
   C. Inspection
   D. Financial Statements
   E. Claims and Liabilities, etc.
   F. Uniformity in Telephone Number and Operations
   G. Meetings and Training Sessions
   H. Signs, Stationery, Specifications, etc.
   I. Purchase of Merchandise and Fifth Wheel Dyna-Kleen Trailer System

VI. OFFICE MANAGEMENT

VII. COMPETITION AND CONFIDENTIALITY
   A. During Term
   B. Following Termination
   C. Public Policy
   D. Services or Products Offered for Sale

VIII. INDEPENDENT CONTRACTOR AND HOLD HARMLESS CLAUSE

IX. INSURANCE AND HOLD HARMLESS
   A. Insurance Premiums

X. OWNERSHIP CHANGES, TRANSFER FEES, DEFAULTS, AND REMEDIES
   A. Sole Proprietorship
   B. Partnerships
   C. Corporations
   D. Incorporation, Transfer of Franchise Agreement, and Buy-Sell Agreements
   E. Shareholder Guarantee
   F. Appraisal
   G. Default, Material Violations, Termination
   H. Discontinue Use of Trade Practices After Termination
   I. Monetary Obligations on Termination

50. Franchise Disclosure Document Components

The Franchise Disclosure Document has 23 sections (referred to as "Items"), as well as exhibits that provide a ton of supplemental information. Here's a guide to understanding the FDD:

Items 1-4: History

Item 1: A general review of the company, including any predecessors or affiliates, and the opportunity being offered. This key overview of the business is one of the sections you'll want to review first.

Item 2: Background data on key officers, directors, employees, and any others who have management responsibility related to the sale or operation of the franchise. It includes a summary of their work experience from the past five years and any other experience they have as officers and/or directors of other companies.

Items 3 and 4: These include disclosures of any past or current litigation or bankruptcy on the part of the company or its key people.

Items 5-7: Fees and Costs

Item 5: Any and all initial fees you have to pay as you begin the franchise business.

Item 6: Any and all other fees that may be required in the subsequent operation of the franchised business, including royalty, advertising, renewal, and transfer fees.

Item 7: An outline of every component of the initial investment you'll be expected to make in the franchise operation, including an allowance for initial advertising and operating capital reserves. This section is extremely important, but the value of the information is limited by the fact that the franchise company is required to express the data in a tabular form involving ranges of potential costs. Review this section with existing franchisees and the franchisor to determine the most accurate estimate possible for your specific location and circumstances.

Items 9, 11, and 15: Contractual Obligations of Franchisee and Franchisor

Item 9: Your obligations (as a franchisee), in a tabular format. The table lists major areas of responsibility in the business (for instance, obligations in relation to finding the real estate site for your business), then provides specific references to the exact sections of both the FDD and the actual franchise agreement contract that define the legal obligations you're assuming. Even though it might seem tedious and burdensome to complete all the cross-referencing that is required by the format chosen for this section, it is essential to your investigation. You should read through the entire FDD and franchise agreement first (to develop a strong overall knowledge base) before coming back to Item 9 and carefully checking each cross reference in the table.

Item 11: The contractual support obligations of the franchisor. This is usually the longest section of the FDD and is very important because it tells you what you'll receive in exchange for the fees you're paying. The section outlines pre-opening assistance as well as ongoing assistance. It also provides extensive detail about the franchisor's training programs and any required franchise systems, such as computer point-of-sale or advertising programs. Keep your highlighter handy in this section to make sure you note all important information as well as any questions you may have.

Item 15: Explanation of exactly what your personal obligations are in relation to the operation of the franchise business.

Item 12: Territory

What you will receive in terms of a protected or exclusive territory. You'll find quite a variance in this provision from franchise to franchise.

Most prospective franchisees believe intuitively that the bigger the protected territory, the better for them. To the contrary, as a general rule, the most successful and well-known franchise systems typically offer territories that are either extremely limited or sometimes no protected territories at all. Discuss this at length with the franchisor to ensure you understand and agree with whatever philosophy it adheres to on this important matter.

Item 17: Exit Strategies and Dispute Resolution Procedures

Any restrictions related to the renewal, termination or transfer of your Franchise Agreement as well as definitions of any required methodology for resolving disputes. You should consider any and all fees and restrictions you face in selling your business long before you get to the point of wanting to sell.

Dispute resolution provisions requiring negotiation and/or mediation before proceeding with legal action are quite common in franchising. It is also fairly common to see requirements for binding arbitration rather than lawsuits in state or federal courts, though this type of provision does not seem as prevalent as it was 20 years ago.

Item 19: Financial Performance Information

Franchisors' representations about the financial performance of their units. This is often the first Item prospective franchisees read to determine the answer to the most commonly asked question in franchising: "How much money can I make in this business?"

But Item 19 will never give you the answer to this question. In fact, the disclaimers of every Item 19 representation you'll ever see will make this point in the clearest and most emphatic language possible. Every franchisee is different, every site is different, and it's simply impossible to predict in advance what future financial performance results you might achieve. What Item 19 can provide—and it is extremely valuable—is helpful clues you can use in your own research to answer the question of how much money you might make.

The typical Item 19 disclosure consists of three types of information: 1) numerical presentations of revenue and/or expense data, 2) notes and explanations outlining the assumptions used in preparing these numerical presentations, and 3) disclaimers that carefully explain the limitations of the usefulness of the data presented.

It's essential to carefully review and analyze the clues you receive from each of the three types of information. If, for example, this Item states that all units used in calculating the numerical presentation were at least two years old at the time the data was gathered, it should be obvious that the presentation won't be relevant in determining what your performance might be like in the first year of the operation of your business.

Item 19 can be one of the most important sources of information you'll receive in the entire FDD. The secret is to be very careful to use the information only within the scope of what it's meant to convey and then to verify this data in your conversations with existing franchisees.

Item 20: Existing Unit Data

Information, in tabular form, about the number and location of the existing units in the franchise system. By requiring franchisors to disclose numbers on the units that have transferred ownership or closed, you get information that may assist you in forming an opinion about growth and success rates for the system.

Items 21 and 22: Financial Statements and Contracts

Item 21: The franchise's audited financial statements for the previous three years. Examine these financial statements to determine the financial strength and stability of the franchisor because you won't receive any future assistance if they go out of business. If this isn't a subject you know well, get assistance from your accountant or someone else familiar with financial statement analysis to help you perform this review and form this opinion.

Item 22: All contracts you may be required to execute in conjunction with becoming a franchisee, including the actual Franchise Agreement contract and other contracts covering personal guarantees, real estate assignments, advertising, co-op rules and conditions, and territorial development schedules.

Other Rules, Restrictions, and Information

Items 8, 10, 13, 14, 16, 18, and 23 all contain important information pertaining to the franchise. Some of these sections relate to rules, such as where you can buy your supplies, what products or services you can offer, and what your obligations are as far as personal participation. Others contain information about any financing programs available through the franchise, any public figures involved in promoting the business, and the status of all trademarks, patents, and copyrights. In addition, there are standard exhibits in every FDD with required listing of state-specific information and other "housekeeping" matters.

51. Operations Manual Outline

I. Introduction
   A. Welcoming Letter from Chief Operations Officer
   B. Introduction to Manual
   C. Biographical Information on Franchisor's Key Personnel

II. Pre-Opening Requirements
   A. Preparation of Chronological Chart by Franchisee, with Franchisor's Assistance, Setting Dates and Time Periods for:
      1. Selection of the site by franchisee
      2. Approval of the site by franchisor
      3. Approval of the lease by franchisor
      4. Execution of a lease
      5. Commencement of construction within required number of days after execution of the lease
      6. Finalization of construction
   B. Preparation of Pro Forma Financial Statements by Franchisee and His/Her Financial Advisors and Accountants
   C. Checklist of All Necessary Permits and Registration Forms
   D. Review of Franchisor's Specifications Regarding Construction and Décor
   E. List of Equipment, Inventory, and Fixtures
   F. Procurement of Necessary Documents, Items, and Services
      1. Suppliers
      2. Telephone systems
      3. Security systems
      4. Cleaning agencies
      5. Trash removal agency
      6. Pest control service
      7. Map services
      8. Fire extinguishers
      9. Background music installation
      10. Bank services
      11. Appropriate licenses
      12. Sales tax permit
      13. Minimum wage and equal opportunity literature
      14. Cleaning supplies
      15. Hand tools
      16. Office forms

III. Pre-Opening and Post-Opening Training Procedures
   A. General Daily Business Operational Policies
   B. Product or Service to Be Sold
      1. Development of menu
      2. Specifications
      3. Purchase lists

C. Preparation of Personnel to Sell Product or Service

D. Décor and Dress Code of Restaurant Personnel

E. Customer Service Procedure Deliveries

F. Delivery Requirements and Techniques

G. Preparation of Sales and Financial Reports

    1. Daily business forms

    2. Inventory strategy

    3. Preparation of daily, weekly, and monthly financial statements

H. Security Procedures

I. Cash Register Operation

J. Store Policy on Tipping

K. In-Store Promotion, Advertising, and Mandatory Direct Mailings

L. Periodic Amendments to Operation Procedures

IV. Bookkeeping and Accounting Methods

V. Grand Opening Procedures

VI. Daily Operational Function

VII. Troubleshooting

VIII. Conclusion

52. Checklist for Evaluating Your Suitability as a Franchisee or Small Business Buyer

Carefully consider these questions before buying your own franchise or small business.

Financial

Yes No

❑ ❑ Have you and your spouse and knowledgeable family members discussed the idea of going into business for yourselves?

❑ ❑ Are you in complete agreement?

❑ ❑ Do you have the financial resources required to buy a franchise or small business? If not, where are you going to get the capital?

❑ ❑ Are you and your spouse ready to make the necessary sacrifices in the way of money and time in order to operate a franchise or small business?

❑ ❑ Will the possible loss of company benefits, including retirement plans, be outweighed by the potential monetary and self-pride rewards that would come from owning your own business?

❑ ❑ Have you made a thorough written balance sheet of your assets and liabilities, as well as liquid cash resources?

❑ ❑ Will your savings provide you with a cushion for at least one year after you have paid for the franchise or small business, allowing a one-year period of time to break even?

❑ ❑ Do you have additional sources of financing, including friends or relatives who might be able to loan you money in the event that your initial financing proves inadequate?

❑ ❑ Do you realize that most new businesses, including franchises, generally do not break even for at least one year after opening?

❑ ❑ Will one of you remain employed at your current occupation while the franchise or small business is in its initial, pre-profit stage?

Personal

Yes No

❑ ❑ Are you and your spouse physically able to handle the emotional and physical strain involved in operating a franchise or small business, caused by long hours and tedious administrative chores?

❑ ❑ Will your family members, particularly small children, suffer from your absence for several years while you build up your business?

❑ ❑ Are you prepared to give up some independence of action in exchange for the advantages the franchise offers you?

❑ ❑ Have you really examined the type of franchise or business you desire and truthfully concluded that you would enjoy running it for several years or until retirement?

❏ ❏ Have you and your spouse had recent physicals?

❏ ❏ Is the present state of your health and that of your spouse good?

❏ ❏ Do you and your spouse enjoy working with others?

❏ ❏ Do you have the ability and experience to work smoothly and profitably with your franchisor, your employees, and your customers?

❏ ❏ Have you asked your friends and relatives for their candid opinions as to your emotional, mental, and physical suitability to running your own business?

❏ ❏ Do you have a capable, willing heir to take over the business if you become disabled?

❏ ❏ If the franchise or new business is not near your present home, do you realize that it would not be beneficial to sell your home and buy one closer until the new venture is successful?

Business

Yes No

❏ ❏ Do you and your spouse have past experience in business that will qualify you for the particular type of franchise or business you desire?

❏ ❏ Is it possible for either you or your spouse to become employed in the type of business you seek to buy before any purchase?

❏ ❏ Have you conducted independent research on the industry you are contemplating entering?

❏ ❏ If you have made your choice of franchises, have you researched the background and experience of your prospective franchisor?

❏ ❏ Have you determined whether the product or service you propose to sell has a market in your prospective territory at the prices you will have to charge?

❏ ❏ What will the market for your product or service be like five years from now?

❏ ❏ What competition exists in your prospective territory already?

❏ ❏ From franchise businesses?

❏ ❏ From non-franchise businesses?

Other Considerations

Yes No

❏ ❏ Do you know an experienced, business-oriented franchise attorney who can evaluate the franchise contract you are considering?

❏ ❏ Do you know an experienced, business-minded accountant?

❏ ❏ Have you prepared a business plan for the franchise or business of your choice?

53. Sample Franchise Agreement Table of Contents

What does a Franchise Agreement Contain?

The agreement will contain provisions covering, in considerable detail, the obligations of the franchiser (the company) and franchisee (you) regarding operating the business; the training and operational support the franchiser will provide (and at what cost); your territory and any exclusivity; the initial duration of the franchise and any renewal rights; how much you must invest; how you must deal with things such as trademarks, patents and signs; what royalties and service fees you will pay; tax issues; what happens if you should want to sell or transfer the franchise; advertising policies; franchisee termination issues; settlement of disputes; by the company, operating practices, cancellation, and attorney fees.

Document Content

1. AGREEMENT TERM

2. TERRITORY

3. REVENUE SHARING

4. FRANCHISOR COMMITMENTS
    4.1. Purchasing
    4.2. Missing Products
    4.3. Payment
    4.4. Marketing
    4.5. Participating Franchises
    4.6. Placement
    4.7. Packing and Shipping
    4.8. Returns/Exchanges
    4.9. Location Count
    4.10. Demographic Information

5. COMMITMENTS
    5.1. Marketing Support

6. ELECTRONIC REPORTING

7. REVIEW

8. TERMINATION
    8.1. Material Breach
    8.2. Insolvency and/or Bankruptcy
    8.3. Failure to Make Payment

9. PUBLIC DISCLOSURE AND CONFIDENTIALITY
    9.1. Public Disclosure
    9.2. Confidential Information

10. NO RIGHT TO USE NAMES

54. State Franchise Guidelines and Offices

Alabama

Alabama has enacted a Deceptive Trade Practices Act that makes it unlawful to make certain misrepresentations in any franchises, distributorships, and seller-assisted marketing plans. ALA. CODE Section 8-19-1.

Arkansas

Arkansas has a franchise relationship act known as the Franchise Practice Act that doesn't require registration or disclosure, but prohibits termination or nonrenewal of franchisees without good cause and protects franchisees from the wrongful acts of franchisors in the misuse of advertising fees. ARK. STAT. Section 79-807 and ANN. Section 4-72-201 through 4-72-210.

California

California has a Franchise Investment Act, which requires full disclosure and registration by the franchisor. CAL. CORP. CODE Section 31000 to 31516. It should be noted that California has a Seller Assisted Marketing Plan Act, which covers certain types of marketing that are akin to franchising. CAL. CIVIL CODE Section 1812-200 to 1812-221. California's Franchise Relations Act became effective January 1, 1981, and pertains to termination with good cause and prior 180-day notification if the franchisor does not intend to renew a contract. The Act further provides for compensation for franchises that have not been renewed but are intended for conversion to company-owned outlets. CAL. BUS. & PROF. CODE Section 20000-20043. Brochures and ads must be submitted in duplicate and avoid any statements regarding success, safe investments, unlikelihood of default, or earnings not supported by Item 19. The ad must be filed with the Department of Corporations at least three business days prior to publishing the ad.

California Corporations Commissioner
Department of Corporations
320 West 4th Street, Suite 750
Los Angeles, CA 90013
213 576-7500

Connecticut

Connecticut has a Business Opportunity Investment Act that requires registration and disclosure by any person who is engaged in the business of selling or offering for sale a business opportunity. CONN. GEN. STAT. Title 36, Ch. 662a, Section 36b-60 through 36b-80. Connecticut also has a Franchise Termination Act that requires good cause for nonrenewal or termination of franchises. CONN. GEN. STAT. Section 42-133e through 42-133g.

Delaware

Delaware has a Franchise Security Law that is a franchisee-franchisor relationship statute requiring good cause for terminations and nonrenewals of franchises. DEL. CODE ANN. Title 6, Section 2551 through 2556.

Florida

Florida's Business Opportunity Act provides for filing, full disclosure, and securing an advertising number. Under certain conditions, an exception from filing can be secured. Certain misrepresentations are prohibited. FLA. STAT. 1995, Ch. 817, Section 559.8 to 559.815, effective Oct. 1, 1998. The Florida Franchise Misrepresentation Act pertains to misrepresentation by franchisors. FLA. STAT. Section 817.416.

Georgia

Georgia has a Business Opportunity Statute pertaining to fraudulent and deceptive practices in the sale of business opportunities. A disclosure must be provided in multilevel distributions. GA. CODE ANN. Section 10-1-410 through 10-1-417.

Hawaii

Hawaii has a Franchise Investment Law pertaining to filing an application and disclosure. HAW. REV. STAT. Section 482E.1 through 482E.5. Hawaii also has a Franchise Rights and Prohibitions Act regarding prohibited actions and good cause requirements for nonrenewals and terminations and an antidiscrimination provision in regard to charges made for royalties, goods, services, equipment, rentals, advertising services unless made at different times and in different circumstances. HAW. REV. STAT. Section 482E. Hawaii does not review advertising.

Hawaii Securities Examiner
1010 Richards Street
Honolulu, HI 96813
808 586-2722

Illinois

Illinois has a Franchise Disclosure Act that regulates full disclosure, registration, good cause termination, and nonrenewal provisions. ILL. COMP. STATS. 1992, Ch. 815, Section 705/1 through 705/44. Illinois has a Business Opportunity Sales Law of 1995. Illinois Laws of 1995, Public Act 89-209; ILL. COMP. STATS. 1996, Ch. 815, Section 60215-1 to 60215-135. [See also Illinois (815 IL CS 705/20).] Illinois does not require a franchisor to amend its registration when a negotiated change is made unless a material change implemented in subsequent sales.

Indiana

Indiana has a Registration Disclosure Statute in addition to a Deceptive Franchise Practices Act (IND. CODE 23-2-217) affecting good cause on nonrenewals and 90-day termination notices. IND. CODE 23-2-2.5-1 to 51. See Business Opportunity Transaction, IND. CODE, Title 24, Art. 5, Ch. 8, Section 1-21 (Par. # 5138.19). Section 23-2-2.5-25 requires advertising copy to be filed with the commission at least five business days prior to first publication.

Indiana Chief Deputy Commissioner
Secretary of State
Franchise Section
Securities Division
302 W Washington Street, Room E-111
Indianapolis, IN 46204
317 232-6681

Iowa

Iowa has two franchise acts: the 1992 Act applies to agreements prior to July 1, 2000 (1992 Act) and the 2000 Act applies to agreements after July 1, 2000 (Section 537 A.10), covering transfers, encroachments, good-cause terminations, good-cause nonrenewals, and a duty of good faith performance. IOWA CODE (2003), Title XIII, Section 523B and 523B 13 and 523H, Section 523H.1 through 523 H.17.

Kentucky

Kentucky has a Business Opportunity Disclosure Act calling for registration of nonexempt offerings. KY. REV. STAT. Section 367.801 et seq. and 367.990.

Louisiana

Louisiana has a Business Opportunity Law that does not provide for filing, but a surety bond is required in certain instances. LA. REV. STAT. Section 51:1801 through 51:1804.

Maine

Maine has a Business Opportunity Act that includes registration of nonexempt offerings and disclosure requirements pertaining to the sale of any business opportunity. ME. REV. STAT. ANN. Chapter 69-B, Section 4691 and Chapters 542 and 597 (Sections 4696-4697).

Maryland

Maryland has a Franchise Registration and Disclosure Law regulating franchises. MD. CODE ANN. Bus. Reg. Section 14-201 et seq. to 14-233. Maryland also has an Equity Participation Investment Program Act, passed for the purpose of encouraging and developing franchises in Maryland, and the Maryland Fair Distributorship Act (1993), regarding cancellation or nonrenewal notices, repurchases, and arbitration between a grantor and a distributor. ANN. CODE of Maryland, Title 14, Section 14-101 through 14-129, Section 14-201 through 14-233, Article of Commercial Law, Title 11, Section 11-1301 through 11-1306.
Maryland Franchise Examiner
Office of the Attorney General
Maryland Division of Securities
200 St. Paul Place, 20th Floor
Baltimore, MD 21202
410 576-7042

Michigan

Michigan has a Franchise Investment Law that includes good cause for termination and renewal provision laws and repurchase requirements for nonrenewals. MICH. COMP. LAWS Section 445.1501 and 445.1545. It also has a Business Opportunity Act requiring a notice filing (MICH. COMP. LAWS Section 445.901 through 445.922) and a Void and Unenforceable Provisions Law (MICH. COMP. LAWS Section 445.1527). See MICH. COMP. LAWS Section 445.1525.
Michigan Franchise Administrator
Consumer Protection Division
Attention: Franchise Administrator
670 Law Building
Lansing, MI 48913
517 373-7117

Minnesota

Minnesota has a Franchise Registration and Full Disclosure Act that also covers Business Opportunities in addition to Pyramid and Unfair Practice Act and requires good cause for terminations and 90 days' prior written notice with a 60-day cure period for nonrenewals. MINN. STAT. Section 80C.01 et seq. to 80C.22. It has an antidiscrimination provision and ads must be filed five business days prior to the first publication.

Commerce Analyst III
Registration Unit
Minnesota Department of Commerce
85 7th Place East, Suite 500
St. Paul, MN 55101-2198
651 296-4026

Mississippi

Mississippi's Franchise Termination Statute also includes provisions regarding profit projections and misrepresenting earnings. Take special notice of the Repurchase of Inventory from Retailers upon Termination of Contract Statute and required 90-day written nonrenewal and termination notices. MISS. CODE ANN. Section 75-24-51 to 75-24-61.

Missouri

Missouri's statute prohibits termination without notice, requires a nonrenewal written 90-day notice, and includes a Pyramid Sales Statute. MO. REV. STAT. Section 407.400 through 407.410, 407.420.

Nebraska

Nebraska's Franchise Practice Act has provisions regarding 60 days' prior written notice and good cause for nonrenewals and terminations. NEB. REV. STAT. Section 87-401 through 87-410. In addition, it has a Business Practice Act that is, in essence, a seller-assisted marketing plans act. NEB. REV. STAT. Section 59-1701 through 59-1761.

New Hampshire

New Hampshire has a Distributor Disclosure Act. N.H. REV. STAT. ANN. Section 339-C1 through 339-C9 and Section 358-E1 through 358-E6.

New Jersey

New Jersey has a Franchise Practice Act requiring 60 days' prior written notice and good cause for terminations, cancellations, and nonrenewals. N.J. REV. STAT. Section 56:10-1 through 56:10-12.

New York

New York's Franchise Registration and Disclosure Statute became effective January 1, 1981, N.Y. GEN. BUS. LAW Section 680 through 695, Laws of 1989 Ch. 61 approved effective April 1, 1989. Franchisors are free to negotiate with prospective franchisees.
Special Deputy Attorney General
Bureau of Investigation
New York State Department of Law
120 Broadway, 23rd Floor
New York, NY 10271
212 416-8211
fax: 212 416-8816

North Carolina

North Carolina's Business Opportunities Disclosure Law requires filing two copies of the disclosure statement that are nonexempt offerings with the secretary of state. N.C. GEN. STAT. Section 66.94 to 66-100.

North Dakota

North Dakota's Franchise Investment Law governs registration, full disclosure, termination, and renewal of provisions. N.D. CENT. CODE ANN. Section 51.19.01 through Section 51.19.17. Ads must be submitted at least five business days prior to first publication.

North Dakota Franchise Examiner
Office of Securities Commission
600 East Boulevard, 5th Floor
Bismarck, ND 58505
701 328-4712

Ohio

Ohio has a non-filing Business Opportunity Act requiring a disclosure be provided to prospective purchasers. OHIO REV. CODE Section 13340.01 through 1334.15 and 1334.99.

Oklahoma

Oklahoma's Business Opportunity Sales Act requires registration of nonexempt offerings. OKLA. STAT. Section 71-4-801 through 828.

Oregon

Oregon's Franchise Transactions Statute requires full disclosure but does not require registration. OR. REV. STAT. Section 650.005 through 650.085. It also has a little FTC Act prohibiting certain misrepresentation actions. OR. REV. STAT. Section 646.605. No advertising filing is required.

Oregon Department of Insurance and Finance
Corporate Securities Section
Labor and Industries Building
Salem, OR 97310
503 378-4140

Rhode Island

Rhode Island's Franchise Distributor Investment Regulation Act requires the franchisor to fully disclose and register. R.I. GEN. LAWS Section 19-28-1 through 19-28.1-34. Franchisors can negotiate changes with prospective franchisees and ads must be filed three business days prior to first publication.

Rhode Island Securities Examiner
Division of Securities
233 Richmond Street, #232
Providence, RI 02903
401 277-3048

South Carolina

South Carolina's Business Opportunity Sales Act requires filing a disclosure with the secretary of state. S.C. CODE Section 39-57-10 to 39-57-80.

South Dakota

South Dakota's Franchises for Brand-Name Goods and Services Law requires registration and full disclosure. S.D. CODIFIED LAWS ANN. Section 37-5A-1 through 37-5A-87. Its Business Opportunity Statute requires filing of business opportunities. S.D. CODIFIED LAWS ANN. Section 37-25A-1 through 37-25A-54.

South Dakota Franchise Administrator
Division of Securities
118 West Capitol Avenue
Pierre, SD 57501
605 773-4013

Texas

Texas has a Business Opportunity Act requiring registration unless the offering is exempt as a franchise offering and a notice of exemption is filed with the secretary of state. TEX. BUS. & COM. CODE, Title 4, Ch. 41, Section 41.001 through 41.303. (See Section 97.21.)
Statutory Document Section
Secretary of State
P.O. Box 12887
Austin, TX 78711
512 475-1769

Utah

Utah has a Business Opportunity Disclosure Act in which it refers to "assisted marketing plans" and requires filing of nonexempt offerings. A notice of claim for exception can be filed with a fee. UTAH CODE ANN. Section 13-15-1 through 13-15-6.

Virginia

Virginia has a Retail Franchise Act that requires disclosure and registration (VA. CODE Section 13.1-557 through 13.1-574) and a Business Opportunity Law that does not require registration (VA. CODE Section 59.1-262 through 59.1-269). It also has a statute requiring good cause for cancellation (VA. CODE Section 13.1-564) and it gives the franchisee the right to negotiate changes.
Virginia Chief Examiner
State Corporation Commission
Division of Securities and Retail Franchising
1300 E. Main Street
Richmond, VA 23219
804 371-9051

Washington

Washington has a Franchise Investment Protection Act, which requires full disclosure and registration (WASH. REV. CODE Section 19.100.10 through 19.100.940), as well as provisions regarding renewal with buyout compensation and good cause termination (WASH. REV. CODE Section 19.100.180 and 19.100.190). It also has a Business Opportunity Fraud Act requiring registration (WASH. REV. CODE Section 19.110.010 through 19.100.930).
Securities Administrator
Department of Financial Institutions
P.O. Box 9033
Olympia, WA 98507-9033
360 902-8760
Washington D.C.

D.C. Franchising Act, D.C. CODE ANN. Section 29-1201, requires good cause for terminations, cancellations, failure to renew, or failure to consent to a transfer with a required 60-day cure period. D.C. has an antidiscrimination provision and franchisors can renegotiate if initiated by the franchisees.

Wisconsin

Wisconsin's Franchise Investment Law requires annual registration by notification on a prescribed form and full disclosure. WIS. STAT. Section 553.01 through 553.78. Its Fair Dealership Law requires "good cause" in order to terminate or fail to renew. WIS. STAT. Section 135.01 to 135.07.

Commissioner of Securities
Registration Division
P.O. Box 1768
Madison, WI 53701-1768
608 266-1064

United States

The Federal Trade Commission (FTC) has a general disclosure act covering franchises and business opportunities (Rule 436.1, entitled Disclosure Requirements and Prohibitions Concerning Franchising and Business Opportunity Ventures). No registration is required (16 C.F.R. Part 436). Legislation is pending regarding franchisor-franchisee relations, including good-cause renewals and terminations and earnings claims.

Note: All states are subject to the FTC Act whether or not they have franchise or business opportunity statutes. The FTC will recognize the Uniform Offering Disclosure of franchise registration states, but business opportunity disclosures must also include the requirements of the FTC disclosure. The FTC does not require registration of the FTC disclosure.

Franchise Rule Coordinator
Federal Trade Commission
Division of Enforcement
Bureau of Consumer Protection
600 Pennsylvania Avenue, N.W.
Washington, DC 20580
202 523-2222
Filing Fees of Franchise Registration States

55. Franchise Area Development Agreement Table of Contents

XYZ Doodads
Development Agreement
Table of Contents

56. Franchise Comparison Worksheet

Use this worksheet to help you determine the attractiveness of each franchise you're considering. Assign each franchise a column number. Answer each question along the left-hand side of the form, assigning a rating of 1-3, with 3 being the strongest. Total each column when finished. The franchise with the highest score will be the most attractive.

The Franchising Organization	Franchise 1	Franchise 2	Franchise 3
Does the franchisor have a good track record?			
Do the primary leaders of the franchise have expertise in the industry?			
Rate the franchisor's financial condition.			
How thoroughly does the franchisor check its prospective franchisees?			
Rate the profitability of the franchisor and its franchisees.			
Column Totals			

The Product or Service			
Is there a demand for the product or service?			
How seasonal is the product or service?			
Are industry sales strong?			
Rate the product or service in comparison to the competition.			
Is the product or service competitively priced?			
What is the potential for industry growth?			
Column Totals			

The Market Area			
Are exclusive territories offered?			
Can you sell franchises in your territory?			
Rate the sales potential of the territory you are considering.			
Is the competition strong in this area?			
How successful are franchisees in close proximity to this area?			
Column Totals			

The Contract	Franchise 1	Franchise 2	Franchise 3
Are the fees and royalties associated with the franchise reasonable?			
How attractive are the renewal, termination and transfer conditions?			
If the franchisor requires you to purchase proprietary inventory, how useful is it?			
If the franchisor requires you to meet annual sales quotas, are they reasonable?			
Column Totals			

Franchisor Support			
Does the franchisor help with site selection, lease negotiations and store layout?			
Is the training program effective and does the franchisor provide ongoing training?			
Does the franchisor provide financing to qualified individuals?			
Are manuals, sales kits, accounting systems, and purchasing guides provided?			
Does the franchisor sponsor an advertising fund to which franchisees contribute?			
How strong are the franchisor's advertising and promotional programs?			
Does the franchisor have favorable national contracts for goods and services?			
Column Totals			
Total Scores			

CHAPTER 5

Legal Ps and Qs
for Partnerships

ORMING A PARTNERSHIP REQUIRES COM-
munication—not only with your state,
but with your business partner, and
family, if applicable. The true definition of a *business partnership* is essentially two
or more people in business for profit, including husbands and wives (if they are in business together and they have not formed any
other type of entity). Included in this chapter
are sample forms you'll need to file legally as
business partners in addition to forms that
will help you legally maintain your business
relationship and determine what it will take
to operate as a successful pair.

To establish a partnership in the eyes of
the IRS, it's required that the partners file
*Form SS-4 Application for Employer Identifi-
cation Number (EIN)*. The EIN is needed to
apply for a business license and for tax
reporting and banking functions.

The *Delaware Certificate of Limited Partnership* is the charter document used by a
limited partnership organized in the State of
Delaware; this form is included as a sample,
but each state uses its own form. The *Sample
General Partnership Agreement* is a simple,
standard agreement between the owners of a
partnership.

A *Partnership Ledger* is a written table listing the owners of a partnership and should
be kept with the partnership agreement. The
ledger must also indicate the percentage held
by each partner. As new partners join the
partnership through the sale of additional
partnership interest (and a new partner's
corresponding capital contribution), the
new ownership is recorded on the ledger.
The partnership ledger should also show
transfers of partners' ownership interests, as
when a partner passes away and transfers his
or her interest through his or her will. Of
course, your partnership ledger may never
change—partners may simply not come and
go from your partnership. Your ledger may
reflect the initial partners and their initial
contributions and percentage interests.

In the real world, most small company
votes are taken by written consent rather

than by notice and meeting and an in-person vote. Use the *Action by Written Consent of Partners* when you wish to take a partnership action in writing, rather than by a noticed meeting. Written consents are important company records and should be maintained in the records book. Compare this consent form to the minutes in the form previous to this one. You'll note that it is often far simpler to take votes by written consent.

57. Application for Employer Identification Number (EIN)

Form **SS-4** (Rev. July 2007) Department of the Treasury Internal Revenue Service	**Application for Employer Identification Number** (For use by employers, corporations, partnerships, trusts, estates, churches, government agencies, Indian tribal entities, certain individuals, and others.) ▶ See separate instructions for each line. ▶ Keep a copy for your records.	OMB No. 1545-0003 EIN

Type or print clearly.

1	Legal name of entity (or individual) for whom the EIN is being requested

2	Trade name of business (if different from name on line 1)	3	Executor, administrator, trustee, "care of" name
4a	Mailing address (room, apt., suite no. and street, or P.O. box)	5a	Street address (if different) (Do not enter a P.O. box.)
4b	City, state, and ZIP code (if foreign, see instructions)	5b	City, state, and ZIP code (if foreign, see instructions)

6	County and state where principal business is located

7a	Name of principal officer, general partner, grantor, owner, or trustor	7b	SSN, ITIN, or EIN

8a	Is this application for a limited liability company (LLC) (or a foreign equivalent)? . . . . ☐ Yes ☐ No	8b	If 8a is "Yes," enter the number of LLC members . . . . ▶
8c	If 8a is "Yes," was the LLC organized in the United States? . . . . ☐ Yes ☐ No		

9a Type of entity   (check only one box).   Caution. If 8a is "Yes," see the instructions for the correct box to check.

☐ Sole proprietor (SSN) _____

☐ Partnership

☐ Corporation (enter form number to be filed) ▶_____

☐ Personal service corporation

☐ Church or church-controlled organization

☐ Other nonprofit organization (specify) ▶_____

☐ Other (specify) ▶

☐ Estate (SSN of decedent) _____

☐ Plan administrator (TIN) _____

☐ Trust (TIN of grantor) _____

☐ National Guard   ☐ State/local government

☐ Farmers' cooperative   ☐ Federal government/military

☐ REMIC   ☐ Indian tribal governments/enterprises

Group Exemption Number (GEN) if any ▶

9b	If a corporation, name the state or foreign country (if applicable) where incorporated	State	Foreign country

10 Reason for applying   (check only one box)

☐ Started new business (specify type) ▶ _____

_____

☐ Hired employees (Check the box and see line 13.)

☐ Compliance with IRS withholding regulations

☐ Other (specify) ▶

☐ Banking purpose (specify purpose) ▶ _____

☐ Changed type of organization (specify new type) ▶ _____

☐ Purchased going business

☐ Created a trust (specify type) ▶ _____

☐ Created a pension plan (specify type) ▶ _____

11	Date business started or acquired (month, day, year). See instructions.	12	Closing month of accounting year

13	Highest number of employees expected in the next 12 months (enter -0- if none).		14	Do you expect your employment tax liability to be $1,000 or less in a full calendar year? ☐ Yes ☐ No (If you expect to pay $4,000 or less in total wages in a full calendar year, you can mark "Yes.")

Agricultural	Household	Other

15	First date wages or annuities were paid (month, day, year). Note. If applicant is a withholding agent, enter date income will first be paid to nonresident alien (month, day, year) . . . . ▶

16 Check one box that best describes the principal activity of your business.

☐ Construction ☐ Rental & leasing ☐ Transportation & warehousing

☐ Real estate ☐ Manufacturing ☐ Finance & insurance

☐ Health care & social assistance

☐ Accommodation & food service

☐ Other (specify)

☐ Wholesale-agent/broker

☐ Wholesale-other ☐ Retail

17	Indicate principal line of merchandise sold, specific construction work done, products produced, or services provided.

18	Has the applicant entity shown on line 1 ever applied for and received an EIN? ☐ Yes ☐ No If "Yes," write previous EIN here ▶

	Complete this section **only** if you want to authorize the named individual to receive the entity's EIN and answer questions about the completion of this form.	
Third Party Designee	Designee's name	Designee's telephone number (include area code) ( )
	Address and ZIP code	Designee's fax number (include area code) ( )

Under penalties of perjury, I declare that I have examined this application, and to the best of my knowledge and belief, it is true, correct, and complete.	Applicant's telephone number (include area code) ( )
Name and title (type or print clearly) ▶	
Signature ▶ Date ▶	Applicant's fax number (include area code) ( )

For Privacy Act and Paperwork Reduction Act Notice, see separate instructions.   Cat. No. 16055N   Form **SS-4** (Rev. 7-2007)

Form SS-4 (Rev. 7-2007) Page **2**

Do I Need an EIN?

File Form SS-4 if the applicant entity does not already have an EIN but is required to show an EIN on any return, statement, or other document. [1] See also the separate instructions for each line on Form SS-4.

IF the applicant...	AND...	THEN...
Started a new business	Does not currently have (nor expect to have) employees	Complete lines 1, 2, 4a–8a, 8b–c (if applicable), 9a, 9b (if applicable), and 10–14 and 16–18.
Hired (or will hire) employees, including household employees	Does not already have an EIN	Complete lines 1, 2, 4a–6, 7a–b (if applicable), 8a, 8b–c (if applicable), 9a, 9b (if applicable), 10–18.
Opened a bank account	Needs an EIN for banking purposes only	Complete lines 1–5b, 7a–b (if applicable), 8a, 8b–c (if applicable), 9a, 9b (if applicable), 10, and 18.
Changed type of organization	Either the legal character of the organization or its ownership changed (for example, you incorporate a sole proprietorship or form a partnership) [2]	Complete lines 1–18 (as applicable).
Purchased a going business [3]	Does not already have an EIN	Complete lines 1–18 (as applicable).
Created a trust	The trust is other than a grantor trust or an IRA trust[4]	Complete lines 1–18 (as applicable).
Created a pension plan as a plan administrator [5]	Needs an EIN for reporting purposes	Complete lines 1, 3, 4a–5b, 9a, 10, and 18.
Is a foreign person needing an EIN to comply with IRS withholding regulations	Needs an EIN to complete a Form W-8 (other than Form W-8ECI), avoid withholding on portfolio assets, or claim tax treaty benefits [6]	Complete lines 1–5b, 7a–b (SSN or ITIN optional), 8a, 8b–c (if applicable), 9a, 9b (if applicable), 10, and 18.
Is administering an estate	Needs an EIN to report estate income on Form 1041	Complete lines 1–6, 9a, 10–12, 13–17 (if applicable), and 18.
Is a withholding agent for taxes on non-wage income paid to an alien (i.e., individual, corporation, or partnership, etc.)	Is an agent, broker, fiduciary, manager, tenant, or spouse who is required to file Form 1042, Annual Withholding Tax Return for U.S. Source Income of Foreign Persons	Complete lines 1, 2, 3 (if applicable), 4a–5b, 7a–b (if applicable), 8a, 8b–c (if applicable), 9a, 9b (if applicable), 10 and 18.
Is a state or local agency	Serves as a tax reporting agent for public assistance recipients under Rev. Proc. 80-4, 1980-1 C.B. 581 [7]	Complete lines 1, 2, 4a–5b, 9a, 10 and 18.
Is a single-member LLC	Needs an EIN to file Form 8832, Classification Election, for filing employment tax returns, or for state reporting purposes [8]	Complete lines 1–18 (as applicable).
Is an S corporation	Needs an EIN to file Form 2553, Election by a Small Business Corporation [9]	Complete lines 1–18 (as applicable).

[1] For example, a sole proprietorship or self-employed farmer who establishes a qualified retirement plan, or is required to file excise, employment, alcohol, tobacco, or firearms returns, must have an EIN. A partnership, corporation, REMIC (real estate mortgage investment conduit), nonprofit organization (church, club, etc.), or farmers' cooperative must use an EIN for any tax-related purpose even if the entity does not have employees.

[2] However, do not apply for a new EIN if the existing entity only (a) changed its business name, (b) elected on Form 8832 to change the way it is taxed (or is covered by the default rules), or (c) terminated its partnership status because at least 50% of the total interests in partnership capital and profits were sold or exchanged within a 12-month period. The EIN of the terminated partnership should continue to be used. See Regulations section 301.6109-1(d)(2)(iii).

[3] Do not use the EIN of the prior business unless you became the "owner" of a corporation by acquiring its stock.

[4] However, grantor trusts that do not file using Optional Method 1 and IRA trusts that are required to file Form 990-T, Exempt Organization Business Income Tax Return, must have an EIN. For more information on grantor trusts, see the Instructions for Form 1041.

[5] A plan administrator is the person or group of persons specified as the administrator by the instrument under which the plan is operated.

[6] Entities applying to be a Qualified Intermediary (QI) need a QI-EIN even if they already have an EIN. See Rev. Proc. 2000-12.

[7] See also Household employer on page 4 of the instructions. Note. State or local agencies may need an EIN for other reasons, for example, hired employees.

[8] Most LLCs do not need to file Form 8832. See Limited liability company (LLC) on page 4 of the instructions for details on completing Form SS-4 for an LLC.

[9] An existing corporation that is electing or revoking S corporation status should use its previously-assigned EIN.

58. Delaware Certificate of Limited Partnership

STATE OF DELAWARE CERTIFICATE OF LIMITED PARTNERSHIP

•**The Undersigned,** desiring to form a limited partnership pursuant to the Delaware Revised Uniform Limited Partnership Act, 6 Delaware Code, Chapter 17, do hereby certify as follows:

•**First:** The name of the limited partnership is _____

_____

_____.

•**Second:** The address of its registered office in the State of Delaware is _____

_____ in the city of _____.

The name of the registered agent at such address is _____

_____

_____.

•**Third:** The name and mailing address of each general partner is as follows:

•**In Witness Whereof,** the undersigned has executed this Certificate of Limited Partnership of

_____ _____ as of _____.

By:

_____

General Partner

Name: _____

(Type or Print Name)

59. Sample General Partnership Agreement

GENERAL PARTNERSHIP AGREEMENT
Between
ANDREW LELAND and
DONALD LELAND

This general partnership agreement is made and entered into as of January 1, 2004, by and among Andrew Leland and Donald Leland (all of whom are hereinafter collectively sometimes referred to as "partners").

The parties hereto desire to form a general partnership (hereinafter referred to as the "Partnership"), under the laws of the State of _____ for the term and upon the conditions set forth in this agreement, and the Partners agree as follows:

1.1. FORMATION OF PARTNERSHIP. The parties hereby form a general partnership, and the name of the partnership shall be _____. This agreement shall supersede any previous partnership agreements between the parties to this agreement.

1.2. DEFINITIONS.

"Act" means the laws governing partnerships in the State of organization .

"Bankruptcy" shall be deemed to have occurred with respect to any Partner 60 days after the happening of any of the following: (1) the filing of an application by a Partner for, or a consent to, the appointment of a trustee of the Partner's assets; (2) the filing by a Partner of a voluntary petition in bankruptcy of the filing of a pleading in any court of record admitting in writing the Partner's inability to pay the Partner's debts as they become due; (3) the making by a Partner of a general assignment for the benefit of creditors; (4) the filing by a Partner of an answer admitting the material allegations of, or consenting to or defaulting in answering a bankruptcy petition filed against the Partner in any bankruptcy proceeding; or (5) the entry of an order, judgment, or decree by any court of competent jurisdiction adjudicating a Partner a bankrupt or appointing a trustee of the Partner's assets, and that order, judgment, or decree continuing unstayed and in effect for a period of 60 days.

"Capital Account" means with respect to each Partner, the account established on the books and records of the Partnership for each Partner under Section 2.1. Each Partner's Capital Account shall initially equal the cash and the agreed value of property (net of liabilities assumed or to which the property is subject) contributed by the Partner to the Partnership, and during the term of the Partnership shall be (1) increased by the amount of (a) Taxable Income allocated to the Partner, other than Taxable Income attributable to the difference between the agreed value and adjusted basis of the property at contribution, and (b) any money and the agreed value of property (net of any liabilities assumed or to which the property is subject) subsequently contributed to the Partnership, and (2) decreased by the amount of (a) Tax Losses allocated to the Partner, except (i) Tax Losses attributable to depreciation of contributed property, which shall decrease Capital Accounts only to the extent of depreciation computed as if the property were purchased by the Partnership at its agreed value, and (ii) Tax Losses attributable to the difference between the agreed value and adjusted basis of property of property at contribution (which shall not decrease the contributing Partner's Capital Account), and (b) all cash and the agreed value of property (net of liabilities assumed or to which the property is subject) distributed to such Partner, and shall otherwise be kept in accordance with applicable Treasury Regulations.

"Contract Price" shall be equal to the fair market value of the selling Partner's Interest as of the date of the event triggering the sale. The fair market value shall be determined within 60 days by a valuation of the selling Partner's Interest as if the net assets of the Partnership were sold for cash and the cash distributed in accordance with Section 9.1.

"Incapacity" or "Incapacitated" means the incompetence, insanity, interdiction, death, disability, or incapacity, as the case may be, of any Partner.

"Interest" means the entire ownership interest of a Partner in the Partnership.

"Managing Partner" means Donald Leland but in the event that he is at any time no longer a Partner, or is replaced by vote of the Partners, the term shall mean the party or parties then acting in that capacity.

"Net Income" with respect to any fiscal period means all cash revenues of the Partnership during that period (including interest or other earning on the funds of the Partnership), less the sum of the following to the extent made from those cash revenues:

(a) All principal and interest payments on any indebtedness of the Partnership.

(b) All cash expenses incurred incident to the operations of the Partnership's business.

(c) Funds set aside as reserves for contingencies, working capital, debt service, taxes, insurance, or other costs or expenses incident to the conduct of the Partnership's business, which the Partners deem reasonably necessary or appropriate.

"Partnership Percentage" means the following percentages:

Name	Percentage
Donald Leland	50%
Andrew Leland	50%

Distributions or allocations made in proportion to or in accordance with the Partnership Percentages of the Partners shall be based upon relative Partnership Percentages as of the record date for distributions and in accordance with Section 706(c) and (d) of the Internal Revenue Code (IRC) for allocations.

"Operating Partner" means Andrew Leland but in the event that he is at any time no longer a Partner, or is replaced by vote of the Partners, the term shall mean the party or parties then acting in that capacity.

"Taxable Income" and "Tax Losses" respectively, shall mean the net income or net losses of the Partnership as determined for federal income tax purposes, and all items required to be separately stated by Section 702 of the IRC and the Regulations thereunder.

1.3. BUSINESS OF THE PARTNERSHIP. The business purpose for which this Partnership is organized is _____. Any modification of the business purpose outlined in this section shall not void this agreement.

1.4. NAMES AND ADDRESSES OF PARTNERS. The names and addresses of the Partners are:

Donald Leland, _____; and

Andrew Leland, _____.

1.5. TERM. The term of the Partnership shall begin on _____ and shall continue until the earlier of December 31, 2050, or until dissolved by an act or event specified in the Agreement or by the law as one effecting dissolution.

1.6. BUSINESS OFFICES. The principal place of business of the Partnership shall be _____. The Partners may, from time to time, change the principal place of business of the Partnership. The Partners may in their discretion establish additional places of business of the Partnership.

2.1 INITIAL CAPITAL CONTRIBUTIONS. The Partner's initial Capital Contributions are deemed made as of this Agreement. The Partners shall initially make Capital Contributions as follows:

(a) Donald Leland shall contribute the following property: _____; and

(b) Andrew Leland shall contribute the following property: _____.

2.2. PARTNER'S ASSESSMENTS. In addition to the Capital Contributions required by Section 2.1, each Partner shall be obligated to make additional Capital Contributions, as needed to maintain the profitability of the Partnership. All additional Capital Contributions shall be made in accordance with the Partnership Percentages and within 30 days after the Partners have received notice thereof from the Managing Partner. The Managing Partner shall call these assessments based upon his estimate of all costs, expenses, or charges with respect to operation of the Partnership, less the expected revenues from such operations. Any increases in the Capital Contributions of the Partners pursuant to this Section shall be noted on Annex A attached hereto and incorporated by reference.

2.3. INTEREST ON CAPITAL CONTRIBUTIONS. No Partner shall be paid interest on any Capital Contribution.

2.4. WITHDRAWAL AND RETURN OF CAPITAL CONTRIBUTIONS. No Partner shall be entitled to withdraw any part of his Capital Contribution, or to receive any distributions from the Partnership except as provided by this Agreement.

2.5. LOANS BY PARTNER. The Partners may (but shall not be obligated to) loan or advance to the Partnership such funds as are necessary for the Partnership's operations, provided, however, that interest on those loans or advances shall not be in excess of five percent.

3.1. DISTRIBUTIONS. Net Income shall be distributed among the Partners in proportion to their Partnership Percentages.

3.2. ALLOCATION OF PROFITS AND LOSSES FOR TAX PURPOSES. The Taxable Income to be allocated among the Partners shall be allocated among them in accordance with the previous section concerning distributions. Tax Losses to allocated among the Partners shall be allocated among them in accordance with their respective Partnership Percentages.

4.1. BOOKS OF ACCOUNT, RECORDS, AND REPORTS. Proper and complete records and books of account shall be kept by the Operating Partner in which shall be entered fully and accurately all transactions and other matters relative to the Partnership's business as are usually entered into records and books of account maintained by persons engaged in businesses of a like character, including a Capital Account for each Partner. The Partnership books and records shall be prepared in accordance with generally accepted accounting practices, consistently applied, and shall be kept on a cash basis except in circumstances in which the Managing Partner determines that another bases of accounting will be in the best interests of the Partnership. The books and records shall at all times be maintained at the principal place of business of the Partnership and shall be open to the inspection and examination of the Partners or their duly authorized representatives during reasonable business hours.

4.2. REPORTS TO PARTNERS. As soon as practicable in the particular case, the Operating Partner shall deliver to every other Partner:

(a) Such information concerning the Partnership after the end of each fiscal year as shall be necessary for the preparation by such a Partner of his income or other tax returns.

(b) An unaudited statement prepared by the Operating Partner setting forth, as of the end of and for each fiscal year, a profit and loss statement and a balance sheet of the Partnership and a statement showing the amounts allocated to or against each Interest during that year.

4.3. FISCAL YEAR. The fiscal year of the Partnership shall end on the thirty-first day of December in each year.

4.4. PARTNERSHIP FUNDS. The funds of the Partnership shall be deposited in such bank account or accounts, or invested in such interest-bearing or non interest-bearing investments, as shall be designated by the Managing Partner. All withdrawals from any such bank accounts shall be made by the duly authorized agent or agents of any Partner. Partnership funds shall be held in the name of the Partnership and shall not be commingled with those of any other person.

5.1. INCAPACITATION. Within 90 days after a Partner becomes Incapacitated, his executor, administrator, committee, or analogous fiduciary (the "Representative") shall sell that Interest to the remaining Partners. The Representative shall notify the other Partners in writing within the 90 day period and the other Partners must purchase the Incapacitated Partner's Interest. The purchase price of an Interest sold pursuant to this Section shall be the Contract Price, and payment for the Interest shall be made in the manner set forth in Section 5.5.

5.2. BANKRUPTCY. At the Bankruptcy of any Partner, that Partner (an "Inactive Partner") or his representative shall cease to have any voice in the conduct of the affairs of the partnership and all acts, consents, and decisions with respect to the Partnership shall thereafter be made by the other Partners. The Inactive Partner shall, nonetheless, remain liable for his share of any losses of the Partnership or contributions to the Partnership as provided herein, and shall be entitled to receive his share of Taxable Income, Tax Losses, and Net Income. For six months from and after the date of the Bankruptcy of any Partner, the other Partners shall have the irrevocable option to purchase the Inactive Partner's Interest in the Partnership. That purchase shall be made in proportion to the respective Partnership Percentages of the other Partners at the time or in such other proportion as they may mutually agree. Should the other Partners exercise their option to purchase the Inactive Partner's Interest, they shall notify the Inactive Partner or his representative of their intention to do so within this six-month period. The purchase price of any Interest purchased pursuant to this Section shall be the Contract Price, and shall be payable at the time and in the manner specified in Section 5.5. Should the other Partners not exercise the option to purchase the Inactive Partner's Interest, the Inactive Partner shall remain such in accordance with the provisions set forth above.

5.3. SALE OF PARTNERSHIP INTEREST. If a Partner desires to offer for sale his Interest in the Partnership, such Partner (the "Selling Partner") shall give written notice to the other Partners (the "Buying Partner[s]"). Within 30 days after receipt of the notice, the Buying Partner(s) shall notify the Selling Partner of their intent to purchase the Interest of the Selling Partner. The purchase price of an Interest sold pursuant to this Section shall be the Contract Price, and payment for the Interest shall be made in the manner set forth in Section 5.5. If the Buying Partners fail to notify the Selling Partner that they intend to purchase his or her interest within the 30-day period, the Selling Partner shall have the right to withdraw from the Partnership. If a Partner withdraws, the Partner shall be entitled to a payment from the Partnership equal to the Contract Price and payable at the time and in the manner set forth in Section 5.5. Any amounts received pursuant to this Section shall constitute complete and full discharge of all amounts owing to the withdrawing Partner on account of his Interest as a Partner in the Partnership.

5.4. ASSIGNMENT. A Partner may not assign any part of his Interest in the Partnership.

5.5. PAYMENT; TIME AND MANNER.

(a) Any Interest transferred to other Partners or the Partnership pursuant to this Agreement shall be paid for, at the purchaser's option, either (1) all in cash at the time of transfer of the Interest, or (2) by a down payment computed in accordance with paragraph (b) below and delivery of a promissory note signed by the purchaser(s).

(b) If the purchaser(s) elects the second option in paragraph (a) above, (s)he shall pay as a down payment 33 percent. The remaining portion shall be represented by a promissory note of the purchasers, and providing for four equal annual installments of the remaining unpaid portion of the Contract Price, each installment due on the anniversary of the transfer of the interest. The promissory note shall provide that interest at an annual rate of 5 percent (compounded semi-annually) shall be paid with each payment of principal (or such higher interest rate as shall be necessary to avoid the imputation of interest pursuant to Section 483 of the IRC), from the date of acquisition of the Interest on the portion of the note remaining unpaid from time to time.

6.1. ADJUSTMENT OF PARTNERSHIP PERCENTAGES. If a Partner withdraws pursuant to Section 5.3, the Partnership Percentages of the remaining Partners shall immediately be recalculated so that each Partner's Partnership Percentage is equal to (1) his Capital Contribution, divided by (2) the aggregate Capital Contributions of all remaining Partners. If the Partners purchase an Interest pursuant to Sections 5.1, 5.2, or 5.3, the Partnership Percentage of the selling Partner shall be added to that of the purchasing Partners, pro rata.

6.2. VOTING. All decisions or actions required by the Partners pursuant to this Agreement (including amendment hereof) shall be made or taken by the affirmative vote (at a meeting or, in lieu thereof, by written consent of the required percentage in Interest) of Partners having 100 percent of the aggregate Partnership Percentages.

7.1. MANAGEMENT AND ADMINISTRATION OF BUSINESS. Except as otherwise provided in this agreement, all Partners shall have the authority to manage the day-to-day operations and affairs of the Partnership and to make decisions regarding the business of the Partnership. Any action taken by any Partner shall constitute the act of and serve to bind the Partnership.

7.2. ACTS REQUIRING UNANIMOUS CONSENT. The following acts may be done only with the unanimous consent of the partners: (a) Borrowing money in the Partnership's name, other than in the ordinary course of the Partnership's business; (b) Capital expenditures in excess of $500.00; and (c) Amendment of this agreement.

8.1. LIABILITY AND INDEMNIFICATION. No Partner shall be liable, responsible, or accountable in damages or otherwise to the Partnership or any Partner for any action taken or failure to act on behalf of the Partnership within the scope of the authority conferred on any Partner by this Agreement or by law unless the act or omission was performed or omitted fraudulently or in bad faith or constituted negligence. The Partnership shall indemnify and hold harmless the Partners from and against any loss, expense, damage, or injury suffered or sustained by them by reason of any acts, omissions arising out of their activities on behalf of the Partnership or in furtherance of the interests of the Partnership, including but not limited to any judgment, award, settlement, reasonable attorneys' fees, and other costs or expenses incurred in connection with the defense of any actual or threatened action, proceeding, or claim, if the acts, omissions, or alleged acts or omissions upon which the actual or threatened action, proceeding, or claims are based were for a purpose reasonably believed to be in the best interests of the Partnership and were not performed or omitted fraudulently or in bad faith or as a result of negligence by a Partner and were not in violation of the Partner's fiduciary obligation to the Partnership. Any such indemnification shall be first from the assets of the Partnership, and then from all Partners and borne among them in accordance with their Partnership Percentages.

8.2. LIMITS ON PARTNERS' POWERS. Anything in this Agreement to the contrary notwithstanding, no Partner shall cause the Partnership to (a) Commingle the Partnership's funds with those of any other person, or employ or permit another to employ those funds or assets in any manner except for the exclusive benefit of the Partnership (except to the extent that funds are temporarily retained by agents of the Partnership), or (b) Reimburse any Partner for expenses incurred by any Partner except for the actual cost to the Partner of goods, materials, or services (including reasonable travel and entertainment expenses) used for or by the Partnership.

9.1. DISSOLUTION OF THE PARTNERSHIP. The happening of any one of the following events shall work an immediate dissolution of the Partnership:

(a) The sale or other disposition of all or substantially all of the assets of the Partnership.

(b) The affirmative vote for dissolution of the Partnership by Partners having at least 34 percent of the aggregate Partnership Percentages.

(c) The Bankruptcy or Incapacity of any Partner; provided that the remaining Partners shall continue the business of the Partnership unless the Partnership is dissolved under subparagraph (b) above.

(d) The expiration of the term of the Partnership.

9.2. WINDING UP. If the Partnership is dissolved and its business is not continued under Section 9.1, the Managing Partner or his/her successor shall commence to wind up the affairs of the Partnership and to liquidate the Partnership's assets. The Partners shall continue to share profits and losses during the period of liquidation in accordance with Sections 3.1 and 3.2. Following the occurrence of any of the events set forth in Section 9.1, the Partners shall determine whether the assets of the Partnership are to be sold or whether the assets are to be distributed to the Partners. If assets are distributed to the Partners, all such assets shall be valued at their then fair market value as determined by the Partners and the difference, if any, of the fair market value over (or under) the adjusted basis of such property to the Partnership shall be credited (or charged) to the Capital Accounts of the Partners in accordance with the provisions of Section 1.2. Such fair market value shall be used for purposes of determining the amount of any distribution to a Partner pursuant to Section 9.3. If the Partners are unable to agree on the fair market value of any asset of the Partnership, the fair market value shall be the average of two appraisals, one prepared by a qualified appraiser selected by Partners having 50 percent or more of the aggregate Partnership Percentages, and the other selected by the remaining Partners.

9.3. DISTRIBUTIONS UPON DISSOLUTION. Subject to the right of the Partners to set up such cash reserves as may be deemed reasonably necessary for any contingent or unforeseen liabilities or obligations of the Partnership, the proceeds of the liquidation and any other funds of the Partnership shall be distributed.

(a) To creditors, in the order of priority as provided by law except those liabilities to Partners in their capacities as Partners.

(b) To the Partners for loans, if any, made by them to the Partnership, or reimbursement for Partnership expenses paid by them.

(c) To the Partners in proportion to their respective Capital Accounts until they have received an amount equal to their Capital Accounts immediately prior to such distribution, but after adjustment for gain or loss with respect to the disposition of the Partnership's assets incident to the dissolution of the Partnership and the winding up of its affairs, whether or not the disposition occurs prior to the dissolution of the Partnership.

(d) To the Partners in accordance with their Partnership Percentages.

9.4. DEFICIT CAPITAL ACCOUNT RESTORATION. If, upon the dissolution and liquidation of the Partnership, after crediting all income upon sale of the Partnership's assets that have been sold and after making the allocations provided for in Section 9.3, any Partner has a negative Capital Account, then the Partner shall be obligated to contribute to the Partnership an amount equal to the negative Capital Account for distribution to creditors, or to Partners with positive Capital Account balances, in accordance with this Section.

10.1. FINAL REPORTS. Within a reasonable time following the completion of the liquidation of the Partnership's properties, the Managing Partner shall supply to each of the other Partners a statement that shall set forth the assets and liabilities of the Partnership as of the date of complete liquidation, and each Partner's portion of distributions pursuant to Section 9.3.

10.2. RIGHTS OF PARTNERS. Each Partner shall look solely to the assets of the Partnership for all distributions with respect to the Partnership and his Capital Contribution (including the return thereof), and share of profits, and shall have no recourse therefor (upon dissolution or otherwise) against any other Partner except as otherwise provided in this agreement.

10.3. TERMINATION. Upon the completion of the liquidation of the Partnership and the distribution of all Partnership funds, the Partnership shall terminate.

10.4. NOTICES. All notices and demands required or permitted under this Agreement shall be in writing and may be sent by certified or registered mail or similar delivery service, postage prepaid, to the Partners at their addresses as shown from time to time on the records of the Partnership, and shall be deemed given when mailed or delivered to the service. Any Partner may specify a different address by notifying the Managing Partner in writing of the different address.

10.5. SEVERABILITY. If any portion of this agreement be deemed by a competent court to be void or unenforceable, the remaining portions shall remain in full force and effect.

10.6. ENTIRE AGREEMENT. This is the entire agreement of the parties. Any oral representations or modifications concerning this instrument shall be of no force or effect unless contained in a subsequent written modification signed by the party to be charged.

IN WITNESS WHEREOF, the undersigned have executed this Agreement as of this date:

_____.

_____
Andrew Leland

_____
Donald Leland

Table A: Name, address and initial capital contribution of the Partners

Name and Address of Partner	Value of Initial Capital Contribution	Nature of Partner's Initial Capital Contribution, i.e., cash, services, property	Percentage Interest of Partner

60. Partnership Ledger

Date of Original Issue	Partner Name	Percentage Interest	Disposition of Shares (transferred or surrendered stock certificate)

61. Action by Written Consent of Partners

Note: In the real world, most small company votes are taken by written consent rather than by notice and meeting and an in-person vote. Use the following form when you wish to take a company action in writing, rather than by a noticed meeting. Keep in mind, however, that your operating agreement and articles may require more than a simple majority to pass certain actions. Written consents are important company records and should be maintained in the record books. Compare this consent form to the minutes in the form just previous to this one. You'll note that it is often far simpler to take votes by written consent.

ACTION BY WRITTEN CONSENT OF PARTNERS OF PALOS VERDES PARTNERS

The undersigned members of Palos Verdes Partners, owning the following number of shares:

John Jones, 50%
Judy Smith, 30%
John Miller, 20%

hereby consent(s) to the following company actions.

1. Lisa Johnson is hereby admitted as a partner to the partnership, and her capital contribution of $10,000 in cash is accepted.

2. The partnership percentages are hereby adjusted to accommodate the new partner; the new partnership percentages would be as follows, effective immediately after this resolution is adopted:

John Jones, 45%
Judy Smith, 27%
John Miller, 18%
Lisa Johnson, 10%

The three current partners all voted in favor of admitting Lisa Johnson.

John Smith and John Miller, both also members, are hereby elected to serve as company managers until the next meeting of members.

Dated _____

_____
John Smith
Percentage Owned _____

Dated _____

_____
John Miller
Percentage Owned _____

Dated _____

_____
Judy Smith
Percentage Owned _____

CHAPTER 6

Legal Forms for Your Business Location

N O MATTER WHERE YOU DECIDE TO establish your business (physically speaking). there are forms involved. Whether your budget accommodates a Class-A floor within a 20-story building or your type of business requires 3,000 square feet of warehouse space, it helps to have a prior understanding of the paperwork involved.

The *Sample Commercial Lease* is an example of one of the generic forms needed to rent space for your business. It's imperative to know in advance that there may be variations depending on the specific space being leased. As with any agreement, it's important to read it thoroughly as several thousand dollars could be at stake when it's all said and done. Once you've established where your business will operate, your next step may include the lease of specific equipment. Equipment leasing agree-

ments differ in each state; however, the *Sample California Agreement to Lease Equipment* is a general template of what to expect. The *Sample Janitorial Service Agreement* is included for business owners whose current commercial contracts don't include janitorial or similar services.

If you own the business, you should have a premium parking space, right? As logical as it may seem, not all business owners are provided with designated parking spaces as part of a commercial lease agreement. The *Sample Parking Agreement* can be a resource for business owners whose current lease agreements don't include a place to park.

As a tenant, you're able to request commercial improvements. Use the sample *Tenant Improvement Form for Property Improvements*, which can help you alter your current working environment.

62. Sample Commercial Lease

This Commercial Lease is hereby made between _____, the "Lessor," and
_____, the "Lessee," concerning the following property:
_____, the "Premises."
Lessee hereby leases from Lessor the Premises.

1. **Term and Rent.** Lessor will lease the above Premises for an initial term of _____ years and
   _____ months, beginning on _____, 20_____ and ending on
   _____, 20_____, as provided herein at the monthly rent of $ _____,
   payable in equal installments in advance on the first day of each month for that month's rental, during
   the term of the lease. All rental payments shall be made to Lessor, at the following address:
   _____.

2. **Use.** Lessee shall use and occupy the Premises for _____. The Premis-
   es shall be used for no other purpose. Lessor represents that the Premises may lawfully be used for
   such purpose.

3. **Care and Maintenance of Premises.** Lessee acknowledges that the Premises are in good order and
   repair, unless otherwise indicated herein. Lessee shall, at his own expense and at all times, maintain
   the Premises in good and safe condition, including electrical wiring, plumbing and heating installations,
   and any other system or equipment upon the Premises and shall surrender the same, at termination
   hereof, in as good a condition as received, normal wear and tear excepted. Lessee shall be responsible
   for all repairs required, excepting the roof, exterior walls, structural foundations, and the following:
   _____, which shall be maintained by Lessor. Lessee shall also maintain in
   good condition such portions adjacent to the Premises, such as sidewalks, driveways, lawns, and
   shrubbery, which would otherwise be required to be maintained by Lessor.

4. **Alterations.** Lessee shall not, without first obtaining the written consent of Lessor, make any alterations, additions, or improvements, in, to, or about the Premises.

5. **Ordinances and Statues.** Lessee shall comply with all statutes, ordinances, and requirements of all
   municipal, state, and federal authorities now in force, or which may hereafter be in force, pertaining to
   the Premises, occasioned by or affecting the use thereof by Lessee.

6. **Assignment and Subletting.** Lessee shall not assign this lease or sublet any portion of the Premises
   without prior written consent of the Lessor, which shall not be unreasonably withheld. Any such
   assignment or subletting without consent shall be void and, at the option of the Lessor, may terminate
   this lease.

7. **Utilities.** All applications and connections for necessary utility services on the demised Premises shall
   be made in the name of Lessee only, and Lessee shall be solely liable for utility charges as they
   become due, including those for sewer, water, gas, electricity, and telephone services.

8. **Entry and Inspection.** Lessee shall permit Lessor or Lessor's agents to enter upon the Premises at reasonable times and upon reasonable notice, for the purpose of inspecting the same, and will permit
   Lessor, at any time within sixty (60) days prior to the expiration of this lease, to place upon the Premis-

es any usual "To Let" or "For Lease" signs and permit persons desiring to lease the same to inspect the Premises thereafter.

9. **Possession.** If Lessor is unable to deliver possession of the Premises at the commencement hereof, Lessor shall not be liable for any damage caused thereby, nor shall this lease be void or voidable, but Lessee shall not be liable for any rent until possession is delivered. Lessee may terminate this lease if possession is not delivered within ten (10) days of the commencement of the term hereof.

10. **Indemnification of Lessor.** Lessor shall not be liable for any damage or injury to Lessee, or any other person, or to any property, occurring on the demised Premises or any part thereof, and Lessee agrees to hold Lessor harmless from any claims for damages, no matter how caused.

11. **Insurance.** Lessee, at his expense, shall maintain public liability insurance including bodily injury and property damage insuring Lessee and Lessor with minimum coverage as follows:

_____

_____

Lessee shall provide Lessor with a Certificate of Insurance showing Lessor as additional insured. The Certificate shall provide for a ten-day written notice to Lessor in the event of cancellation or material change of coverage. To the maximum extent permitted by insurance policies that may be owned by Lessor or Lessee, Lessee and Lessor, for the benefit of each other, waive any and all rights of subrogation that might otherwise exist.

12. **Eminent Domain.** If the Premises or any part thereof or any estate therein, or any other part of the building materially affecting Lessee's use of the Premises, shall be taken by eminent domain, this lease shall terminate on the date when title vests pursuant to such taking. The rent, and any additional rent, shall be apportioned as of the termination date, and any rent paid for any period beyond that date shall be repaid to Lessee. Lessee shall not be entitled to any part of the award for such taking or any payment in lieu thereof, but Lessee may file a claim for any taking of fixtures and improvements owned by Lessee and for moving expenses.

13. **Destruction of Premises.** In the event of a partial destruction of the Premises during the term hereof, from any cause, Lessor shall forthwith repair the same, provided that such repairs can be made within sixty (60) days under existing governmental laws and regulations, but such partial destruction shall not terminate this lease, except that Lessee shall be entitled to a proportionate reduction of rent while such repairs are being made, based upon the extent to which the making of such repairs shall interfere with the business of Lessee on the Premises. If such repairs cannot be made within said sixty (60) days, Lessor, at his option, may make the same within a reasonable time, this lease continuing in effect with the rent proportionately abated as aforesaid, and in the event that Lessor shall not elect to make such repairs that cannot be made within sixty (60) days, this lease may be terminated at the option of either party. In the event that the building in which the demised Premises may be situated is destroyed to an extent of not less than one-third of the replacement costs thereof, Lessor may elect to terminate this lease whether the demised Premises be injured or not. A total destruction of the building in which the Premises may be situated shall terminate this lease.

14. **Lessor's Remedies on Default.** If Lessee defaults in the payment of rent, or any additional rent, or defaults in the performance of any of the other covenants or conditions hereof, Lessor may give

Lessee notice of such default and if Lessee does not cure any such default within sixty (60) days, after the giving of such notice (or if such other default is of such nature that it cannot be completely cured within such period, if Lessee does not commence such curing within such sixty (60) days and thereafter proceed with reasonable diligence and in good faith to cure such default), then Lessor may terminate this lease on not less than thirty (30) days' notice to Lessee. On the date specified in such notice, the term of this lease shall terminate and Lessee shall then quit and surrender the Premises to Lessor, but Lessee shall remain liable as hereinafter provided. If this lease shall have been so terminated by Lessor, Lessor may at any time thereafter resume possession of the Premises by any lawful means and remove Lessee or other occupants and their effects. No failure to enforce any term shall be deemed a waiver.

15. **Common Area Expenses.** In the event the Premises are situated in a shopping center or in a commercial building in which there are common areas, Lessee agrees to pay his pro-rata share of maintenance, taxes, and insurance for the common areas.

16. **Attorney's Fees.** In case suit should be brought for recovery of the Premises, or for any sum due hereunder, or because of any act which may arise out of the possession of the Premises, by either party, the prevailing party shall be entitled to all costs incurred in connection with such action, including a reasonable attorney's fee.

17. **Notices.** Any notice that either party may or is required to give shall be given by mailing the same, postage prepaid, to Lessee at the Premises, or Lessor at the address shown below [give address], or at such other places as may be designated by the parties from time to time.

18. **Heirs, Assigns, Successors.** This lease is binding upon and inures to the benefit of the heirs, assigns, and successors in interest to the parties.

19. **Subordination.** This lease is and shall be subordinated to all existing and future liens and encumbrances against the property.

20. **Entire Agreement.** The foregoing constitutes the entire agreement between the parties and may be modified only by a writing signed by both parties. The following Exhibits, if any, have been made a part of this lease before the parties' execution hereof:

[Insert any exhibits here]

Signed this _____ day of _____, 20_____.

_____
Signature of Lessor

_____
Signature of Lessee

63. Sample California Agreement to Lease Equipment

This agreement to lease equipment ("Lease") is made effective _____ [Date], between

_____ , ("Lessor") and

_____ ,("Lessee").

Lessor desires to lease ("Equipment") to Lessee, and Lessee desires to lease from Lessor.

In consideration of the mutual covenants and promises hereinafter set forth, the parties hereto agree as follows:

1. **Lease.**

   Lessor hereby leases to Lessee, and Lessee hereby leases from Lessor, the following described equipment (the "Equipment"):

2. **Term.**

   The term of this Lease is effective _____ [Effective Date] and ends _____ [End Date] thereafter.

3. **Shipping.**

   Lessee shall be responsible for shipping the Equipment to Lessee's premises.

4. **Rent and Deposit (Installments).**

A. The monthly rent for the Equipment shall be paid in advance in installments of _____ [Installment Amount] each month, beginning on _____ [Date of First Payment] and on the first day of each month thereafter through the effective dates of the contract. Payments will be given to Lessee or mailed to address designated by Lessee at [Address for Payments]. Any installment payment not made by the_____(day) of the month shall be considered overdue and in addition to Lessor's other remedies, Lessor may levy a late payment charge equal to ____(%) per month on any overdue amount. Rent for any partial month shall be prorated.

B. Lessee shall pay a deposit in the following amount prior to taking possession of the Equipment: _____ [Deposit Amount]. The deposit will be refunded to Lessee following Lessee's performance of all obligations in this Lease.

5. **Use.**

   Lessee shall use the Equipment in a careful and proper manner and shall comply with and conform to all national, state, municipal, police and other laws, ordinances and regulations in any way relating to the possession, use or maintenance of the Equipment.

   _____

   _____

   _____

64. Sample Janitorial Service Agreement

Company (Janitorial)_____

Address: _____

Effective Date: _____

("Janitor") and _____ located at _____ ("Company") hereby agree to enter into this contract on the terms and conditions set forth on _____ and continuing till _____ (duration of contract). In consideration of the premises and the obligations hereinafter set forth and for other good and valuable consideration, the receipt and sufficiency of which are hereby acknowledged, the parties agree as follows:

1. **Services.** Company accepts Janitor's proposal dated _____ ("Proposal") to provide cleaning services at Company's facilities as described in the proposal, and Janitor agrees to perform the services described in the Proposal as modified by the terms and conditions contained in this agreement.

2. **Access Requirements.** Janitor shall assign to Company only Janitor employees that have completed, to Company's satisfaction, Company's standard safety training program. Company has the right to refuse access to its facilities to Janitor employees who have not completed such training and shall not be obligated in any manner to Janitor by such refusal.

3. **Cost.** Company shall pay Janitor for actual time which Janitor employees work at Company at the rate of ($_____) per hour, pro-rated for any partial hour worked, not to exceed _____ (_____) hours per week.

4. **Payment Schedule.** Janitor shall bill Company every four (4) weeks from the Effective Date for actual time worked at Company during the previous four (4) week period. Company shall not be obligated to pay any payment due at a time when Janitor is in breach of this Agreement until the breach is remedied to the satisfaction of Company.

5. **Renewal.** This Agreement shall automatically renew under the terms specified herein for a one (1) year period on the expiration of the current term unless either party notifies the other in writing at least thirty (30) days prior to the expiration of the current term that this Agreement shall not be renewed.

6. **Cancellation for Convenience.** Either party may terminate this Agreement by sending written notice to the other party thirty (30) days prior to the date on which the Agreement shall terminate.

7. **Presence of Hazardous Materials.** Janitor acknowledges that Company stores and uses hazardous materials throughout Company's facilities. Janitor assumes the risk of harm to its employees, their property or the property of Janitor resulting from contact with hazardous materials while Janitor's employees or property are on Company's.

8. **Compliance with Laws.** All services rendered by Janitor and its employees pursuant to this Agreement shall conform with and be in full compliance with all applicable laws, rules, ordinances and regulations adopted or required by any federal, state, or local government. Janitor shall be entirely and solely responsible for the payment of employee and employer payroll taxes, contributions, and/or assessments, whether pertaining to federal, state, or local requirements, workers' compensation insurance, or other insurance for Janitor and all of its employees providing the services specified in this Agreement.

9. **Insurance.** Janitor agrees to maintain insurance in commercially reasonable amounts calculated to protect Company and Janitor from any and all claims of any kind or nature for worker's compensation, as required by the state where this contract is performed, and for damage to property or personal injury, including death, arising from acts or omissions of Janitor in performing its duties under this agreement, whether the acts or omissions are those of Janitor, its employees, or agents, or anyone directly or indirectly engaged or employed by Janitor or its agents.

10. **Independent Contractor Status.** The parties intend this Agreement to create an independent contractor relationship. Neither Janitor nor its employees or agents are to be considered agents or employees of Company for any purpose, including that of federal and state taxation, federal, state, and local employment laws, or employee benefits. Janitor, not Company, shall furnish all labor, tools, equipment, vehicles, licenses, and registrations necessary to perform the services.

11. **Assignment/Sub-Contracting.** Janitor shall not assign its rights, delegate its duties, or subcontract any part of its obligations under this Agreement without prior written consent of Company.

12. **Conflicts between Agreements.** The terms of this Agreement shall control over any conflicting terms in the Proposal or any referenced agreement or document.

13. **Indemnification.** Janitor shall indemnify, defend and hold Company, its parent company, subsidiaries, officers and employees harmless from and against any and all claims, actions, suits, demands, assessments or judgments asserted and any and all losses, liabilities, damages, costs and expenses (including, without limitation, reasonable attorneys' fees to the extent permitted by law, accounting fees and investigation costs) alleged or incurred by third Parties arising out of or relating to any operations, acts or omissions of Janitor or any of its employees or agents in the exercise of Janitor's rights or the performance or observance of Janitor's obligations under this Agreement.

14. **Survival.** All provisions that logically ought to survive termination of this Agreement shall survive.

15. **Severability.** If any provision of this Agreement, or the application thereof to any person or circumstance, shall be held invalid or unenforceable by any court of competent jurisdiction, the remainder of this Agreement or the application of such provisions to persons or circumstances, other than those as to which it is held invalid or unenforceable, shall not be affected thereby.

16. **Entire Agreement.** This Agreement, consisting of the Proposal and this document, constitutes the entire agreement with respect to the subject matter herein and supersedes all prior or contemporaneous oral or written agreements concerning such services.

IN WITNESS WHEREOF, the Parties have executed this Agreement as of the date first written above.

Janitor Company   _____ [Name of Other Company]

a _____ corporation   a _____ corporation

By: _____   By: _____

Name: _____   Name: _____

Its: _____   Its: _____

65. Sample Parking Space Agreement

Name: _____

Company: _____

Address: _____

Date of Agreement:

On (date) _____, between "Tenant"_____, of _____(company) and hereinafter referred to as "Landlord"_____, of _____("Landlord Company")_____.

Landlord desires to lease to Tenant and Tenant desires to lease from Landlord the premises generally described as _____(description of leased space).

It is agreed as follows:

Landlord hereby leases to "Tenant" parking space located at the following designated space:

(space number) _____

(effective dates) _____

Payment Terms:

Tenant agrees to pay $_____in advance on (date)_____of each month to Landlord by mail or in person at the following address:_____.

Upon Receipt of Payment:

Once Landlord receives payment, Landlord agrees to issue:

■ Receipt stating the name of Tenant

■ Designated parking space

■ Total rent paid

■ Effective dates

Landlord shall not be liable for any damage or theft of property from said parking space.

The vehicle(s) to be parked in "parking space" shall have current registration and insurance, as verified by Landlord.

Verified: Date:_____

IN WITNESS WHEREOF, the parties hereto have executed this Agreement on the date first above written.

_____

_____

66. Tenant Improvement Form for Property Improvements

Tenant:_____

Building Address:_____

Description of Work:

_____

_____

_____

_____

_____

_____

_____

In consideration of approval, the Tenant agrees:

1.

2.

3.

CHAPTER 7

Forms to Establish Business Ethics

ESTABLISHING A FOUNDATION OF ETHICAL business practices can prevent a host of legal issues from surfacing. An ethical office is one that has a common understanding of cultural and legal morals specific to the working environment. It's up to the business owner and supporting staff to create and implement these moral standards to assure the highest levels of ethical behaviors.

Instituting what is and isn't appropriate behavior is not always easy. The ethics forms included in this chapter help small businesses not only establish ethical operations but enforce them, as well.

Use the *Common Tax Forms for Small Business Checklist* to ensure you take care of employee forms such as the W2 or the 1099 if you employ subcontractors.

An operating code of ethics is often part of a company's employee handbook. Legally, a code of ethics can provide a framework for how staff and management should operate individually and in a way that respects others

and prevents legal problems. Use the *Guide to Writing a Code of Ethics* to establish what is right or wrong in a business context relevant to your own business. Implement *SCORE's Five Tips for Ethical Training* to create an effective ethics training program.

A dress code is commonplace in most organizations. While dress codes are established to portray a company in one way or another, they can also prevent potential legal situations from surfacing. A sample dress code policy provides an example of what a conservative organization may mandate as far as clothing goes and how it's worn.

It's important to prevent discrimination against noncitizens in the workplace. The Immigration and Nationality Act (INA) governs immigration and citizenship in the U.S. and is especially relevant to small business owners since it includes provisions addressing employment eligibility, employment verification, and nondiscrimination. The U.S. government's official INA guide, included in this chapter, describes these rules in detail.

67. Common Tax Forms for Small Business

Universal

If you pay quarterly estimated income tax payments, use Form 1040-ES.
www.irs.gov/pub/irs-pdf/f1040es.pdf

Form W-2 for employees
www.irs.gov/pub/irs-pdf/fw2.pdf

Form W-3 is sent to the IRS, along with Copy A of any Forms W-2 you issued.
www.irs.gov/pub/irs-pdf/fw3.pdf

Form 941 payroll tax
www.irs.gov/pub/irs-pdf/f941.pdf

Form 940 unemployment tax
www.irs.gov/pub/irs-pdf/f940.pdf

Form 1099-MISC
For independent contractors who were paid at least $600
www.irs.gov/pub/irs-pdf/f1099msc.pdf

Form 1096 is sent to the IRS, along with Copy A of any Forms 1099-MISC issued.
www.irs.gov/pub/irs-pdf/f1096.pdf

Form 4868 for a 6-month extension to file the return.
www.irs.gov/pub/irs-pdf/f4868.pdf

Sole Proprietors

File the Following with your 1040

Schedule SE self-employment tax
www.irs.gov/pub/irs-pdf/f1040sse.pdf

Form 4562 equipment and other depreciable property deductions
www.irs.gov/pub/irs-pdf/f4562.pdf

Schedule C report your business income and expenses
www.irs.gov/pub/irs-pdf/f1040sc.pdf

Form 8829 (to deduct a home office)
www.irs.gov/pub/irs-pdf/f8829.pdf

Partnership and LLCs

Form 1065 annual business income tax return
www.irs.gov/pub/irs-pdf/f1065.pdf

Form 7004 for a 6-month extension of time to file Form 1065
www.irs.gov/pub/irs-pdf/f7004.pdf

Corporations

File—Form 1120-W
www.irs.gov/pub/irs-pdf/f1120w.pdf

Form 1120—annual corporate income tax return for regular "C" corporations.
www.irs.gov/pub/irs-pdf/f1120.pdf

Form 1120S—the annual corporate income tax return for "S" corporations.
www.irs.gov/pub/irs-pdf/f1120s.pdf

68. A Guide to Writing a Code of Ethics

A Codes of Ethics is implemented by companies big and small to establish an office-wide understanding and acceptance of how individuals will conduct themselves in a business context. In addition, a code can be used to promote your company's values and attract an audience that values the same. Legally, a working code of ethics can help prevent issues such as stealing, harassment, and lying that could easily end up in court and cost thousands of dollars all on top of bad press.

Use this guide to develop your company's own code and imprint it as the organization's modus operandi.

1. Behavioral Brainstorm
Gather the key players in your office together for a brainstorm session that establishes what your company represents beyond its products and services. The answer may be in the company's tagline. Review marketing material, engage each other in conversation, and have someone write down all the unique qualities that embody the organization.

2. A Historical Review
As a business owner, think back to the start and assess what problems existed, how or if they were resolved, and how a code of conduct could prevent those or similar issues from occurring again.

3. External Review
People who know your business well, and don't work for you, can provide a fresh perspective on your company. Consult customers, vendors, online communities, and social media, to gather different perspectives on how your company comes off to the public. You may be dealt with a full range of issues that might confront your organization, causing potential legal problems down the road.

4. Who will write the document?
Determine whether an internal employee will write the company's code of conduct, or if it's best outsourced to a professional. Whichever method you chose, the Code should represent the organization's core values and principles.

5. Establish a Clear Code for All
Ultimately, a code should make clear who within your organization it applies to. Depending on the size of your organization you may need to specify position-specific language in the code.

6. Putting the Code into Practice
A mass email with an attachment of your latest code of conduct will not do it justice. Announcing and implementing an effective code of conduct takes planning and clarity. Consider employee reactions when asked to commit to an ethical way of handling themselves at work and even outside of work as representatives of the company. The standards expressed in the document should be clear and logical for those who have to follow them. In addition, the implementation of the code, understanding how it will factor into daily operations, and the ensuing consequences if it is not followed, should officially communicated to all it applies to.

7. Determine how often the document will be reviewed and updated
Use this time to review your current code for efficacy and relevancy. Coordinate a team to assess these aspects and make the appropriate updates.

69. SCORE's Five Tips on Ethics Training

1. Know that a strong ethics program can protect your company's reputation and enhance profits. Employees need to understand what's expected of them.

2. Begin by creating a statement of values and a code of ethics for your company, involving employees in the process.

3. Set up a training process. Having managers (including the CEO) train direct reports can be very effective.

4. Keep in mind that some employees may need special training because certain jobs, such as purchasing, expose them to more ethical lapses.

5. A good source of information is *www.bsr.org*, the website of the organization, Business for Social Responsibility.

70. Sample Dress Code

Business-Casual

The purpose of 'Company's' Business Casual Dress Policy is to establish a working environment where employees can dress comfortably and represent the company professionally at the same time. Business casual dress standards are as follows:

Acceptable Women's Attire

- Shirt with a collar and/or a sweater
- Turtlenecks
- Blouses
- Cardigans
- Khakis
- Dress pants
- Capri pants
- Moderate length skirts (knee-length or longer)
- Professional sandals, flats, or pumps
- Head Covers that are required for religious purposes or to honor cultural tradition

Unacceptable Women's Attire:

- Workout wear
- T-shirts
- Mid-rifs
- Flip-flops, sneakers
- Sweat-suits
- Jeans
- Leggings
- Short shorts
- Mini skirts

Acceptable Attire for Men

- Polo shirts
- Collared shirts
- Dress shirts
- Sweaters
- Khakis
- Dress Pants
- Head Covers that are required for religious purposes or to honor cultural tradition
  *Ties are not required

Unacceptable Attire for Men

- Team-related clothing (i.e. NFL jerseys)
- Caps
- T-shirts
- Jeans

- Sweatpants
- Sweatshirts
- Exercise pants
- Bermuda shorts
- Flip flops / opened toed sandals

In addition clothing that has words, terms, or pictures that may be offensive to other employees is prohibited.

Non-Cooperation

If management and/or human resources deems that clothing fails to meet these standards, the employee will be given a warning and asked not to wear the inappropriate item to work again. Upon the employee's second violation of these rules, a second warning will be issued along with dismissal from work for the remaining day. All other policies about personal time use will apply. Appropriate disciplinary action will be applied if dress code violations continue.

70. Your Guide to Fair Employment

Introduction

This guide is designed to help you, the employer, understand and comply with the Immigration and Nationality Act (INA). In short, INA requires you to hire and/or retain only those persons authorized to work in the United States. It also requires you to protect workers against discrimination on the basis of immigration status, nationality, accent, or appearance. This guide provides the steps for both verifying employees' work eligibility and for ensuring that their civil rights are not violated when you are making hiring decisions. First, the guide defines INA fully. It describes how the law affects you and explains how to avoid immigration-related employment discrimination. It outlines easy-to-follow procedures for hiring employees and explains the Employment Eligibility Verification Process. (Form I-9). The guide includes a list of documents that are acceptable in determining employment eligibility. Finally, it provides you with questions and answers to tricky hypothetical situations. If you have further questions about how to comply with INA, please contact the Office of Special Counsel (OSC) for Immigration-Related Unfair Employment Practices of the U.S. Department of Justice. Another excellent source of information on this topic is The Handbook for Employers published by the Immigration and Naturalization Service (INS). To obtain a copy of the Handbook, please contact the INS.

Staying in compliance with INA's antidiscrimination provisions and avoiding costly penalties and fines is a simple matter. Just look at the facts, not at the faces when making hiring decisions, and follow these three basic rules:

- Fill out an Employment Eligibility Verification form (INS Form I-9) for every new employee, including U.S. citizens.
- Allow your employees to show you documents of their choice as long as the documents prove identity and work eligibility and appear on INS list of acceptable documents. You may not ask for specific documents.
- Do not ask for more documents than required.

What Is INA?

The Immigration and Nationality Act (INA) as amended by the Immigration Reform and Control Act of 1986 (IRCA) was the first Federal law making it illegal for employers to knowingly hire persons who are not authorized to work in the United States. The law was an attempt to reduce the stream of undocumented workers entering this country in search of jobs. INA requires that you, as an employer, check documents to confirm the identity and work eligibility of all persons hired after November 1986. To remain in compliance, you must.

- Hire only those persons authorized to work in the United States.
- Ask all new employees to show documents that establish both identity and work authorization.
- Complete the INS Employment Eligibility Verification Form I-9 for every new employee. U.S. citizens and noncitizens.

Noncompliance with the Form I-9 requirements may result in sanctions against employers.

Congress also recognized that these employer sanctions might discourage you from hiring certain eligible workers if they looked or sounded foreign. Therefore, the law also prohibits discrimination in hiring and firing on the basis of citizenship status or national origin. Employers who discriminate may be required to pay fines and penalties, to hire or rehire the employee, and to pay back wages.

How Does INA Affect You?

As an employer:

- INA makes it unlawful for an employer to knowingly hire, recruit, or refer for a fee any individual who is not authorized to work in the United States. It is also unlawful to continue to employ an undocumented worker or one who loses authorization to work. (Those hired before November 6, 1986, do not fall within this category.)
- You may hire anyone whose documents prove identity and work authorization in accordance with the I-9 requirements. There are many documents and combinations of documents that are acceptable, as long as they appear to be reasonably genuine. (For a list of acceptable documents, see the back of the I-9 form.)
- You must treat all job applicants and employees equally.whether they are U.S. citizens or noncitizens. This means you may not discriminate in hiring, firing, recruiting, or referring for a fee, nor are you permitted to retaliate against an employee who has filed a discrimination charge or participated in an investigation.

Types of Immigration-Related Employment

Discrimination:

- Citizenship status discrimination refers to unequal treatment because of citizenship or immigration status.
- National origin discrimination refers to unequal treatment because of nationality, which includes place of birth, appearance, accent, and can include language.
- The Office of Special Counsel (OSC) enforces the provisions against discrimination. OSC covers all cases of discrimination based on citizenship status by employers of four or more employees. It covers national origin discrimination with employers of four to fourteen employees. The Equal Employment Opportunity Commission has jurisdiction over employers of 15 or more.

What Are INA's I-9 Requirements?

I-9. is short for Form I-9, the .Employment Eligibility Verification. form developed by INS as a way for employers to document the fact that they are hiring only persons who are authorized to work in the United States. Over time, the term .I-9 requirements. has come to describe the entire process of verifying worker eligibility outlined out in INA.

As an employer, to comply with INA.s I-9 requirements, you must.

- Complete the I-9 form and keep it on file for at least 3 years from the date of employment or for 1 year after the employee leaves the job, whichever is later. You must also make the forms available for government inspection upon request.
- Verify, on the I-9 form, that you have seen documents establishing identity and work authorization for all your new employees. U.S. citizens and noncitizens alike hired after November 6, 1986.
- Accept any valid documents presented to you by your employee. You may not ask for more documents than those required and may not demand to see specific documents, such as a green card.

Remember that work authorization documents must be renewed on or before their expiration date and the

I-9 form must be updated. This is also called reverification. At this time, you must accept any valid documents your employee chooses to present, whether or not they are the same documents provided initially.

(Note: You don.t need to see an identity document when the I-9 is updated.)

Remember, you are free to hire anyone who can show documents establishing his or her identity and authorization to work. Any of the documents (or combination of documents) listed on the back of Form I-9 are acceptable as long as they appear to be reasonably genuine.

How Can You Avoid Immigration-Related Employment Discrimination?
- Avoid citizens only. hiring policies or requiring that applicants have a particular immigration status. In most cases, these practices are illegal.
- Give out the same job information over the telephone, and use the same application form for all applicants.
- Base all decisions about firing on job performance and/or behavior, not on appearance, accent, name, or citizenship status of your employees.

As an employer, to comply with INA's antidiscrimination provisions, you should.
- Let the employee choose which documents to present, as long as they prove identity and work authorization and are included in the acceptable list on the back of the I-9 form.
- Accept documents that appear to be genuine. As an employer, to avoid employment discrimination based on nationality or citizenship status, you must.
- Treat all people the same in announcing the job, taking applications, interviewing, offering the job, verifying eligibility to work, hiring, and firing.
- Remember that U.S. citizenship, or nationality, belongs to all individuals born of a U.S. citizen and all persons born in Puerto Rico, Guam, the Virgin Islands, Northern Mariana Islands, American Samoa, and Swains Island. Citizenship is granted to legal immigrants after they complete the naturalization process.

What Would You Do?

Read each of the cases below. Circle Yes or No. Answers are given below.

1. Saving Time. Your crew boss catches you before you start interviewing people for a job. He says, .Find out if those two near the door have their .green cards. before you waste your time. Did you discriminate in hiring?   Yes   No

2. The Cooperative Executive. You are president of a company. After hearing about INA's penalties for hiring undocumented workers, you issue a memo stating, "Let's go along with the government on this one. Please be careful when hiring people who look like they crossed the border illegally." Have you committed national origin discrimination?   Yes   No

How about citizenship status discrimination? Yes   No

3. On the Way Out. The rainy spring caused your lettuce harvest to be less abundant than usual. You need fewer farm workers than you hired for the season. In deciding between Héctor Fernández and José González, you keep Héctor because he is a legal permanent resident and José, an asylee, only has a temporary work permit. Have you committed citizenship status discrimination?   Yes   No

4. A Stitch in Time. You gladly hire Lily Chou because she told you how she beaded sweaters in Taiwan.

You are surprised when she hands you a California driver's license and an unrestricted Social Security card for the I-9 form. (Note: Some Social Security cards are restricted and bear the inscription "Valid Only with INS Authorization" or "Not Valid for Employment.") Miss Chou,. you say, I must see a card from the INS. Does Lily Chou have a case against you?   Yes   No

5. Hire American. You manufacture precision cast parts. Ordinarily, any one of your 12 employees knows someone who can fill an open position. You tell them unofficially that you prefer that they bring applicants who are U.S. citizens.and you fill out the I-9 form for everyone they bring. Are you in compliance with INA? Yes   No

6. Temporary Workers. You hire Billy, John, Paul, and Sam just for a weekend to clean windows in your office building. You would have hired Ngo except that he looked too foreign. Are you violating the antidiscrimination provisions?   Yes   No

7. Frenchman With a Fault. Three men apply to manage the front desk of your four-star hotel. One has more experience than the other two, but you refuse to hire him because all he has for the I-9 form is an unexpired French passport with an unexpired work authorization stamp. You ask him for "a driver's license, anything." The next person has only a temporary resident card that expires in nine days. That's too close for comfort. So, you hire the third applicant, who has a valid Canadian driver's license. Are you discriminating? Yes   No

8. Useless Regret. The person you chose to run your jacquard loom was unable to show documentation for the I-9 form. She said she would send for it, but you turned her down because you didn.t want to get into as much paperwork as Martha required the last time. You hired your second choice, a woman with less experience but valid papers in hand. Did you violate INA?   Yes   No

Answer s

1. Saving Time
Yes. First of all, it is recommended that you wait until you hire an individual before asking him/her for papers to verify his/her identity and work authorization. However, if you ask for papers ahead of time only from people who appear to be foreign, you are discriminating on the basis of national origin. You must treat all applicants equally, and, when you review their papers, you cannot insist on seeing particular documents if they have already shown you valid documents. Otherwise, you are engaging in document abuse.

2. The Cooperative Executive
Yes, you are engaging in both types of discrimination (national origin and citizenship status). When you ask new hires to fill out the I-9, you must do so for all new hires. Also, you must treat all new hires in the same way when verifying work eligibility, regardless of whether they are immigrants or members of a particular nationality.

3. On the Way Out
Yes. This is definitely citizenship status discrimination. You cannot fire a protected individual under INA because he/she has a temporary work permit as opposed to legal permanent residency. A protected individual is a U.S. citizen, national, permanent resident, temporary resident, refugee, or an asylee. In any event, your firing decision cannot be based on this factor. Otherwise, your actions will be considered discriminatory by OSC.

4. A Stitch in Time

Yes. Lily Chou has a very strong case against you. You should have let her choose which valid documents to present as proof of her identity and work authorization. A California driver's license proves identity, and an unrestricted Social Security card proves work authorization. Your insistence on seeing an INS card is called document abuse, and this is a discriminatory practice.

5. Hire American

No, you are not in compliance with INA. Unless otherwise required by law, you cannot have citizens-only hiring policies. If you insist on doing so, you are engaging in citizenship status discrimination.

6. Temporary Workers

Yes. You cannot deny work to individuals because they looked too .foreign.. This is national origin discrimination. And, if you wrongly assumed that Ngo was unauthorized to work, you have also committed citizenship status discrimination.

7. Frenchman with a Fault

Yes, you are discriminating. The unexpired French passport, with an unexpired work authorization attached is sufficient documentation to show that the applicant is work-authorized. So is the person with the temporary resident card. When the card expires in nine days, you can ask him/her to reverify work authorization in Section 3 of the I-9 form. The third applicant did not show sufficient documents to establish work authorization. A Canadian driver's license is a permissible document to establish identity, but it does not establish authorization to work in the United States. Therefore, the applicant would also need to show you a document from List C.

Remember, for reverification purposes, the individual again has the right to show the valid documents of his/her choice. These documents don't have to be the same ones that he/she presented initially. If you insist on seeing the same documents, you are engaging in document abuse.

8. Useless Regret

Probably. Although you may choose not to allow applicants 3 days to present valid documents, you must treat all applicants equally. The paperwork requirements are the same for citizens and noncitizens alike.

CHAPTER 8

The Lawful Way to Employ Immigrants

AN ESTIMATED 17.7 MILLION IMMIGRANTS currently work in the United States. Businesses in all industries employ immigrants; however, not all do so within the legal constructs set forth by the federal government and specifically, the Immigration and Naturalization Services and U.S. Citizen and Immigration Services.

As a small business owner, it's important to be mindful of the legal issues relating to hiring aliens and immigrants. Legally speaking, an *alien* is a person who was not born in the United States and comes into the country from outside. Once an alien is legally in the U.S. and intends to remain, he or she is identified as an *immigrant*.

According to law and the Immigration Reform and Control Act of 1986, employers should hire only U.S. citizens and aliens who are authorized to work in the United States. The law requires every employer to verify the employment eligibility of every worker hired to avoid civil fines and criminal penalties for failure to comply with the law's record keep-ing requirements. The law also requires each company to follow fixed guidelines regardless of company size or the number of employees being hired.

The Immigration and Naturalization Service has developed a Form I-9 (found on the website supporting this book) that employers must complete and retain to verify employment eligibility for all employees. A sample I-9 form is included in this chapter to help readers become familiar with the language and required information.

Form I-129 (found on the website) is a petition that must be completed to hire a non-immigrant worker. For example, employers looking to hire foreign workers to perform services or labor or to receive training may file an I-129 petition. Form I-129 is also used to petition for an extension of stay in the U.S.

A non-U.S. citizen entrepreneur in the United States who is seeking to legally immigrate to the United States may file *Form I-526*. Form I-526 requires a non-U.S. citizen entrepreneur to invest an amount of $1 million toward a particular regulated area in a new commercial enterprise. This is found the website, also.

Form 9035 specifies the prevailing wage that is set forth, and a promise from the U.S. company to pay at least the prevailing wage. Form 9035 is to be filed as stipulated by the H-1B program, which allows an employer to temporarily employ a foreign worker in the U.S. on a nonimmigrant basis in a specialty occupation.

Finally, *Form 9142 Application for Temporary Employment Certification* is just that—a form employers need to file if looking to employ foreign workers for temporary employment in the U.S.

72. Form 9035 and 9035E Application for Nonimmigrant Workers

OMB Approval: 1205-0310
Expiration Date: 01/31/2012

Labor Condition Application for Nonimmigrant Workers
ETA Form 9035 & 9035E
U.S. Department of Labor

Electronic Filing of Labor Condition Applications
For The H-1B Nonimmigrant Visa Program

This Department of Labor, Employment and Training Administration (ETA), electronic filing system enables an employer to file a Labor Condition Application (LCA) and obtain certification of the LCA. This Form must be submitted by the employer or by someone authorized to act on behalf of the employer.

A) I understand and agree that, upon my receipt of ETA's certification of the LCA by electronic response to my submission, I must take the following actions at the specified times and circumstances:
- print and sign a hardcopy of the electronically filed and certified LCA;
- maintain a signed hardcopy of this LCA in my public access files;
- submit a signed hardcopy of the LCA to the United States Citizenship and Immigration Services (USCIS) in support of the I-129, on the date of submission of the I-129;
- provide a signed hardcopy of this LCA to each H-1B nonimmigrant who is employed pursuant to the LCA.

❏ Yes ❏ No

B) I understand and agree that, by filing the LCA electronically, I attest that all of the statements in the LCA are true and accurate and that I am undertaking all the obligations that are set out in the LCA (Form ETA 9035E) and the accompanying instructions (Form ETA 9035CP).

❏ Yes ❏ No

C) I hereby choose one of the following options, with regard to the accompanying instructions:

❏ I choose to have the Form ETA 9035CP electronically attached to the certified LCA, and to be bound by the LCA obligations as explained in this form

❏ I choose not to have the Form ETA 9035CP electronically attached to the certified LCA, but I have read the instructions and I understand that I am bound by the LCA obligations as explained in this form

---

ETA Form 9035/9035E Attestation **FOR DEPARTMENT OF LABOR USE ONLY** Page 1 of 1

Case Number:_____ Case Status: _____ Period of Employment: _____ to _____

OMB Approval: 1205-0310
Expiration Date: 01/31/2012

Labor Condition Application for Nonimmigrant Workers
ETA Form 9035 & 9035E
U.S. Department of Labor

*Please read and review the filing instructions carefully before completing the ETA Form 9035 or 9035E. A copy of the instructions can be found at http://www.foreignlaborcert.doleta.gov/. In accordance with Federal Regulations at 20 CFR 655.730(b), incomplete or obviously inaccurate Labor Condition Applications (LCAs) will not be certified by the Department of Labor. If the employer has received permission from the Administrator of the Office of Foreign Labor Certification to submit this form non-electronically, ALL required fields/items containing an asterisk (*) must be completed as well as any fields/items where a response is conditional as indicated by the section (§) symbol.*

A. Employment-Based Nonimmigrant Visa Information

1. Indicate the type of visa classification supported by this application *(Write classification symbol)*: *

B. Temporary Need Information

1. Job Title *

2. SOC (ONET/OES) code *	3. SOC (ONET/OES) occupation title *

4. Is this a full-time position? *	**Period of Intended Employment**	
☐ Yes ☐ No	5. Begin Date * *(mm/dd/yyyy)*	6. End Date * *(mm/dd/yyyy)*

7. Worker positions needed/basis for the visa classification supported by this application

    Total Worker Positions Being Requested for Certification *

Basis for the visa classification supported by this application
(indicate the total workers in each applicable category based on the total workers identified above)

a. New employment *

b. Continuation of previously approved employment * without change with the same employer

c. Change in previously approved employment *

d. New concurrent employment *

e. Change in employer *

f. Amended petition *

C. Employer Information

1. Legal business name *

2. Trade name/Doing Business As (DBA), if applicable

3. Address 1 *

4. Address 2

5. City *	6. State *	7. Postal code *

8. Country *	9. Province

10. Telephone number *	11. Extension

12. Federal Employer Identification Number (FEIN from IRS) *	13. NAICS code (must be at least 4-digits) *

ETA Form 9035/9035E   **FOR DEPARTMENT OF LABOR USE ONLY**   Page 1 of 5

Case Number:_____ Case Status:_____ Period of Employment:_____ to _____

OMB Approval: 1205-0310
Expiration Date: 01/31/2012

Labor Condition Application for Nonimmigrant Workers
ETA Form 9035 & 9035E
U.S. Department of Labor

D. Employer Point of Contact Information

Important Note: The information contained in this Section must be that of an employee of the employer who is authorized to act on behalf of the employer in labor certification matters. The information in this Section <u>must be</u> <u>different</u> from the agent or attorney information listed in Section E, unless the attorney is an employee of the employer.

1. Contact's last (family) name *	2. First (given) name *	3. Middle name(s) *
4. Contact's job title *		
5. Address 1 *		
6. Address 2		
7. City *	8. State *	9. Postal code *
10. Country *	11. Province	
12. Telephone number *	13. Extension	14. E-Mail address

E. Attorney or Agent Information (If applicable)

1. Is the employer represented by an attorney or agent in the filing of this application? * If "Yes", complete the remainder of Section E below.		☐ Yes ☐ No
2. Attorney or Agent's last (family) name §	3. First (given) name §	4. Middle name(s) §
5. Address 1 §		
6. Address 2		
7. City §	8. State §	9. Postal code §
10. Country §	11. Province	
12. Telephone number §	13. Extension	14. E-Mail address
15. Law firm/Business name §		16. Law firm/Business FEIN §
17. State Bar number (only if attorney) §	18. State of highest court where attorney is in good standing (only if attorney) §	
19. Name of the highest court where attorney is in good standing (only if attorney) §		

ETA Form 9035/9035E   **FOR DEPARTMENT OF LABOR USE ONLY**   Page 2 of 5

Case Number:_____ Case Status: _____ Period of Employment: _____ to _____

OMB Approval: 1205-0310
Expiration Date: 01/31/2012

Labor Condition Application for Nonimmigrant Workers
ETA Form 9035 & 9035E
U.S. Department of Labor

F. Rate of Pay

1. Wage Rate (Required)	2. Per: (Choose only one) *
From: $ _____ . ____ * To: $ _____ . ____	☐ Hour ☐ Week ☐ Bi-Weekly ☐ Month ☐ Year

G. Employment and Prevailing Wage Information

<u>Important Note</u>: It is important for the employer to define the place of intended employment with as much geographic specificity as possible The place of employment address listed below <u>must be a physical location and cannot be a P.O. Box</u>. The employer may use this section to identify up to three (3) physical locations and corresponding prevailing wages covering each location where work will be performed and the electronic system will accept up to 3 physical locations and prevailing wage information. If the employer has received approval from the Department of Labor to submit this form non-electronically and the work is expected to be performed in more than one location, an attachment must be submitted in order to complete this section.

a. Place of Employment 1

1. Address 1 *	
2. Address 2	
3. City *	4. County *
5. State/District/Territory *	6. Postal code *

Prevailing Wage Information (corresponding to the place of employment location listed above)	
7. Agency which issued prevailing wage §	7a. Prevailing wage tracking number (if applicable) §
8. Wage level * ☐ I ☐ II ☐ III ☐ IV ☐ N/A	
9. Prevailing wage * $ _____ . ____	10. Per: (Choose only one) * ☐ Hour ☐ Week ☐ Bi-Weekly ☐ Month ☐ Year
11. Prevailing wage source (Choose only one) * ☐ OES ☐ CBA ☐ DBA ☐ SCA ☐ Other	
11a. Year source published *	11b. If "OES", <u>and</u> SWA/NPC did not issue prevailing wage **OR** "Other" in question 11, specify source §

H. Employer Labor Condition Statements

❗ <u>Important Note</u>: In order for your application to be processed, you <u>MUST</u> read Section H of the Labor Condition Application – General Instructions Form ETA 9035CP under the heading "Employer Labor Condition Statements" and agree to all four (4) labor condition statements summarized below:

   (1) **Wages:** Pay nonimmigrants at least the local prevailing wage or the employer's actual wage, whichever is higher, and pay for non-productive time. Offer nonimmigrants benefits on the same basis as offered to U.S. workers.
   (2) **Working Conditions:** Provide working conditions for nonimmigrants which will not adversely affect the working conditions of workers similarly employed.
   (3) **Strike, Lockout, or Work Stoppage:** There is no strike, lockout, or work stoppage in the named occupation at the place of employment.
   (4) **Notice:** Notice to union or to workers has been or will be provided in the named occupation at the place of employment. A copy of this form will be provided to each nonimmigrant worker employed pursuant to the application.

1. <u>I have read and agree to</u> Labor Condition Statements 1, 2, 3, and 4 above and as fully explained in Section H of the Labor Condition Application – General Instructions – Form ETA 9035CP. *	☐ Yes ☐ No

ETA Form 9035/9035E	**FOR DEPARTMENT OF LABOR USE ONLY**	Page 3 of 5

Case Number:_____ Case Status:_____ Period of Employment:_____ to _____

OMB Approval: 1205-0310
Expiration Date: 01/31/2012

**Labor Condition Application for Nonimmigrant Workers
ETA Form 9035 & 9035E
U.S. Department of Labor**

I. Additional Employer Labor Condition Statements – H-1B Employers ONLY

! **Important Note**: In order for your H-1B application to be processed, you <u>MUST</u> read Section I – Subsection 1 of the Labor Condition Application – General Instructions Form ETA 9035CP under the heading "Additional Employer Labor Condition Statements" and answer the questions below.

a. Subsection 1

1. Is the employer H-1B dependent? §	☐ Yes ☐ No
2. Is the employer a willful violator? §	☐ Yes ☐ No
3. If "Yes" is marked in questions I.1 and/or I.2, you must answer "Yes" or "No" regarding whether the employer will use this application <u>ONLY</u> to support H-1B petitions or extensions of status for exempt H-1B nonimmigrants? §	☐ Yes ☐ No ☐ N/A

If you marked "Yes" to questions I.1 and/or I.2 and "No" to question I.3, you <u>MUST</u> read Section I – Subsection 2 of the Labor Condition Application – General Instructions Form ETA 9035CP under the heading "Additional Employer Labor Condition Statements" and indicate your agreement to all three (3) additional statements summarized below.

b. Subsection 2

A. **Displacement:** Non-displacement of the U.S. workers in the employer's workforce
B. **Secondary Displacement:** Non-displacement of U.S. workers in another employer's workforce; and
C. **Recruitment and Hiring:** Recruitment of U.S. workers and hiring of U.S. workers applicant(s) who are equally or better qualified than the H-1B nonimmigrant(s).

4. <u>I have read and agree</u> to Additional Employer Labor Condition Statements A, B, and C above and as fully explained in Section I – Subsections 1 and 2 of the Labor Condition Application – General Instructions Form ETA 9035CP. §	☐ Yes ☐ No

J. Public Disclosure Information

! **Important Note**: You <u>must</u> select from the options listed in this Section.

1. Public disclosure information will be kept at: *	☐ Employer's principal place of business ☐ Place of employment

K. Declaration of Employer

By signing this form, I, on behalf of the employer, attest that the information and labor condition statements provided are true and accurate; that I have read sections H and I of the Labor Condition Application – General Instructions Form ETA 9035CP, and that I agree to comply with the Labor Condition Statements as set forth in the Labor Condition Application – General Instructions Form ETA 9035CP and with the Department of Labor regulations (20 CFR part 655, Subparts H and I). I agree to make this application, supporting documentation, and other records available to officials of the Department of Labor upon request during any investigation under the Immigration and Nationality Act. Making fraudulent representations on this Form can lead to civil or criminal action under 18 U.S.C. 1001, 18 U.S.C. 1546, or other provisions of law.

1. Last (family) name of hiring or designated official *	2. First (given) name of hiring or designated official *	3. Middle initial *
4. Hiring or designated official title *		
5. Signature *	6. Date signed *	

ETA Form 9035/9035E   **FOR DEPARTMENT OF LABOR USE ONLY**   Page 4 of 5

Case Number:_____   Case Status:_____   Period of Employment:_____ to _____

OMB Approval: 1205-0310
Expiration Date: 01/31/2012

Labor Condition Application for Nonimmigrant Workers
ETA Form 9035 & 9035E
U.S. Department of Labor

L. LCA Preparer

Important Note: Complete this section if the preparer of this LCA is a person other than the one identified in either Section D (employer point of contact) or E (attorney or agent) of this application.

1. Last (family) name §	2. First (given) name §	3. Middle initial §

4. Firm/Business name §

5. E-Mail address §

M. U.S. Government Agency Use (ONLY)

By virtue of the signature below, the Department of Labor hereby acknowledges the following:

This certification is valid from _____ to _____.

_____
Department of Labor, Office of Foreign Labor Certification

_____
Determination Date (date signed)

_____
Case number

_____
Case Status

The Department of Labor is not the guarantor of the accuracy, truthfulness, or adequacy of a certified LCA.

N. Signature Notification and Complaints

The signatures and dates signed on this form will not be filled out when electronically submitting to the Department of Labor for processing, but **MUST** be complete when submitting non-electronically. If the application is submitted electronically, any resulting certification **MUST** be signed *immediately upon receipt* from the Department of Labor before it can be submitted to USCIS for further processing.

Complaints alleging misrepresentation of material facts in the LCA and/or failure to comply with the terms of the LCA may be filed using the WH-4 Form with any office of the Wage and Hour Division, Employment Standards Administration, U.S. Department of Labor. A listing of the Wage and Hour Division offices can be obtained at http://www.dol.gov/esa. Complaints alleging failure to offer employment to an equally or better qualified U.S. worker, or an employer's misrepresentation regarding such offer(s) of employment, may be filed with the U.S. Department of Justice, Office of the Special Counsel for Immigration-Related Unfair Employment Practices, 950 Pennsylvania Avenue, NW, Washington, DC, 20530. Please note that complaints should be filed with the Office of Special Counsel at the Department of Justice only if the violation is by an employer who is H-1B dependent or a willful violator as defined in 20 CFR 655.710(b) and 655.734(a)(1)(ii).

O. OMB Paperwork Reduction Act *(1205-0310)*

These reporting instructions have been approved under the Paperwork Reduction Act of 1995. Persons are not required to respond to this collection of information unless it displays a currently valid OMB control number. Obligations to reply are mandatory (Immigration and Nationality Act, Section 212(n) and (t) and 214(c). Public reporting burden for this collection of information, which is to assist with program management and to meet Congressional and statutory requirements is estimated to average 1 hour per response, including the time to review instructions, search existing data sources, gather and maintain the data needed, and complete and review the collection of information. Send comments regarding this burden estimate or any other aspect of this collection of information, including suggestions for reducing this burden, to the U.S. Department of Labor, Room C-4312, 200 Constitution Ave. NW, Washington, DC 20210. (Paperwork Reduction Project OMB 1205-0310.) **Do NOT send the completed application to this address.**

ETA Form 9035/9035E   **FOR DEPARTMENT OF LABOR USE ONLY**   Page 5 of 5

Case Number:_____ Case Status:_____ Period of Employment: _____ to _____

73. Form 9142 Application for Temporary Employment Certification

OMB Approval: 1205-0466
Expiration Date: 11/30/2011

Application for Temporary Employment Certification
ETA Form 9142
U.S. Department of Labor

*Please read and review the filing instructions carefully before completing the ETA Form 9142. A copy of the instructions can be found at http://www.foreignlaborcert.doleta.gov/. In accordance with Federal Regulations, incomplete or obviously inaccurate applications will not be certified by the Department of Labor. If submitting this form non-electronically, ALL required fields/items containing an asterisk (*) must be completed as well as any fields/items where a response is conditional as indicated by the section (§) symbol.*

A. Employment-Based Nonimmigrant Visa Information

1. Indicate the type of visa classification supported by this application *(Write classification symbol)*: *

B. Temporary Need Information

1. Job Title *

2. SOC (ONET/OES) code *

3. SOC (ONET/OES) occupation title *

4. Is this a full-time position? *

☐ Yes   ☐ No

Period of Intended Employment

5. Begin Date *
(mm/dd/yyyy)

6. End Date *
(mm/dd/yyyy)

7. Worker positions needed/basis for the visa classification supported by this application

Total Worker Positions Being Requested for Certification *

Basis for the visa classification supported by this application
(indicate the total workers in each applicable category based on the total workers identified above)

a. New employment *

d. New concurrent employment *

b. Continuation of previously approved employment *
without change with the same employer

e. Change in employer *

c. Change in previously approved employment *

f. Amended petition *

8. Nature of Temporary Need: (Choose only one of the standards) *

☐ Seasonal   ☐ Peakload   ☐ One-Time Occurrence   ☐ Intermittent or Other Temporary Need

9. Statement of Temporary Need *

ETA Form 9142

FOR DEPARTMENT OF LABOR USE ONLY

Page 1 of 6

Case Number: _____   Case Status: _____   Validity Period: _____ to _____

OMB Approval: 1205-0466
Expiration Date: 11/30/2011

Application for Temporary Employment Certification
ETA Form 9142
U.S. Department of Labor

C. Employer Information

Important Note: Enter the full name of the individual employer, partnership, or corporation and all other required information in this section. For joint employer or master applications filed on behalf of more than one employer under the H-2A program, identify the main or primary employer in the section below and then submit a separate attachment that identifies each employer, <u>by name, mailing address, and total worker positions needed</u>, under the application.

1. Legal business name *		
2. Trade name/Doing Business As (DBA), if applicable		
3. Address 1 *		
4. Address 2		
5. City *	6. State *	7. Postal code *
8. Country *	9. Province	
10. Telephone number *	11. Extension	
12. Federal Employer Identification Number (FEIN from IRS) *	13. NAICS code (must be at least 4-digits) *	

14. Type of employer application (choose only one box below) *

☐ Individual Employer   ☐ Association – Sole Employer (H-2A only)
☐ H-2A Labor Contractor or   ☐ Association – Joint Employer (H-2A only)
    Job Contractor   ☐ Association – Filing as Agent (H-2A only)

D. Employer Point of Contact Information

Important Note: The information contained in this Section must be that of an employee of the employer who is authorized to act on behalf of the employer in labor certification matters. The information in this Section <u>must be different</u> from the agent or attorney information listed in Section E, unless the attorney is an employee of the employer. For joint employer or master applications filed on behalf of more than one employer under the H-2A program, enter <u>only</u> the contact information for the main or primary employer (e.g., contact for an association filing as joint employer) under the application.

1. Contact's last (family) name *	2. First (given) name *	3. Middle name(s) *
4. Contact's job title *		
5. Address 1 *		
6. Address 2		
7. City *	8. State *	9. Postal code *
10. Country *	11. Province	
12. Telephone number *	13. Extension	14. E-Mail address

ETA Form 9142	**FOR DEPARTMENT OF LABOR USE ONLY**	Page 2 of 6
Case Number: _____	Case Status: _____	Validity Period: _____ to _____

OMB Approval: 1205-0466
Expiration Date: 11/30/2011

**Application for Temporary Employment Certification
ETA Form 9142
U.S. Department of Labor**

E. Attorney or Agent Information (If applicable)

1. Is/are the employer(s) represented by an attorney or agent in the filing of this application (including associations acting as agent under the H-2A program)? If "Yes", complete Section E. *		☐ Yes ☐ No
2. Attorney or Agent's last (family) name §	3. First (given) name §	4. Middle name(s) §

5. Address 1 §

6. Address 2

7. City §	8. State §	9. Postal code §
10. Country §	11. Province	
12. Telephone number §	13. Extension	14. E-Mail address

15. Law firm/Business name §	16. Law firm/Business FEIN §
17. State Bar number (only if attorney) §	18. State of highest court where attorney is in good standing (only if attorney) §

19. Name of the highest court where attorney is in good standing (only if attorney) §

F. Job Offer Information

a. Job Description

1. Job Title *

2. Number of hours of work per week Basic *: _____ Overtime: _____	3. Hourly Work Schedule * A.M. *(h:mm):* ___ : ____ P.M. *(h:mm):* ___ : ____
4. Does this position supervise the work of other employees? * ☐ Yes ☐ No	4a. If yes, number of employees worker will supervise (if applicable) § _____

5. Job duties – A description of the duties to be performed **MUST** begin in this space. If necessary, add attachment to <u>continue and complete</u> description. *

OMB Approval: 1205-0466
Expiration Date: 11/30/2011

Application for Temporary Employment Certification
ETA Form 9142
U.S. Department of Labor

F. Job Offer Information *(continued)*

b. Minimum Job Requirements

1. Education: minimum U.S. diploma/degree required *   ☐ None ☐ High School/GED ☐ Associate's ☐ Bachelor's ☐ Master's ☐ Doctorate (PhD) ☐ Other degree (JD, MD, etc.)

1a. If "Other degree" in question 1, specify the diploma/ degree required §	1b. Indicate the major(s) and/or field(s) of study required § (May list more than one related major and more than one field)

2. Does the employer require a second U.S. diploma/degree? *	☐ Yes ☐ No
2a. If "Yes" in question 2, indicate the second U.S. diploma/degree and the major(s) and/or field(s) of study required §	

3. Is training for the job opportunity required? *	☐ Yes ☐ No

3a. If "Yes" in question 3, specify the number of <u>months</u> of training required §	3b. Indicate the field(s)/name(s) of training required § (May list more than one related field and more than one type)

4. Is employment experience required? *	☐ Yes ☐ No

4a. If "Yes" in question 4, specify the number of <u>months</u> of experience required §	4b. Indicate the occupation required §

5. Special Requirements - List specific skills, licenses/certifications, and requirements of the job opportunity. *

c. Place of Employment Information

1. Worksite address 1 *

2. Address 2

3. City *	4. County *

5. State/District/Territory *	6. Postal code *

7. Will work be performed in multiple worksites within an area of intended employment or a location(s) other than the address listed above? *	☐ Yes ☐ No

7a. If Yes in question 7, identify the geographic place(s) of employment with as much specificity as possible. If necessary, submit an attachment to <u>continue and complete</u> a listing of all anticipated worksites. §

ETA Form 9142	**FOR DEPARTMENT OF LABOR USE ONLY**	Page 4 of 6

Case Number: _____ Case Status: _____ Validity Period: _____ to _____

OMB Approval: 1205-0466
Expiration Date: 11/30/2011

Application for Temporary Employment Certification
ETA Form 9142
U.S. Department of Labor

I. Declaration of Employer and Attorney/Agent

In accordance with Federal regulations, the employer must attest that it will abide by certain terms, assurances and obligations as a condition for receiving a temporary labor certification from the U.S. Department of Labor. <u>Applications that fail to attach Appendix A.2 or Appendix B.1 will be considered incomplete and not accepted for processing by the ETA application processing center.</u>

1. For H-2A Applications ONLY, please confirm that you have read and agree to all the applicable terms, assurances and obligations contained in **Appendix A.2**. §	❑ Yes ❑ No ❑ N/A
2. For H-2B Applications ONLY, please confirm that you have read and agree to all the applicable terms, assurances and obligations contained in **Appendix B.1**. §	❑ Yes ❑ No ❑ N/A

J. Preparer

Complete this section if the preparer of this application is a person other than the one identified in either Section D (employer point of contact) or E (attorney or agent) of this application.

1. Last (family) name §	2. First (given) name §	3. Middle initial §
4. Job Title §		
5. Firm/Business name §		
6. E-Mail address §		

K. U.S. Government Agency Use (ONLY)

Pursuant to the provisions of Section 101 (a)(15)(h)(ii) of the Immigration and Nationality Act, as amended, I hereby certify that there are not sufficient U.S. workers available and the employment of the above will not adversely affect the wages and working conditions of workers in the U.S. similarly employed. By virtue of the signature below, the Department of Labor hereby acknowledges the following:

This certification is valid from _____ to _____.

_____
Department of Labor, Office of Foreign Labor Certification

_____
Determination Date (date signed)

_____
Case number

_____
Case Status

L. OMB Paperwork Reduction Act *(1205-0466)*

Persons are not required to respond to this collection of information unless it displays a currently valid OMB control number. Respondent's reply to these reporting requirements is mandatory to obtain the benefits of temporary employment certification (Immigration and Nationality Act, Section 101 (a)(15)(H)(ii)). Public reporting burden for this collection of information is estimated to average 2 hours 10 minutes per response for H-2A and 2 hours 45 minutes for H-2B, including the time for reviewing instructions, searching existing data sources, gathering and maintaining the data needed, and completing and reviewing the collection of information. Send comments regarding this burden estimate to the Office of Foreign Labor Certification * U.S. Department of Labor * Room C4312 * 200 Constitution Ave., NW * Washington, DC * 20210. **Do NOT send the completed application to this address.**

OMB Approval: 1205-0466
Expiration Date: 11/30/2011

Application for Temporary Employment Certification
ETA Form 9142
U.S. Department of Labor

I. Declaration of Employer and Attorney/Agent

In accordance with Federal regulations, the employer must attest that it will abide by certain terms, assurances and obligations as a condition for receiving a temporary labor certification from the U.S. Department of Labor. <u>Applications that fail to attach Appendix A.2 or Appendix B.1 will be considered incomplete and not accepted for processing by the ETA application processing center</u>.

1. For H-2A Applications ONLY, please confirm that you have read and agree to all the applicable terms, assurances and obligations contained in **Appendix A.2**. §	❑ Yes ❑ No ❑ N/A
2. For H-2B Applications ONLY, please confirm that you have read and agree to all the applicable terms, assurances and obligations contained in **Appendix B.1**. §	❑ Yes ❑ No ❑ N/A

J. Preparer

Complete this section if the preparer of this application is a person other than the one identified in either Section D (employer point of contact) or E (attorney or agent) of this application.

1. Last (family) name §	2. First (given) name §	3. Middle initial §
4. Job Title §		
5. Firm/Business name §		
6. E-Mail address §		

K. U.S. Government Agency Use (ONLY)

Pursuant to the provisions of Section 101 (a)(15)(h)(ii) of the Immigration and Nationality Act, as amended, I hereby certify that there are not sufficient U.S. workers available and the employment of the above will not adversely affect the wages and working conditions of workers in the U.S. similarly employed. By virtue of the signature below, the Department of Labor hereby acknowledges the following:

This certification is valid from _____ to _____.

_____
Department of Labor, Office of Foreign Labor Certification

_____
Determination Date (date signed)

_____
Case number

_____
Case Status

L. OMB Paperwork Reduction Act *(1205-0466)*

Persons are not required to respond to this collection of information unless it displays a currently valid OMB control number. Respondent's reply to these reporting requirements is mandatory to obtain the benefits of temporary employment certification (Immigration and Nationality Act, Section 101 (a)(15)(H)(ii). Public reporting burden for this collection of information is estimated to average 2 hours 10 minutes per response for H-2A and 2 hours 45 minutes for H-2B, including the time for reviewing instructions, searching existing data sources, gathering and maintaining the data needed, and completing and reviewing the collection of information. Send comments regarding this burden estimate to the Office of Foreign Labor Certification * U.S. Department of Labor * Room C4312 * 200 Constitution Ave., NW * Washington, DC * 20210. **Do NOT send the completed application to this address.**

ETA Form 9142	**FOR DEPARTMENT OF LABOR USE ONLY**	Page 6 of 6

Case Number: _____   Case Status: _____   Validity Period: _____ to _____

CHAPTER 9

Legally Navigating Online Activity

ONLINE OPERATIONS ARE REGULATED just as heavily as brick and mortar businesses. Transparency is key, and providing an experience with minimal ambiguity for the general online audience is essential. This means explaining exactly who you and your company are, what you're offering, and what the intended final outcome will be. The Federal Trade Commission is the controlling force and has the goal of preventing fraud, deception, and unfair business practices online. This chapter includes forms that help you establish legal polices on your website(s), in addition to forms that can be used for common online agreements.

When working with a freelance graphic designer or others, use the *Agreement to Sell Works of Art* before the designer can schedule or begin this job to establish the terms so you can use the original work.

Before working with any freelance web designer, advise that an *Art Approvals Sheet* will be used to assess the final work before it is officially accepted. The *Creative Review Checklist* is to be used by clients to complete a thorough review of artistic proofs and/or final drafts and should be used to account for any changes and recommendations within the terms of the original contract.

The sample *Change-Order Form* may be accepted by some outsourced designers to indicate on the record that an original assignment has been revised and establishes whether or not it will continue.

Online identity theft is a type of fraud that occurs when someone (or something) pretends to act as someone else by illegally using personally identifiable information such as one's name, address, credit card number(s), or even social security number. The *Identity Theft Victim's Complaint and Affidavit* is a voluntary form for filing a report with law enforcement, and disputes with credit reporting agencies and creditors about identity theft-related problems. As a business owner conducting operations online, it's important to have this information handy to protect yourself and your business from online fraud.

One tactic many online companies employ is linking to other websites with high page ranks. Without getting into website technicalities, these links are basically quick connections to other web pages, and ideally quality web pages that optimize the rankings of the host site. With millions of websites in existence, it's important to have a legal linking agreement in place to establish what's permitted with regard to the sites being connected to.

If you've heard the statement, "content is king" as far as Internet marketing goes, you may also know that a lot of content is shared. While millions of excerpts, articles, white papers, and more are shared on the fly every day, standard copyrights still exist. Before you cut and paste an article that would mesh with your business's audience, use the sample *Permission Request Form* to make sure you have the content provider's OK in writing.

Use the *Valuing an Internet Business Form* to assess the dynamic differences including the unique legal components involved in an internet business.

With more than 50 percent of companies in the U.S. operating online in some capacity, it's important to abide by the rules that govern the web. The *Web Site Terms of Service* is a strongly worded legal disclaimer for any business that operates a website. In addition, two sample letters are included to use with the *Digital Millennium Copyright Act of 1998*, which updates U.S. copyright law for the Internet. The Act protects online service providers from civil and criminal liability for copyright infringement under some circumstances. If a copyright holder discovers that his or her content appears on the Internet without proper authorization, the holder may take advantage of the Act's "notification and takedown" provisions to have the content removed from the website where it appears. Those provisions govern the process of notification by copyright holders and the rights and responsibilities of online service providers once they receive notice of infringing material. The copyright owner would deliver to the online service provider the *Notification of Infringement Letter Under the Digital Millennium Copyright Act*. A subscriber who feels his or her material is not infringing then may deliver a *Counter-Notification Letter Under the Digital Millennium Copyright Act* to respond to the notice.

Finally ensure your website's terms of service are clear with the sample *Website Terms of Service Form*. Standard FTC-stipulated terms relating to data collection and the ways a party gathers, uses, discloses, and manages a customer's data are generally addressed in the terms of service.

74. Agreement to Sell Works of Art

Company Name: _____

Address: _____

Phone: _____ Fax: _____ E-mail: _____

Your tax ID (Social Security) number: _____

Art Commission Contract

This Agreement must be signed and returned before Artist can schedule or begin this job.

Name of Client/Company: _____

Address: _____

Phone: _____ Fax: _____ E-mail: _____

Name of Person Commissioning Art

Job number (will also be the invoice number);

ProjectTitle: _____

Project Description: _____

_____

Project Due Date(s): _____

Terms
1. Original Art: _____

_____

2. Credits and Reproduction: _____

_____

3. Cancellation: _____

_____

4. Payment Terms: _____

_____

5. Additional Expenses: _____

_____

6. Permissions and Releases: _____

_____

This agreement shall be governed by and construed in accordance with the laws of the State of _____
and shall be binding upon and inure to the benefit of the respective executors, administrators, successors
and assigns of the parties.

Date: _____

Buyer: _____

_____
[Buyer's Signature]

_____
[Buyer's Printed Name]

Artist: _____

_____
[Artist's Signature]

_____
[Artist's Printed Name]

75. Art Approval Form

Date: _____

Artist:_____

Address:_____

Phone: _____ Fax: _____ E-mail: _____

Client: _____

Address:_____

Phone: _____ Fax: _____ E-mail: _____

Job#_____

Job Description:_____

_____

_____

Please review the attached proof for errors and omissions. By signing below, you accept of full responsibility for all errors, omissions and legal and ethical compliance in this document. Artist is not liable for errors not mentioned on this approval form. Any changes from your previously approved copy will be charged extra based on the cost of time and materials.

Please check if:

Job is OK as is: _____

Job is ok with stated corrections: _____

Provide New Proof_____

Artist Comments: _____

_____

Artist Signature: _____

Client Comments: _____

_____

Client Signature: _____

76. Change Order Form

Order Change

Date: _____

Client: _____

Address: _____

Phone: _____ Fax: _____ E-mail: _____

Website: _____

Project # _____

Project Description: _____

_____

_____

Details of change(s): _____

_____

_____

_____

Schedule impact: _____

Budget impact: _____

OKAY TO PROCEED ❑ Yes   ❑ No

DO NOT PROCEED ❑ Yes   ❑ No

Please advise if there are any questions or if the information is incorrect.

Client Signature: _____

Print Name_____

Title: _____

Date: _____

77. Creative Review Checklist

Date: _____

Client: _____

Project Description: _____

_____

_____

Job # _____

Point of Contact: _____

Job Specifications

Primary Goal: _____

_____

Secondary Goal: _____

_____

Product/Service

Yes No NA

❏ ❏ ❏ Meets creative concept

❏ ❏ ❏ Accurately portrays product/service

❏ ❏ ❏ Benefits and Features are established

❏ ❏ ❏ Brand elements including logos, taglines etc. are shown

❏ ❏ ❏ Creative and brand trademarks and copyrights are shown

Creative Concept

❏ ❏ ❏ Attention getting

❏ ❏ ❏ Style compliments product/service

❏ ❏ ❏ Organization is accurately represented

❏ ❏ ❏ Key benefits/call to action are easily recognized

❏ ❏ ❏ Overall style is effective

❏ ❏ ❏ Overall style is consistent

❏ ❏ ❏ Concept is persuasive

❏ ❏ ❏ Contact information is apparent

Implementation

Yes No NA

❏ ❏ ❏   Job meets formatting specifications

❏ ❏ ❏   Job materials (originals and final) are provided

❏ ❏ ❏   Related time and resources are accounted for

Comments: _____

_____

Client Signature: _____

Print Name: _____

Date: _____

78. Identity Theft Victim's Complaint and Affidavit

Average time to complete: 10 minutes

Identity Theft Victim's Complaint and Affidavit

A voluntary form for filing a report with law enforcement, and disputes with credit reporting agencies and creditors about identity theft-related problems. Visit ftc.gov/idtheft to use a secure online version that you can print for your records.

Before completing this form:
1. Place a fraud alert on your credit reports, and review the reports for signs of fraud.
2. Close the accounts that you know, or believe, have been tampered with or opened fraudulently.

About You *(the victim)*

Now

(1) My full legal name: _____
First   Middle   Last   Suffix

(2) My date of birth: _____
mm/dd/yyyy

(3) My Social Security number: _____-_____-_____

(4) My driver's license: _____ _____
State   Number

(5) My current street address:

_____
Number & Street Name   Apartment, Suite, etc.

_____
City   State   Zip Code   Country

(6) I have lived at this address since _____
mm/yyyy

(7) My daytime phone: (____)_____

My evening phone: (____)_____

My email: _____

> Leave (3) blank until you provide this form to someone with a legitimate business need, like when you are filing your report at the police station or sending the form to a credit reporting agency to correct your credit report.

At the Time of the Fraud

(8) My full legal name was: _____
First   Middle   Last   Suffix

(9) My address was: _____
Number & Street Name   Apartment, Suite, etc.

_____
City   State   Zip Code   Country

(10) My daytime phone: (____)_____ My evening phone: (____)_____

My email: _____

> Skip (8) - (10) if your information has not changed since the fraud.

The Paperwork Reduction Act requires the FTC to display a valid control number (in this case, OMB control #3084-0047) before we can collect – or sponsor the collection of – your information, or require you to provide it.

Victim's Name _____   Phone number (___)_____   *Page 2*

About You (the victim) (Continued)

Declarations

(11) I ☐ did OR ☐ did not authorize anyone to use my name or personal information to obtain money, credit, loans, goods, or services — or for any other purpose — as described in this report.

(12) I ☐ did OR ☐ did not receive any money, goods, services, or other benefit as a result of the events described in this report.

(13) I ☐ am OR ☐ am not willing to work with law enforcement if charges are brought against the person(s) who committed the fraud.

About the Fraud

(14) I believe the following person used my information or identification documents to open new accounts, use my existing accounts, or commit other fraud.

| (14): Enter what you know about anyone you believe was involved (even if you don't have complete information). |

Name: _____
  First   Middle   Last   Suffix

Address: _____
  Number & Street Name   Apartment, Suite, etc.

_____
  City   State   Zip Code   Country

Phone Numbers: (___)_____   (___)_____

Additional information about this person: _____

_____

_____

_____

_____

_____

_____

_____

_____

_____

_____

Victim's Name _____ *Phone number (_____)_____* *Page 3*

(15) Additional information about the crime (for example, how the identity thief gained access to your information or which documents or information were used):

_____

_____

_____

_____

_____

_____

_____

_____

> (14) and (15): Attach additional sheets as needed.

Documentation

(16) I can verify my identity with these documents:

☐ A valid government-issued photo identification card (for example, my driver's license, state-issued ID card, or my passport).
If you are under 16 and don't have a photo-ID, a copy of your birth certificate or a copy of your official school record showing your enrollment and legal address is acceptable.

☐ Proof of residency during the time the disputed charges occurred, the loan was made, or the other event took place (for example, a copy of a rental/lease agreement in my name, a utility bill, or an insurance bill).

> (16): Reminder: Attach copies of your identity documents when sending this form to creditors and credit reporting agencies.

About the Information or Accounts

(17) The following personal information (like my name, address, Social Security number, or date of birth) in my credit report is inaccurate as a result of this identity theft:

(A) _____

(B) _____

(C) _____

(18) Credit inquiries from these companies appear on my credit report as a result of this identity theft:

Company Name: _____

Company Name: _____

Company Name: _____

Victim's Name _____ *Phone number* (____)_____ *Page 4*

(19)   Below are details about the different frauds committed using my personal information.

Name of Institution	Contact Person	Phone	Extension
Account Number	Routing Number	Affected Check Number(s)	

Account Type: ☐ Credit   ☐ Bank   ☐ Phone/Utilities   ☐ Loan
☐ Government Benefits   ☐ Internet or Email   ☐ Other

Select ONE:
☐ This account was opened fraudulently.
☐ This was an existing account that someone tampered with.

Date Opened or Misused (mm/yyyy)   Date Discovered (mm/yyyy)   Total Amount Obtained ($)

Name of Institution	Contact Person	Phone	Extension
Account Number	Routing Number	Affected Check Number(s)	

Account Type: ☐ Credit   ☐ Bank   ☐ Phone/Utilities   ☐ Loan
☐ Government Benefits   ☐ Internet or Email   ☐ Other

Select ONE:
☐ This account was opened fraudulently.
☐ This was an existing account that someone tampered with.

Date Opened or Misused (mm/yyyy)   Date Discovered (mm/yyyy)   Total Amount Obtained ($)

Name of Institution	Contact Person	Phone	Extension
Account Number	Routing Number	Affected Check Number(s)	

Account Type: ☐ Credit   ☐ Bank   ☐ Phone/Utilities   ☐ Loan
☐ Government Benefits   ☐ Internet or Email   ☐ Other

Select ONE:
☐ This account was opened fraudulently.
☐ This was an existing account that someone tampered with.

Date Opened or Misused (mm/yyyy)   Date Discovered (mm/yyyy)   Total Amount Obtained ($)

(19):
If there were more than three frauds, copy this page blank, and attach as many additional copies as necessary.

Enter any applicable information that you have, even if it is incomplete or an estimate.

If the thief committed two types of fraud at one company, list the company twice, giving the information about the two frauds separately.

Contact Person: Someone you dealt with, whom an investigator can call about this fraud.

Account Number: The number of the credit or debit card, bank account, loan, or other account that was misused.

Dates: Indicate when the thief began to misuse your information and when you discovered the problem.

Amount Obtained: For instance, the total amount purchased with the card or withdrawn from the account.

Victim's Name _____ *Phone number (____)_____* *Page 5*

Your Law Enforcement Report

(20) One way to get a credit reporting agency to quickly block identity theft-related information from appearing on your credit report is to submit a detailed law enforcement report ("Identity Theft Report"). You can obtain an Identity Theft Report by taking this form to your local law enforcement office, along with your supporting documentation. Ask an officer to witness your signature and complete the rest of the information in this section. It's important to get your report number, whether or not you are able to file in person or get a copy of the official law enforcement report. Attach a copy of any confirmation letter or official law enforcement report you receive when sending this form to credit reporting agencies.

> (20):
> Check "I have not..." if you have not yet filed a report with law enforcement or you have chosen not to. Check "I was unable..." if you tried to file a report but law enforcement refused to take it.
>
> *Automated report:* A law enforcement report filed through an automated system, for example, by telephone, mail, or the Internet, instead of a face-to-face interview with a law enforcement officer.

Select ONE:

☐ I have not filed a law enforcement report.
☐ I was unable to file any law enforcement report.
☐ I filed an automated report with the law enforcement agency listed below.
☐ I filed my report in person with the law enforcement officer and agency listed below.

_____
Law Enforcement Department   State

_____   _____
Report Number   Filing Date (mm/dd/yyyy)

_____
Officer's Name (please print)   Officer's Signature

_____   _____
Badge Number   Phone Number

Did the victim receive a copy of the report from the law enforcement officer?   ☐ Yes   OR   ☐ No

Victim's FTC complaint number (if available): _____

Victim's Name _____ Phone number (____)_____ *Page 6*

Signature

As applicable, sign and date *IN THE PRESENCE OF* a law enforcement officer, a notary, or a witness.

(21) I certify that, to the best of my knowledge and belief, all of the information on and attached to this complaint is true, correct, and complete and made in good faith. I understand that this complaint or the information it contains may be made available to federal, state, and/or local law enforcement agencies for such action within their jurisdiction as they deem appropriate. I understand that knowingly making any false or fraudulent statement or representation to the government may violate federal, state, or local criminal statutes, and may result in a fine, imprisonment, or both.

_____   _____
Signature   Date Signed (mm/dd/yyyy)

Your Affidavit

(22) If you do not choose to file a report with law enforcement, you may use this form as an Identity Theft Affidavit to prove to each of the companies where the thief misused your information that you are not responsible for the fraud. While many companies accept this affidavit, others require that you submit different forms. Check with each company to see if it accepts this form. You should also check to see if it requires notarization. If so, sign in the presence of a notary. If it does not, please have one witness (non-relative) sign that you completed and signed this Affidavit.

_____
(Notary)

Witness:

_____   _____
(signature)   (printed name)

_____   _____
(date)   (telephone number)

79. Sample Linking Agreement

XYZ Company, Inc.
WEBSITE LINKING AGREEMENT

THIS WEBSITE LINKING AGREEMENT (the "Agreement") made as of this ___ day of _____, 20___ (the "Effective Date"), by and among XYZ Company, Inc. ("Company") and _____, ("Owner"), under the following circumstances:

RECITALS

A. COMPANY maintains a website with the current URL of www.Company.com (this website or any successor website referred to as the "COMPANY Website") on which COMPANY offers information relating to COMPANY's health care benefits.

B. Owner maintains a website with the current URL(s) of

www._____

www._____

www._____

www._____

C. Owner desires that a hyperlink be provided to COMPANY's website and that Owner shall prominently display the hyperlink to the website.

NOW, THEREFORE, in consideration of the premises and the mutual covenants and obligations hereinafter set forth, and other good and valuable consideration, the legal sufficiency of which is hereby acknowledged, the parties hereto agree as follows:

1. Linking Obligations.
   1.1 Owner's Linking Obligations. Owner shall prominently display a hyperlink [on each main introductory page] OR [at a location to be determined in the sole discretion of Owner] of the Owner Website to the COMPANY Website with information provided by COMPANY.

D. Standards and Notifications
   ___ Source Site shall maintain its site in accordance with industry standards and upon notice from Destination Site shall promptly remove the Link if required. Source Site shall promptly notify Destination Site of any change to the Link or changes to the Source Site affecting the Link.

By: _____   By: _____

Date: _____   Date: _____

Source Site Title: _____   Destination Site Title: _____

Source Site Mailing Address: _____   Destination Site Mailing Address: _____

_____   _____

e-mail: _____   e-mail: _____

80. Permission Request Form (online images and text)

Requestor Information

Name: _____

Title: _____

Company: _____

Address: _____

Phone: _____ Fax: _____ E-mail: _____

Proposed Use

Provide a detailed description of the image, trademark, text or other content you wish to use. Describe how you wish to use the creative material. Provide attachments of all applicable creative material (images for example.)

Indicate your intended use: _____

_____

❏ Commercial

❏ Non-Commercial

Describe where the creative content will be used: _____

_____

Website: _____

Describe audience that the creative content is intended for: _____

Enter the start and end date that you wish to use the creative content: _____

81. Valuing an Internet Business

These questions are designed to remind you of some the dynamic differences involved in an internet business.

1. Does a new product, with a prototype but not yet in the marketplace, have a value that can be calculated and that could raise the selling price of a business?

2. What are some of the reasons why a company might acquire an internet business even though it has not yet shown a profit?

3. What are the two things most small-business buyers need after acquiring a company?

4. How many years should a buyer pay on a purchase money promissory note for the balance of a purchase price?

5. What is the internet?

6. What is the difference between a website and a conventional storefront?

7. What is the value of a domain name?

8. In what ways can the value of website visits be calculated?

82. Notification of Infringement Letter Under the Digital Millennium Copyright Act

Date: _____

To:

_____

_____

_____

_____

To Whom It May Concern:

I am writing to you to avail myself of my rights under the Digital Millennium Copyright Act (DMCA). This letter is a Notice of Infringement as authorized in § 512(c) of the U.S. Copyright Law. I wish to report an instance or what I feel in good faith is an instance of copyright infringement. The infringing material appears on a service for which you are the designated agent.

You are registered with the U.S. Copyright Office as the Designated Service Provider Agent to receive notifications of alleged Copyright infringement with respect to users of the Service for which you are the Designated Agent.

1. The material that I contend belongs to me and that appears illegally on the service is the following: [describe the infringing material: e.g., "a song entitled "Legal Battle Blues" and a song entitled "A Little Litigation," both performed by Lawyers in Love].

2. The material appears at the Web site address: [provide the full Web site address and a link to the page on which the material appears].

3. My contact information is as follows: [provide your name, address, telephone number, and e-mail address].

4. I have a good-faith belief that the use of the material that appears on the service is not authorized by the copyright owner, by its agent, or by operation of law.

5. The information in this notice is accurate and I am either the copyright owner or authorized to act on behalf of the copyright owner.

I declare under the perjury laws of the United States of America that this notification is true and correct.

_____

Signature

_____

Printed Name

83. Counter-Notification Letter Under the Digital Millennium Copyright Act

Date: _____

To:

_____

_____

_____

_____

To Whom It May Concern:

I am writing to you to avail myself of my rights under the Digital Millennium Copyright Act (DMCA). You recently provided me with a copy of Notice of Infringement from [Name the party who submitted the Notice of Infringement]. This letter is a Counter-Notification as authorized in § 512(g) of the U.S. Copyright Law. I have a good-faith belief that the material that was removed or disabled as a result of the Notice of Infringement as a result of mistake or misidentification of the material. I therefore request that the material be replaced and/or no longer disabled.

You are registered with the U.S. Copyright Office as the Designated Service Provider Agent to receive notifications of alleged copyright infringement with respect to users of the Service for which you are the Designated Agent.

1. The material in question formerly appeared at the Web site address: [provide the full Web site address and a link to the page on which the material appears].

2. My contact information is as follows: [provide your name, address, telephone number, and e-mail address].

3. I consent to the jurisdiction of the Federal District Court for the judicial district in which my address is located (solely for the purposes of the resolution of this dispute) and I agree to accept service of process from the person who provided the Notice of Infringement.

4. I have a good-faith belief that the material removed or disabled following the Notice of Infringement was removed or disabled because of mistake or misidentification of the material. I therefore request that the material be replaced and/or no longer disabled.

I declare under the perjury laws of the United States of America that this notification is true and correct.

_____
Signature

_____
Printed Name

84. Mutual Nondisclosure Agreement

This agreement is made effective on _____ (date) by and between _____ (first party) and _____ (second party) (collectively, the "Parties"), to ensure the protection and preservation of the confidential and/or proprietary nature of information disclosed or made available or to be disclosed or made available to each other. For the purposes of this agreement, each Party shall be deemed to include any subsidiaries, internal divisions, agents, and employees. Any signing party shall refer to and bind the individual and the entity that he or she represents.

Whereas the Parties desire to ensure the confidential status of the information that may be disclosed to each other.

Now, therefore, in reliance upon and in consideration of the following undertakings, the Parties agree as follows:

1. Subject to limitations set forth in paragraph 2, all information disclosed to the other party shall be deemed to be "Proprietary Information." In particular, Proprietary Information shall be deemed to include any information, marketing technique, publicity technique, public relations technique, process, technique, algorithm, program, design, drawing, mask work, formula, test data research project, work in progress, future development, engineering, manufacturing, marketing, servicing, financing or personal matter relating to the disclosing party, its present or future products, sales, suppliers, clients, customers, employees, investors or business, whether in oral, written, graphic or electronic form.'

2. The term "Proprietary Information" shall not be deemed to include information that (i) is now, or here-after becomes, through no act or failure to act on the part of the receiving party, generally known or available information, (ii) is known by the receiving party at the time of receiving such information as evidenced by its records, (iii) is hereafter furnished to the receiving party by a third party, as a matter of right and without restriction on disclosure, (iv) is independently developed by the receiving party without reference to the information disclosed hereunder, or (v) is the subject of a written permission to disclose provided by the disclosing party.

    Not withstanding any other provision of this Agreement, disclosure of Proprietary Information shall not be precluded if such disclosure:

    a. is in response to a valid order of a court or other governmental body of the United States or any political subdivision thereof,

    b. is otherwise required by law, or,

    c. is otherwise necessary to establish rights or enforce obligations under this agreement, but only to the extent that any such disclosure is necessary.

In the event that the receiving party is requested in any proceedings before a court or any other governmental body to disclose Proprietary Information, it shall give the disclosing party prompt notice of such request so that the disclosing party may seek an appropriate protective order. If, in the absence of a protective order, the receiving party is nonetheless compelled to disclose Proprietary Information, the receiving party may disclose such information without liability hereunder, provided, however, that such party gives the disclosing party advance written notice of the information to be disclosed and, upon the request and at the expense of the disclosing party, uses its best efforts to obtain assurances that confidential treatment will be accorded to such information.

3. Each party shall maintain in trust and confidence and not disclose to any third party or use for any unauthorized purpose any Proprietary Information received from the other party. Each party may use such Proprietary Information in the extent required to accomplish the purpose of the discussions with respect to the subject. Proprietary Information shall not be used for any purpose or in any manner that would constitute a violation on law regulations, including without limitation the export control laws of the United States of America. No other rights or licenses to trademarks, inventions, copyrights or patents are implied or granted under this Agreement.

4. Proprietary Information supplied shall not be reproduced in any form except as required to accomplish the intent of this Agreement.

5. The responsibilities of the Parties are limited to using their efforts to protect the Proprietary Information received with the same degree of care used to protect their own Proprietary Information from unauthorized use or disclosure. Both Parties shall advise their employees or agents who might have access to such Proprietary Information of the confidential nature thereof and that by receiving such information they are agreeing to be bound by this Agreement. No Proprietary Information shall be disclosed to any officer, employee, or agent of either party who does not have a need for such information for the purpose of the discussions with respect to the subject.

6. All Proprietary Information (including all copies thereof) shall remain the property of the disclosing party and shall be returned to the disclosing party after the receiving party's need for it has expired, or upon request of the disclosing party, and in any event, upon completion or termination of this Agreement. The receiving party further agrees to destroy all notes and copies thereof made by its officers and employees containing or based on any Proprietary Information and to cause all agents and representatives to whom or to which Proprietary Information has been disclosed to destroy all notes and copies in their possession that contain Proprietary Information.

7. This Agreement shall survive any termination of the discussion with respect to the subject and shall continue in full force and effect until such time as Parties mutually agree to terminate it.

8. This Agreement shall be governed by the laws of the United States of America and as those laws that are applied to contracts entered into and to be performed in all states. Should any revision of this Agreement be determined to be void, invalid or otherwise unenforceable by any court or tribunal of competent jurisdiction, such determination shall not affect the remaining provisions of this Agreement, which shall remain in full force and effect.

9. This Agreement contains final, complete, and exclusive agreement of the Parties relative to the subject matter hereof and supersedes any prior agreement of the Parties, whether oral or written. This Agreement may not be changed, modified, amended or supplemented except by a written instrument signed by both Parties.

10. Each party hereby acknowledges and agrees that, in the event of any breach of this Agreement by the other party, including, without limitations, the actual or threatened disclosure of a disclosing party's

Proprietary Information without the prior express written consent of the disclosing party, the disclosing party will suffer an irreparable injury such that no remedy at law will afford it adequate protection against or appropriate compensation for such injury. Accordingly, each party hereby agrees that the other party shall be entitled to specific performance of a receiving party's obligations under this Agreement as well as further injunctive relief as may be granted by a court of competent jurisdiction.

11. The term of this agreement is for two (2) years, commencing on the "Effective Date."

AGREED TO:

Signature: _____

Printed Name: _____

Date: _____

AGREED TO:

Signature: _____

Printed Name: _____

Date: _____

85. Website Terms of Service

Terms of Service

Some or all of the information on this website(s) is provided by _____ ("Company") on one or more Company websites. The Company websites include the following websites: _____. Company provides this service to you, subject to the following Terms of Service ("TOS"), which may be updated by us anytime without notice to you. When using particular Company services, you shall be subject to any posted guidelines or rules applicable to such services that may be posted from time to time. All such guidelines or rules are hereby incorporated by reference into the TOS. For specific services, Company also may put forth specific Terms of Service that differ from this TOS. It is your responsibility to periodically review the TOS. If you do not agree with or understand the TOS, do not use a Company site.

The TOS apply to both "Affiliates" (persons or entities that receive the Service, as defined below, for redistribution and/or republication on a non-Company website) and "Users" (all persons, including Affiliates, that make any use whatsoever of any Service, as defined below). Company currently provides Affiliates and Users with several resources, including news feeds, message boards, financial calculators, articles, and stock quotes (the "Service"). Unless expressly stated otherwise, new resources added to the current Service shall be subject to the TOS. You understand and agree that the Service is provided "as is" and that Company assumes no responsibility for the timeliness, deletion, misdelivery, or failure to store any user communications or personalization settings.

In consideration of your use of the Service, you agree to (a) provide true, accurate, current, and complete information about yourself as prompted by the Service's registration form (such information being the "Registration Data") and (b) maintain and promptly update the Registration Data to keep it truthful, accurate, current, and complete. If you provide any information that is untrue, inaccurate, not current, or incomplete, or Company has reasonable grounds to suspect that such information is untrue, inaccurate, not current, or incomplete, Company has the right to suspend or terminate your account and refuse any and all current or future use of the Service (or any portion thereof). You will receive a password and account designation upon completing the registration process for the use of some Services. You are responsible for maintaining the confidentiality of the password and account and are fully responsible for all activities that occur under your password or account. You agree to (a) immediately notify Company of any unauthorized use of your password or account or any other breach of security and (b) ensure that you exit from your account at the end of each session. Company cannot and will not be liable for any loss or damage arising from your failure to comply with this Paragraph.

You understand that all information, data, text, software, music, sound, photographs, graphics, video, messages, or other materials ("Content"), whether publicly posted or privately transmitted, are the sole responsibility of the person from which such Content originated. This means that you, and not Company, are entirely responsible for all Content that you upload, post, e-mail, or otherwise transmit via the Service. Company does not control the Content posted via the Service and thus does not guarantee its accuracy, integrity, or quality. By using the Service, you may be exposed to Content that is offensive, indecent, or objectionable. Under no circumstances will Company be liable in any way for any Content, including, but not limited to, for any errors or omissions in any Content, or for any loss or damage of any kind incurred as a result of the use of any Content posted, e-mailed, or otherwise transmitted via the Service.

You agree to not use the Service to:

i. upload, post, e-mail, or otherwise transmit any Content that is unlawful, harmful, threatening, abusive, harassing, defamatory, vulgar, obscene, libelous, invasive of another's privacy, hateful, or racially, ethnically, or otherwise objectionable;

ii. impersonate any person or entity or falsely state or otherwise misrepresent your affiliation with a person or entity;

iii. forge headers or otherwise manipulate identifiers in order to disguise the origin of any Content transmitted through the Service;

iv. upload, post, e-mail, or otherwise transmit any Content that you do not have a right to transmit under any law or under contractual or fiduciary relationships;

v. upload, post, e-mail, or otherwise transmit any Content that infringes any patent, trademark, trade secret, copyright, or other proprietary rights ("Rights") of any party;

vi. upload, post, e-mail, or otherwise transmit any unsolicited or unauthorized advertising, promotional materials, "junk mail," "spam," "chain letters," "pyramid schemes," or any other form of solicitation, except in areas designated for such purpose;

vii. upload, post, e-mail, or otherwise transmit any material that contains software viruses or any other computer code, files, or programs designed to interrupt, destroy, or limit the functionality of any computer software or hardware or telecommunications equipment;

viii. interfere with or disrupt the Service or servers or networks connected to the Service, or disobey any requirements, procedures, policies, or regulations of networks connected to the Service;

ix. intentionally or unintentionally violate any applicable local, state, national, or international law, including, but not limited to, regulations promulgated by the U.S. Securities and Exchange Commission, any rules of any national or other securities exchange, including, without limitation, the New York Stock Exchange, the American Stock Exchange, or the NASDAQ, and any regulations having the force of law; or

x. "stalk" or otherwise harass another or collect or store personal data about other Users.

You acknowledge that Company does not pre-screen Content, but that Company and its designees shall have the right (but not the obligation) in their sole discretion to refuse or move any Content that is available via the Service. Without limiting the foregoing, Company and its designees shall have the right to remove any Content that violates the TOS or is otherwise objectionable. You agree that you must evaluate, and bear all risks associated with, the use of any Content, including any reliance on the accuracy, completeness, or usefulness of such Content. In this regard, you acknowledge that you may not rely on any Content created by Company or submitted to Company, including without limitation information in Company Message Boards and in all other parts of the Service.

You acknowledge and agree that Company may preserve Content and may also disclose Content if required to do so by law or in the good faith belief that such preservation or disclosure is reasonably necessary to (a) comply with legal process; (b) enforce the TOS; (c) respond to claims that any Content violates the rights of third parties; or (d) protect the rights, property, or personal safety of Company, its Users, and the public.

You understand that the technical processing and transmission of the Service, including your Content, may involve (a) transmissions over various networks and (b) changes to conform and adapt to technical requirements of connecting networks or devices.

Recognizing the global nature of the Internet, you agree to comply with all local rules regarding online conduct and acceptable Content. Specifically, you agree to comply with all applicable laws regarding the transmission of technical data exported from the United States or the country in which you reside.

With respect to all Content you elect to post to other publicly accessible areas of the Service, you grant Company the royalty-free, perpetual, irrevocable, non-exclusive, and fully sublicensable right and license to use, reproduce, modify, adapt, publish, translate, create derivative works from, distribute, perform, and display such Content (in whole or part) worldwide and/or to incorporate it in other works in any form, media, or technology now known or later developed.

You agree to indemnify and hold Company and its subsidiaries, Affiliates, officers, agents, co-branders or other partners, and employees harmless from any claim or demand, including reasonable attorneys' fees, made by any third party due to or arising out of Content you submit, post to, or transmit through the Service, your use of the Service, your connection to the Service, your violation of the TOS, or your violation of any rights of another.

You agree not to reproduce, duplicate, copy, sell, resell, or exploit for any commercial purposes any portion of the Service, use of the Service, or access to the Service, except in accordance with the TOS.

You acknowledge that Company may establish general practices and limits concerning use of the Service, including without limitation the maximum number of days Content will be retained by the Service, the maximum number of messages that may be sent from or received by an account on the Service, the maximum size of any message that may be sent from or received by an account on the Service, the maximum disk space that will be allotted on Company's servers on your behalf, and the maximum number of times and the maximum duration for which you may access the Service in a given period of time. You agree that Company has no responsibility or liability for the deletion or failure to store any messages and other communications or other Content maintained or transmitted by the Service. You acknowledge that Company reserves the right to log off accounts that are inactive for an extended period of time. You further acknowledge that Company reserves the right to change these general practices and limits at any time, in its sole discretion, with or without notice.

Company reserves the right at any time and from time to time to modify or discontinue, temporarily or permanently, the Service (or any part thereof), with or without notice. You agree that Company shall not be liable to you or to any third party for any modification, suspension, or discontinuance of the Service.

You agree that Company, in its sole discretion, may terminate your password, account (or any part thereof), or use of the Service and remove and discard any Content within the Service for any reason. Company may also, in its sole discretion and at any time, discontinue providing the Service, or any part thereof, or may change the price for the Service, all with or without notice. You agree that any termination of your access to the Service under any provision of this TOS may be affected without prior notice, and acknowledge and agree that Company may immediately deactivate or delete your account and all related information and files in your account and/or bar any further access to such files or the Service. Further, you agree that Company shall not be liable to you or any third party for any termination of your access to the Service.

Your correspondence or business dealings with, or participation in promotions of, advertisers found on or through the Service, including payment and delivery of related goods or services, and any other terms, conditions, warranties, or representations associated with such dealings, are solely between you and such advertiser. You agree that Company shall not be responsible or liable for any loss or damage of any sort incurred as the result of any such dealings or as the result of the presence of such advertisers on the Service.

The Service or third parties may provide links to other World Wide Web sites or resources. Because Company has no control over such sites and resources, you acknowledge and agree that Company is not responsible for the availability of such external sites or resources and does not endorse and is not responsible or liable for any Content, advertising, products, or other materials on or available from such sites or resources. You further acknowledge and agree that Company shall not be responsible or liable, directly or indirectly, for any damage or loss caused or alleged to be caused by or in connection with use of or reliance on any such Content, goods, or services available on or through any such site or resource.

You acknowledge and agree that the Service and any necessary software used in connection with the Service (the "Software") contain proprietary and confidential information that is protected by applicable intellectual property and other laws. You further acknowledge and agree that Content contained in sponsor advertisements or information presented to you through the Service or advertisers is protected by copyrights, trademarks, service marks, patents, or other proprietary rights and laws. Except as expressly authorized by Company or advertisers, you agree not to modify, rent, lease, loan, sell, distribute, or create derivative works based on the Service or the Software, in whole or in part.

Company grants you a personal, non-transferable, and non-exclusive right and license to use the object code of its Software on a single computer, provided that you do not (and do not allow any third party to) copy, modify, create a derivative work of, reverse engineer, reverse assemble, or otherwise attempt to discover any source code, sell, assign, sublicense, grant a security interest in, or otherwise transfer any right in the Software. You agree not to modify the Software in any manner or form or to use modified versions of the Software, including (without limitation) for the purpose of obtaining unauthorized access to the Service. You agree not to access the Service by any means other than through the interface that is provided by Company for use in accessing the Service.

YOU EXPRESSLY UNDERSTAND AND AGREE THAT:

a. YOUR USE OF THE SERVICE IS AT YOUR SOLE RISK. THE SERVICE IS PROVIDED ON AN "AS IS" AND "AS AVAILABLE" BASIS. COMPANY EXPRESSLY DISCLAIMS ALL WARRANTIES OF ANY KIND, WHETHER EXPRESS OR IMPLIED, INCLUDING, BUT NOT LIMITED TO, THE IMPLIED WARRANTIES OF MERCHANTABILITY, FITNESS FOR A PARTICULAR PURPOSE, AND NON-INFRINGEMENT.

b. COMPANY MAKES NO WARRANTY THAT (i) THE SERVICE WILL MEET YOUR REQUIREMENTS, (ii) THE SERVICE WILL BE UNINTERRUPTED, TIMELY, SECURE, OR ERROR-FREE, (iii) THE RESULTS THAT MAY BE OBTAINED FROM THE USE OF THE SERVICE WILL BE ACCURATE OR RELIABLE, (iv) THE QUALITY OF

ANY PRODUCTS, SERVICES, INFORMATION, OR OTHER MATERIAL PURCHASED OR OBTAINED BY YOU THROUGH THE SERVICE WILL MEET YOUR EXPECTATIONS, AND (V) ANY ERRORS IN THE SOFTWARE WILL BE CORRECTED.

c. ANY MATERIAL DOWNLOADED OR OTHERWISE OBTAINED THROUGH THE USE OF THE SERVICE IS DONE AT YOUR OWN DISCRETION AND RISK AND THAT YOU WILL BE SOLELY RESPONSIBLE FOR ANY DAMAGE TO YOUR COMPUTER SYSTEM OR LOSS OF DATA THAT RESULTS FROM THE DOWNLOAD OF ANY SUCH MATERIAL.

d. NO ADVICE OR INFORMATION, WHETHER ORAL OR WRITTEN, OBTAINED BY YOU FROM COMPANY OR THROUGH OR FROM THE SERVICE, SHALL CREATE ANY WARRANTY NOT EXPRESSLY STATED IN THE TOS.

YOU EXPRESSLY UNDERSTAND AND AGREE THAT COMPANY SHALL NOT BE LIABLE FOR ANY DIRECT, INDIRECT, INCIDENTAL, SPECIAL, CONSEQUENTIAL, OR EXEMPLARY DAMAGES, INCLUDING BUT NOT LIMITED TO DAMAGES FOR LOSS OF PROFITS, GOODWILL, USE, DATA, OR OTHER INTANGIBLE LOSSES (EVEN IF COMPANY HAS BEEN ADVISED OF THE POSSIBILITY OF SUCH DAMAGES) RESULTING FROM (i) THE USE OR THE INABILITY TO USE THE SERVICE; (ii) THE COST OF PROCUREMENT OF SUBSTITUTE GOODS AND SERVICES RESULTING FROM ANY GOODS, DATA, INFORMATION, OR SERVICES PURCHASED OR OBTAINED OR MESSAGES RECEIVED OR TRANSACTIONS ENTERED INTO THROUGH OR FROM THE SERVICE; (iii) UNAUTHORIZED ACCESS TO OR ALTERATION OF YOUR TRANSMISSIONS OR DATA; (iv) STATEMENTS OR CONDUCT OF ANY THIRD PARTY ON THE SERVICE; OR (v) ANY OTHER MATTER RELATING TO THE SERVICE.

SOME JURISDICTIONS DO NOT ALLOW THE EXCLUSION OF CERTAIN WARRANTIES OR THE LIMITATION OR EXCLUSION OF LIABILITY FOR INCIDENTAL OR CONSEQUENTIAL DAMAGES. ACCORDINGLY, SOME OF THE ABOVE LIMITATIONS OF LIABILITY MAY NOT APPLY TO YOU.

THE SERVICE IS PROVIDED FOR INFORMATIONAL PURPOSES ONLY AND NO CONTENT INCLUDED IN THE SERVICE IS INTENDED FOR TRADING OR INVESTING PURPOSES. COMPANY SHALL NOT BE RESPONSIBLE OR LIABLE FOR THE ACCURACY, USEFULNESS, OR AVAILABILITY OF ANY INFORMATION TRANSMITTED VIA THE SERVICE AND SHALL NOT BE RESPONSIBLE OR LIABLE FOR ANY TRADING OR INVESTMENT DECISIONS MADE BASED ON SUCH INFORMATION.

Company respects the intellectual property of others and we ask our Users to do the same. If you believe that your work has been copied in a way that constitutes copyright infringement, please contact Company:

_____

_____

_____

The TOS constitute the entire agreement between you and Company and govern your use of the Service, superseding any prior agreements between you and Company. You also may be subject to additional terms and conditions that may apply when you use affiliate services, third-party content, or third-party software. The TOS and the relationship between you and Company shall be governed by the laws of the State of California without regard to its conflict of law provisions. You and Company agree to submit to the personal and exclusive jurisdiction of the courts located within the county of _____, _____. The failure of Company to exercise or enforce any right or provision of the TOS shall not constitute a waiver of such right or provision. If any provision of the TOS is found by a court of competent jurisdiction to be invalid, the parties nevertheless agree that the court should endeavor to give effect to the parties' intentions as reflected in the provision and that the other provisions of the TOS remain in full force and effect. You agree that, regardless of any statute or law to the contrary, any claim or cause of action arising out of or related to use of the Service or the TOS must be filed within one (1) year after such claim or cause of action arose or be forever barred.

CHAPTER 10

Create Legal Contracts and Agreements

A S A BUSINESS OWNER, YOU WILL RECEIVE and administer all kinds of contracts and agreements, the most common legal transactions you will be involved in when running a business. Properly executed contracts provide grounds to legally enforce and dispute business matters.

The surest way to maintain clear understandings with your customers and vendors is to document your arrangements in written agreements. We have included here several useful and universal contracts and agreements.

Use the *Bill of Sale* to record the terms of a simple sale of goods or property. The *Unsecured Promissory Note* is a legal document that documents a promise to pay money at a future date. Use this document to memorialize simple business or personal loans. The *Secured Promissory Note and Security Agreement* is a legal document that memorializes a loan, but it goes a step farther: it grants to the lender the right to repossess property in the event the loan is not repaid. The *Secured*

Promissory Note and Security Agreement gives the lender greater rights and power than the *Unsecured Promissory Note*.

The *Consulting Services Agreement* is a general and universal agreement suitable for nearly all types of consulting services firms. Customize the agreement to cover the particular services that you offer.

The *Multimedia Development Contract* is a contract suitable for use by Web developers, programmers, and print and graphic designers. Keep in mind, however, that you'll need to customize the contract to cover the particular services you offer.

The *Mutual Compromise Agreement and Mutual Release* is an agreement to finally and forever settle a dispute between two parties. Use this agreement to finalize the resolution of conflicts and lawsuits between you and third parties.

Use the *Checklist for a Buyer's Purchase Order* for quality assurance, knowing that the final order is correct in its wording as to all terms and conditions. The *Checklist for Modi-*

fying or Extending an Existing Contracts ensures the changes you make to a signed agreement are compliant and correctly communicate all amendments, redefined terms, and other changes.

If your company is the seller, refer to the *Checklist for Purchase Orders Where Your Company Is the Seller* to confirm you've clearly established the terms and conditions of the sale, including pricing, loss assessment, shipping, and delivery dates.

Use the *Checklist for Sales Agreements Where Your Company Is the Seller* to ensure the correct legal name of parties, set effective dates of the contract, the terms, and more.

Refer to the sample *Terms of Purchase* to help you establish the contractual obligations of the buyer. In addition, the seller can use the sample *Terms of Sale* form to establish the delivery and payment terms agreed on between your company and the buyer.

If your contract will require legal counsel, refer to the *Examples of Legal "Boilerplate"* for assigning a lawyer, lawyer fees, and venue, and defining the overall legal contract.

Use the *Lawyer Engagement Letter* as a sample letter to request legal representation from your chosen firm. Once your company is set to work with outside counsel, refer to the *Terms and Conditions for Outside Legal Counsel* to establish the framework of the relationship.

Finally, if your company requires outside service that may involve diagnostic testing and/or the use of specialized equipment, use the sample *Service Evaluation and Repair Agreement* to document the description of work, costs, liability, and warranties.

86. Bill of Sale

BILL OF SALE

This Bill of Sale is made on this _____ day of 20____ between _____ ("Seller") and _____ ("Buyer").

Seller, in exchange for consideration of $_____, the receipt of which funds is acknowledged, hereby do grant, sell, transfer, and deliver to Buyer the following goods:
_____.

Buyer shall have full rights and title to the goods described above.

Seller is the lawful owner of the goods and the goods are free from all encumbrances. Seller has good right to sell the goods and will warrant and defend the right against the lawful claims and demands of all persons.

_____
Signature of Seller

_____
Signature of Buyer

87. Unsecured Promissory Note

UNSECURED PROMISSORY NOTE

Amount: $_____

Date: _____

For value received, _____ ("Borrower") hereby covenants and promises to pay to _____ ("Lender") _____ Dollars ($_____.00) in lawful money of the United States of America, together with interest thereon computed from the date hereof at the rate of ten percent (10%) per annum, on an actual day/365 day basis. All interest, principal, and other costs hereunder shall be due and payable to the holder ("Holder") of this Promissory Note (this "Note") on or before _____ (the "Due Date").

Payments of principal and interest will be made in legal tender of the United States of America. Borrower shall have the right to prepay without penalty all or any part of the unpaid balance of this Note at any time. Borrower shall not be entitled to re-borrow any prepaid amounts of the principal, interest, or other costs or charges. All payments made pursuant to this Note will be first applied to accrued and unpaid interest, if any, then to other proper charges under this Note, and the balance, if any, to principal.

This Note shall be paid as follows: monthly payments of $_____ shall be made upon this Note on the first day of each month, commencing with the date of _____, and shall continue until _____ (the "Repayment Date"), at which time all sums due hereunder shall be paid.

Notwithstanding anything in this Note to the contrary, the entire unpaid principal amount of this Note, together with all accrued but unpaid interest thereon and other unpaid charges hereunder, will become immediately all due and payable without further notice at the option of the Holder if Borrower fails to timely make any payment hereunder when such payment becomes first due and such failure continues for a period of ten days after written notice from Holder to Borrower.

If any amount payable to Holder under this Note is not received by Holder on or before the Due Date, then such amount (the "Delinquent Amount") will bear interest from and after the Due Date until paid at an annual rate of interest equal to the greater of (i) fifteen percent (15%) or (ii) the maximum rate then permitted by law (the "Default Rate"). If the maximum rate then permitted by law is lower than 15%, the maximum legal rate shall be the Default Rate.

All rights, remedies, undertakings, obligations, options, covenants, conditions, and agreements contained in this Note are cumulative and no one of them will be exclusive of any other. Any notice to any party concerning this Note will be delivered as set forth in the Financing Agreement.

Borrower for itself and its legal representatives, successors, and assigns expressly waives presentment, protest, demand, notice of dishonor, notice of nonpayment, notice of maturity, notice of protest, presentment for the purpose of accelerating maturity, and diligence in collection, and consents that Holder may extend the time for payment or otherwise modify the terms of payment or any part or the whole of the debt evidenced hereby.

The prevailing party in any action, litigation, or proceeding, including any appeal or the collection of any judgment concerning this Note, will be awarded, in addition to any damages, injunctions, or other relief, and without regard to whether or not such matter be prosecuted to final judgment, such party's costs and expenses, including reasonable attorneys' fees, and Lender shall be entitled to recover all of its attorneys' fees and costs should Lender place this Note in the hands of an attorney for collection.

_____ ("Borrower")

Signature _____

Date _____

88. Secured Promissory Note and Security Agreement

SECURED PROMISSORY NOTE

Amount: $_____

Date: _____

For value received, _____ ("Borrower") hereby covenants and promises to pay to _____ ("Lender")

_____ Dollars ($_____) in lawful money of the United States of America, together with interest thereon computed from the date hereof at the rate of ten percent (10%) per annum, on an actual day/365 day basis. All interest, principal, and other costs hereunder shall be due and payable to the holder ("Holder") of this Promissory Note (this "Note") on or before _____ (the "Due Date").

Payments of principal and interest will be made in legal tender of the United States of America. Borrower shall have the right to prepay without penalty all or any part of the unpaid balance of this Note at any time. Borrower shall not be entitled to re-borrow any prepaid amounts of the principal, interest, or other costs or charges. All payments made pursuant to this Note will be first applied to accrued and unpaid interest, if any, then to other proper charges under this Note, and the balance, if any, to principal.

This Note is secured by a security interest in Borrower's assets, as more particularly described in the Security Agreement attached to this Note.

This Note shall be paid as follows: monthly payments of $_____ shall be made upon this Note on the first day of each month, commencing with the date of _____, and shall continue until _____ (the "Repayment Date"), at which time all sums due hereunder shall be paid.

Notwithstanding anything in this Note to the contrary, the entire unpaid principal amount of this Note, together with all accrued but unpaid interest thereon and other unpaid charges hereunder, will become immediately all due and payable without further notice at the option of the Holder if Borrower fails to timely make any payment hereunder when such payment becomes first due and such failure continues for a period of ten days after written notice from Holder to Borrower.

If any amount payable to Holder under this Note is not received by Holder on or before the Due Date, then such amount (the "Delinquent Amount") will bear interest from and after the Due Date until paid at an annual rate of interest equal to the greater of (i) fifteen percent (15%) or (ii) the maximum rate then permitted by law (the "Default Rate"). If the maximum rate then permitted by law is lower than 15%, the maximum legal rate shall be the Default Rate.

All rights, remedies, undertakings, obligations, options, covenants, conditions, and agreements contained in this Note are cumulative and no one of them will be exclusive of any other. Any notice to any party concerning this Note will be delivered as set forth in the Financing Agreement.

Borrower for itself and its legal representatives, successors, and assigns expressly waives presentment, protest, demand, notice of dishonor, notice of nonpayment, notice of maturity, notice of protest, presentment for the purpose of accelerating maturity, and diligence in collection and consents that Holder may extend the time for payment or otherwise modify the terms of payment or any part or the whole of the debt evidenced hereby.

The prevailing party in any action, litigation, or proceeding, including any appeal or the collection of any judgment concerning this Note, will be awarded, in addition to any damages, injunctions, or other relief, and without regard to whether or not such matter be prosecuted to final judgment, such party's costs and expenses, including reasonable attorneys' fees, and Lender shall be entitled to recover all of its attorneys' fees and costs should Lender place this Note in the hands of an attorney for collection.

_____ ("Borrower")

Signature _____

Date _____

This Security Agreement is made on this ____ day of _____ between _____ ("Borrower") and _____ ("Lender").

SECURITY AGREEMENT ACCOMPANYING SECURED PROMISSORY NOTE

1. Security Interest. Borrower grants to Lender a "Security Interest" in the following property (the "Collateral"):

_____

_____

_____

_____

_____

The Security Interest shall secure the payment and performance of Borrower's promissory note of given date herewith in the principal amount of _____ Dollars (\$_____) and the payment and performance of all other liabilities and obligations of Borrower to Lender of every kind and description, direct or indirect, absolute or contingent, due or to become due, now existing or hereafter arising.

2. Covenants. Borrower hereby warrants and covenants:

    a. The parties intend that the collateral is and will at all times remain personal property despite the fact and irrespective of the manner in which it is attached to realty.

    b. The Borrower will not sell, dispose, or otherwise transfer the collateral or any interest therein without the prior written consent of Lender, and the Borrower shall keep the collateral free from unpaid charges (including rent), taxes, and liens.

    c. The Borrower shall execute alone or with Lender any Financing Statement or other document or procure any document, and pay the cost of filing the same in all public offices wherever filing is deemed by Lender to be necessary.

    d. Borrower shall maintain insurance at all times with respect to all collateral against risks of fire, theft, and other such risks and in such amounts as Lender may require. The policies shall be payable to both the Lender and the Borrower as their interests appear and shall provide for ten (10) days' written notice of cancellation to Lender.

e.   The Borrower shall make all repairs, replacements, additions, and improvements necessary to maintain any equipment in good working order and condition. At its option, Lender may discharge taxes, liens, or other encumbrances at any time levied or placed on the collateral, may pay rent or insurance due on the collateral, and may pay for the maintenance and preservation of the collateral. Borrower agrees to reimburse Lender on demand for any payment made or any expense incurred by Lender pursuant to the foregoing authorization.

3.   Default. The Borrower shall be in default under this Agreement if it is in default under the Note. Upon default and at any time thereafter, Lender may declare all obligations secured hereby immediately due and payable and shall have the remedies of a Lender under the Uniform Commercial Code. Lender may require the Borrower to make it available to Lender at a place that is mutually convenient. No waiver by Lender of any default shall operate as a waiver of any other default or of the same default on a future occasion. This Agreement shall inure to the benefit of and bind the heirs, executors, administrators, successors, and assigns of the parties. This Agreement shall have the effect of an instrument under seal.

_____ ("Borrower")

Signature _____

Date_____

89. Consulting Services Agreement

CONSULTING SERVICES AGREEMENT

This Consulting Services Agreement (this "Agreement") is hereby made between
_____ ("Client") and _____ ("Consultant"). Consultant agrees to provide the "Services," as more fully defined below, to Client and Client agrees to pay to Consultant the Consultant Services Fee, as more fully defined below.

1. Definitions. The following definitions shall apply to this Agreement.

   a. The "Services Fee Payment Schedule" (if applicable) shall include the compensation outlined in Exhibit A, and shall be paid according to the terms outlined in the table attached to this Agreement as Exhibit B.

   b. The "Agreement Term" shall begin with the Commencement Date and shall end with the Termination Date.

   c. The "Commencement Date" shall be the later of (i) the last date upon which a party executes this Agreement or (ii) the first date upon which Services are rendered.

   d. The "Termination Date" shall be any of the following: (i) the one-year anniversary of the Commencement Date or (ii) the date of receipt by either party of a Termination Notice.

2. Services. Consultant shall perform the duties and tasks outlined in the table attached to this Agreement as Exhibit C (the "Services"). The Services may include a development schedule and milestones.

3. Payment. Client shall pay the "Consulting Services Fee" as outlined in the table attached to this Agreement as Exhibit A, and shall pay such Consulting Services Fee according to the "Services Fee Payment Schedule" (if applicable) as outlined in the table attached to this Agreement as Exhibit B.

4. Termination. Either party may without cause terminate this Agreement by delivering to the other party written notice via U.S. Mail, facsimile, or personal delivery (but not by electronic mail transmission) expressing a desire to terminate this Agreement (a "Termination Notice"). Termination shall be effective immediately upon receipt of a Termination Notice.

5. Representations and Warranties. The parties to this Agreement make the following representations and warranties.

   a. Both parties represent and warrant to the other party that they have the full power to enter into this agreement without restriction.

   b. This Agreement shall not establish an employer/employee relationship between the parties. Consultant shall be an independent contractor and shall not enjoy the benefits normally afforded to employees provided either by Client's policy or by law.

   c. Consultant shall not include in the Material (as defined in Paragraph 5, below) any copyrights, trade secrets, trademarks, service marks, patents, or other property that to the Consultant's knowledge would infringe on the rights of third parties.

   d. Consultant shall not be an agent or representative of Client, except as specifically defined in this Agreement. Consultant shall have no authority to, and shall not attempt to, bind Client to contracts with third parties.

6. Confidential Information. Neither party shall, at any time, either directly or indirectly, use for its own benefit, nor shall it divulge, disclose, or communicate any information received from the other party that has been identified as Confidential. Both parties agree to execute standard nondisclosure agreements in connection with this Agreement.

7. Copyrights. Consultant, in the absence of any agreement to the contrary, agrees to irrevocably assign and convey to Client all rights, title, and interest to the copyrights, trade secrets, trademarks, service marks, patents, or other property created or to be created in connection with the performance of the Services (the "Material"). Client shall be deemed the author of such material and the Material shall be a "work for hire" as defined in 17 U.S.C. § 201 and the cases interpreting it.

8. Limitation of Damages. NEITHER PARTY SHALL BE LIABLE TO THE OTHER PARTY FOR ANY INCIDENTAL, CONSEQUENTIAL, SPECIAL, OR PUNITIVE DAMAGES OF ANY KIND OR NATURE, INCLUDING, WITHOUT LIMITATION, THE BREACH OF THIS AGREEMENT OR ANY TERMINATION OF THIS AGREEMENT, WHETHER SUCH LIABILITY IS ASSERTED ON THE BASIS OF CONTRACT, TORT, OR OTHERWISE, EVEN IF EITHER PARTY HAS BEEN WARNED OR WARNED OF THE POSSIBILITY OF ANY SUCH LOSS OR DAMAGE.

9. General Provisions. This Agreement constitutes the entire agreement of the parties and supersedes all prior understandings and agreements of the parties, whether oral or written. If any provision of this Agreement shall be held to be invalid or unenforceable for any reason, (i) the remaining provisions shall continue to be valid and enforceable; or (ii) if by limiting such provision it would become valid and enforceable, then such provision shall be deemed to be written, construed, and enforced as so limited. This Agreement shall be governed by the laws of the State of California. This Agreement is to be performed in (and venue shall lie exclusively in) _____ County, _____. This Agreement shall not be strictly construed against any party to this Agreement. Any controversy or claim arising out of or relating to this Agreement, or the breach thereof, shall be resolved by either (i) adjudication in a small claims court (subject to jurisdictional limitations) or (ii) in binding arbitration administered under the rules of the American Arbitration Association in accordance with its applicable rules.

Date _____   Date _____

_____   _____
Consultant   Client

Exhibit A: The "Consulting Services Fee" shall include the following payments and shall be according to the terms outlined herein:

The "Consulting Services Fee" shall include:

$_____, payable per hour for the time that Consultant devotes to the performance of the Services and for which written itemization for individual tasks is provided to Client (the "Hourly Rate"). The Hourly Rate shall be recorded in increments of time no greater than 1/10 of an hour (6 minutes). Payment shall be made within 15 days of the receipt of a written invoice by Client.

The "Consulting Services Fee" shall include:

$_____, payable in cash, by negotiable draft(s), or by transfer(s) to Client's bank account, according to the Services Fee Payment Schedule, which appears as Exhibit B.

Exhibit B: The "Services Fee Payment Schedule" shall include the following payments and according to the terms outlined herein:

The "Consulting Services Fee" shall be paid as follows:

$_____ shall accrue to the consultant upon the completion of each calendar month of service. Partial months shall be prorated on a daily basis. Payment shall be made within 15 days following the later of (a) the end of any applicable calendar month or (b) the submission of a written invoice to Client.

Exhibit C: The "Services" to be performed under the Agreement shall include the following:

Describe services to be performed.

90. Multimedia Development Contract

MULTIMEDIA DEVELOPMENT CONTRACT

This agreement is entered into by and between _____("Client") and _____ ("Developer") (together, the "Parties").

The effective date of this agreement is _____ ("Effective Date").

Recitals

WHEREAS, Developer offers the following services and related services: digital media design and development, corporate identity design and development, print design, Web site design and development, interactive kiosk design and development, CD-ROM design and development, logo design and development, computer graphics design and development.

WHEREAS, Client wishes to have Developer provide services for compensation.

NOW, THEREFORE, in consideration of the promises and mutual covenants and agreements set forth herein, Client and Developer agree as follows:

Definitions

"Existing Client Content" means the material provided by Client to be incorporated into the Product.

"Developer Tools" means the software tools of general application, whether owned or licensed to Developer, which are used to develop the Product.

"Development Schedule" shall be, only when applicable, as set forth in Schedule B to this Agreement, which lists the deliverable items contracted for ("Deliverables") and the deadlines for their delivery.

"Error" means, only when applicable, any failure of a Deliverable or Product to (i) meet the Specifications, if any, or (ii) to properly operate.

"Payment Schedule" shall be set forth in Schedule C to this Agreement and is the schedule by which payments under this agreement shall be made.

"Product" means the material that is the subject of this agreement, as further described in paragraph 1.1, below.

"Specifications" for the product, only when applicable, shall be set forth in Schedule A.

DEVELOPMENT AND DELIVERY OF DELIVERABLES, PAYMENT

1.1. Developer agrees to develop, on behalf of Client, the following (the "Product"): (describe what you are making, e.g., interactive Kiosk, educational CD-ROM, Web site, etc.).

1.2. Developer shall use his best efforts to develop each Deliverable and/or Product in accordance with the Specifications, if any.

1.3. All development work will be performed by Developer or his employees or by approved independent contractors who have executed confidentiality agreements, where appropriate.

1.4. Developer shall deliver all Deliverables and/or Product within the times specified in the Development Schedule and in accordance with the Specifications, if any.

1.5. Developer agrees to comply with all reasonable requests of Client as to the manner of delivery of all Deliverables, which may include delivery by electronic means.

1.6. Client agrees to pay according to the Payment Schedule.

1.7. If the Client, following the execution of this Agreement, alters the Specifications, or alters the nature and/or scope of the project as described in paragraph 1.1, or requests additional work, Developer reserves the right, upon notification to the Client, to (i) modify the Payment Schedule or (ii) charge Client on an hourly basis for the additional time at the rate of $_____ per hour.

1.8. Except as expressly provided in this Agreement or in a later writing signed by the Client, Developer shall bear all expenses arising from the performance of its obligations under this Agreement.

1.9. Except as expressly provided in this Agreement, this Agreement does not include any maintenance work on the Product or later enhancements to the product.

TESTING AND ACCEPTANCE

2.1. All Deliverables shall be thoroughly tested by Developer (if applicable) and all necessary corrections as a result of such testing shall be made, prior to delivery to Client.

2.2. When applicable, in the event that a Deliverable or Product delivered to Client has an Error, Client shall notify Developer within 7 days of delivery or shall waive its objections. Upon notification to Developer, Developer shall have 7 days to make a correction to the Deliverable or Product and present the repaired Deliverable or Product to Client. If the Payment Schedule calls for work under this Agreement to be paid by piece rate, time spent correcting Errors is to be included in the amounts in the Payment Schedule. If the Payment Schedule calls for work under this Agreement to be paid by hourly rate, time spent correcting Errors shall be billed to Client according to the hourly rate in the Payment Schedule.

COPYRIGHTS

3.1. Client will retain copyright ownership of Existing Client Content.

3.2. Developer will retain copyright ownership of the following material ("Developer's Components") to be created in the development of the Product and to include any and all of the following:

   a. Developer's existing tools, such as (source code, pre-existing code, scripts, stock images—basically your tools that you bring to the project: these should be non-negotiable items and should appear here in every contract.)

   b. Content created in connection with development of the Product, including: (simply insert the components that you are creating to which you wish to retain the rights—HTML code, source code, Java code, computer code in any language, images, animations, scripts, script code, text, logos).

3.3. Client will retain copyright ownership of, and Developer agrees to irrevocably assign and convey to Client all rights, title, and interest in the same, the following material ("Client's Components") to be created in the development of the Product and to include any and all of the following: (HTML code, source code, Java code, computer code in any language, images, animations, scripts, script code, text, logos—simply insert the components that you are creating to which you wish to give the rights).

3.4. Developer will retain copyright ownership of any copyrights not specifically granted to either party by this Agreement ("Non-specified Components").

3.5. Developer, however, grants to Client a royalty-free, worldwide, perpetual, irrevocable, non-exclusive license, with the right to sublicense through multiple tiers of sub-licensees, to use, reproduce, distribute, modify, publicly perform, and publicly display the Developer's Components and Non-specified Components in any medium and in any manner, unless such rights are specifically limited by this Agreement. This license includes the right to modify such copyrighted material.

3.6. Client, however, grants to Developer a royalty-free, worldwide, perpetual, irrevocable, non-exclusive license, to use, reproduce, distribute, modify, publicly perform, and publicly display its Existing Client Content and Client's Components (if any) for the sole and limited purpose of use in Developer's portfolio as self-promotion and not for direct commercial sale.

3.7. For the purposes of this agreement, "copyright" shall be deemed to include copyrights, trade secrets, patents, trademarks, and other intellectual property rights.

3.8. If any third party content or Developer Tools are used in the development of the Product, Developer shall be responsible for obtaining and/or paying for any necessary licenses to use third party content.

CONFIDENTIALITY

4.1. The terms of this Agreement, Existing Client Content, and other sensitive business information are confidential ("Confidential Information"). Developer and Client agree, except as authorized in writing, not to disclose to any third party Confidential Information. Developer agrees to return to Client promptly, upon completion of the Product, all Existing Client Content.

WARRANTIES, COVENANTS, AND INDEMNIFICATION

5.1. Developer represents and warrants to Client the following: (i) Developer has the full power to enter into this agreement without restriction, (ii) except with respect to Existing Client Content, and properly licensed materials, the performance, distribution, or use of the Product will not violate the rights of any third parties, and (iii) Developer agrees to defend, hold harmless, and indemnify Client and its representatives from and against all claims, defense costs, judgments, and other expenses arising out of the breach of the foregoing warranties.

5.2. Client represents and warrants to Developer the following: (i) Client has the full power to enter into this agreement without restriction, (ii) the performance of this Agreement will not violate the rights of any third parties, and (iii) Client agrees to defend, hold harmless, and indemnify Developer and its representatives from and against all claims, defense costs, judgments, and other expenses arising out of the breach of the foregoing warranties.

TERMINATION

6.1. If Developer fails to correct an Error according to paragraph 2.2 after 3 attempts, Client may terminate this agreement without making any further payments according to the Payment Schedule.

6.2. No termination of this Agreement by any party shall affect Developer's rights to receive his hourly rate for all time spent producing Deliverables and/or Product.

MISCELLANEOUS PROVISIONS

7.1. This Agreement contains the entire understanding and agreement of the parties, supersedes all prior written or oral understandings or agreements, and may not be altered, modified, or waived except in a signed writing.

7.2. EXCEPT AS PROVIDED ABOVE WITH RESPECT TO THIRD PARTY INDEMNIFICATION, NEITHER PARTY SHALL BE LIABLE TO THE OTHER PARTY FOR ANY INCIDENTAL, CONSEQUENTIAL, SPECIAL, OR PUNITIVE DAMAGES OF ANY KIND OR NATURE, INCLUDING, WITHOUT LIMITATION, THE BREACH OF THIS AGREEMENT OR ANY TERMINATION OF THIS AGREEMENT, WHETHER SUCH LIABILITY IS ASSERTED ON THE BASIS OF CONTRACT, TORT, OR OTHERWISE, EVEN IF EITHER PARTY HAS BEEN WARNED OR WARNED OF THE POSSIBILITY OF ANY SUCH LOSS OR DAMAGE.

_____

Developer

_____

Client

Schedule A

Specifications

(This will depend on the job, obviously, and may not apply to all jobs.)

Schedule B

Development Schedule

(This will depend on the job, obviously, and may not apply to all jobs.)

Schedule C

Payment Schedule

(For hourly rate:)

Developer shall be paid on an hourly basis, and his rates and billing procedures are as follows: Charges are $_____ per hour. The minimum billing increment is six minutes or 1/10 of an hour. Time spent on individual tasks is rounded up to the next 10th of an hour.

(For piece rate:)

Deliverables	Due Date	Payment Due
Down payment (1/3)	_____	$_____
Milestone 1	_____	$_____
Milestone 2	_____	$_____
Final Completion	_____	$_____
Total Payment	_____	$_____

91. Mutual Compromise Agreement and Mutual Release

THIS MUTUAL COMPROMISE AGREEMENT AND MUTUAL RELEASE ("Agreement") is entered into as of _____, by and between _____ ("Debtor") and _____ ("Creditor") (collectively "Parties or Party"). For the purposes of the Agreement, "Party" includes subsidiaries and parents of a Party and includes individuals serving as directors, officers, employees, agents, consultants, and advisors to or of a Party.

A. BACKGROUND

1. Debtor and Creditor entered into an agreement or series of agreements (the "Contract") whereby Debtor provided a series of services to Creditor for an agreed-upon fee.

2. Since the time of entering into the Contract, the Parties have determined that a settlement of the mutual obligations between them is appropriate and would best serve the interests of all of the Parties. This Agreement is intended to express the Parties' intent to equitably settle the obligations arising from or related to the Contract.

B. AGREEMENT

NOW, THEREFORE, IN CONSIDERATION OF THE FOLLOWING, THE FOREGOING, THE MUTUAL COVENANTS, PROMISES, AGREEMENTS, REPRESENTATIONS, AND RELEASES CONTAINED HEREIN, AND IN EXCHANGE FOR OTHER GOOD AND VALUABLE CONSIDERATION, THE RECEIPT, SUFFICIENCY, AND ADEQUACY OF WHICH IS HEREBY ACKNOWLEDGED, THE PARTIES HEREBY AGREE AS FOLLOWS:

1. Settlement.

   a. Debtor shall pay the following amounts to Creditor: _____, such payment to be made no later than _____ date.

   b. Debtor shall owe no further liability or obligation to Creditor in connection with any services.

2. Confidentiality. Debtor and Creditor shall keep the terms of the Agreement confidential and shall not disclose such terms to any other Party except as is necessary for the proper conduct of the disclosing Party's business.

3. No Other Payments. No additional funds shall be required to be paid or transferred by Creditor to Debtor or by Debtor to Creditor.

4. Nature and Effect of Agreement and Conditions Thereon. This Agreement consists of a compromise and settlement by the Parties of claims arising from the Contract described in Section A, Paragraph 2, above, and a release given by the Parties relinquishing their claims against the other. By executing this Agreement, the Parties intend to and do hereby extinguish the obligations heretofore existing between them and arising from that dispute.

   The nature and effect of this agreement, and the enforcement of any of the provisions found herein, is strictly conditioned upon the actions described in Paragraph 1. The shares must bear the medallion guaranteed signature of an authorized officer of the entity whose name appears on the face of the certificate and the shares must be accompanied by a resolution of the board authorizing transfer of the shares.

5. Admissions. This Agreement is not, and shall not be treated as, an admission of liability by either Party for any purpose, and shall not be admissible as evidence before any tribunal or court.

6. Compromise Agreement. The Parties hereby compromise and settle any and all past, present, or future claims, demands, obligations, or causes of action for compensatory or punitive damages, costs, losses, expenses, and compensation, whether based on tort, contract, or other theories of recovery, which the Parties have or which may later accrue to or be acquired by one Party against the other, the other's predecessors and successors in interest, heirs, and assigns, past, present, and future officers, directors, shareholders, agents, employees, parent and subsidiary organizations, affiliates, and partners, arising from the subject matter of the claim described in Section A, Paragraph 2, above, and agree that this compromise and settlement shall constitute a bar to all such claims. The Parties agree that this compromise and settlement shall constitute a bar to all past, present, and future claims arising out of the subject matter of the action described in Section A, Paragraph 2, above.

7. Release and Discharge. The Parties hereby release and discharge the other, the other's predecessors and successors in interest, heirs, and assigns, past, present, and future officers, directors, shareholders, agents, employees, parent and subsidiary organizations, affiliates, and partners from, and relinquish, any and all past, present, or future claims, demands, obligations, or causes of action for compensatory or punitive damages, costs, losses, expenses, and compensation, whether based on tort, contract, or other theories of recovery, which the Parties have or which may later accrue to or be acquired by one Party against the other arising from the subject of the claim described in Section A, Paragraph 2, above.

8. Unknown Claims. The Parties acknowledge and agree that, upon execution of the release, this Agreement applies to all claims for damages or losses that either Party may have against the other, whether those damages or losses are known or unknown, foreseen or unforeseen, and in the event that this Agreement is deemed executed in California, the Parties thereby waive application of California Civil Code Section 1542.

The Parties certify that each has read the following provisions of California Civil Code Section 1542: "A general release does not extend to claims which the creditor does not know or suspect to exist in his favor at the time of executing the release, which if known by him must have materially affected his settlement with the debtor."

The Parties understand and acknowledge that the significance and consequence of this waiver of California Civil Code Section 1542 is that even if one Party should eventually suffer additional damages arising out of the facts referred to in Section A, Paragraph 2, above, that Party will not be able to make any claim for these damages. Furthermore, the Parties acknowledge that they intend these consequences even as to claims for damages that may exist as of the date of this release but that the damaged or harmed Party does not know exist and that, if known, would materially affect that Party's decision to execute this release, regardless of whether the damaged Party's lack of knowledge is the result of ignorance, oversight, error, negligence, or any other cause.

9. Conditions of Execution. Each Party acknowledges and warrants that its execution of this compromise agreement and release is free and voluntary.

10. Representation of Understanding. All Parties and signatories to this Agreement acknowledge and agree that the terms of this Agreement are contractual and not mere recital, and all Parties and signatories

represent and warrant that they have carefully read this Agreement, have fully reviewed its provisions with their attorneys, know and understand its contents, and sign the same as their own free acts and deeds. It is understood and agreed by all Parties and signatories to this Agreement that execution of this Agreement may affect rights and liabilities of substantial extent and degree and, with the full understanding of that fact, they represent that the covenants and releases provided for in this Agreement are in their respective best interests.

11. Construction. The provisions of this Agreement shall not be construed against either Party.

12. Entire Agreement. This Agreement constitutes the entire agreement between the Parties and signatories and all prior and contemporaneous conversation, negotiations, possible and alleged agreements, and representations, covenants, and warranties, express or implied, or written, with respect to the subject matter hereof, are waived, merged herein, and superseded hereby. There are no other agreements, representations, covenants, or warranties not set forth herein. The terms of this Agreement may not be contradicted by evidence of any prior or contemporaneous agreement. The Parties further intend and agree that this Agreement constitutes the complete and exclusive statement of its terms and that no extrinsic evidence whatsoever may be introduced in any judicial or arbitration proceeding, if any, involving this Agreement. No part of this Agreement may be amended or modified in any way unless such amendment or modification is expressed in writing signed by all Parties to this Agreement.

13. Counterparts. This Agreement may be executed in multiple counterparts, each of which shall be deemed an original but all of which together shall constitute one and the same instrument. When all of the Parties and signatories have executed any copy hereof, such execution shall constitute the execution of this Agreement, whereupon it shall become effective.

14. Governing Law. THIS AGREEMENT WILL BE GOVERNED AND CONSTRUED IN ACCORDANCE WITH THE LAW OF THE STATE OF _____ AND THE UNITED STATES OF AMERICA, WITHOUT REGARD TO CONFLICT OF LAW PRINCIPLES. This Agreement shall not be strictly construed against any Party to this Agreement. Any controversy or claim arising out of or relating to this Agreement, or the breach thereof, shall be resolved by arbitration administered under the rules of the American Arbitration Association in accordance with its applicable rules. Such arbitration shall take place within San Mateo County, California, and shall be binding upon all Parties, and any judgment upon or any an award rendered by the arbitrator may be entered in any court having jurisdiction thereof.

15. Binding Effect. The provisions of this Agreement shall be binding upon and inure to the benefit of each of the Parties and their respective successors and assigns. Nothing expressed or implied in this Agreement is intended, or shall be construed, to confer upon or give any person, partnership, or corporation, other than the Parties, their successors and assigns, any benefits, rights, or remedies under or by reason of this Agreement, except to the extent of any contrary provision herein contained.

16. Authority. The Parties hereto represent and warrant that they possess the full and complete authority to covenant and agree as provided in this Agreement and, if applicable, to release other Parties and signatories as provided herein. If any Party hereto is a corporation or limited liability company, the signatory for any such corporation or limited liability company represents and warrants that such signatory possesses the authority and has been authorized by the corporation or limited liability company to enter

into this Agreement, whether by resolution of the board of, upon the instruction by an authorized officer of, as authorized in the bylaws of the corporation on whose behalf the signatory is executing this Agreement, or otherwise.

17. Severability. If any provision of this Agreement is held by a court to be unenforceable or invalid for any reason, the remaining provisions of this Agreement shall be unaffected by such holding.

18. Exchanges by Fax. The exchange of a fully executed Agreement in counterparts or otherwise by fax shall be sufficient to bind the Parties to the terms and conditions of this Agreement.

IN WITNESS WHEREOF, the Parties and signatories execute this Agreement on the dates indicated.

_____, "Debtor"

Date _____

Signature _____

_____, "Creditor"

Date _____

Signature _____

92. Checklist for a Buyer's Purchase Order

❏ Definitions for capitalized terms

❏ Limit right to take actions affecting agreement to authorized buyer and member of management

❏ Order acceptance
- On written acceptance from seller
- On expiration of time period
- On shipment
- Payment not final acceptance
- Acceptance not waiver of latent defects
- Testing and inspection at anytime during and after manufacture

❏ Products
- Must meet specifications
- No substitutions without consent

❏ Seller may not manufacture in advance of buyer's needs

❏ Buyer has right to require progress reports on orders

❏ Product rejection
- At buyer's option may return for credit or replacement, halt at plant for correction, or keep if adjustment in price

❏ Buyer's changes to order
- Process for initiating changes
- Changes at any time
- Changes can be specifications, delivery date, drawings, designs, packaging, destination, schedule, inspection, quantities, and suspension of manufacture
- Notification of additional charges
- Notification of additional time for delivery

❏ Price
- As stated in buyer's PO
- No extra charges
- No greater than lowest prevailing price offered to any customer

❏ Invoices
- What is to be included in invoice detail
- Cash discount and how calculated
- When time period for determining cash discounts begins
- Payment due dates
- Invoice intervals
- Payments in what currency
- Payments to be made by cash, check, electronic funds transfer or other

- ■ Buyer has right to set off any amounts owed by seller
- ❏ Shipping
  - ■ Notification of drop shipment
  - ■ Notification of actual or expected delay
  - ■ Title and risk of loss passes at delivery to buyer

- ❏ Designation of carrier
  - ■ Packaging and labeling requirements
  - ■ No advance delivery
  - ■ If advance delivery, returned or stored at seller's cost
  - ■ Seller to pay rush delivery if needed to meet delivery date

- ❏ Time of essence to buyer only

- ❏ Returns - process

- ❏ Warranty
  - ■ Passed on to buyer's customer
  - ■ Free from defects in design, workmanship, and materials
  - ■ Conforms to specifications, drawings, samples, advertising literature
  - ■ Warranty period—period of time, period of use, or period of performance
  - ■ Warranty period for repaired products
  - ■ Warranty period for refurbished products
  - ■ Merchantable
  - ■ Fit for intended purpose
  - ■ Free of defects in title
  - ■ Does not infringe any patent, copyright, mask work or other intellectual property right
  - ■ Packaged to protect from damage
  - ■ Remedies for breach of warranty at buyer's option
  - ■ Remedies include repair, replace, refund or buyer may fix and charge seller
  - ■ Remedies not exclusive

- ❏ Buyer expressly objects to any conflicting terms in seller's PO

- ❏ Corrective action plan required on notice by buyer

- ❏ No credit hold without notice

- ❏ Taxes included in price

- ❏ No gratuities to staff or families of staff

- ❏ Patent Infringement
  - ■ Indemnification for all products
  - ■ Includes claims of unfair competition
  - ■ Retain right to defend and settle
  - ■ Seller must procure for buyer right to use product
  - ■ Seller must modify product to become non-infringing

- Seller must replace product with non-infringing product
- Seller must refund price

❏ Termination provision
  - For cause

❏ Any breach or material breach

❏ Fails to perform

❏ Performs unsatisfactorily

❏ Fails to make progress

❏ Right to cure period
  - For convenience

❏ At any time

❏ Work stops immediately

❏ If partial cancellation, work continues on remainder of order

❏ Amount of payment to seller for cancellation of custom products by period of time between cancellation and delivery date

❏ Amount of payment for cancellation of stock products if any

❏ Limit on time to claim payment for a cancellation
  - Insolvency
  - Bankruptcy
  - Assignment for benefit of creditors
  - Receiver appointed
  - Initiates reorganization

❏ Closes business

❏ Stops operating

❏ Buyer has right to manufacture if seller ceases business

❏ Conflicting language between agreements resolved in what manner

❏ Confidential information
  - How defined
  - What are acceptable uses and disclosures
  - Term of confidentiality obligations
  - Duties towards confidential information
  - Exceptions to duties of confidentiality

❏ No implied licenses to buyer's information or property

❏ Alternative dispute resolution

- Negotiation
- Mediation
- Arbitration
- If don't want any of these include provision specifically rejecting
- Is alternative exclusive or required before litigation
- Who pays for alternative
- Who specifically is required to participate in alternative
- Qualifications of neutral party officiating over the alternative
- What is the timeframe for alternative
- Where does alternative dispute forum occur
- What rules govern alternative dispute forum
- If neutral party renders a decision is it binding

❑ Indemnity
  - Seller to provide
  - To buyer, officers, employees, consultants, directors, agents, parent, subsidiary
  - Claims, liabilities, losses, damages, costs, charges, attorneys' fees, legal costs, liens, death, personal injury, accidents, property damage.
  - Arising out of actual or alleged defects in material and workmanship, negligence, gross negligence, breach of the contract, claims of liens or encumbrances

❑ Limitation on liability
  - Consequential damages- special, indirect, incidental, exemplary
  - Limit on damages

❑ Requirement to obtain and maintain insurance
  - Contract liability, comprehensive, general, automobile liability, workers' compensation, product liability.
  - Insurance certificates required to be produced
  - Named insured

❑ Compliance with laws
  - Requirement to obtain permits and licenses
  - Comply with OSHA, hazardous materials laws

❑ Safety
  - Label hazardous materials
  - Provide material safety data sheet on any chemicals
  - If hazardous materials in products, inform in writing
  - If defects become known must inform buyer

❑ Publicity
  - Allow with other party's written consent not to be unreasonably withheld
  - Allow for your company at its discretion
  - Prohibit entirely

❏ Choice of law to interpret contract

❏ Recovery of prevailing party's expenses in litigation
  ▪ Attorneys fees
  ▪ Legal costs
  ▪ Expert witness fees

❏ Investigation costs

❏ Severability–illegal or otherwise unenforceable provisions can be severed

❏ Waiver–waiver of breach not agreement to waive all breaches

❏ Assignment/subcontracting permitted
  ▪ Preclude partial or complete assignment but allow subcontracting
  ▪ Preclude subcontracting but allow partial or complete assignment
  ▪ Allowed with consent not to be withheld unreasonably
  ▪ Allowed with consent at other party's sole discretion
  ▪ Allowed if a party is sold
  ▪ Allowed if a party is transferred to an affiliate or subsidiary
  ▪ If subcontractor's permitted will sub be required to maintain company confidential information

❏ Choice of venue for litigation

❏ Rights provided in contract are cumulative or exclusive

❏ Force Majeure–consider inclusion of fire, accident, acts of public enemy, terrorism, severe weather, acts of God, labor disruption, flood, failure of suppliers to deliver, difficulty obtaining supplies, epidemics, nuclear strike, government intervention, government or freight embargo, quarantine, difficulty obtaining transportation
  ▪ Notice required if event occurs
  ▪ Right to terminate if event lasts specified amount of time
  ▪ Integration (or Entire Agreement) provision
  ▪ All documents making up the agreement referenced

❏ Notice provision
  ▪ Are both parties addresses included
  ▪ Acceptable delivery methods
  ▪ Time that the other party is deemed to have received the notice specified

❏ No joint venture, agency, partnership, trust, or association

❏ Successors and assigns – agreement binding on

❏ Survival–certain terms of the agreement may survive termination

❏ Written modification – all modifications in writing and signed

❏ If terms on back of a form, does the front call attention to the terms

❏ Will Buyer provide tooling or otherwise have its own property at seller

- Seller must insure it, label it as buyers, separate it from other property, return it in good condition, and secure it
- Buyer may enter and inspect it at any time

93. Checklist for Modifying or Extending an Existing Contract

❑ Document is numbered in title

❑ Clearly states it is an amendment, modification or supplement

❑ Refers to name and date of original agreement

❑ Refers to parties of original agreement

❑ States parties have received good and valuable consideration for modification

❑ Effective date

❑ States term being deleted and states its replacement

❑ States term being modified and how it is modified

❑ Includes terms to be added

❑ Correct signature blocks and dates

❑ Agreement signed and initialed on all pages by both parties

94. Checklist for Sales Agreements Where Your Company Is the Seller

❏ The checklist for purchase orders is applicable for sales agreements with the addition that a ?sales agreement needs:

❏ Correct legal name of parties

❏ Effective date of contract

❏ Term

❏ No third party beneficiaries

❏ Correct signature blocks

❏ Agreement signed and each page initialed by both parties

95. Terms of Purchase

Indemnification. Each Party shall indemnify and hold harmless the other, its parent, subsidiaries, affiliates, successors, assigns, employees, officers, directors, agents, or subcontractors from and against any and all suits, claims, losses, forfeitures, demands, fees, damages, liabilities, costs, expenses, obligations, proceedings, or injuries, of any kind or nature, including reasonable attorneys fees which that Party may hereafter incur, become responsible for, or pay out as a result of the other Party's breach of any term or provision of this Agreement, or a claim of lien or encumbrances made by third parties.

Assignment. Neither Party may assign or otherwise transfer this Agreement without the prior written consent of the other.

LIMITATION OF LIABILITY. IN NO EVENT SHALL EITHER PARTY BE LIABLE IN CONTRACT, TORT OR OTHERWISE FOR INCIDENTAL OR CONSEQUENTIAL DAMAGES OF ANY KIND, INCLUDING, WITHOUT LIMITATION, ECONOMIC DAMAGE OR LOST PROFITS, REGARDLESS OF WHETHER EITHER PARTY SHALL BE ADVISED, SHALL HAVE OTHER REASON TO KNOW, OR IN FACT SHALL KNOW OF THE POSSIBILITY.

Forum and Legal Fees. Should legal action arise concerning this Agreement, the prevailing party shall be entitled to recover all reasonable attorneys' fees and related costs, in addition to any other relief which may be awarded by any court or other tribunal. The Parties agree that prior to initiating any legal proceedings against the other, the Parties will engage a neutral mediator who will be charged with assisting the parties to reach a mutually agreeable resolution of all contested matters. The mediation shall take place in Ingut, Noodle USA and will be conducted in the English language. The mediator shall be chosen by mutual agreement of the Parties and the mediator's fees shall be borne equally by the Parties. In the event that a mediator cannot be agreed on by the Parties, each Party shall chose a mediator and the two mediators shall together chose a third mediator who will conduct the mediation. The costs of the two mediators chosen to choose the third mediator shall be borne equally by the Parties. The Parties agree to participate in the mediation in good faith.

Severability. If any provision of this Agreement is held by a court of law to be illegal, invalid or unenforceable, that provision shall be deemed amended to achieve as nearly as possible the same economic effect as the original provision, and the legality, validity and enforceability of the remaining provisions of this Agreement shall not be affected or impaired.

Waiver. No term or provision hereof will be considered waived and no breach of this Agreement excused unless such waiver or consent is in writing. The waiver or consent to a breach of any provision of this Agreement shall not operate or be construed as a waiver of, consent to, or excuse of any other or subsequent breach.

Conflicts Between Documents. These terms shall control over any conflicting terms in any other document which might be exchanged related to this transaction.

Force Majeure. Neither Party shall be held responsible for any delay or failure in performance of any part of this Agreement to the extent such delay or failure is caused by fire, flood, explosion, terrorism, war, embargo, government requirement, civil or military authority, act of God, or other similar causes beyond its control and without the fault or negligence of the delayed or non-performing Party. The Party so affected shall notify the non-affected Party in writing within ten (10) days after the beginning of any such cause that would affect the Party's performance.

Successors and Assigns. The Parties intend this Agreement to bind any and all of the Parties' successors, heirs, and assigns.

Survival. All provisions that logically ought to survive termination of this Agreement shall survive.

Entire Agreement. This Agreement supersedes, terminates, and otherwise renders null and void any and all prior written or oral agreements or understandings between the Parties relating to the subject matter of this Agreement. Except as otherwise provided in this Agreement, only a written instrument signed by both Parties may modify this Agreement.

96. Terms of Sale

1. **Order Acceptance.** Acceptance of buyer's order is subject to credit approval.

2. **Price.** Prices shall be those in effect at time of shipment.

3. **Shipping.** Goods shall be shipped F.O.B. shipping point.

4. **Payment.** Invoices are eligible for cash discount if paid by the 10th of the month following the invoice date. All invoices are due on the 15th of the month following the invoice date. Payments not made when due shall incur a monthly service charge of the lesser of 1-1/2 percent or the maximum permitted by law.

5. **Taxes.** Prices do not include sales or other taxes imposed on the sale of goods which shall be separately invoiced unless Buyer provides Seller with an acceptable tax exemption certificate.

6. **Returns.** With Seller's prior approval, goods may be returned for credit against unpaid invoices. The amount of the credit will be reduced by a restocking fee equal to 10% of the price of the returned goods.

7. **Delivery.** Seller shall not be liable for any delay in delivery that is the result of acts not under Seller's control such as weather, strikes, and acts of God. Delivery dates are best estimates only.

8. **WARRANTIES.** SELLER WARRANTS THAT ALL GOODS SOLD ARE FREE OF ANY SECURITY INTEREST. SELLER MAKES NO OTHER EXPRESS OR IMPLIED WARRANTIES, AND SPECIFICALLY MAKES NO IMPLIED WARRANTIES OF MERCHANTABILITY OR FITNESS FOR PURPOSE.

9. **Limitation of Liability.** Seller's liability shall be limited to either repair or replacement of the goods or refund of the purchase price, all at Seller's option, and in no case shall Seller be liable for incidental or consequential damage of any kind for any reason.

10. **Waiver.** The failure of Seller to insist on the performance of any of the terms or conditions of this contract or to exercise any right hereunder shall not be a waiver of such terms, conditions or rights in the future, nor shall it be deemed to be a waiver of any other term, condition, or right under this contract.

11. **Modification of Terms and Conditions.** No terms and conditions other than those stated herein, and no modification of these terms or conditions, shall be binding on Seller without Seller's written consent.

97. Examples of Legal "Boilerplate"

Assignment/Subcontracting: Four Alternatives

Neither party shall have the right to assign or subcontract any part of its obligations under this agreement.

Neither party shall have the right to assign or subcontract any of its obligations or duties under this agreement without the prior written consent of the other party, which consent shall not be unreasonably withheld or delayed.

Neither party shall have the right to assign or subcontract any of its obligations or duties under this agreement, without the prior written consent of the other party, which consent shall be in the sole determination of the party with the right to consent.

Notwithstanding the foregoing, either party may, without the consent of the other party, assign the agreement to an affiliate or subsidiary or to any person that acquires all or substantially all of the assets of a party.

Attorneys Fees

The non-prevailing party in any dispute under this Agreement shall pay all costs and expenses, including expert witness fees and attorneys' fees, incurred by the prevailing party in resolving such dispute.

Choice of Law or Governing Law

This Agreement shall be governed by and construed in accordance with the internal laws of the State of _____ U.S.A., without reference to any conflicts of law provisions.

Choice of Venue

Each party hereby submits to the exclusive jurisdiction of, and waives any venue or other objection against, any federal court sitting in the State of _____, U.S.A., or any _____ state court in any legal proceeding arising out of or relating to this Contract. Each party agrees that all claims and matters may be heard and determined in any such court and each party waives any right to object to such filing on venue, forum non convenient or similar grounds.

Compliance with Laws

Each party shall comply in all respects with all applicable legal requirements governing the duties, obligations, and business practices of that party and shall obtain any permits or licenses necessary for its operations. Neither party shall take any action in violation of any applicable legal requirement that could result in liability being imposed on the other party.

Conflicts

The terms of this Agreement shall control over any conflicting terms in any referenced agreement or document.

Cumulative Rights

Any specific rights or remedy provided in this contract will not be exclusive but will be cumulative of all other rights and remedies.

Force Majeure

Neither Party shall be held responsible for any delay or failure in performance of any part of this Agreement to the extent such delay or failure is caused by fire, flood, explosion, war, embargo, government requirement, civil or military authority, act of God, or other similar causes beyond its control and without the fault or negligence of the delayed or non-performing Party. The affected party will notify the other party in writing within ten (10) days after the beginning of any such cause that would affect its performance. Notwithstanding, if a party's performance is delayed for a period exceeding thirty (30) days from the date the other party receives notice under this paragraph, the non-affected party will have the right, without any liability to the other party, to terminate this agreement.

Indemnity

Each Party shall indemnify, defend and hold the other Party harmless from and against any and all claims, actions, suits, demands, assessments or judgments asserted and any and all losses, liabilities, damages, costs and expenses (including, without limitation, attorneys' fees, accounting fees and investigation costs to the extent permitted by law) alleged or incurred arising out of or relating to any operations, acts or omissions of the indemnifying Party or any of its employees, agents, and invitees in the exercise of the indemnifying Party's rights or the performance or observance of the indemnifying Party's obligations under this Agreement. Prompt notice must be given of any claim, and the Party who is providing the indemnification will have control of any defense or settlement.

Insurance

Each party agrees to maintain insurance in commercially reasonable amounts covering claims of any kind or nature for damage to property or personal injury, including death, made by anyone, that may arise from activities performed or facilitated by this contract, whether these activities are performed by that company, its employees, agents, or anyone directly or indirectly engaged or employed by that party or its agents.

Integration Provision or Entire Agreement

This Agreement sets forth and constitutes the entire agreement and understanding of the parties with respect to the subject matter hereof. This Agreement supersedes any and all prior agreements, negotiations, correspondence, undertakings, promises, covenants, arrangements, communications, representations and warranties, whether oral or written of any party to this Agreement.

Limit of Liability: Two Alternatives

IN NO EVENT SHALL EITHER PARTY BE LIABLE TO THE OTHER OR ANY THIRD PARTY IN CONTRACT, TORT OR OTHERWISE FOR INCIDENTAL OR CONSEQUENTIAL DAMAGES OF ANY KIND, INCLUDING, WITHOUT LIMITATION, PUNITIVE OR ECONOMIC DAMAGES OR LOST PROFITS, REGARDLESS OF WHETHER EITHER PARTY SHALL BE ADVISED, SHALL HAVE OTHER REASON TO KNOW, OR IN FACT SHALL KNOW OF THE POSSIBILITY.

IN NO EVENT SHALL EITHER PARTY BE LIABLE FOR ANY INCIDENTAL OR CONSEQUENTIAL DAMAGES. SELLER'S LIABILITY AND BUYER'S EXCLUSIVE REMEDY FOR ANY CAUSE OF ACTION ARISING IN CONNECTION WITH THIS CONTRACT OR THE SALE OR USE OF THE GOODS, WHETHER BASED ON NEGLIGENCE,

STRICT LIABILITY, BREACH OF WARRANTY, BREACH OF CONTRACT, OR EQUITABLE PRINCIPLES, IS EXPRESSLY LIMITED TO, AT SELLER'S OPTION, REPLACEMENT OF, OR REPAYMENT OF THE PURCHASE PRICE FOR THAT PORTION OF THE GOODS WITH RESPECT TO WHICH DAMAGES ARE CLAIMED. ALL CLAIMS OF ANY KIND ARISING IN CONNECTION WITH THIS CONTRACT OR THE SALE OR USE OF THE GOODS SHALL BE DEEMED WAIVED UNLESS MADE IN WRITING WITHIN SIXTY (60) DAYS FROM THE DATE OF SELLER'S DELIVERY, OR THE DATE FIXED FOR DELIVERY IN THE EVENT OF NONDELIVERY.

Notices

All notices shall be in writing and shall be delivered personally, by United States certified or registered mail, postage prepaid, return receipt requested, or by a recognized overnight delivery service. Any notice must be delivered to the parties at their respective addresses set forth below their signatures or to such other address as shall be specified in writing by either party according to the requirements of this section. The date that notice shall be deemed to have been made shall be the date of delivery, when delivered personally; on written verification of receipt if delivered by overnight delivery; or the date set forth on the return receipt if sent by certified or registered mail.

Relationship of the Parties

The relationship of the parties under this Agreement is that of an independent contractor and the company hiring the contractor. In all matters relating to this Agreement each Party hereto shall be solely responsible for the acts of its employees and agents, and employees or agents of one Party shall not be considered employees or agents of the other Party. Except as otherwise provided herein, no Party shall have any right, power or authority to create any obligation, express or implied, on behalf of any other Party. Nothing in this Agreement is intended to create or constitute a joint venture, partnership, agency, trust or other association of any kind between the Parties or persons referred to herein.

Severability

If any provision of this Agreement shall be declared by any court of competent jurisdiction to be illegal, void, or unenforceable, the other provisions shall not be affected but shall remain in full force and effect. If the non-solicitation or non-competition provisions are found to be unreasonable or invalid, these restrictions shall be shall enforced to the maximum extent valid and enforceable.

Successors and Assigns

This Agreement shall be binding on and inure to the benefit of the parties hereto and their respective heirs, legal or personal representatives, successors and assigns.

Survival

All provisions that logically ought to survive termination of this Agreement shall survive.

Termination for Cause

If either party breaches any provision of this Agreement and if such breach is not cured within thirty (30) days after receiving written notice from the other party specifying such breach in reasonable detail, the non-breaching party shall have the right to terminate this Agreement by giving written notice thereof to the party in breach, which termination shall go into effect immediately on receipt.

Termination for Convenience

This Agreement may be terminated by either party on thirty (30) days advance written notice effective as of the expiration of the notice period.

Termination on Insolvency

Either party has the right to terminate this agreement where the other party becomes insolvent, fails to pay its bills when due, makes an assignment for the benefit of creditors, goes out of business or ceases production.

Waiver

Failure of either party to insist on strict compliance with any of the terms, covenants, and conditions of this Agreement shall not be deemed a waiver of such terms, covenants, and conditions or of any similar right or power hereunder at any subsequent time.

Warranty Disclaimers

EXCEPT AS EXPRESSLY STATED IN THIS AGREEMENT, THE SELLER EXPRESSLY DISCLAIMS AND NEGATES ANY IMPLIED OR EXPRESS WARRANTY OF MERCHANTABILITY, ANY IMPLIED OR EXPRESS WARRANTY OF FITNESS FOR A PARTICULAR PURPOSE, AND ANY IMPLIED OR EXPRESS WARRANTY OF CONFORMITY TO MODELS OR SAMPLES OF MATERIALS.

Written Modification

This Agreement may be amended or modified only by a writing executed by both parties.

98. Lawyer Engagement Letter

Dear _____,

The purpose of this letter ("Engagement Letter") is to confirm the engagement of your firm to represent _____ in the following legal matter: _____.

Our policy regarding retention of legal services is:

1. No expenditure of time or costs should be made without pre-approval of a budget defining the tasks, time, hourly rate and name of staff person conducting the task, or part thereof. I have found that this is the best way for both of us to have the same understanding about what is being done and what it will cost. _____ will not be liable for legal fees or costs exceeding this budget without written pre-approval of such fees and costs.

2. The attached Terms and Conditions, along with this Engagement Letter, comprise the contract governing your firm's provision of legal services to _____. The performance of legal services to _____ signifies your firm's agreement to this contract.

3. Correspondence and bills should be directed to me.

4. I will forward a letter similar to this regarding each matter in which we engage your firm. I have found that this practice clarifies, for both parties, when a discussion rises to the level of legal advice which you expect to be paid for and we expect to be billed for. Please feel free to decline to discuss matters that you expect to be paid for where you have not received an engagement letter.

We look forward to working with you on this and other matters

Sincerely,

99. Terms and Conditions for Engagement of Outside Counsel

I. Introduction

This sets forth the Terms and Conditions ("Terms) for the engagement of outside legal counsel who provide services to _____.

The Legal Department seeks to provide and arrange for the highest quality legal services, provided in an expeditious and cost effective manner, consistent with the values and mission of _____. _____ expects that outside counsel will not only provide high quality, cost effective legal services, but will also offer constructive and forward thinking suggestions regarding the efficient delivery of legal services in each matter for which counsel is engaged.

In evaluating the quality, effectiveness and efficiency of outside counsel's services, _____ will consider the following:

A. How effectively outside counsel works with in-house attorneys and the senior executive staff, with particular emphasis on clear, concise communications;

B. The utilization of a practical, common sense approach to problem solving;

C. Judgment in balancing the need for high quality legal services against the high cost of legal representation generally;

D. Whether innovative, creative approaches to resolving problems are identified, considered and implemented;

E. The reasonableness of the time spent on tasks and projects involved in the representation;

F. The continuity of staffing on matters;

G. Whether personnel are performing work appropriate to the billing rates;

H. The appropriateness and effectiveness of outside resources suggested or used by outside counsel.

II. Working with the _____ Legal Department

The _____ Legal Department has responsibility for the retention and management of outside counsel for _____. As such, the Legal Department expects outside counsel to work closely with the responsible in-house attorney. Assignments, communication with third parties, as well as litigation and transaction strategies should be discussed with _____'s in-house counsel at the commencement of the engagement and regularly throughout its term.

The Legal Department will from time to time involve other outside counsel in transactions or disputes that warrant such involvement. This involvement may require that outside counsel work cooperatively with other attorneys outside _____, although coordination and supervision of all outside counsel remains a Legal Department responsibility. Courtesy and professionalism is expected in connection with all interactions between and among outside counsel and in-house attorneys and _____ executives.

III. Standards of Engagements

All engagements of outside counsel require that attorneys observe the following standards when representing _____:

A. **Confidentiality and Privacy.** _____ is subject to laws requiring the protection of confidential and private information. Outside counsel agree to maintain the confidentiality and privacy of all records and information arising from outside counsel's representation of _____.

B. **Strategy.** Litigation or transaction strategy should be discussed with the responsible _____ attorney and agreed upon at an early stage. Strategy should be reviewed from time to time and should not be changed without prior concurrence of the responsible _____ attorney.

C. **Periodic Reporting.** The responsible _____ attorney should be advised promptly of any unusual adverse or positive developments such as counterclaims, new case law, or affirmative defenses that may apply. While no reporting frequency is universally required, reports should be made at reasonable intervals and whenever specific circumstances warrant. Both _____ and outside counsel are well served by regular communication. Often outside counsel will be expected to communicate both with a responsible _____ attorney and a responsible business executive in the matter for which outside counsel has been engaged.

D. **Prior Document Review.** Although prior review of all documents is not required, certain key documents in litigation or transactions should be submitted in draft form to the Legal Department prior to filing or communicating with clients. For example, contracts, legal opinions, pleadings and appellate briefs should be submitted to the responsible _____ attorney with ample time for review.

E. **Research.** The selection of outside counsel is often based on the expertise and experience of a particular lawyer or lawyers within a firm. As such, basic research should not be billed to _____ without specific authorization from the responsible Legal Department attorney.

F. **Timing.** As time considerations are often a critical element in the selection of outside counsel, any delay or unanticipated complications that may result in delay should be reported to the responsible _____ attorney as soon as possible.

G. **Staffing.** _____ will require that a specific attorney or attorneys be assigned to each particular matter. It is expected that, absent unforeseen circumstances, personnel specified in an engagement letter will be the only attorneys and paralegals to work on any given matter from start to finish. _____ will not be billed for "start up" costs of educating new staff due to personnel changes within the firm. Therefore, it is expected both as a matter of client relations and professional responsibility that attorneys assigned have the requisite skill and expertise necessary to represent _____ effectively. _____ will not be billed for time required for attorneys to become competent in areas outside of their acknowledged expertise. Every effort should be made with regard to maintaining the continuity of staffing a particular matter. The number of different lawyers who work on a particular matter should be held to the minimum number of lawyers needed to handle the matter efficiently. We encourage the use of less experienced attorneys and paralegals where appropriate. Attorneys should not perform a task for which a paralegal is qualified nor should a paralegal perform a task for which an administrative assistant is qualified. We expect only one attorney from the firm to attend meetings, depositions and arguments, unless prior arrangements and approval have been received from the responsible _____ attorney.

H. **Billing Matters.** _____ will not pay for time spent in administrative tasks such as opening a file, clearing conflicts of interest, preparing or reviewing invoices, discussions with in-house counsel regarding the contents of an invoice or time spent on matters solely for the convenience of out-side counsel. Time spent on preparing a strategic plan or budget will be paid for at the agreed upon billing rates. Travel time however is not reimbursed unless the time is actually used in performing services for _____ or is otherwise arranged with the responsible _____ attorney.

I. **Media Coverage.** _____ has an experienced communications department and does not routinely authorize outside counsel to discuss _____ matters with the media. Any media inquiries relating to _____ or a matter for which outside counsel has been engaged, should be referred to the _____ attorney. In some cases, the _____ Communications Department may request that outside counsel represent _____ with the media, but such arrangements must be made in advance and is solely within the discretion of the responsible _____ attorney.

IV. Consultations

_____ values outside counsel's expertise and advice and is always interested in steps that may be taken by _____ to reduce legal exposure. Therefore outside counsel will periodically meet with the responsible _____ attorney to review complex transactions, or cases in progress and discuss recommendations for a particular matter and for future business planning. Depending upon the circumstances, meetings may be held with General Counsel or other _____ lawyers, management staff, or members of the research staff or board of directors.

V. Client Communications/Representation

All client contact, information and communication should take place through the Legal Department. All requests for _____ or its affiliates' documents, results of internal investigations, data, or interviews should be coordinated through the Legal Department unless the responsible _____ attorney directs otherwise. Outside counsel may be asked to represent _____ affiliate corporations and sometimes the officers, directors and employees of these corporations. Therefore, although outside counsel may have multiple clients through such arrangement, the Legal Department will continue to be responsible to coordinate all legal services and communication with all such clients should include the responsible _____ attorney unless conflicts or other considerations necessitate otherwise.

VI. Service of Process/Documents

_____'s statutory agent for Service of Process will insure that any Service of Process, including any summons and complaints or other pleadings that are served on _____ will be forwarded to outside counsel in a timely manner. It is the responsibility of outside counsel to establish a litigation file and docket all pleadings so that timely responses are filed and no default is entered against _____ or any _____ affiliate.

VII. Billing Practices and Format

Use of proper billing practices and billing formats are of critical importance to insure payment for outside counsel services. As such all outside counsel providing services are requested to comply with following standards for billing.

A. **Billing Rates.** Before the commencement of work, an engagement letter must be executed. It will include the hourly rates agreed upon for all attorneys and paralegals providing services on a particular matter. There should be no increase in the hourly rates established for the individuals working on _____ matters during the calendar year. Any proposed increase in hourly rates should be communicated to the Legal Department before January 1.

B. **Billing.** A task-based billing format should be used for all invoices submitted to _____. Task-based billing formats require three elements: First, the outside counsel must record time in a single activity entry. Second, the time records must demonstrate a minimum amount of descriptive detail so that the billing data is intelligible upon review. Third, the time records should organize billing data on a task basis showing exactly what work was done during the billing period, who performed it and how much time was spent on each task and the hourly rate for that individual. Office conferences and third party communications should always identify the other participant to the topic discussed.

C. **No Block Billing.** Counsel should not combine different tasks performed by an attorney during one day that relate to a single billable matter into a single "block" entry. This practice makes it impossible to understand how much time was devoted to each of the several tasks combined in a single entry. _____ will not honor invoices submitted using this format.

D. **Costs and Disbursements.** All costs and disbursements (including lodging, travel, out-of-pocket expenses, copying service, transcripts and the like) must be included in the firm's statements with supporting documentation for all lodging and travel expenses (other than nominal amounts) and for any individual item whose cost is $25 or more. All expenses shall be the reasonable necessary actual net costs incurred and paid by the firm. All expenses are to be billed at cost. Please note that air travel, if any, must be at coach rates, advance purchase discount travel, otherwise expressly authorized by the responsible _____ attorney. Expenses for lodging, meals and transportation shall be at reasonable rates and counsel must exercise prudence at incurring such expenses. Travel time, including time spent traveling from a local office to our facilities, will not be reimbursed unless the time is actually spent performing services for _____. Non-reimbursable expenses include avoidable charges for unused guaranteed hotel reservations and charges for hotel movies and airline headsets, recreation and health club facilities, personal trip insurance, and other personal expenditures.

E. **Overhead Expenses.** Routine overhead costs, including, for example, administrative services, library services, clerical support, office supplies, postage, office copying, telecopying or fax filing, local telephone, file indexing, bill preparations, staff overtime, word processing and meals and snacks (unless while traveling out of town) shall be considered as included in the firm's hourly fees and not charged to

_____. _____ will not pay for time spent in firm administrative tasks, such as opening a file, clearing conflicts of interest, preparing and reviewing invoices, discussion with in-house counsel regarding the contents of an invoice or time spent on matters solely for the convenience of counsel.

VIII. Budgets

_____ expects outside counsel to develop a project budget for each matter. _____ understands the difficulty of predicting the amount of work required in a particular case or transaction; much depends upon the action and reactions of third parties. A request for a budget is a request that outside counsel make a conscientious effort to advise _____ of the various components of work that will be required in any representation and to consider how much work might reasonably cost so that the _____ Legal Department can make an informed decision regarding whether and how to proceed with the matter. Budgets should address the following:

A. **Transaction Matters:**

1. Identify the attorneys proposed to work on the transaction team. This should have been already reflected in the Engagement Letter.

2. Describe the broad paths expected to be required, e.g., key documents to be drafted, issues to be researched. If these are known, identify them specifically and approximate the number of hours required to perform them.

3. Describe the broad tasks that might be required. Even if the particular tasks are only a possibility rather than a likelihood, describe them and approximate the number of hours required in case the need arises.

4. Describe any travel and/or out of town meetings that are to be expected and the approximate cost of each.

5. If you feel that the budgeted numbers reflect an amount that does not adequately address the full range of a firm's work on a particular transaction or case, provide the additional information necessary in order to enable the responsible attorney to obtain a realistic picture of what the costs of the engagement may involve.

B. **Litigation:** Depending on the type of case, a budget will be required either for the complete handling of a case (from assignment through trial) or for particular periods, (e.g., the first 3 months of the case, followed by another budget for the following period; or for a period through discovery; then pretrial motions and then through trial).

IX. Settlement

The Legal Department is responsible to work with outside counsel regarding settlement of any litigation matter. The settlement of any case in litigation requires the approval of the General Counsel. Certain substantial settlements will also require the involvement of _____'s President.

X. Conflicts of Interest

_____ not, as a policy matter, prohibit a lawyer or law firm in all cases from representing clients whose interest have been or could become adverse to _____. However _____ retains the prerogative, where a conflict could arise or has arisen, to object to the representation and require the withdrawal of counsel in accordance with applicable professional rules. _____ requires that outside counsel identify and discuss with the responsible _____ attorney any potential legal conflicts or business conflicts that may arise affecting the engagement of the firm.

100. Service Evaluation and Repair Agreement

Equipment Owner Information:

NAME: _____

ADDRESS: _____

CITY: _____ STATE: _____ ZIP: _____

HOME PHONE: _____ WORK PHONE: _____

Description of Equipment:

MAKE: _____ MODEL: _____

SERIAL NUMBER: _____ COLOR: _____

APPROX. AGE: _____ PROBLEM:

_____

_____

_____

Diagnostic Fee (Must be paid prior to service evaluation)

$_____ Date Paid _____

Agreement

1. **Terms.** The Diagnostic Fee must be paid when the item is checked in for service and is non-refundable. When Company has completed its examination of the equipment, Company will contact the owner listed above to discuss the results of the examination. Owner may be presented with a Repair Price Quote. If a Repair Price Quote is provided, Owner must authorize the repair before Company will proceed to repair the Equipment. If the Repair is authorized the Diagnostic fee paid by Owner will be credited towards the Repair Price Quote

2. **Repair Price Quotes.** The price quoted to repair the Equipment is good for 5 business days from the date the Owner is notified by phone of the Quote. On the expiration of the fifth business day the Quote will no longer be honored and the Equipment must be picked up by Owner within thirty (30) days. Company relies on the Owner to accurately describe all problems in order to properly determine the cost of repair. If the problem description proves to be inaccurate or incomplete, additional charges may apply. Company may not be able to repair your Equipment through no fault of Company's and you will be informed if this is the case.

3. **Warranty.** Company's technicians will use generally recognized commercial practices and standards to resolve all reported issues. Company will re-repair any repair not performed in accordance with the foregoing warranty, provided that Company receives notice from Owner within thirty (30) days after the Equipment is returned to Owner. If Company is unable within a reasonable time to re-repair the Equipment, Company will refund the Repair Price Quote paid by Owner. These warranties will not apply if

Company determines that the re-repair is due to improper or inadequate maintenance or calibration or improper use or operation of the Equipment. THE ABOVE WARRANTIES ARE EXCLUSIVE AND NO OTHER WARRANTY, WHETHER WRITTEN OR ORAL, IS EXPRESSED OR IMPLIED. COMPANY SPECIFICALLY DISCLAIMS THE IMPLIED WARRANTIES OF MERCHANTABILITY AND FITNESS FOR A PARTICULAR PURPOSE.

4. **Abandonment.** Equipment not picked up by the Owner within 30 days of the date the Diagnostic Fee is paid is considered abandoned without notice and becomes the sole property of Company, which may dispose of the Equipment in any manner it chooses without payment or notice to Owner.

5. **Limitation of Liability.** COMPANY'S LIABILITY TO OWNER UNDER THIS AGREEMENT FOR DAMAGES OR LOSSES OF ANY KIND OR NATURE RESULTING FROM COMPANY'S BREACH OF THIS AGREEMENT OR NEGLIGENT CONDUCT SHALL BE LIMITED TO THE AMOUNT PAID TO COMPANY BY OWNER UNDER THIS AGREEMENT.

6. **Complete Agreement.** This agreement constitutes the complete agreement between Company and Owner and supersedes all prior or contemporaneous agreements or representations, written or oral, concerning the subject matter of this agreement. This agreement may not be modified or amended except in writing signed by Company and Owner (no other act, document, usage or custom shall be deemed to amend or modify this agreement).

Acceptance of Terms and Authorization for Evaluation

My signature below indicates that I accept these terms and conditions and authorize Company to conduct any and all evaluations which it, in its sole discretion, determines are necessary to diagnose the condition of the equipment listed above.

Owner: _____ Date: _____

Repair Price Quote

Date of Quote: _____ Technician: _____

Who was contacted: _____ How/At what number: _____

Repair Authorized: _____ Date Promised: _____

Acknowledgement of Return of Equipment

I acknowledge that the Equipment referenced above has been returned to me:

Owner: _____ Date: _____

CHAPTER 11

When Business and Family Mix

BUSINESS OWNERS ARE GENERALLY MORE apt to dive into a strategic plan than one that pertains to their estate plan. There are a number of ways to use an estate plan, and as a business owner, it's wise to understand the legal framework surrounding your assets. Minimize potential legal problems and financial insecurities with the estate planning forms in this chapter. These forms help business owners plan for business succession or transition. Whether you want to leave a charitable economic legacy or give everything to your children, there are forms in this chapter to help you plan your estate legally and effectively.

The example of a *Simple Will* included in this chapter shows a properly executed legal document transferring property or money to one's heirs or beneficiaries through a probate proceeding.

Use the *Asset Value Test* to determine the amount attributable to each share if the company closes. Keep in mind that the true value of the assets may not be the total values shown by a company's balance sheet, since it's not the function of balance sheets to value assets.

Determine the dollar value required to insure your business and life with the *Calculating Your Life Insurance Needs Form*. This form can help you understand exactly how much life insurance you should have to protect future earnings. You'll find the more you know about your personal and business finances, the more accurate your needs analysis will be.

Use the *Family Documentation Form* to define your genealogical connections. The family documentation form enables you to identify your spouse, former spouses, children, parents, siblings, spouse's siblings, and even former spouse's siblings if applicable. Customize the form to distinguish who the members of your your family are.

The *Sample Family Trust* (included on the website that supports this book shows what a discretionary trust set up to hold a family's assets or to conduct a family business looks like. A family trust allows family members to share the tax burden and also protects family assets.

Use the *Common Distribution of Provisions Form* to show how beneficiaries in a simple will are specified and designated to receive assets or a percentage of an asset's value. Meanwhile, the *Common Trust Distribution Form* is a simplified example of how to state who will receive how much of the estate's assets and when.

To get a full picture of your combined business and personal finances, use the *Financial Summary Worksheet* to quickly calculate a current picture of your personal and business finances. The *Total Assets and Liabilities Worksheet* helps itemize investment assets and can be used as a reference for progress measurements. It is broken into three parts to help you better understand your investments, your total financial picture, and your annual progress.

A *fiduciary*—the person(s) who holds in trust property in which another person has the titles or benefits—files the *IRS Form 1041 U.S. Income Tax Return for Estates and Trusts* to report income, deductions, gains, and losses associated with the estate or trust. *Form 104-K* should be filled out for each beneficiary of a trust or estate to itemize the various categories of income, such as dividends and capital gains. One such form should be sent to each beneficiary each year, and there is a box to be checked on the form to indicate if it's the final year of payments from the estate or trust.

Refer to *IRS Form 706* to see what information needs to be filed on certain estates of a deceased resident or citizen. *IRS Form 709 for Gift Tax Returns* is used to report transfers subject to the federal gift and certain generation-skipping transfer (GST) taxes, and to figure the tax, if any, due on those transfers.

Use *Publication 950* (on the Web) to understand estate and gift tax filing requirements. According to the IRS, if you give someone money or property during your life, you may be subject to federal gift tax. The money and property you own when you die (your estate) may be subject to federal estate tax, and the gross income of your estate may be subject to federal income tax. The purpose of this publication is to give you a general understanding of when these taxes apply and when they do not.

101. A Simplified Simple Will

LAST WILL OF BONITA K. TOVAH

I, Bonita K. Tovah, formerly known by my maiden name, Bonita Sansei, and my prior married name, Bonita Bellfleur, a resident of Orange County, California, declare that this is my will. I hereby revoke all prior wills and codicils.

[Your will should identify all names that you have formerly used, including your maiden name, any prior married names, and any variation that you may have used. For example, if Bonita also goes by her middle name, she should include the phase: "also known as Katherine Tovah."]

ARTICLE ONE. INTRODUCTORY PROVISIONS

1.1. Disposal of Property. I intend that this will dispose of all of my property.

[One of the things that gives a will legal effect is a clear expression that you intend for it to function as a will and transfer your property.]

1.2. Exercise of Power of Appointment. I do not exercise any power of appointment that I now possess or that hereafter may be conferred on me.
[Sometimes your spouse or your parents–and on rare occasions someone else–will designate in their will or trust that you can designate who will ultimately receive assets that they have set aside (with the ultimate distribution occurring either upon their death or upon your death). This is called a "power of appointment." If you intend to designate someone (for example, your children) to receive these assets, this provision in your will should specifically refer to the document giving you the power of appointment, and indicate to whom you elect to leave the property.]

1.3. Contract Affecting Will. I have not made any agreement requiring me to leave assets to anyone.
[Although rare, occasionally contracts are entered into obligating a person to leave assets to a specified person or group of people. For example, a divorce settlement may obligate one spouse, or both, to leave certain assets only to the children from the marriage.]

ARTICLE TWO. IDENTITY OF SPOUSE AND CHILDREN

2.1. Spouse. I am married to Moses R. Tovah, and all references to "my husband" are to him.

2.2. Children. I have two children from a prior marriage, whose father is Sam Bellfleur, Sr., as follows:

Name	Date of Birth
Sam Bellfleur, Jr.	December 23, 1996
Sarah Bellfleur	November 18, 2001

All references in this will to my "child," "children," or "issue," refer to the above children and any children later born to or adopted by me.

2.3. Deceased Children. I have no deceased children

ARTICLE THREE. SPECIFIC GIFTS

3.1. Specific Gifts. I give the following items of property as indicated below:

(a) I give to my daughter, Sarah Bellfleur, all of my jewelry if she survives me. If she does not survive me, I leave my jewelry to my female grandchildren, to be distributed among them as they shall agree (or if they cannot agree, as my executor determines). If my daughter is not alive and I have no female grandchildren, then this gift shall lapse and become part of the residue of my estate.

[Aside from being sexist, this provision works to get some specific property to your daughter. When leaving property to anyone, you need to think about what you want to happen to the property if your chosen beneficiary passes away before you do. This provision addresses the issue by leaving the jewelry to an entirely new group of people (as opposed to "Sarah's children") since the female grandchildren may be either Sarah's daughters or Sam's daughters.]

(b) I give to my son, Sam Bellfleur, my 2003 Mustang convertible, if he survives me. If he does not survive me, then this gift shall lapse and become part of the residue of my estate.

[This provision may or may not work, depending on what is your real intent. If you are leaving Sam the Mustang convertible because he always loved that car, then the provision works well. However, if you are leaving the car to Sam to offset leaving the jewelry to his sister, this provision will not work if you have replaced the Mustang before you die. Even if you now own a Porsche convertible, that won't benefit

Sam because this provision is very specific: Sam gets the Mustang convertible. If you no longer own the Mustang, Sam does not receive anything under this provision (and the Porsche will go wherever you have left assets not specifically assigned to a named individual, sometimes referred to as the "residue of your estate").]

(c) I give to my friend, Erica D. Grate, $50,000, if she survives me. If she does not survive me, this gift shall lapse and become part of the residue of my estate.

[Be very careful when leaving cash bequests since the rule of law is that "specific" bequests will be paid first. This means if your estate has gone down drastically in value, either due to bad investments or to huge medical bills, Erica will still get the full $50,000 and your residuary beneficiaries may get less than you intended. For example, if you were worth $1 million when you wrote your will, it made sense to leave your friend, Erica, $50,000 since your spouse and children will still receive $950,000. If your medical bills for the last year of your life are $800,000, then leaving $50,000 to Erica and $150,000

split between your spouse and children probably doesn't make sense. When I draft documents leaving cash bequests, I usually use language like: "I leave Erica the lesser of $50,000 or 5 percent of the then-value of my estate." That way, if the estate is only worth $200,000 when you die, Erica will get $10,000 and your spouse and children will share $190,000.]

ARTICLE FOUR. RESIDUARY PROVISIONS

4.1. Disposition of Residue. I leave the residue of my estate as follows: (1) two-thirds (2/3) to my husband, if he survives me, and (2) one-third (1/3) to my children, in equal shares. If my husband does not survive me, his share should become part of the share for my children. If either child of mine does not survive me, that child's share should go to that child's issue, in equal shares. If a child of mine does not survive me and does not have any living issue at the time of my death, then that child's share should go to my other child (or, if that child is also not living, then to that child's issue). If neither child survives me, and neither child has issue living at the time of my death, then my children's share should go to my spouse.

[This provision does some things well and other things not so well. Note the detailed provisions for handling property if one or more of your beneficiaries die before you. Thinking those distribution provisions through carefully is good. On the other hand, if you have any ownership interest in the house that you and your spouse have been living in, this provision may not be good since it does nothing to make sure your spouse can continue living in the house. You need to consider whether you own any assets that should be solely in one person's control before including language that divides your assets between two or more individuals.]

ARTICLE FIVE. EXECUTOR

5.1. Executor. I nominate my husband as executor of this will.

5.2. Successor Executors. If my husband is unable (for any reason) or unwilling to serve as executor, I appoint the following as successor executor, in the order indicated,:

First, my friend, Erica D. Grate;
Second, National Trust Company.

[Selection of an executor is important. This person will be responsible for collecting all of your assets and seeing that they are distributed as you have directed in your will. During the probate process, it may be necessary for your executor to make decisions regarding investment of the assets during the year or two that probate is ongoing, to decide whether or not to challenge any claims made by people claiming to be owed money by you, or to mediate disagreements among your beneficiaries. Make sure the person you select for this job is someone who is completely trustworthy, has the common sense to make the necessary decisions (and will know when to seek the help of professional advisors), and is able and willing to deal with any stress that may arise from disputes among your beneficiaries. If you cannot think of someone who has all the characteristics needed, then consider designating a bank or trust company to serve as executor. It will cost money, but the job will be done properly.]

5.4. Bond. No bond or undertaking shall be required of any executor nominated in this will.

[A bond is an insurance policy that will reimburse your estate for any missing assets if your executor acts improperly. The premium for the bond, if you require one, will be paid from the assets in your estate (and reduce the amount going to your beneficiaries). Bond is not required for a bank or trust company, but should be considered if you are appointing an individual. As a general rule, do not appoint someone—friend or relative—unless you have known them a long time and observed them in a variety of

situations, so that you are sure they have the integrity needed for the job. If you have any doubts regarding their integrity, I recommend that you cross them off the list rather than require a bond.]

5.5. Independent Administration. The executor shall have full authority to administer my estate under the California Independent Administration of Estates Act.

["Independent" or "unsupervised" administration of your estate is a simplified process that allows your executor to take most actions necessary to collect your assets, sell assets that need to be sold, and prepare to distribute your assets, with minimal court supervision. If you do not expressly permit independent administration of your estate, a good number of the actions your executor will need to take can only be accomplished after scheduling a hearing and getting express approval from the judge (unless your beneficiaries unanimously agree to waive this requirement). This can delay distribution of assets to your beneficiaries and can result in increased costs of administration. You should consider permitting independent administration unless you anticipate disagreements between your beneficiaries (in which case, the additional court supervision may help keep the disputes under control).]

5.6. Powers of Executor. Subject to any limitations stated elsewhere in this will, the executor shall have, in addition to all of the powers now or hereafter conferred on executors by law, and any powers enumerated elsewhere in this will, the power to perform any of the acts specified in this section:

[An exhaustive list of powers should be included here, so that your executor will be equipped to deal with everything that comes up in your probate.]

5.7. Incapacitated Persons. If any beneficiary is a minor, or it appears to the executor that any beneficiary is incapacitated, incompetent, or for any reason not able to receive payments or make intelligent or responsible use of the payments, then the executor may make payments to the beneficiary's conservator or guardian; to the beneficiary's custodian under the Uniform Gifts to Minors Act or Uniform Transfers to Minors Act of any state (including a custodian selected by the executor); to one or more suitable persons deemed proper by the executor (such as a relative of the beneficiary, or to accounts in the beneficiary's name with financial institutions. The receipt of payments by any of the above shall satisfy the executor's obligation to distribute assets to that beneficiary.

[Make sure that a provision like this is in your will so your executor will not be faced with the expensive proposition of bringing a court proceeding to appoint a conservator if one of your beneficiaries is under 18 or is physically or mentally incapacitated at the time the assets are to be distributed.]

ARTICLE SIX. CONCLUDING PROVISIONS

6.1. Simultaneous Death. If any beneficiary under this will and I die simultaneously, or if it cannot be established by clear and convincing evidence whether that beneficiary or I died first, I shall be deemed to have survived that beneficiary, and this will shall be construed accordingly.

6.2. Period of Survivorship. For the purposes of this will, a beneficiary shall not be deemed to have survived me if that beneficiary dies within thirty (30) days after my death.

6.3. No Contest Clause. If any person (including any entity or charity), directly or indirectly, contests the validity of this will, or any codicil to this will, in whole or in part, or opposes, objects to, or seeks to invalidate any of its provisions, or seeks to succeed to any part of my estate otherwise than in the manner specified in this will, any gift or other interest given to that person under this will shall be revoked and shall be disposed of as if he or she had predeceased me without issue.

[This can be a very important part of your will. Will contests can tie up your estate for several years, and can easily cost hundreds of thousands of dollars in legal fees. A "no-contest" provision disinherits any beneficiary who challenges your will. However, if you have intentionally left nothing to one of your children, the no-contest clause has no affect since that child has nothing to lose. Unless you are so upset with that child (or spouse) that you cannot bring yourself to leave him or her anything, it is usually better to leave enough to the disfavored child so that there is something to lose by contesting the will. Also, note the last two words of the no-contest clause; "without issue." These words are important. Without them, if a child of yours successfully contests the will, the no-contest clause would prevent the child from receiving any portion of your estate, but that child's share could go to his or her children. Often, this is an acceptable outcome for your child and he or she will not be deterred from bringing the legal challenge. By adding the words "without issue," you are disinheriting any child who challenges your will and also disinheriting that child's children and grandchildren. The result is that the child cannot benefit, even indirectly, from challenging the will.]

6.4. Definition of Incapacity. For purposes of this will, a person shall be deemed "incapacitated" if and for so long as a court of competent jurisdiction has made a finding to that effect, or a guardian or conservator of that person's estate or person duly appointed by a court of competent jurisdiction is serving, or upon certification by two physicians licensed to practice under the laws of the state where the person is domiciled at the time of the certification, that the person is unable properly to care for himself or herself or for his or her property. The latter certification shall be made by each physician in a written declaration under penalty of perjury.

Executed on _____, 20_____, at _____, California.

_____

Bonita K. Tovah

[Witness Page]

On the date written above, we, the undersigned, each being present at the same time, witnessed the signing of this instrument by Bonita K. Tovah. At that time, Bonita K. Tovah appeared to us to be of sound mind and memory and, to the best of our knowledge, was not acting under fraud, duress, menace, or undue influence. Understanding this instrument, which consists of _____ pages including the

pages on which the signature of Bonita K. Tovah and our signatures appear, to be the will of Bonita K. Tovah, we subscribe our names as witnesses thereto.

We declare under penalty of perjury under the laws of the State of California that the foregoing is true and correct.

Executed on _____, 20_____, at _____, California.

_____ residing at _____
Signature

_____,
Print Name

_____ residing at _____
Signature

_____
Print Name

[This witness page is critical. Without two witnesses—three in some states—your will is not valid. The witnesses should be at least 18 years old, legally competent, and not receiving assets under the will. A neighbor, co-worker, or friend, can be an excellent witness. If you prepare your own will without the help of any estate planning attorney, make sure you comply with all the formalities required in your state. Do not, do not, DO NOT use this form as it is incomplete and may not meet the formalities required in your state. This form is only useful in illustrating the issues that you need to consider in designing your estate plan.]

102. Asset Value Test

Spouse			Children		
Asset	FMV	Debt	Asset	FMV	Debt
Residence	650,000	320,000	Life Ins.	250,000	–
Bank Acct.	70,000	–	Bank Acct.	50,000	–
401(k)	150,000	–			
Car	25,000	15,000			
Total	895,000	335,000	Total	300,000	–
Total FMV	895,000		Total FMV	300,000	
Less Total Debt	335,000		Less Total Debt	0	
Net Value	660,000		Net Value	300,000	

103. Calculating Your Life Insurance Needs

While there are hundreds of ways to compute your life insurance needs, this simple formula works for many families.

This example assumes a family with two children (who will attend college at a cost of $120,000 each), a mortgage balance of $350,000, existing savings totaling $135,000, and monthly living expenses of $7,000 (including a mortgage payment of $2,300).

Mortgage payoff	$ 350,000
College expenses	240,000
Monthly income fund[1]	1,128,000
Total needed	$1,718,000
Less existing savings	$135,000
Total policy needed	$1,583,000

1. This is the amount necessary to generate $4,700 each month ($7,000 less the $2,300 mortgage payment), assuming it is invested at a 5% rate of return. ($4,700 x 12 = $56,400 per year. $56,400 ÷ .05 = $1,128,000.)

104. Your Family Documentation

You:

Name: _____ Birth date _____ Soc Sec #_____

Prior Names:_____

Spouse:

Name: _____ Birth date _____ Soc Sec #_____

Prior Names:_____

Date of Marriage: _____ City/State of Ceremony _____

Residences During Marriage:

Current: _____ Since _____

Prior City/State: _____ From _____To _____

Prior City/State: _____ From _____To _____

Prior City/State: _____ From _____To _____

Prior City/State: _____ From _____To _____

Children of this Marriage:

Name: _____ Birth date _____ Soc Sec #_____

Address: _____ Phone:_____

Name: _____ Birth date _____ Soc Sec #_____

Address: _____ Phone:_____

Name: _____ Birth date _____ Soc Sec #_____

Address: _____ Phone:_____

Name: _____ Birth date _____ Soc Sec #_____

Address: _____ Phone:_____

Your Prior Marriages:

Prior Spouse: _____ Marriage Date: _____ Disso. Date: _____

Child: _____ Birth date _____ Soc Sec #_____

Address: _____ Phone:_____

Child: _____ Birth date _____ Soc Sec #_____

Address: _____ Phone:_____

Child: _____ Birth date _____ Soc Sec #_____

Address: _____ Phone:_____

Child: _____ Birth date _____ Soc Sec #_____

Address: _____ Phone:_____

Spouse's Prior Marriages:

Prior Spouse: _____Marriage Date: _____ Dissolution Date: _____

Child: _____ Birth date _____ Soc Sec #_____

Address: _____ Phone:_____

Child: _____ Birth date _____ Soc Sec #_____

Address: _____ Phone:_____

Child: _____ Birth date _____ Soc Sec #_____

Address: _____ Phone:_____

Child: _____ Birth date _____ Soc Sec #_____

Address: _____ Phone:_____

Child: _____ Birth date _____ Soc Sec #_____

Grandchildren:

Name: _____ Child of: _____

Name: _____ Child of: _____

Name: _____ Child of: _____

Name: _____ Child of: _____

Name: _____ Child of: _____

Name: _____ Child of: _____

Name: _____ Child of: _____

Your Parents (if living):

Father's Name: _____ Address: _____ Phone: _____

Mother's Name: _____ Address: _____ Phone: _____

Spouse's Parents (if living):

Father's Name: _____ Address: _____ Phone: _____

Mother's Name: _____ Address: _____ Phone: _____

Your Siblings:

Name: _____ Address: _____ Phone: _____

Name: _____ Address: _____ Phone: _____

Name: _____ Address: _____ Phone: _____

Name: _____ Address: _____ Phone: _____

Name: _____ Address: _____ Phone: _____

Name: _____ Address: _____ Phone: _____

Nieces/Nephews:

Name: _____ Child of: _____

Name: _____ Child of: _____

Name: _____ Child of: _____

Name: _____ Child of: _____

Name: _____ Child of: _____

Name: _____ Child of: _____

Name: _____ Child of: _____

Almost Family (people you may consider including in your will; for example, close friends, former in-laws, former stepchildren, former stepparent)

Name: _____ Address: _____ Phone: _____

Name: _____ Address: _____ Phone: _____

Name: _____ Address: _____ Phone: _____

Name: _____ Address: _____ Phone: _____

Charities You Support (and that you may desire to include in your estate plan)

Name: _____ Address: _____

Name: _____ Address: _____

Name: _____ Address: _____

105. Common Distribution Provisions and Common Trust Distribution Provisions

Will

I hereby leave my assets as follows:

- My jewelry and personal effects to my wife if she is alive, or alternately to my children in equal shares.

- My personal residence to my wife.

- My car to my son, Mario.

- Bank account of Dad, number 121855, to my daughter, Dakota.

- $10,000 to Easter Seals Disability Services.

- The balance of my estate to my wife if she is alive, or alternatively to my children in equal shares.

Trust

- After my death, the trustee should distribute money to my children from time to time, as necessary to maintain the lifestyle each child had immediately prior to my death.

- As each child turns 27, the trustee should distribute to that child 15% of his or her share of the trust.

- As each child turns 30, the trustee should distribute to that child 30% of his or her share of the trust.

- As each child turns 33, the trustee should distribute to that child the balance of his or her share of the trust.

106. Financial Summary Worksheet

ASSETS

Checking Accounts:

Bank name: _____ Account No. _____ Balance _____

Bank name: _____ Account No. _____ Balance _____

Total Checking Accounts _____

Savings Accounts:

Bank name: _____ Account No. _____ Balance _____

Bank name: _____ Account No. _____ Balance _____

Bank name: _____ Account No. _____ Balance _____

Bank name: _____ Account No. _____ Balance _____

Total Savings Accounts _____

Brokerage Accounts:

Brokerage name: _____ Account No. _____ Balance _____

Brokerage name: _____ Account No. _____ Balance _____

Total Brokerage Accounts _____

Certificates of Deposit:

Bank name: _____ Account No. _____ Balance _____

Bank name: _____ Account No. _____ Balance _____

Bank name: _____ Account No. _____ Balance _____

Total Certificates of Deposit _____

Money Market Accounts:

Bank name: _____ Account No. _____ Balance _____

Bank name: _____ Account No. _____ Balance _____

Total Money Market Accounts _____

Mutual Funds:

Fund Name: _____ Account No. _____ Value _____

Fund Name: _____ Account No. _____ Value _____

Fund Name: _____ Account No. _____ Value _____

Fund Name: _____ Account No. _____ Value _____

Total Value Mutual Funds _____

Stocks:

Stock: _____ No. of shares _____ Value _____

Stock: _____ No. of shares _____ Value _____

Stock: _____ No. of shares _____ Value _____

Stock: _____ No. of shares _____ Value _____

Total Value Stocks _____

Retirement Accounts:

Bank/Brokerage: _____ Account No. _____ Value _____

Primary Beneficiary _____ Alternate _____

Bank/Brokerage: _____ Account No. _____ Value _____

Primary Beneficiary _____ Alternate _____

Bank/Brokerage: _____ Account No. _____ Value _____

Primary Beneficiary _____ Alternate _____

Total Value Retirement Accounts _____

Business Interests:

Description _____ Value _____

Description _____ Value _____

Total Business Interests Value _____

REAL ESTATE

Family Residence:

Address: _____ Mortgage _____ Fair Market Value _____

Family Residence Value _____

Rental Property:

Address: _____ Mortgage _____ Fair Market Value _____

Address: _____ Mortgage _____ Fair Market Value _____

Address: _____ Mortgage _____ Fair Market Value _____

Total Rental Property Value _____

Total Rental Property Mortgage _____

Other Real Estate:

Address: _____ Mortgage _____ Fair Market Value _____

Address: _____ Mortgage _____ Fair Market Value _____

Address: _____ Mortgage _____ Fair Market Value _____

Total Other Real Estate Value _____

Total Other Real Estate Mortgage _____

Automobiles:

Make _____ Model _____ Year _____ Value _____

Loan Balance _____

Make _____ Model _____ Year _____ Value _____

Loan Balance _____

Make _____ Model _____ Year _____ Value _____

Loan Balance _____

Total Automobile Value _____

Total Automobile Loans _____

Collectibles (valuable jewelry, antiques, or artwork):

Description _____ Value _____

Description _____ Value _____

Description _____ Value _____

Description _____ Value _____

Description _____ Value _____

Description _____ Value _____

Total Collectibles Value _____

107. Total Assets and Liabilities Worksheet

Assets

Total Checking Accounts _____

Total Savings Accounts _____

Total Brokerage Accounts _____

Total Certificates of Deposit _____

Total Money Market Accounts _____

Total Mutual Funds _____

Total Stocks _____

Total Retirement Accounts _____

Total Business Interests Value _____

Family Residence Value _____

Total Rental Property Value _____

Total Other Real Estate Value _____

Total Automobile Value _____

Total Collectibles Value _____

Total Life Insurance Benefits _____

Total Life Insurance Cash Value _____

Total Assets _____

Liabilities

Family Residence Mortgage _____

Total Rental Property Mortgage _____

Total Other Real Estate Mortgage _____

Total Automobile Loans _____

Total Life Insurance Loan Balance _____

Total Other Loan Balance _____

Total Liabilities _____

Net Assets (Assets less Liabilities) _____

108. Form 1041 U.S. Income Tax Return for Estates and Trusts

Form **1041**	Department of the Treasury—Internal Revenue Service **U.S. Income Tax Return for Estates and Trusts**	**2009**	OMB No. 1545-0092

A Type of entity (see instr.):	For calendar year 2009 or fiscal year beginning , 2009, and ending , 20	
☐ Decedent's estate	Name of estate or trust (If a grantor type trust, see page 14 of the instructions.)	C Employer identification number
☐ Simple trust		
☐ Complex trust	Name and title of fiduciary	D Date entity created
☐ Qualified disability trust		
☐ ESBT (S portion only)	Number, street, and room or suite no. (If a P.O. box, see page 15 of the instructions.)	E Nonexempt charitable and split-interest trusts, check applicable boxes (see page 16 of the instr.):
☐ Grantor type trust		☐ Described in section 4947(a)(1)
☐ Bankruptcy estate–Ch. 7		
☐ Bankruptcy estate–Ch. 11	City or town, state, and ZIP code	☐ Not a private foundation
☐ Pooled income fund		☐ Described in section 4947(a)(2)

B Number of Schedules K-1 attached (see instructions) ▶	F Check applicable boxes:	☐ Initial return ☐ Final return ☐ Amended return ☐ Change in fiduciary ☐ Change in fiduciary's name	☐ Change in trust's name ☐ Change in fiduciary's address

G Check here if the estate or filing trust made a section 645 election . . . . ▶ ☐

Income	1	Interest income	1	
	2a	Total ordinary dividends	2a	
	b	Qualified dividends allocable to: (1) Beneficiaries _____ (2) Estate or trust _____		
	3	Business income or (loss). Attach Schedule C or C-EZ (Form 1040)	3	
	4	Capital gain or (loss). Attach Schedule D (Form 1041)	4	
	5	Rents, royalties, partnerships, other estates and trusts, etc. Attach Schedule E (Form 1040)	5	
	6	Farm income or (loss). Attach Schedule F (Form 1040)	6	
	7	Ordinary gain or (loss). Attach Form 4797	7	
	8	Other income. List type and amount _____	8	
	9	Total income. Combine lines 1, 2a, and 3 through 8 . . . . ▶	9	
Deductions	10	Interest. Check if Form 4952 is attached ▶ ☐	10	
	11	Taxes	11	
	12	Fiduciary fees	12	
	13	Charitable deduction (from Schedule A, line 7)	13	
	14	Attorney, accountant, and return preparer fees	14	
	15a	Other deductions not subject to the 2% floor (attach schedule)	15a	
	b	Allowable miscellaneous itemized deductions subject to the 2% floor	15b	
	16	Add lines 10 through 15b . . . . ▶	16	
	17	Adjusted total income or (loss). Subtract line 16 from line 9 17		
	18	Income distribution deduction (from Schedule B, line 15). Attach Schedules K-1 (Form 1041)	18	
	19	Estate tax deduction including certain generation-skipping taxes (attach computation) . .	19	
	20	Exemption	20	
	21	Add lines 18 through 20 . . . . ▶	21	
Tax and Payments	22	Taxable income. Subtract line 21 from line 17. If a loss, see page 23 of the instructions . . .	22	
	23	Total tax (from Schedule G, line 7)	23	
	24	Payments: a 2009 estimated tax payments and amount applied from 2008 return . . .	24a	
	b	Estimated tax payments allocated to beneficiaries (from Form 1041-T)	24b	
	c	Subtract line 24b from line 24a	24c	
	d	Tax paid with Form 7004 (see page 24 of the instructions)	24d	
	e	Federal income tax withheld. If any is from Form(s) 1099, check ▶ ☐	24e	
		Other payments: f Form 2439 _____ ; g Form 4136 _____ ; Total ▶	24h	
	25	Total payments. Add lines 24c through 24e, and 24h . . . . ▶	25	
	26	Estimated tax penalty (see page 24 of the instructions)	26	
	27	Tax due. If line 25 is smaller than the total of lines 23 and 26, enter amount owed	27	
	28	Overpayment. If line 25 is larger than the total of lines 23 and 26, enter amount overpaid . .	28	
	29	Amount of line 28 to be: a Credited to 2010 estimated tax ▶ ; b Refunded ▶	29	

Sign Here — Under penalties of perjury, I declare that I have examined this return, including accompanying schedules and statements, and to the best of my knowledge and belief, it is true, correct, and complete. Declaration of preparer (other than taxpayer) is based on all information of which preparer has any knowledge.

▶ Signature of fiduciary or officer representing fiduciary	Date	▶	EIN of fiduciary if a financial institution	May the IRS discuss this return with the preparer shown below (see instr.)? ☐ Yes ☐ No

Paid Preparer's Use Only	Preparer's signature ▶	Date	Check if self-employed ☐	Preparer's SSN or PTIN
	Firm's name (or yours if self-employed), address, and ZIP code ▶		EIN	
			Phone no.	

For Privacy Act and Paperwork Reduction Act Notice, see the separate instructions.   Cat. No. 11370H   Form **1041** (2009)

Form 1041 (2009)   Page **2**

Schedule A	Charitable Deduction. Do not complete for a simple trust or a pooled income fund.		
1	Amounts paid or permanently set aside for charitable purposes from gross income (see page 25)	1	
2	Tax-exempt income allocable to charitable contributions (see page 25 of the instructions) . . .	2	
3	Subtract line 2 from line 1	3	
4	Capital gains for the tax year allocated to corpus and paid or permanently set aside for charitable purposes	4	
5	Add lines 3 and 4	5	
6	Section 1202 exclusion allocable to capital gains paid or permanently set aside for charitable purposes (see page 25 of the instructions)	6	
7	Charitable deduction. Subtract line 6 from line 5. Enter here and on page 1, line 13	7	

Schedule B	Income Distribution Deduction		
1	Adjusted total income (see page 26 of the instructions)	1	
2	Adjusted tax-exempt interest	2	
3	Total net gain from Schedule D (Form 1041), line 15, column (1) (see page 26 of the instructions) .	3	
4	Enter amount from Schedule A, line 4 (minus any allocable section 1202 exclusion)	4	
5	Capital gains for the tax year included on Schedule A, line 1 (see page 26 of the instructions) . .	5	
6	Enter any gain from page 1, line 4, as a negative number. If page 1, line 4, is a loss, enter the loss as a positive number	6	
7	Distributable net income. Combine lines 1 through 6. If zero or less, enter -0-	7	
8	If a complex trust, enter accounting income for the tax year as determined under the governing instrument and applicable local law .	8		
9	Income required to be distributed currently	9	
10	Other amounts paid, credited, or otherwise required to be distributed	10	
11	Total distributions. Add lines 9 and 10. If greater than line 8, see page 27 of the instructions . .	11	
12	Enter the amount of tax-exempt income included on line 11	12	
13	Tentative income distribution deduction. Subtract line 12 from line 11	13	
14	Tentative income distribution deduction. Subtract line 2 from line 7. If zero or less, enter -0- . .	14	
15	Income distribution deduction. Enter the smaller of line 13 or line 14 here and on page 1, line 18	15	

Schedule G	Tax Computation (see page 27 of the instructions)			
1	Tax: a Tax on taxable income (see page 27 of the instructions) . .	1a		
	b Tax on lump-sum distributions. Attach Form 4972	1b		
	c Alternative minimum tax (from Schedule I (Form 1041), line 56)	1c		
	d Total. Add lines 1a through 1c . . . . ▶	1d		
2a	Foreign tax credit. Attach Form 1116	2a		
b	Other nonbusiness credits (attach schedule)	2b		
c	General business credit. Attach Form 3800	2c		
d	Credit for prior year minimum tax. Attach Form 8801	2d		
3	Total credits. Add lines 2a through 2d . . . . ▶	3		
4	Subtract line 3 from line 1d. If zero or less, enter -0-	4		
5	Recapture taxes. Check if from: ☐ Form 4255 ☐ Form 8611	5		
6	Household employment taxes. Attach Schedule H (Form 1040)	6		
7	Total tax. Add lines 4 through 6. Enter here and on page 1, line 23 . . . . ▶	7		

	Other Information	Yes	No
1	Did the estate or trust receive tax-exempt income? If "Yes," attach a computation of the allocation of expenses Enter the amount of tax-exempt interest income and exempt-interest dividends ▶ $ _____		
2	Did the estate or trust receive all or any part of the earnings (salary, wages, and other compensation) of any individual by reason of a contract assignment or similar arrangement?		
3	At any time during calendar year 2009, did the estate or trust have an interest in or a signature or other authority over a bank, securities, or other financial account in a foreign country? . . . . See page 30 of the instructions for exceptions and filing requirements for Form TD F 90-22.1. If "Yes," enter the name of the foreign country ▶ _____		
4	During the tax year, did the estate or trust receive a distribution from, or was it the grantor of, or transferor to, a foreign trust? If "Yes," the estate or trust may have to file Form 3520. See page 30 of the instructions		
5	Did the estate or trust receive, or pay, any qualified residence interest on seller-provided financing? If "Yes," see page 30 for required attachment		
6	If this is an estate or a complex trust making the section 663(b) election, check here (see page 30) . . ▶ ☐		
7	To make a section 643(e)(3) election, attach Schedule D (Form 1041), and check here (see page 30) . . ▶ ☐		
8	If the decedent's estate has been open for more than 2 years, attach an explanation for the delay in closing the estate, and check here ▶ ☐		
9	Are any present or future trust beneficiaries skip persons? See page 30 of the instructions		

Form **1041** (2009)

109. Form 706 U.S. Estate (and Generation-Skipping Transfer) Tax Return

Form **706** (Rev. October 2006) Department of the Treasury Internal Revenue Service	**United States Estate (and Generation-Skipping Transfer) Tax Return** Estate of a citizen or resident of the United States (see separate instructions). To be filed for decedents dying after December 31, 2005, and before January 1, 2007.	OMB No. 1545-0015

Part 1—Decedent and Executor

1a Decedent's first name and middle initial (and maiden name, if any)	1b Decedent's last name	2 Decedent's Social Security No.

3a County, state, and ZIP code, or foreign country, of legal residence (domicile) at time of death	3b Year domicile established	4 Date of birth	5 Date of death

6b Executor's address (number and street including apartment or suite no. or rural route; city, town, or post office; state; and ZIP code) and phone no.

6a Name of executor (see page 4 of the instructions)	

6c Executor's social security number (see page 4 of the instructions)	Phone no. ( )

7a Name and location of court where will was probated or estate administered	7b Case number

8 If decedent died testate, check here ▶ ☐ and attach a certified copy of the will.   9 If you extended the time to file this Form 706, check here ▶ ☐

10 If Schedule R-1 is attached, check here ▶ ☐

Part 2—Tax Computation

1	Total gross estate less exclusion (from Part 5—Recapitulation, page 3, item 12)	1
2	Tentative total allowable deductions (from Part 5—Recapitulation, page 3, item 22)	2
3a	Tentative taxable estate (before state death tax deduction) (subtract line 2 from line 1)	3a
b	State death tax deduction	3b
c	Taxable estate (subtract line 3b from line 3a)	3c
4	Adjusted taxable gifts (total taxable gifts (within the meaning of section 2503) made by the decedent after December 31, 1976, other than gifts that are includible in decedent's gross estate (section 2001(b)))	4
5	Add lines 3c and 4	5
6	Tentative tax on the amount on line 5 from Table A on page 4 of the instructions	6
7	Total gift tax paid or payable with respect to gifts made by the decedent after December 31, 1976. Include gift taxes by the decedent's spouse for such spouse's share of split gifts (section 2513) only if the decedent was the donor of these gifts and they are includible in the decedent's gross estate (see instructions)	7
8	Gross estate tax (subtract line 7 from line 6)	8
9	Maximum unified credit (applicable credit amount) against estate tax .	9
10	Adjustment to unified credit (applicable credit amount). (This adjustment may not exceed $6,000. See page 6 of the instructions.)	10
11	Allowable unified credit (applicable credit amount) (subtract line 10 from line 9)	11
12	Subtract line 11 from line 8 (but do not enter less than zero)	12
13	Credit for foreign death taxes (from Schedule(s) P). (Attach Form(s) 706-CE.)	13
14	Credit for tax on prior transfers (from Schedule Q)	14
15	Total credits (add lines 13 and 14)	15
16	Net estate tax (subtract line 15 from line 12)	16
17	Generation-skipping transfer (GST) taxes payable (from Schedule R, Part 2, line 10)	17
18	Total transfer taxes (add lines 16 and 17)	18
19	Prior payments. Explain in an attached statement	19
20	Balance due (or overpayment) (subtract line 19 from line 18)	20

Under penalties of perjury, I declare that I have examined this return, including accompanying schedules and statements, and to the best of my knowledge and belief, it is true, correct, and complete. Declaration of preparer other than the executor is based on all information of which preparer has any knowledge.

Signature(s) of executor(s)	Date

Signature of preparer other than executor	Address (and ZIP code)	Date

For Privacy Act and Paperwork Reduction Act Notice, see page 28 of the separate instructions for this form.   Cat. No. 20548R   Form **706** (Rev. 10-2006)

Form 706 (Rev. 10-2006)

Estate of:

Part 3—Elections by the Executor

Please check the "Yes" or "No" box for each question (see instructions beginning on page 6).
Note. Some of these elections require the posting of bonds or liens.

			Yes	No
1	Do you elect alternate valuation?	1		
2	Do you elect special-use valuation? If "Yes," you must complete and attach Schedule A–1.	2		
3	Do you elect to pay the taxes in installments as described in section 6166? . . . . If "Yes," you must attach the additional information described on pages 9 and 10 of the instructions. Note. By electing section 6166, you agree to provide security for estate tax deferred under section 6166 and interest in the form of a surety bond or a section 6324A special lien.	3		
4	Do you elect to postpone the part of the taxes attributable to a reversionary or remainder interest as described in section 6163?	4		

Part 4—General Information
(Note. Please attach the necessary supplemental documents. You must attach the death certificate.) (see instructions on page 11)

Authorization to receive confidential tax information under Regs. sec. 601.504(b)(2)(i); to act as the estate's representative before the IRS; and to make written or oral presentations on behalf of the estate if return prepared by an attorney, accountant, or enrolled agent for the executor:

Name of representative (print or type)	State	Address (number, street, and room or suite no., city, state, and ZIP code)

I declare that I am the ☐ attorney/ ☐ certified public accountant/ ☐ enrolled agent (you must check the applicable box) for the executor and prepared this return for the executor. I am not under suspension or disbarment from practice before the Internal Revenue Service and am qualified to practice in the state shown above.

Signature	CAF number	Date	Telephone number

1 Death certificate number and issuing authority (attach a copy of the death certificate to this return).

2 Decedent's business or occupation. If retired, check here ► ☐ and state decedent's former business or occupation.

3 Marital status of the decedent at time of death:
☐ Married
☐ Widow or widower —Name, SSN, and date of death of deceased spouse ► . . . .
☐ Single
☐ Legally separated
☐ Divorced —Date divorce decree became final ►

4a Surviving spouse's name	4b Social security number	4c Amount received (see page 11 of the instructions)

5 Individuals (other than the surviving spouse), trusts, or other estates who receive benefits from the estate (do not include charitable beneficiaries shown in Schedule O) (see instructions).

Name of individual, trust, or estate receiving $5,000 or more	Identifying number	Relationship to decedent	Amount (see instructions)

All unascertainable beneficiaries and those who receive less than $5,000 . . . . ►

Total . . . .

Please check the "Yes" or "No" box for each question.	Yes	No
6 Does the gross estate contain any section 2044 property (qualified terminable interest property (QTIP) from a prior gift or estate) (see page 11 of the instructions)?		
7a Have federal gift tax returns ever been filed? If "Yes," please attach copies of the returns, if available, and furnish the following information:		

7b Period(s) covered	7c Internal Revenue office(s) where filed

(continued on next page)

Page 2

Form 706 (Rev. 10-2006)

Part 4—General Information   (continued)

	If you answer "Yes" to any of questions 8–16, you must attach additional information as described in the instructions.	Yes	No
8a	Was there any insurance on the decedent's life that is not included on the return as part of the gross estate?		
b	Did the decedent own any insurance on the life of another that is not included in the gross estate?		
9	Did the decedent at the time of death own any property as a joint tenant with right of survivorship in which (a) one or more of the other joint tenants was someone other than the decedent's spouse, and (b) less than the full value of the property is included on the return as part of the gross estate? If "Yes," you must complete and attach Schedule E		
10	Did the decedent, at the time of death, own any interest in a partnership or unincorporated business or any stock in an inactive or closely held corporation?		
11	Did the decedent make any transfer described in section 2035, 2036, 2037, or 2038 (see the instructions for Schedule G beginning on page 13 of the separate instructions)? If "Yes," you must complete and attach Schedule G		
12a	Were there in existence at the time of the decedent's death any trusts created by the decedent during his or her lifetime?		
b	Were there in existence at the time of the decedent's death any trusts not created by the decedent under which the decedent possessed any power, beneficial interest, or trusteeship?		
c	Was the decedent receiving income from a trust created after October 22, 1986 by a parent or grandparent? If "Yes," was there a GST taxable termination (under section 2612) upon the death of the decedent?		
d	If there was a GST taxable termination (under section 2612), attach a statement to explain. Provide a copy of the trust or will creating the trust, and give the name, address, and phone number of the current trustee(s).		
e	Did decedent at any time during his or her lifetime transfer or sell an interest in a partnership, limited liability company, or closely held corporation to a trust described in question 12a or 12b? If "Yes," provide the EIN number to this transferred/sold item. ▶		
13	Did the decedent ever possess, exercise, or release any general power of appointment? If "Yes," you must complete and attach Schedule H		
14	Was the marital deduction computed under the transitional rule of Public Law 97-34, section 403(e)(3) (Economic Recovery Tax Act of 1981)? If "Yes," attach a separate computation of the marital deduction, enter the amount on item 20 of the Recapitulation, and note on item 20 "computation attached."		
15	Was the decedent, immediately before death, receiving an annuity described in the "General" paragraph of the instructions for Schedule I or a private annuity? If "Yes," you must complete and attach Schedule I		
16	Was the decedent ever the beneficiary of a trust for which a deduction was claimed by the estate of a pre-deceased spouse under section 2056(b)(7) and which is not reported on this return? If "Yes," attach an explanation		

Part 5—Recapitulation

Item number	Gross estate		Alternate value	Value at date of death
1	Schedule A—Real Estate	1		
2	Schedule B—Stocks and Bonds	2		
3	Schedule C—Mortgages, Notes, and Cash	3		
4	Schedule D—Insurance on the Decedent's Life (attach Form(s) 712)	4		
5	Schedule E—Jointly Owned Property (attach Form(s) 712 for life insurance)	5		
6	Schedule F—Other Miscellaneous Property (attach Form(s) 712 for life insurance)	6		
7	Schedule G—Transfers During Decedent's Life (att. Form(s) 712 for life insurance)	7		
8	Schedule H—Powers of Appointment	8		
9	Schedule I—Annuities	9		
10	Total gross estate (add items 1 through 9)	10		
11	Schedule U—Qualified Conservation Easement Exclusion	11		
12	Total gross estate less exclusion (subtract item 11 from item 10). Enter here and on line 1 of Part 2—Tax Computation	12		

Item number	Deductions		Amount
13	Schedule J—Funeral Expenses and Expenses Incurred in Administering Property Subject to Claims	13	
14	Schedule K—Debts of the Decedent	14	
15	Schedule K—Mortgages and Liens	15	
16	Total of items 13 through 15	16	
17	Allowable amount of deductions from item 16 (see the instructions for item 17 of the Recapitulation)	17	
18	Schedule L—Net Losses During Administration	18	
19	Schedule L—Expenses Incurred in Administering Property Not Subject to Claims	19	
20	Schedule M—Bequests, etc., to Surviving Spouse	20	
21	Schedule O—Charitable, Public, and Similar Gifts and Bequests	21	
22	Tentative total allowable deductions (add items 17 through 21). Enter here and on line 2 of the Tax Computation	22	

Page 3

110. Form 709 U.S. Gift (and Generation-Skipping Transfer) Tax Return

Form **709**	United States Gift (and Generation-Skipping Transfer) Tax Return	OMB No. 1545-0020
Department of the Treasury Internal Revenue Service	(For gifts made during calendar year 2006) ▶ See separate instructions.	**2006**

Part 1—General Information

1 Donor's first name and middle initial	2 Donor's last name		3 Donor's social security number
4 Address (number, street, and apartment number)			5 Legal residence (domicile) (county and state)
6 City, state, and ZIP code			7 Citizenship

		Yes	No
8	If the donor died during the year, check here ▶ ☐ and enter date of death .... , ...		
9	If you extended the time to file this Form 709, check here ▶ ☐		
10	Enter the total number of donees listed on Schedule A. Count each person only once. ▶		
11a	Have you (the donor) previously filed a Form 709 (or 709-A) for any other year? If "No," skip line 11b		
11b	If the answer to line 11a is "Yes," has your address changed since you last filed Form 709 (or 709-A)?		
12	Gifts by husband or wife to third parties. Do you consent to have the gifts (including generation-skipping transfers) made by you and by your spouse to third parties during the calendar year considered as made one-half by each of you? (See instructions.) (If the answer is "Yes," the following information must be furnished and your spouse must sign the consent shown below. If the answer is "No," skip lines 13–18 and go to Schedule A.		
13	Name of consenting spouse	14 SSN	
15	Were you married to one another during the entire calendar year? (see instructions)		
16	If 15 is "No," check whether ☐ married ☐ divorced or ☐ widowed/deceased, and give date (see instructions) ▶		
17	Will a gift tax return for this year be filed by your spouse? (If "Yes," mail both returns in the same envelope.)		
18	Consent of Spouse. I consent to have the gifts (and generation-skipping transfers) made by me and by my spouse to third parties during the calendar year considered as made one-half by each of us. We are both aware of the joint and several liability for tax created by the execution of this consent.		

Consenting spouse's signature ▶ _____ Date ▶ _____

Part 2—Tax Computation

1	Enter the amount from Schedule A, Part 4, line 11	1	
2	Enter the amount from Schedule B, line 3	2	
3	Total taxable gifts. Add lines 1 and 2	3	
4	Tax computed on amount on line 3 (see Table for Computing Gift Tax in separate instructions)	4	
5	Tax computed on amount on line 2 (see Table for Computing Gift Tax in separate instructions)	5	
6	Balance. Subtract line 5 from line 4	6	
7	Maximum unified credit (nonresident aliens, see instructions)	7	345,800	00
8	Enter the unified credit against tax allowable for all prior periods (from Sch. B, line 1, col. C)	8	
9	Balance. Subtract line 8 from line 7	9	
10	Enter 20% (.20) of the amount allowed as a specific exemption for gifts made after September 8, 1976, and before January 1, 1977 (see instructions)	10	
11	Balance. Subtract line 10 from line 9	11	
12	Unified credit. Enter the smaller of line 6 or line 11	12	
13	Credit for foreign gift taxes (see instructions)	13	
14	Total credits. Add lines 12 and 13	14	
15	Balance. Subtract line 14 from line 6. Do not enter less than zero	15	
16	Generation-skipping transfer taxes (from Schedule C, Part 3, col. H, Total)	16	
17	Total tax. Add lines 15 and 16	17	
18	Gift and generation-skipping transfer taxes prepaid with extension of time to file	18	
19	If line 18 is less than line 17, enter balance due (see instructions)	19	
20	If line 18 is greater than line 17, enter amount to be refunded	20	

Sign Here

Under penalties of perjury, I declare that I have examined this return, including any accompanying schedules and statements, and to the best of my knowledge and belief, it is true, correct, and complete. Declaration of preparer (other than donor) is based on all information of which preparer has any knowledge.

▶ _____ _____
  Signature of donor   Date

Paid Preparer's Use Only

Preparer's signature ▶		Date	Check if self-employed ▶ ☐
Firm's name (or yours if self-employed), address, and ZIP code		Phone no. ▶ ( )	

Attach check or money order here.

For Disclosure, Privacy Act, and Paperwork Reduction Act Notice, see page 12 of the separate instructions for this form.   Cat. No. 16783M   Form **709** (2006)

Form 709 (2006) Page **2**

| SCHEDULE A | Computation of Taxable Gifts | (Including transfers in trust) (see instructions) |

A   Does the value of any item listed on Schedule A reflect any valuation discount? If "Yes," attach explanation . . . . . . Yes ☐ No ☐

B   ☐ ◄ Check here if you elect under section 529(c)(2)(B) to treat any transfers made this year to a qualified tuition program as made ratably over a 5-year period beginning this year. See instructions. Attach explanation.

Part 1—Gifts Subject Only to Gift Tax. Gifts less political organization, medical, and educational exclusions. See instructions.

A Item number	B • Donee's name and address • Relationship to donor (if any) • Description of gift • If the gift was of securities, give CUSIP no. • If closely held entity, give EIN	C	D Donor's adjusted basis of gift	E Date of gift	F Value at date of gift	G For split gifts, enter ½ of column F	H Net transfer (subtract col. G from col. F)
1							

Gifts made by spouse —complete only if you are splitting gifts with your spouse and he/she also made gifts.

Total of Part 1.   Add amounts from Part 1, column H . . . . ►

Part 2—Direct Skips. Gifts that are direct skips and are subject to both gift tax and generation-skipping transfer tax. You must list the gifts in chronological order.

A Item number	B • Donee's name and address • Relationship to donor (if any) • Description of gift • If the gift was of securities, give CUSIP no. • If closely held entity, give EIN	C 2632(b) election out	D Donor's adjusted basis of gift	E Date of gift	F Value at date of gift	G For split gifts, enter ½ of column F	H Net transfer (subtract col. G from col. F)
1							

Gifts made by spouse —complete only if you are splitting gifts with your spouse and he/she also made gifts.

Total of Part 2.   Add amounts from Part 2, column H . . . . ►

Part 3—Indirect Skips. Gifts to trusts that are currently subject to gift tax and may later be subject to generation-skipping transfer tax. You must list these gifts in chronological order.

A Item number	B • Donee's name and address • Relationship to donor (if any) • Description of gift • If the gift was of securities, give CUSIP no. • If closely held entity, give EIN	C 2632(c) election	D Donor's adjusted basis of gift	E Date of gift	F Value at date of gift	G For split gifts, enter ½ of column F	H Net transfer (subtract col. G from col. F)
1							

Gifts made by spouse —complete only if you are splitting gifts with your spouse and he/she also made gifts.

Total of Part 3.   Add amounts from Part 3, column H . . . . ►

(If more space is needed, attach additional sheets of same size.) Form **709** (2006)

Form 709 (2006) — Page 3

Part 4—Taxable Gift Reconciliation

1	Total value of gifts of donor. Add totals from column H of Parts 1, 2, and 3	1
2	Total annual exclusions for gifts listed on line 1 (see instructions)	2
3	Total included amount of gifts. Subtract line 2 from line 1	3

Deductions (see instructions)

4	Gifts of interests to spouse for which a marital deduction will be claimed, based on item numbers _____ of Schedule A	4
5	Exclusions attributable to gifts on line 4	5
6	Marital deduction. Subtract line 5 from line 4	6
7	Charitable deduction, based on item nos. _____ less exclusions	7
8	Total deductions. Add lines 6 and 7	8
9	Subtract line 8 from line 3	9
10	Generation-skipping transfer taxes payable with this Form 709 (from Schedule C, Part 3, col. H, Total)	10
11	Taxable gifts. Add lines 9 and 10. Enter here and on page 1, Part 2—Tax Computation, line 1	11

Terminable Interest (QTIP) Marital Deduction. (See instructions for Schedule A, Part 4, line 4.)

If a trust (or other property) meets the requirements of qualified terminable interest property under section 2523(f), and:

a. The trust (or other property) is listed on Schedule A, and

b. The value of the trust (or other property) is entered in whole or in part as a deduction on Schedule A, Part 4, line 4, then the donor shall be deemed to have made an election to have such trust (or other property) treated as qualified terminable interest property under section 2523(f).

If less than the entire value of the trust (or other property) that the donor has included in Parts 1 and 3 of Schedule A is entered as a deduction on line 4, the donor shall be considered to have made an election only as to a fraction of the trust (or other property). The numerator of this fraction is equal to the amount of the trust (or other property) deducted on Schedule A, Part 4, line 6. The denominator is equal to the total value of the trust (or other property) listed in Parts 1 and 3 of Schedule A.

If you make the QTIP election, the terminable interest property involved will be included in your spouse's gross estate upon his or her death (section 2044). See instructions for line 4 of Schedule A. If your spouse disposes (by gift or otherwise) of all or part of the qualifying life income interest, he or she will be considered to have made a transfer of the entire property that is subject to the gift tax. See Transfer of Certain Life Estates Received From Spouse on page 4 of the instructions.

12 Election Out of QTIP Treatment of Annuities

☐ ◄ Check here if you elect under section 2523(f)(6) not to treat as qualified terminable interest property any joint and survivor annuities that are reported on Schedule A and would otherwise be treated as qualified terminable interest property under section 2523(f). See instructions. Enter the item numbers from Schedule A for the annuities for which you are making this election ► _____

SCHEDULE B — Gifts From Prior Periods

If you answered "Yes" on line 11a of page 1, Part 1, see the instructions for completing Schedule B. If you answered "No," skip to the Tax Computation on page 1 (or Schedule C, if applicable).

A Calendar year or calendar quarter (see instructions)	B Internal Revenue office where prior return was filed	C Amount of unified credit against gift tax for periods after December 31, 1976	D Amount of specific exemption for prior periods ending before January 1, 1977	E Amount of taxable gifts

1	Totals for prior periods	1
2	Amount, if any, by which total specific exemption, line 1, column D, is more than $30,000	2
3	Total amount of taxable gifts for prior periods. Add amount on line 1, column E and amount, if any, on line 2. Enter here and on page 1, Part 2—Tax Computation, line 2	3

(If more space is needed, attach additional sheets of same size.)

Form 709 (2006)

Form 709 (2006)   Page **4**

SCHEDULE C	Computation of Generation-Skipping Transfer Tax

Note. Inter vivos direct skips that are completely excluded by the GST exemption must still be fully reported (including value and exemptions claimed) on Schedule C.

Part 1—Generation-Skipping Transfers

A Item No. (from Schedule A, Part 2, col. A)	B Value (from Schedule A, Part 2, col. H)	C Nontaxable portion of transfer	D Net Transfer (subtract col. C from col. B)
1			
Gifts made by spouse (for gift splitting only)			

Part 2 —GST Exemption Reconciliation (Section 2631) and Section 2652(a)(3) Election

Check here ▶ ☐ if you are making a section 2652(a)(3) (special QTIP) election (see instructions)

Enter the item numbers from Schedule A of the gifts for which you are making this election ▶ ....

1	Maximum allowable exemption (see instructions)	1
2	Total exemption used for periods before filing this return	2
3	Exemption available for this return. Subtract line 2 from line 1	3
4	Exemption claimed on this return from Part 3, column C total, below	4
5	Automatic allocation of exemption to transfers reported on Schedule A, Part 3 (see instructions)	5
6	Exemption allocated to transfers not shown on line 4 or 5, above.　You must attach a Notice of Allocation. (see instructions)	6
7	Add lines 4, 5, and 6	7
8	Exemption available for future transfers. Subtract line 7 from line 3	8

Part 3—Tax Computation

A Item No. (from Schedule C, Part 1)	B Net transfer (from Schedule C, Part 1, col. D)	C GST Exemption Allocated	D Divide col. C by col. B	E Inclusion Ratio (subtract col. D from 1.000)	F Maximum Estate Tax Rate	G Applicable Rate (multiply col. E by col. F)	H Generation-Skipping Transfer Tax (multiply col. B by col. G)
1					46% (.46)		
					46% (.46)		
					46% (.46)		
					46% (.46)		
					46% (.46)		
					46% (.46)		
Gifts made by spouse (for gift splitting only)							
					46% (.46)		
					46% (.46)		
					46% (.46)		
					46% (.46)		
					46% (.46)		
					46% (.46)		
Total exemption claimed. Enter here and on Part 2, line 4, above. May not exceed Part 2, line 3, above		Total generation-skipping transfer tax.　Enter here; on page 3, Schedule A, Part 4, line 10; and on page 1, Part 2—Tax Computation, line 16					

(If more space is needed, attach additional sheets of same size.)

Form **709** (2006)

♻ Printed on recycled paper

CHAPTER 12

Employ Legally and Effectively

ATTRACTING AND HIRING THE RIGHT employees for your firm are essential to your business success. In this chapter, you will find forms and worksheets to help you attract and evaluate suitable candidates. These forms are applicable to nearly any industry and serve as examples of legal records and contracts between the company and its employees.

You will find two employment applications, the *Application for Employment—Short Form* and the *Application for Employment—Long Form*. The short form will likely be sufficient for most hires, while the long form is more appropriate for longer-term and executive positions.

As part of the employment application process, insist that your applicants execute the *Authorization to Release Employment Applicant Information*. This important form authorizes the applicant's former employer to release information about the applicant's work history and personal characteristics. Most former employers will insist on receiving such an authorization before divulging any information.

You will also find two versions of a *Pre-Employment Reference Check via Phone*. These two forms are scripts that you can use when making telephone contact with an applicant's former employer. If you wish to contact your applicant's former employer by letter, use the *Pre-Employment Reference Check via Letter* form.

Once you have narrowed your employee search to a handful of candidates, summarize their critical strengths and weaknesses with the *Applicant Comparison Summary Form*. Rate each candidate's qualifications for critical job requirements, such as computer skills, foreign languages, and the like. You can rate each applicant's individual skills with *Applicant Rating Form, Part One* and *Applicant Rating Form, Part Two*.

Once you have found your ideal candidate, you can use the *Offer of Employment and Employment Contract*. This form formally announces the offer of employment and documents the terms of the employment agreement. Save a copy in the employee's file.

All employees come to a company looking for a job and many leave looking for a job. This section is brief, but important. When an employee is terminated from your firm, make sure that all documents are in order before you part ways. The past few decades have witnessed a significant increase in litigation brought by former employees for wrongful termination. While some of these suits are valid, others are groundless and abusive and exploit poor record keeping by employers; thus, the importance of properly documenting the separation. This will allow you to more successfully defend yourself if you are sued for wrongful termination.

If an employee chooses to leave voluntarily, have him or her execute the *Voluntary Resignation Form*. This form serves as a nearly indisputable record of the employee's willing termination of employment. This form may also go a long way to extinguishing an employee's right to charge your business's unemployment insurance for unemployment benefits. The *Employee's Separation Checklist* advises an employee of outstanding issues that must be resolved before separation. The *Manager's Pre-Dismissal Checklist* ensures that all loose ends are well tied before an employee departs. Finally, the *Employee Exit Interview* helps company and employee communicate their final thoughts before terminating the employment relationship.

Now that you've got the best candidate in the door, it's important to keep him or her there and to maintain adequate records. You should maintain a master database of your employees with the *Employee Master Database*. With this form you can maintain an accurate and convenient master list of the name, Social Security number, date of birth, address, and hire date of each current or former employee. (Always maintain records for five years after an employee leaves.) You can also maintain records of whether the employee is current or former and full- or part-time. The Employee Master Database also contains columns for whether your employees have executed an employment agreement, stock option agreement, employee handbook acknowledgment, nondisclosure agreement, and W-4 form. Once you have these documents on file, indicate this by writing "OF" in the appropriate cell.

111. Application for Employment–Short Form

Our policy is to provide equal employment opportunity to all qualified persons without regard to race, creed, color, religious belief, sex, age, national origin, ancestry, physical or mental disability, or veteran status.

Name

Last _____ First _____ Middle_____

Date _____

Street Address _____

City _____ State _____ ZIP _____

Telephone _____

Social Security # _____

Position applied for _____

How did you hear of this opening? _____

When can you start? _____ Desired Wage $_____

Are you a U.S. citizen or otherwise authorized to work in the U.S. on an unrestricted basis? (You may be required to provide documentation.) ❏ Yes ❏ No

Are you looking for full-time employment? ❏ Yes ❏ No

If no, what hours are you available? _____

Are you willing to work swing shift? ❏ Yes ❏ No

Are you willing to work graveyard? ❏ Yes ❏ No

Have you ever been convicted of a felony? (This will not necessarily affect your application.) ❏ Yes ❏ No
If yes, please describe conditions. _____
_____
_____
_____
_____

Education	School Name and Location	Year	Major	Degree
High School	_____	____	_____	_____
College	_____	____	_____	_____
College	_____	____	_____	_____
Post-College	_____	____	_____	_____
Other Training	_____	____	_____	_____

In addition to your work history, are there other skills, qualifications, or experience that we should consider?
_____
_____
_____
_____
_____
_____

Employment History (Start with most recent employer)
Company Name _____
Address _____ Telephone _____
Date Started _____ Starting Wage _____ Starting Position _____
Date Ended _____ Ending Wage _____ Ending Position _____
Name of Supervisor _____
May we contact? ❑ Yes ❑ No
Responsibilities _____
Reason for leaving _____

Company Name _____
Address _____ Telephone _____
Date Started _____ Starting Wage _____ Starting Position _____
Date Ended _____ Ending Wage _____ Ending Position _____
Name of Supervisor _____
May we contact? ❑ Yes ❑ No
Responsibilities _____
Reason for leaving _____

Company Name _____
Address _____ Telephone _____
Date Started _____ Starting Wage _____ Starting Position _____
Date Ended _____ Ending Wage _____ Ending Position _____
Name of Supervisor _____
May we contact? ❑ Yes ❑ No
Responsibilities _____
Reason for leaving _____

Attach additional information if necessary.

I certify that the facts set forth in this application for employment are true and complete to the best of my knowledge. I understand that if I am employed, false statements on this application shall be considered sufficient cause for dismissal. This company is hereby authorized to make any investigations of my prior educational and employment history.

I understand that employment at this company is "at will," which means that either I or this company can terminate the employment relationship at any time, with or without prior notice, and for any reason not prohibited by statute. All employment is continued on that basis. I understand that no supervisor, manager, or executive of this company, other than the president, has any authority to alter the foregoing.

Signature_____ Date _____

112. Application for Employment—Long Form

Our policy is to provide equal employment opportunity to all qualified persons without regard to race, creed, color, religious belief, sex, age, national origin, ancestry, physical or mental disability, or veteran status.

Name
Last _____ First _____ Middle_____
Date _____
Street Address _____
City _____ State _____ ZIP _____
Telephone _____
Social Security # _____

Position applied for _____
How did you hear of this opening? _____
When can you start? _____ Desired Wage $_____

Are you a U.S. citizen or otherwise authorized to work in the U.S. on an unrestricted basis? (You may be required to provide documentation.) ❑ Yes ❑ No
Are you looking for full-time employment? ❑ Yes ❑ No
If no, what hours are you available? _____
Are you willing to work swing shift? ❑ Yes ❑ No
Are you willing to work graveyard? ❑ Yes ❑ No

Have you ever been convicted of a felony? (This will not necessarily affect your application.) ❑ Yes ❑ No
If yes, please describe conditions. _____
_____
_____
_____
_____

Employment Desired
Have you ever applied for employment here? ❑ Yes ❑ No
When? _____
Where? _____
Have you ever been employed by this company? ❑ Yes ❑ No
When? _____
Where? _____
Are you presently employed? ❑ Yes ❑ No
May we contact your present employer? ❑ Yes ❑ No
Are you available for full-time work? ❑ Yes ❑ No
Are you available for part-time work? ❑ Yes ❑ No
Will you relocate? ❑ Yes ❑ No
Are you willing to travel? ❑ Yes ❑ No If yes, what percent? _____
Date you can start _____
Desired position _____

Desired starting salary _____

Please list applicable skills _____

_____

_____

Education: School Name and Location   Year   Major   Degree

High School _____   _____ _____ _____

College _____   _____ _____ _____

College _____   _____ _____ _____

Post-College _____   _____ _____ _____

Other Training _____   _____ _____ _____

In addition to your work history, are there other skills, qualifications, or experience that we should consider?

_____

_____

_____

_____

Please list any scholastic honors received and offices held in school.

_____

_____

Are you planning to continue your studies?   ❏ Yes   ❏ No

If yes, where and what courses of study?

_____

_____

Company Name _____

Address _____ Telephone _____

Date Started _____ Starting Wage _____ Starting Position _____

Date Ended _____ Ending Wage _____ Ending Position _____

Name of Supervisor _____

May we contact? ❏ Yes   ❏ No

Responsibilities _____

_____

Reason for leaving _____

Company Name _____

Address _____ Telephone _____

Date Started _____ Starting Wage _____ Starting Position _____

Date Ended _____ Ending Wage _____ Ending Position _____

Name of Supervisor _____

May we contact? ❏ Yes   ❏ No

Responsibilities _____

_____

Reason for leaving _____

Company Name _____
Address _____ Telephone _____
Date Started _____ Starting Wage _____ Starting Position _____
Date Ended _____ Ending Wage _____ Ending Position _____
Name of Supervisor _____
May we contact? ❏ Yes ❏ No
Responsibilities _____
_____
Reason for leaving _____

Company Name _____
Address _____ Telephone _____
Date Started _____ Starting Wage _____ Starting Position _____
Date Ended _____ Ending Wage _____ Ending Position _____
Name of Supervisor _____
May we contact? ❏ Yes ❏ No
Responsibilities _____
_____
Reason for leaving _____

Company Name _____
Address _____ Telephone _____
Date Started _____ Starting Wage _____ Starting Position _____
Date Ended _____ Ending Wage _____ Ending Position _____
Name of Supervisor _____
May we contact? ❏ Yes ❏ No
Responsibilities _____
_____
Reason for leaving _____

Company Name _____
Address _____ Telephone _____
Date Started _____ Starting Wage _____ Starting Position _____
Date Ended _____ Ending Wage _____ Ending Position _____
Name of Supervisor _____
May we contact? ❏ Yes ❏ No
Responsibilities _____
_____
Reason for leaving _____

References
List three personal references, not related to you, who have known you for more than one year.

Name _____ Phone _____ Years Known_____
Address _____

Name _____ Phone _____Years Known_____
Address _____

Name _____ Phone _____Years Known_____
Address _____

Emergency Contact

In case of emergency, please notify:_____

Name _____ Phone _____
Address _____

Name _____ Phone _____
Address _____

Please Read Before Signing:

I certify that all information provided by me on this application is true and complete to the best of my knowledge and that I have withheld nothing that, if disclosed, would alter the integrity of this application.

I authorize my previous employers, schools, or persons listed as references to give any information regarding employment or educational record. I agree that this company and my previous employers will not be held liable in any respect if a job offer is not extended, or is withdrawn, or employment is terminated because of false statements, omissions, or answers made by myself on this application. In the event of any employment with this company, I will comply with all rules and regulations as set by the company in any communication distributed to the employees.

In compliance with the Immigration Reform and Control Act of 1986, I understand that I am required to provide approved documentation to the company that verifies my right to work in the United States on the first day of employment. I have received from the company a list of the approved documents that are required.

I understand that employment at this company is "at will," which means that either I or this company can terminate the employment relationship at any time, with or without prior notice, and for any reason not prohibited by statute. All employment is continued on that basis. I hereby acknowledge that I have read and understand the above statements.

Signature _____ Date _____

Immigration Reform and Control Act Requirement

In compliance with the Immigration Reform and Control Act of 1986, you are required to provide approved documentation that verifies your right to work in the United States prior to your employment with this company. Please be prepared to provide us with the following documentation in the event you are offered and accept employment with our company:

Any one of the following: (These establish both identity and employment authorization.)
1. U.S. Passport.

2. Certificate of U.S. Citizenship (issued by USCIS).
3. Certificate of Naturalization (issued by USCIS).
4. Resident alien card or other alien unexpired endorsement card, with photo or other approved identifying information which evidences employment authorization.
5. Unexpired foreign passport with unexpired endorsement authorizing employment.

Or one from List A and List B:

List A (These establish employment authorization.)
1. Social Security card.
2. Birth Certificate or other documentation that establishes U.S. nationality or birth.
3. Other approved documentation.

List B
1. Driver's license or similar government identification card with photo or other approved identifying information.
2. Other approved documentation of identity for applicants under age 16 or in a state that does not issue an I.D. card (other than a driver's license).

113. Authorization to Release Employment Applicant Information

Employment Applicant:

_____

_____

_____

_____

To:

_____

_____

_____

_____

I have applied for a position with _____.

I have been requested to provide information for their use in reviewing my background and qualifications. Therefore, I authorize the investigation of my past and present work, character, education, military, and employment qualifications.

The release in any manner of all information by you is authorized, whether such information is of record or not, and I do hereby release all persons, agencies, firms, companies, etc., from any damages resulting from providing such information.

This authorization is valid for 90 days from the date of my signature below. Please keep this copy of my release request for your files. Thank you for your cooperation.

Signature_____ Date_____

Note: Medical information is often protected by state laws and civil codes. Consult your attorney if you wish to seek this information.

Note: Many employers are reluctant to provide information on previous employees. If you ask each applicant to distribute this form to his or her references before you contact them, the prior employers may be more willing to release information.

114. Pre-Employment Reference Check via Phone

Applicant's Name_____ Applying for_____

"My name is _____ from _____Company.
_____ has applied for a position with our company.
I would like to verify the information provided us by _____
and _____ has given us permission to contact you."

Person Contacted_____ Company_____

Phone_____ ❏ Personnel Department ❏ Ex-Supervisor ❏ Other _____

Comments: _____

_____

Job Title _____
Employment Date _____
Job Responsibilities _____
Attendance _____
Rehire _____

Person Contacted_____ Company_____
Phone_____ ❏ Personnel Department ❏ Ex-Supervisor ❏ Other _____
Comments: _____

_____

Job Title _____
Employment Date _____
Job Responsibilities _____
Attendance _____
Rehire _____

Person Contacted_____ Company_____
Phone_____ ❏ Personnel Department ❏ Ex-Supervisor ❏ Other _____
Comments: _____

_____

Job Title _____
Employment Date _____
Job Responsibilities _____
Attendance _____
Rehire _____

References Checked by _____ Date _____

Checker's Comments _____

_____

_____

115. Pre-Employment Reference Check via Letter

From:

_____

_____

_____

To:

_____

_____

_____

We would appreciate your assistance in verifying the information listed below regarding an employment application. It is to be understood that all information is confidential and will be treated as such in our company personnel files. Attached, please find an authorization to release information signed by the applicant. A self-addressed, stamped envelope is enclosed for your convenience in replying. We appreciate your assistance in this matter. Thank you.

Yours truly,

Personnel Manager

The following information was provided to us by the applicant. Please make any appropriate corrections:

Name _____ SS # _____

Job Title _____ Final Salary $_____

Date of Employment _____

Reason for Termination

_____

Please complete the following requested information:

Would you rehire this applicant? ❑ Yes ❑ No

If no, why not? _____

Please review and rate the applicant in these areas:

	Unsatisfactory		Average		Outstanding
Attendance	1	2	3	4	5
Quality of work	1	2	3	4	5
Quantity of work	1	2	3	4	5
Cooperation	1	2	3	4	5
Responsibility	1	2	3	4	5

Signed _____ Title _____ Date _____

116. Applicant Comparison Summary Form

Position _____ Date Interviewed _____

Interviewed
by _____

Candidate
1 _____

Candidate
2 _____

Candidate
3 _____

Candidate
4 _____

Critical Job Requirements	Candidate #1	#2	#3	#4	Comments

Legend:
✓ Meets critical job requirements
+ Exceeds critical job requirements
– Does not meet critical job requirements

117. Applicant Rating Form, Part One

Applicant's Name _____

Position and Department _____

Interviewed by _____ Date _____

Critical Job Requirements	Below Average			Average		Above Average			Excellent	
_____	1	2	3	4	5	6	7	8	9	10
_____	1	2	3	4	5	6	7	8	9	10
_____	1	2	3	4	5	6	7	8	9	10
_____	1	2	3	4	5	6	7	8	9	10
_____	1	2	3	4	5	6	7	8	9	10
_____	1	2	3	4	5	6	7	8	9	10
_____	1	2	3	4	5	6	7	8	9	10
_____	1	2	3	4	5	6	7	8	9	10
_____	1	2	3	4	5	6	7	8	9	10
_____	1	2	3	4	5	6	7	8	9	10
_____	1	2	3	4	5	6	7	8	9	10
_____	1	2	3	4	5	6	7	8	9	10
_____	1	2	3	4	5	6	7	8	9	10
_____	1	2	3	4	5	6	7	8	9	10
_____	1	2	3	4	5	6	7	8	9	10
_____	1	2	3	4	5	6	7	8	9	10
_____	1	2	3	4	5	6	7	8	9	10

Comments:

Strong Points _____

_____

Weak Areas _____

_____

Other _____

_____

118. Applicant Rating Form, Part Two

Applicant's Name _____

Position and Department _____

Interviewed by _____ Date _____

Job Experience:	Poor				Outstanding
Relevance to Position	1	2	3	4	5
Accomplishments	1	2	3	4	5
Analytical/Problem Solving	1	2	3	4	5
Leadership	1	2	3	4	5
Career Goals	1	2	3	4	5

Academics:					
Relevance of Studies to Job	1	2	3	4	5
Extent, Variety in Activities	1	2	3	4	5
Abilities as a Student	1	2	3	4	5

Characteristics:					
Grooming	1	2	3	4	5
Bearing	1	2	3	4	5
Initiative	1	2	3	4	5
Grasp of Ideas	1	2	3	4	5
Stability	1	2	3	4	5
Personality	1	2	3	4	5

Preparation for Interview:					
Knowledge of Company	1	2	3	4	5
Relevance of Questions	1	2	3	4	5

Summary of Strength and Shortcomings:

Talent, Skills, Knowledge, Energy _____

_____

Motivation, Interests _____

_____

Personal Qualities, Effectiveness _____

_____

Other Comments _____

_____

119. Offer of Employment and Employment Contract

Date
Employee Name _____
Address _____
_____

Dear _____:

We are pleased to offer you a position with _____ ("Company"). Your start date, manager, compensation, benefits, and other terms of employment will be as set forth below and on EXHIBIT A.

TERMS OF EMPLOYMENT

1. **Position and Duties.** Company shall employ you, and you agree to competently and professionally perform such duties as are customarily the responsibility of the position as set forth in the job description attached as EXHIBIT A and as reasonably assigned to you from time to time by your Manager as set forth in EXHIBIT A.

2. **Outside Business Activities.** During your employment with Company, you shall devote competent energies, interests, and abilities to the performance of your duties under this Agreement. During the term of this Agreement, you shall not, without Company's prior written consent, render any services to others for compensation or engage or participate, actively or passively, in any other business activities that would interfere with the performance of your duties hereunder or compete with Company's business.

3. **Employment Classification.** You shall be a Full-Time Employee and shall not be entitled to benefits except as specifically outlined herein.

4. **Compensation/Benefits.**
   4.1 Wage. Company shall pay you the wage as set forth in the job description attached as EXHIBIT A.
   4.2 Reimbursement of Expenses. You shall be reimbursed for all reasonable and necessary expenses paid or incurred by you in the performance of your duties. You shall provide Company with original receipts for such expenses.
   4.3 Withholdings. All compensation paid to you under this Agreement, including payment of salary and taxable benefits, shall be subject to such withholdings as may be required by law or Company's general practices.
   4.4 Benefits. You will also receive Company's standard employee benefits package (including health insurance), and will be subject to Company's vacation policy as such package and policy are in effect from time to time.

5. **At-Will Employment.** Either party may terminate this Agreement by written notice at any time for any reason or for no reason. This Agreement is intended to be and shall be deemed to be an at-will employment Agreement and does not constitute a guarantee of continuing employment for any term.

6. **Nondisclosure Agreement.** You agree to sign Company's standard Employee Nondisclosure Agreement and Proprietary Rights Assignment as a condition of your employment. We wish to impress upon you that we do not wish you to bring with you any confidential or proprietary material of any former employer or to violate any other obligation to your former employers.

7. **Authorization to Work.** Because of federal regulations adopted in the Immigration Reform and Control Act of 1986, you will need to present documentation demonstrating that you have authorization to work in the United States.

8. **Further Assurances.** Each party shall perform any and all further acts and execute and deliver any documents that are reasonably necessary to carry out the intent of this Agreement.

9. **Notices.** All notices or other communications required or permitted by this Agreement or by law shall be in writing and shall be deemed duly served and given when delivered personally or by facsimile, air courier, certified mail (return receipt requested), postage and fees prepaid, to the party at the address indicated in the signature block or at such other address as a party may request in writing.

10. **Governing Law.** This Agreement shall be governed and interpreted in accordance with the laws of the State of California, as such laws are applied to agreements between residents of California to be performed entirely within the State of California.

11. **Entire Agreement.** This Agreement sets forth the entire Agreement between the parties pertaining to the subject matter hereof and supersedes all prior written agreements and all prior or contemporaneous oral Agreements and understandings, expressed or implied.

12. **Written Modification and Waiver.** No modification to this Agreement, nor any waiver of any rights, shall be effective unless assented to in writing by the party to be charged, and the waiver of any breach or default shall not constitute a waiver of any other right or any subsequent breach or default.

13. **Assignment.** This Agreement is personal in nature, and neither of the parties shall, without the consent of the other, assign or transfer this Agreement or any rights or obligations under this Agreement, except that Company may assign or transfer this Agreement to a successor of Company's business, in the event of the transfer or sale of all or substantially all of the assets of Company's business, or to a subsidiary, provided that in the case of any assignment or transfer under the terms of this Section, this Agreement shall be binding on and inure to the benefit of the successor of Company's business, and the successor of Company's business shall discharge and perform all of the obligations of Company under this Agreement.

14. **Severability.** If any of the provisions of this Agreement are determined to be invalid, illegal, or unenforceable, such provisions shall be modified to the minimum extent necessary to make such provisions enforceable, and the remaining provisions shall continue in full force and effect to the extent the economic benefits conferred upon the parties by this Agreement remain substantially unimpaired.

15. **Arbitration of Disputes.** Any controversy or claim arising out of or relating to this contract, or the breach thereof, shall be settled by arbitration administered by the American Arbitration Association under its National Rules for the Resolution of Employment Disputes, and judgment upon the award rendered by the arbitrator(s) may be entered by any court having jurisdiction thereof.

We look forward to your arrival and the start of a long and mutually satisfying work relationship.
Sincerely,
Company
By: _____

Date: _____

Acknowledged, Accepted, and Agreed

_____

Employee Signature

120. Voluntary Resignation

Employee Name _____

Department _____

I voluntarily resign my employment with

_____

Effective: Month _____ Day _____ Year_____

My reasons for leaving are:

_____

_____

_____

_____

_____

_____

_____

_____

_____

Forwarding Address: _____

_____

_____

Employee Signature _____ Date_____

Manager Signature _____ Date_____

121. Employee's Separation Checklist

Employee Name _____

Date of Termination _____

The following items are to have been collected prior to your separation with the company. Please have all these below listed items returned to your manager prior to your separation date. Thank you.

❏ All keys returned.

❏ Company vehicle keys returned.

❏ Company vehicle returned.

❏ Company credit cards returned.

❏ Company phone credit cards returned.

❏ Company equipment (portable phones, beepers, PCs) returned.

❏ COBRA election forms signed and returned.

❏ 401(k) election forms signed and returned.

❏ Profit-sharing election forms signed and returned.

Your files, desk, and work area will be inventoried for all equipment and work utensils given to you by the company.

❏ Desk and working premises inventoried.

122. Manager's Pre-Dismissal Checklist

Employee Name

_____

Date of Termination

_____

Collect the following items from the employee prior to separation from the company:

❏ All keys returned.

❏ Company vehicle keys returned.

❏ Company vehicle returned.

❏ Company credit cards returned.

❏ Company phone credit cards returned.

❏ Company equipment (e.g., portable phones, beepers, credit cards, laptop computers) returned.

❏ COBRA election forms signed and returned.

❏ 401(k) election forms signed and returned.

❏ Profit-sharing election forms signed and returned.

❏ Company documents and files inventoried.

❏ Desk and working premises inventoried.

❏ Personnel and Payroll Departments notified of departure.

❏ Final expense report received, reviewed, and approved; expense check prepared.

❏ Final check prepared (including all accrued vacation pay, sick pay, accrued wages, bonus, etc.).

❏ Exit interview prepared.

❏ Exit interview given.

❏ Final checks (payroll and expense) given to terminating employee.

All of the above duties have been completed in a satisfactory manner.

Company has no further liability with the terminating employee.

Manager Signature _____ Date _____

123. Employee Exit Interview

Employee Name _____

Title _____

Department _____

Date _____

What did you like best about your current position?

_____

_____

_____

What did you like least about your current position?

_____

_____

_____

What did you like best about the company?

_____

_____

_____

What did you like least about the company?

_____

_____

_____

What are your feelings toward your supervisor?

_____

_____

_____

Why are you leaving the company at this time? What company and position are you going to?

_____

_____

_____

What are your comments about the company's salary and benefits?

_____

_____

_____

What suggestions do you have for improving your current position and other aspects within the company?

_____

_____

_____

Interviewed by _____ Date _____

Interviewer's remarks

_____

_____

_____

_____

_____

124. Employee Master Database

Employee File Information

OF = On File

Current Employee	Name	SS Number	DOB	Home Address	Date Hired	Full/Part Time	Employm't Contract	Stock Opt. Agreement	Emp Hdbk Ack	Signed NDA	W-4 on File	US Dept Just EEV

CHAPTER 13

When Business Becomes Litigious

SMALL BUSINESSES SEE THEIR FAIR SHARE OF legal action, whether it stems from employee matters, contractual agreements, or even website jargon. This chapter includes forms that can help small business owners better understand what's legal and what's not, and what to do should a small claims situation occur.

Your company may possess proprietary information or trade secrets that need to be kept confidential. This information may also be your company's bread and butter, whether it includes business plans, marketing strategies, technology, and other information. To protect proprietary information internally and with potential business partners, refer to the *Sample Mutual Nondisclosure Agreement*, that serves to prevent multiple parties from revealing information that pertains to the other parties involved.

Use the *Sample Cease and Desist Letter* to demand in writing that the recipient refrain from a specific action that in a business situation can include debt collections, patent, copy-right, or trademark infringement, libel or slander. A sample form of a *Trademark Infringement Cease and Desist Letter* (on the Web) shows how to draft a cease and desist letter for a specific violation, which in this case is when you feel that a party is using a trademark or service mark for which you have priority rights.

As a business owner, you may find yourself in small claims court either as a plaintiff or defendant. This chapter includes forms for both plaintiffs and defendants that help you file, dispute, and settle the matter in a legal framework. As a plaintiff, you may file small claims against the defendant who wrote your business a bad check or have an unpaid promissory note. Defendants can use the forms in this chapter to properly respond and even negotiate claims.

If you have a case to state to an opponent or potential opponent, use the *Sample Demand Letter* (on the Web) to construct your argument(s) and send to the opponent before the demand is filed in court (unless your state does not require so).

As a defendant, refer to the *Sample Letter by Defendant to Plaintiff in a Collections Matter*, which lays out reasons why the parties should compromise.

Refer to the *Sample Settlement and Compromise Agreement* as an example of how to format the binding agreement if you and the opponent agree on a preliminary settlement.

In the event you settled your claim and received a check that bounced, use the *Bad Check Demand Letter* (on the Web) to insist that proper monies be received within a specified time frame.

Should the need arise to take your case to a small claims court, as a plaintiff you would need to file a small claims complaint form that provides basic facts about your action. A sample *California Small Claims Complaint Form* is included in this chapter as a reference. These forms differ in each state.

Use the *Sample Debtor's Order of Examination* (on the Web) to order the debtor to appear in court. The sample *Judgment Debtor's Exam Form* (on the Web) allows a judgment creditor (anyone who is owed money by order of a court) to make the debtor answer questions about his or her assets, like jewelry, cars, stocks, bank accounts, valuable memorabilia, etc.

In some cases you may have need to command a witness's testimony to support your case. To command a witness, a written subpoena is the written device used to compel the appearance of a third party at a small claims trial. The law and forms used for subpoenas vary widely from state to state. A *Sample Connecticut Subpoena Form* is included on the Web as a general reference.

If you're a plaintiff and won a judgment, the next step is to collect it. Refer to the *Sample Post-Judgment Demand Letter* that would be used in real life as an opening to your collection efforts. Depending on your state's requirements, use a form similar to this chapter's *California Debtors Statement of Assets* to inquire into the debtor's personal property in the event he or she has not responded to your other collection efforts. To garnish a debtor's wages or other assets, refer to the sample *Writ of Execution Form* and *California Complaint Form* as examples of the types of documents you can present to a court clerk for approval and further direction.

As a plaintiff, the ultimate goal is to have your judgment satisfied. If finally the judgment is paid, the plaintiff files a Satisfaction of Judgment with the court. A sample *California Satisfaction of Judgment* is is on the Web as a reference.

125. Sample Cease and Desist Letter

Your Name

Address
City, State Zip

Debt Collector's Name
Address
City, State Zip

Re: (account #)

Dear (Name of Debt Collection Company or Employee):

Pursuant to my rights under federal debt collection laws, I am requesting that you cease and desist communication with me, in addition to my family and friends. This request in response to the
_____(alleged debts) you claim I owe.

This letter servers as notification that should your and (insert name of debt collection company) not comply with this request, I will immediately file a complaint with the Federal Trade Commission and the [your state] Attorney General's office. Civil and criminal claims will be pursued.

Sincerely,

(your name)

126. Sample Demand Letter

Michael Samuels
731 9th Avenue Suite E
San Diego, CA 92101
619.501.3825
fax: 419.735.2386

January 15, 2008

Kevin R. Baker
Big Bob's International Inc.
Royal Bank Building
Suite 2000
335 8th Ave. S.W.
New York, New York 10001
VIA U.S. MAIL

RE: Demand for Payment under Professional Services Agreement

Dear Mr. Baker,

As you know, I am president of I-Storm, Inc. ("I-Storm"), and I am writing to you about claims that I-Storm has against your company, Big Bobs International Inc. ("Big Bobs") under the Professional Services Agreement ("Agreement") dated March 17, 2006.

This letter shall serve as our final demand for payments under the agreement.

Under the terms of the Agreement, I-Storm is entitled to $13,000. Our records show that we have received $8,500. This leaves a remaining balance of $4,500.

Furthermore, I-Storm performed extra work beyond the terms of the Agreement in the form of additional software modules and changes from the specifications outlined in the Agreement ("Overages"). Our invoices show $2,800 in Overages.

With the preceding in mind, we therefore submit the following demand.

1. The remaining balance of $4,500 must be paid within 5 days of the date of this letter in the name of I-Storm, Inc.

2. With respect to the balance for Overages of $2,800, we will accept $500, also to be paid within 5 days of the date of this letter in the name of I-Storm, Inc.

3. Upon receiving the full balances due under the Agreement, I-Storm will grant a full license to Big Bobs of all work product under the Agreement.

4. You must agree in principle to the terms outlined herein within 2 days of the date of this letter. Thereafter, I will draft a settlement agreement formalizing these terms before the 5-day deadline for payment of the outstanding balances.

This offer is not subject to negotiation, including any arguments that Big Bobs might impose with respect to issues of performance under the Agreement. If you do not accept the offer outlined in this demand in writing within 2 days of the date of this letter, this offer will be automatically and permanently withdrawn.

Upon the withdrawal of this offer due to your non-acceptance, you are instructed (i) to return to I-Storm all work product under the Agreement, including, but not limited to, all software code, files, documentation, and other materials; (ii) that I-Storm shall terminate the Agreement pursuant to the "Breach and Termination" clause, and pursuant to such clause, all sums under the Agreement shall become due and payable and shall bear 1% interest per month from the date of invoice; and (iii) that I-Storm shall take immediate and permanent steps to ensure that Big Bobs never receive a license to the work product under the Agreement.

Thereafter, we will pursue the case through the court system. It is only fair to warn you that we may report this matter to the credit reporting bureau, and that that event, your credit rating may suffer. You can avoid the time and expense of court by resolving this matter. Our offer is generous, and we sincerely hope you accept it.

I await your response, and sincerely hope that you accept the terms of our demand on behalf of Big Bobs.

Yours truly,

Michael Samuels

President, I-Storm, Inc.

127. Sample Letter by Defendant to Plaintiff in a Collections Matter

December 1, 2010

Joe Plaintiff
Ace Collection Agency
1000 Collection Avenue
NY, NY 10001

Dear Joe,

I received your demand letter. While I sympathize with your position, I strongly suggest that you compromise this claim. Otherwise you are likely to receive nothing, even if you go to court. I am making this offer as a good-faith gesture to you.

I hope to spare us both the hassle and time of preparing paperwork, serving each other with papers, serving witnesses with subpoenas, going to court, and then the substantial efforts that you'll need to expend to collect on any judgment you might get.

We have already talked about my defenses and counterclaims. But I wish to remind you that I am steadfast in pursuing my side of the case. Small claims decisions are not reliable, so really neither of us truly know what is going to happen in court. In light of all this risk, I hope you accept my offer.

But really the main point is that even if you win a judgment for the full amount that you are seeking, you'll still need to expend a lot of effort to collect the debt. Unfortunately, I cannot and will not offer you my cooperation to collect on the judgment if you take me to court, but I do offer my cooperation to settle this case today. While I am now employed, I am considering leaving my job and moving out of state. If I do, you'll need to take the judgment to my new home state to collect. As far as assets, I don't have much, so I can't offer you much.

In order to settle the case, and without admitting any fault or waiving any evidentiary objections, I will agree to settle this case for 25% of what you are seeking, or $250. This is the most I can afford to pay, so this is my final offer.

Please let me know within three days if you accept this offer of settlement.

Yours very truly,

John Debtor

128. Sample Settlement and Compromise Agreement

MUTUAL RELEASE AND WAIVER AGREEMENT

THIS MUTUAL WAIVER AGREEMENT AND MUTUAL RELEASE ("Agreement") is entered into as of March _____, 2008, by and between Muirfield Furniture Company, Inc. ("Debtor") and Elizabeth Berkey, d/b/a Berkey Design ("Creditor") (collectively "Parties or Party"). For the purposes of the Agreement, "Party" includes subsidiaries and parents of a Party and includes owners as well as individuals serving as directors, officers, employees, agents, consultants, and advisors to or of a Party.

A. BACKGROUND

1. Debtor and Creditor entered into an agreement or series of agreements (the "Contract") whereby creditor provided graphic design, marketing, and other creative services to debtor.

2. Since the time of entering into the Contract, the Parties have determined that a settlement of the mutual obligations between them is appropriate and would best serve the interests of all of the Parties, and this Agreement is intended to express the Parties' intent to equitably settle the obligations arising from or related to the Contract.

B. AGREEMENT

NOW, THEREFORE, IN CONSIDERATION OF THE FOLLOWING, THE FOREGOING, THE MUTUAL COVENANTS, PROMISES, AGREEMENTS, REPRESENTATIONS AND RELEASES CONTAINED HEREIN, AND IN EXCHANGE FOR OTHER GOOD AND VALUABLE CONSIDERATION, THE RECEIPT, SUFFICIENCY AND ADEQUACY OF WHICH IS HEREBY ACKNOWLEDGED, THE PARTIES HEREBY AGREE AS FOLLOWS:

1. **Payment to Creditor.**
   a. Debtor shall pay $4,000.00 to Creditor, such payment to be made no later than 72 hours following the execution of this Agreement. Payment under this paragraph is a precondition to the effectiveness of this Agreement.
   b. Debtor shall owe no further liability or obligation to Creditor in connection with any services.

2. **No other Payments.** No additional funds shall be required to be paid or transferred by Creditor to Debtor, or by Debtor to Creditor.

3. **Nature and Effect of Agreement and Conditions Thereon.** By executing this Agreement, the Parties intend to and do hereby extinguish the obligations heretofore existing between them and arising from the Contract.

4. **Admissions.** This Agreement is not, and shall not be treated as, an admission of liability by either Party for any purpose, and shall not be admissible as evidence before any tribunal or court.

5. **Release and Discharge.** The Parties hereby compromise and settle any and all past, present, or future claims, demands, obligations, or causes of action for compensatory or punitive damages, costs, losses, expenses, and compensation whether based on tort, contract, or other theories of recovery, which the Parties have or which may later accrue to or be acquired by one Party against the other, the other's predecessors and successor in interest, heirs, and assigns, past present and future officers, directors, shareholders, agents, employees, parent and subsidiary organizations, affiliates, and partners, arising

from the subject matter of the Contract.

6. **Unknown Claims.** The Parties acknowledge and agree that upon execution of the release, this Agreement applies to all claims for damages or losses either Party may have against the other whether those damages or losses are known or unknown, foreseen or unforeseen.

[Note: the remainder of Paragraph 6 is only for use in the State of California]

In the event that this Agreement is deemed executed in California, the Parties thereby waive application of California Civil Code Section 1542.

The Parties certify that each has read the following provisions of California Civil Code Section 1542:

"A general release does not extend to claims which the Debtor does not know or suspect to exist in his favor at the time of executing the release, which if known by him must have materially affected his settlement with the debtor."

The Parties understand and acknowledge that the significance and consequence of this waiver of California Civil Code Section 1542 is that even if one Party should eventually suffer additional damages arising out of the facts referred to in Section A, above, it will not be able to make any claim for these damages. Furthermore, the Parties acknowledge that they intend these consequences even as to claims for damages that may exist as of the date of this release but which the damaged or harmed Party does not know exists, and which, if known, would materially affect that Party's decision to execute this release, regardless of whether the damaged Party's lack of knowledge is the result of ignorance, oversight, error, negligence, or any other cause.

7. **Conditions of Execution.** Each Party acknowledges and warrants that its execution of this compromise agreement and release is free and voluntary. All Parties and signatories to this Agreement acknowledge and agree that the terms of this Agreement are contractual and not mere recital, and all Parties and signatories represent and warrant that they have carefully read this Agreement, have fully reviewed its provisions with their attorneys and know and understand its contents. It is understood and agreed by all Parties and signatories to this Agreement that execution of this Agreement may affect rights and liabilities of substantial extent and degree and with the full understanding of that fact, they represent that the covenants and releases provided for in this Agreement are in their respective best interests.

8. **Entire Agreement.** This Agreement constitutes the entire agreement between the Parties and signatories and all prior and contemporaneous conversation, negotiations, possible and alleged agreements, and representations, covenants, and warranties, express or implied, or written, with respect to the subject matter hereof, are waived, merged herein and superseded hereby. There are no other agreements, representations, covenants or warranties not set forth herein. The terms of this Agreement may not be contradicted by evidence of any prior or contemporaneous agreement. The Parties further intend and agree that this Agreement constitutes the complete and exclusive statement of its terms and that no extrinsic evidence whatsoever may be introduced in any judicial or arbitration proceeding, if any, involving this Agreement. No part of this Agreement may be amended or modified in any way unless such amendment or modification is expressed in writing signed by all Parties to this Agreement.

9. **Counterparts.** This Agreement may be executed in multiple counterparts, each of which shall be deemed an original but all of which together shall constitute one and the same instrument. When all of the Parties and signatories have executed any copy hereof, such execution shall constitute the execution of this Agreement, whereupon it shall become effective.

10. **Governing Law.** THIS AGREEMENT WILL BE GOVERNED AND CONSTRUED IN ACCORDANCE WITH THE LAW OF THE STATE OF CALIFORNIA AND THE UNITED STATES OF AMERICA, WITHOUT REGARD TO CONFLICT OF LAW PRINCIPLES. This Agreement shall not be strictly construed against any Party to this Agreement. Any controversy or claim arising out of or relating to this Agreement, or the breach thereof, shall be resolved by arbitration administered under the rules of the American Arbitration Association in accordance with its applicable rules. Such arbitration shall take place within Marin County, California, and shall be binding upon all Parties, and any judgment upon or any an award rendered by the arbitrator may be entered in any court having jurisdiction thereof.

IN WITNESS WHEREOF, the Parties and signatories execute this Agreement on the dates indicated.

Muirfield Furniture Company, Inc., Debtor: Elizabeth Berkey/Berkey Design, Creditor:

_____   _____

Donald LeBuhn, President   Elizabeth Berkey

129. California Complaint Form

Case Number: _____

Plaintiff *(list names):* _____

(1) The Plaintiff (the person, business, or public entity that is suing) is:

Name: _____ Phone: (___) _____

Street address: _____
                  Street   *City*   *State*   *Zip*

Mailing address *(if different):* _____
                          Street   *City*   *State*   *Zip*

If more than one Plaintiff, list next Plaintiff here:

Name: _____ Phone: (___) _____

Street address: _____
                  Street   *City*   *State*   *Zip*

Mailing address *(if different):* _____
                          Street   *City*   *State*   *Zip*

☐ *Check here if more than 2 Plaintiffs and attach Form SC-100A.*

☐ *Check here if either Plaintiff listed above is doing business under a fictitious name. If so, attach Form SC-103.*

(2) The Defendant (the person, business, or public entity being sued) is:

Name: _____ Phone: (___) _____

Street address: _____
                  Street   *City*   *State*   *Zip*

Mailing address *(if different):* _____
                          Street   *City*   *State*   *Zip*

If more than one Defendant, list next Defendant here:

Name: _____ Phone: (___) _____

Street address: _____
                  Street   *City*   *State*   *Zip*

Mailing address *(if different):* _____
                          Street   *City*   *State*   *Zip*

☐ *Check here if more than 2 Defendants and attach Form SC-100A.*

☐ *Check here if any Defendant is on active military duty, and write his or her name here:* _____

(3) The Plaintiff claims the Defendant owes $ _____ . *(Explain below):*

a. Why does the Defendant owe the Plaintiff money? _____

_____

_____

b. When did this happen? *(Date):* _____

If no specific date, give the time period: *Date started:* _____ *Through:* _____

c. How did you calculate the money owed to you? *(Do not include court costs or fees for service.)* _____

_____

☐ *Check here if you need more space. Attach one sheet of paper or Form MC-031 and write "SC-100, Item 3" at the top.*

| Revised January 1, 2007 | **Plaintiff's Claim and ORDER to Go to Small Claims Court** (Small Claims) | **SC-100**, Page 2 of 5 → |

Case Number:

Plaintiff *(list names):* _____

4 **You must ask the Defendant (in person, in writing, or by phone) to pay you before you sue. Have you done this?** ☐ Yes ☐ No

If no, explain why not: _____

5 **Why are you filing your claim at this courthouse?**
This courthouse covers the area *(check the one that applies):*

a. ☐ (1) Where the Defendant lives or does business.   (4) Where a contract (written or spoken) was made,
      (2) Where the Plaintiff's property was damaged.   signed, performed, or broken by the Defendant *or*
      (3) Where the Plaintiff was injured.   where the Defendant lived or did business when
                                          the Defendant made the contract.

b. ☐ Where the buyer or lessee signed the contract, lives now, or lived when the contract was made, if this claim is about an offer or contract for personal, family, or household goods, services, or loans. *(Code Civ. Proc., § 395(b).)*

c. ☐ Where the buyer signed the contract, lives now, or lived when the contract was made, if this claim is about a retail installment contract (like a credit card). *(Civil Code, § 1812.10.)*

d. ☐ Where the buyer signed the contract, lives now, or lived when the contract was made, or where the vehicle is permanently garaged, if this claim is about a vehicle finance sale. *(Civil Code, § 2984.4.)*

e. ☐ Other *(specify):* _____

6 **List the zip code of the place checked in ⑤ above** *(if you know):* _____

7 **Is your claim about an attorney-client fee dispute?** ☐ Yes ☐ No
If yes, and if you have had arbitration, fill out Form SC-101, attach it to this form, and check here: ☐

8 **Are you suing a public entity?** ☐ Yes ☐ No
If yes, you must file a written claim with the entity first. ☐ *A claim was filed on (date):* _____
If the public entity denies your claim or does not answer within the time allowed by law, you can file this form.

9 **Have you filed more than 12 other small claims within the last 12 months in California?**
☐ Yes ☐ No   *If yes, the filing fee for this case will be higher.*

10 **I understand that by filing a claim in small claims court, I have no right to appeal this claim.**

11 I have not filed, and understand that I cannot file, more than two small claims cases for more than $2,500 in California during this calendar year.

I declare, under penalty of perjury under California State law, that the information above and on any attachments to this form is true and correct.

Date:_____
     Plaintiff types or prints name here   ▶ *Plaintiff signs here*

Date:_____
     Second Plaintiff types or prints name here   ▶ *Second Plaintiff signs here*

Requests for Accommodations
Assistive listening systems, computer-assisted, real-time captioning, or sign language interpreter services are available if you ask at least 5 days before the trial. Contact the clerk's office for Form MC-410, *Request for Accommodations by Persons With Disabilities and Order. (Civil Code, § 54.8.)*

Revised January 1, 2007   **Plaintiff's Claim and ORDER**   **SC-100,** Page 3 of 5
                              to Go to Small Claims Court   →
                                       (Small Claims)

130. Debtor's Order of Examination (California)

Name and Address of Court:

SMALL CLAIMS CASE NO.:

PLAINTIFF/DE MANDANTE *(Name, street address, and telephone number of each):*

DEFENDANT/DEMANDADO *(Name, street address, and telephone number of each):*

Telephone No.:

Telephone No.:

☐ See attached sheet for additional plaintiffs and defendants.

ORDER TO PRODUCE STATEMENT OF ASSETS
AND TO APPEAR FOR EXAMINATION

1. TO JUDGMENT DEBTOR *(name):*

2. YOU ARE ORDERED

   a. to pay the judgment and file proof of payment (a canceled check or money order or cash receipt, and a written declaration that shows full payment of the judgment, including postjudgment costs and interest) with the court before the hearing date shown in the box below, **OR**

   b. to (1) personally appear in this court on the date and time shown in the box below, and (2) bring with you a completed *Judgment Debtor's Statement of Assets* (form SC-133). (At the hearing you will be required to explain why you did not complete and mail form SC-133 to judgment creditor within 30 days after the *Notice of Entry of Judgment* (form SC-130) was mailed or handed to you by the clerk, and to answer questions about your income and assets.)

HEARING DATE FECHA DEL JUICIO		DATE	DAY	TIME	PLACE	COURT USE
	1.					
	2.					
	3.					

If you fail to appear and have not paid the judgment, including postjudgment costs and interest, a bench warrant may be issued for your arrest, you may be held in contempt of court, and you may be ordered to pay penalties.	Si usted no se presenta y no ha pagado el monto del fallo judicial, inclusive las costas e intereses posterlores al fallo, la corte puede expedir una orden de detencion contra usted, declararle en desacato y ordenar clue pague multas.

3. This order may be served by a sheriff, marshal, or registered process server.

Date:

▶

(SIGNATURE OF JUDGE)

APPLICATION FOR THIS ORDER

A. Judgment creditor (the person who won the case) *(name):*   applies for an order requiring judgment debtor (the person or business who lost the case and owes money) *(name):*

   to (1) pay the judgment or (2) personally appear in this court with a completed *Judgment Debtor's Statement of Assets* (form SC-133), explain why judgment debtor did not pay the judgment or complete and mail form SC-133 to judgment creditor within 30 days after the *Notice of Entry of Judgment* was mailed or handed to judgment debtor, and answer questions about judgment debtor's income and assets.

B. Judgment creditor states the following:

   (1) Judgment debtor has not paid the judgment.

   (2) Judgment debtor either did not file an appeal or the appeal has been dismissed or judgment debtor lost the appeal.

   (3) Judgment debtor either did not file a motion to vacate or the motion to vacate has been denied.

   (4) More than 30 days have passed since the *Notice of Entry of Judgment* form was mailed or delivered to judgment debtor.

   (5) Judgment creditor has not received a completed *Judgment Debtor's Statement of Assets* form from judgment debtor.

   (6) The person to be examined resides or has a place of business in this county or within 150 miles of the place of examination.

I declare under penalty of perjury under the laws of the State of California that the foregoing is true and correct.

Date:

▶

· · · · · · · · · · · (TYPE OR PRINT NAME) · · · · · · · · · (See Instructions on reverse)   (DECLARANT)

— The county provides small claims advisor services free of charge. —

Page 1 of 2

Form Adopted for Mandatory Use
Judicial Council of California
SC-134 [Rev. January 1, 2007]

APPLICATION AND ORDER TO PRODUCE STATEMENT OF ASSETS AND TO APPEAR FOR EXAMINATION
(Small Claims)

Code of Civil Procedure §§ 11 6.820,116.830
www.courtinfo.ca.gov

American LegalNet, Inc.
www.FormsWorkflow.com

SC-134

INSTRUCTIONS FOR JUDGMENT CREDITOR

1. To set a hearing on an *Application for Order to Produce Statement of Assets and to Appear for Examination,* you must complete this form, present it to the court clerk, and pay the fee for an initial hearing date or a reset hearing date.

2. After you file this form, the clerk will set a hearing date, note the hearing date on the form, and return two copies or an original and one copy of the form to you.

3. You must have a copy of this form and a blank copy of the *Judgment Debtor's Statement of Assets* (form SC-133) personally served on the judgment debtor by a sheriff, marshal, or registered process server at least 10 calendar days before the date of the hearing, and have a proof of service filed with the court. The law provides for a new fee if you reset the hearing.

4. If the judgment is paid, including all postjudgment costs and interest, you must immediately complete the *Acknowledgment of Satisfaction of Judgment form* on the reverse of the *Notice of Entry of Judgment* (form SC-130) and file a copy with the court.

5. You must attend the hearing unless the judgment has been paid.

6. This form is intended to be an easy tool to enforce your right to receive a completed *Judgment Debtor's Statement of Assets* (form SC-133). This form is not intended to replace the *Application and Order for Appearance and Examination* (form EJ-125), often called an "Order for Examination." The *Application and Order for Appearance and Examination* may still be used to enforce a small claims judgment if you are not seeking at the same time to make the debtor complete a *Judgment Debtor's Statement of Assets.*

SC-134 [Rev. January 1, 2007]

APPLICATION AND ORDER TO PRODUCE STATEMENT OF ASSETS AND TO APPEAR FOR EXAMINATION (Small Claims)

Page 2 of 2

131. Connecticut Subpoena

SUBPOENA/CIVIL
JD-CL-43 Rev. 3-06
C.G.S. § 52-143, 52-144
Pr. Bk. Secs. 7-19, 24-22

STATE OF CONNECTICUT
SUPERIOR COURT
www.jud.ct.gov

COURT USE ONLY

SUBISSU

INSTRUCTIONS: Do NOT use this subpoena if the witness is being summoned by the state or by the attorney general or an assistant attorney general or by any public defender or assistant public defender acting in his/her official capacity.

NAME OF CASE	DOCKET NO.

				ADDRESS OF COURT (No., street and town)
☐ Judicial District	☐ Housing Session	☐ G.A. No. ____	☐ Small Claims Area	

TO: (Name and address)

DATE AND TIME YOU ARE TO APPEAR	TIME ___ . m.	REPORT TO
		☐ CLERK'S OFFICE
		☐ COURTROOM NO. _____
		☐ PERSON REQUESTING SUBPOENA

BY AUTHORITY OF THE STATE OF CONNECTICUT, you are hereby commanded to appear before the Superior Court in session at the above address on the date indicated above or to such day thereafter and within sixty days hereof on which the action named above is legally to be tried, to testify what you know in said action pending in the court.

YOU ARE FURTHER COMMANDED TO BRING WITH YOU AND PRODUCE:

HEREOF FAIL NOT, UNDER PENALTY OF THE LAW.
To any proper officer or indifferent person to serve and return.

NAME OF PERSON REQUESTING SUBPOENA	TELEPHONE NO.

SIGNED (Clerk, Commissioner of Superior Court)	ON (Date)	AT

NOTICE TO THE PERSON SUMMONED

You must report to the court at the time and address shown above and remain until this case is disposed of and you are discharged by the court. Present this subpoena when you report.

If you do not appear in court on the day and at the time stated, or on the day and at the time to which your appearance may have been postponed or continued by order of an officer of the court, and one day's attendance and traveling fees have been tendered to you, the court may order that you be arrested. In addition, if the aforementioned fees have been paid to you and you fail to appear and testify, without reasonable excuse, you shall be fined not more than twenty-five dollars and pay all damages to the aggrieved party. The party requesting the subpoena is responsible for paying the witness fees.

Any questions regarding this subpoena should be directed to the person who requested it.

RETURN OF SERVICE

JUDICIAL DISTRICT OF	DATE
ss. _____ , Connecticut	

Then and there I made service of the within subpoena not less than eighteen hours prior to the time designated for the person summoned to appear, by reading the same in the presence and hearing/leaving a true and attested copy hereof in the hands/at the last usual place of abode of each of the within-named persons, viz:	**FEES**
	COPY
	ENDORSEMENT
	SERVICE
	TRAVEL (Show miles & amount)

ATTEST (Signature of proper officer or indifferent person)	TITLE (If applicable)	TOTAL

DISTRIBUTION: ORIGINAL - Court COPY1 - Witness COPY2 - File

132. Sample Post-Judgment Demand Letter

The following demand letter is a post-judgment demand in a case concerning a software development contract.

Michael Samuels
731 9th Avenue Suite E
San Diego, CA 92101
619.501.3825
fax: 419.735.2386

January 15, 2008

Kevin R. Baker
Big Bob's International Inc.
Royal Bank Building
Suite 2000
335 8th Ave. S.W.
New York, New York 10001

VIA U.S. MAIL

RE: Demand for Post-Judgment Payment, Case No. 07-0245

Dear Mr. Baker,

As you know, I am president of I-Storm, Inc. ("I-Storm"), and I am writing to you to demand payment of the Judgment (Case No. 07-0245) against your company, Big Bobs International Inc. ("Big Bobs") in the amount of $4,500.

 Yours truly,

Michael Samuels
President, I-Storm, Inc.

133. Debtor's Statement of Assets (California)

MAIL TO THE JUDGMENT CREDITOR DO NOT FILE WITH THE COURT	SC-133

JUDGMENT CREDITOR (the person or business who won the case) *(name):*

JUDGMENT DEBTOR (the person or business who lost the case and owes money) *(name):*

SMALL CLAIMS CASE NO.:

NOTICE TO JUDGMENT DEBTOR: You *must* (1) pay the judgment or (2) appeal or (3) file a motion to vacate. If you fail to pay or take one of the other two actions, you must complete and mail this form to the judgment creditor. If you do not, you may have to go to court to answer questions and may have penalties imposed on you by the court.	**AVISO AL DEUDOR POR FALLO JUDICIAL: Usted debe (1) pagar el monto del fallo judicial, o (2) presentar un recurso de apelación o (3) presentar un recurso de nulidad.** Si usted no paga el fallo o presenta uno de estos dos recursos, deberá llenar y enviar por correo este formulario a su acreedor por fallo judicial. Si no lo hace, es posible que deba presentarse ante la corte para contestar preguntas y pagar las multas que la corte le pueda imponer.

INSTRUCTIONS

The small claims court has ruled that you owe money to the judgment creditor.

1. You may appeal a judgment against you only on the other party's claim. You may *not* appeal a judgment against you on *your* claim.

   a. If you appeared at the trial and you want to appeal, you must file a *Notice of Appeal* (form SC-140) within 30 days after the date the *Notice of Entry of Judgment* (form SC-130) was mailed or handed to you by the clerk.

   b. If you did not appear at the trial, before you can appeal, you must first file a *Notice of Motion to Vacate Judgment and Declaration* (form SC-135) and pay the required fee within 30 days after the date the *Notice of Entry of Judgment* was mailed or handed to you. The judgment cannot be collected until the motion is decided. If your motion is denied, you then have 10 days after the date the notice of denial was mailed to file your appeal.

2. Unless you **pay the judgment or appeal the judgment or file a motion to vacate, you must fill out this form and mail it to the person who won the case** within **30 days** after the *Notice of Entry of Judgment* was mailed or handed to you by the clerk. Mailing this completed form does not stay enforcement of the judgment.

3. If you lose your appeal or motion to vacate, you must pay the judgment, including postjudgment costs and interest. As soon as the small claims court denies your motion to vacate and the denial is not appealed, or receives the dismissal of your appeal or judgment from the superior court after appeal, the judgment is no longer suspended and may be immediately enforced against you by the judgment creditor.

4. Unless you have paid the judgment, complete and mail this form to the judgment creditor within **30 days** after the date the clerk mails or delivers to you (a) the denial of your motion to vacate, or (b) the dismissal of your appeal, or (c) the judgment against you on your appeal.

If you were sued as an individual, skip this box and begin with item 1 below. Otherwise, check the applicable box, attach the documents indicated, and complete item 15 on the reverse.

   a. ☐ *(Corporation or partnership)* Attached to this form is a statement describing the nature, value, and exact location of all assets of the corporation or the partners, and a statement showing that the person signing this form is authorized to submit this form on behalf of the corporation or partnership.

   b. ☐ *(Governmental agency)* Attached to this form is the statement of an authorized representative of the agency stating when the agency will pay the judgment and any reasons for its failure to do so.

JUDGMENT DEBTOR'S STATEMENT OF ASSETS

EMPLOYMENT

1. What are your sources of income and occupation? *(Provide job title and name of division or office in which you work.)*

2. a. Name and address of your business or employer *(include address of your payroll or human resources department, if different):*

   b. If not employed, names and addresses of all sources of income *(specify):*

3. How often are you paid?
   ☐ daily   ☐ every two weeks   ☐ monthly
   ☐ weekly   ☐ twice a month   ☐ other *(explain):*

4. What is your gross pay each pay period? $

5. What is your take-home pay each pay period? $

6. If your spouse earns any income, give the name of your spouse, the name and address of the business or employer, job title, and division or office *(specify):*

Page 1 of 2

Form Adopted for Mandatory Use Judicial Council of California SC-133 [Rev. January 1, 2004]	**JUDGMENT DEBTOR'S STATEMENT OF ASSETS** **(Small Claims)**	Code of Civil Procedure, §§ 116.620(a), 116.830
		American LegalNet, Inc. www.USCourtForms.com

CASH, BANK DEPOSITS

7. How much money do you have in cash? . . . . $

8. How much other money do you have in banks, savings and loans, credit unions, and other financial
institutions either in your own name or jointly *(list):*

Name and address of financial institution	Account number	Individual or joint?	Balance
a.			$
b.			$
c.			$

PROPERTY

9. List all automobiles, other vehicles, and boats owned in your name or jointly:

Make and year	License and vehicle identification (VIN) numbers	Value	Legal owner if different from registered owner	Amount owed
a.		$		$
b.		$		$
c.		$		$
d.		$		$

10. List all real estate owned in your name or jointly:

Address of real estate	Fair market value	Amount owed
a.	$	$
b.	$	$

OTHER PERSONAL PROPERTY (*Do not list household furniture and furnishings, appliances, or clothing.*)

11. List anything of value not listed above owned in your name or jointly (*continue on attached sheet if necessary*):

Description	Value	Address where property is located
a.	$	
b.	$	
c.	$	

12. Is anyone holding assets for you? ☐ Yes. ☐ No. If yes, describe the assets and give the name and address of the
person or entity holding each asset *(specify):*

13. Have you disposed of or transferred any asset within the last 60 days? ☐ Yes. ☐ No. If yes, give the name and
address of each person or entity who received any asset and describe each asset *(specify):*

14. If you are not able to pay the judgment in one lump sum, you may be able to make payment arrangements with the person or
business who won the case (the judgment creditor). State the amount that you can pay each month: $, beginning
on *(date):*   . If you are unable to agree, you may also ask the court for permission to
make installment payments by filing a *Request to Pay Judgment in Installments* (form SC-106).

15. I declare under penalty of perjury under the laws of the State of California that the foregoing is true and correct.

Date:

▶

_____   _____
(TYPE OR PRINT NAME)   (SIGNATURE)

Mail or deliver this completed form to the judgment creditor at the address shown on the **Notice of Entry of Judgment** *form.*

SC-133 [Rev. January 1, 2004]   **JUDGMENT DEBTOR'S STATEMENT OF ASSETS**   Page 2 of 2
                                                            (Small Claims)

134. Writ of Execution (California)

EJ-130

ATTORNEY OR PARTY WITHOUT ATTORNEY *(Name, State Bar number and address):*

FOR COURT USE ONLY

TELEPHONE NO.:   FAX NO. *(Optional):*

E-MAIL ADDRESS *(Optional):*

ATTORNEY FOR *(Name):*

☐ ATTORNEY FOR   ☐ JUDGMENT CREDITOR   ☐ ASSIGNEE OF RECORD

SUPERIOR COURT OF CALIFORNIA, COUNTY OF

STREET ADDRESS:

MAILING ADDRESS:

CITY AND ZIP CODE:

BRANCH NAME:

PLAINTIFF:

DEFENDANT:

WRIT OF

☐ **EXECUTION (Money Judgment)**
☐ **POSSESSION OF**   ☐ **Personal Property**
       ☐ **Real Property**
☐ **SALE**

CASE NUMBER:

1. **To the Sheriff or Marshal of the County of:**

   You are directed to enforce the judgment described below with daily interest and your costs as provided by law.

2. **To any registered process server:** You are authorized to serve this writ only in accord with CCP 699.080 or CCP 715.040.

3. *(Name):*

   is the ☐ judgment creditor ☐ assignee of record   whose address is shown on this form above the court's name.

4. **Judgment debtor** *(name and last known address):*

   ☐ Additional judgment debtors on next page

5. **Judgment entered on** *(date):*

6. ☐ **Judgment renewed on** *(dates):*

7. **Notice of sale** under this writ
   a. ☐ has not been requested.
   b. ☐ has been requested *(see next page).*
8. ☐ Joint debtor information on next page.

[SEAL]

9. ☐ See next page for information on real or personal property to be delivered under a writ of possession or sold under a writ of sale.

10. ☐ This writ is issued on a sister-state judgment.

11. Total judgment . . . . $

12. Costs after judgment (per filed order or memo CCP 685.090) . . . . $

13. Subtotal *(add 11 and 12)* . . . . $

14. Credits . . . . $

15. Subtotal *(subtract 14 from 13)* . . . . . . $

16. Interest after judgment (per filed affidavit CCP 685.050) (not on GC 6103.5 fees). . . $

17. Fee for issuance of writ . . . . $

18. **Total** *(add 15, 16, and 17)* . . . . $

19. Levying officer:
    (a) Add daily interest from date of writ *(at the legal rate on 15)* (not on GC 6103.5 fees) of. . . . . . $
    (b) Pay directly to court costs included in 11 and 17 (GC 6103.5, 68511.3; CCP 699.520(i)) . . . . $

20. ☐ The amounts called for in items 11–19 are different for each debtor. These amounts are stated for each debtor on Attachment 20.

Issued on *(date):*

Clerk, by _____ , Deputy

NOTICE TO PERSON SERVED: SEE NEXT PAGE FOR IMPORTANT INFORMATION.

Page 1 of 2

Form Approved for Optional Use
Judicial Council of California
EJ-130 [Rev. January 1, 2006]

WRIT OF EXECUTION

American LegalNet, Inc.
www.USCourtForms.com

Code of Civil Procedure, §§ 699.520, 712.010,
Government Code, § 6103.5
www.courtinfo.ca.gov

135. Satisfaction of Judgment (California)

EJ-100

ATTORNEY OR PARTY WITHOUT ATTORNEY *(Name, State Bar number, and address):*
After recording return to:

TELEPHONE NO.:
FAX NO. *(Optional):*
E-MAIL ADDRESS *(Optional):*
ATTORNEY FOR *(Name):*

SUPERIOR COURT OF CALIFORNIA, COUNTY OF
STREET ADDRESS:
MAILING ADDRESS:
CITY AND ZIP CODE:
BRANCH NAME:

FOR RECORDER'S OR SECRETARY OF STATE'S USE ONLY

PLAINTIFF:

DEFENDANT:

CASE NUMBER:

ACKNOWLEDGMENT OF SATISFACTION OF JUDGMENT
☐ **FULL** ☐ **PARTIAL** ☐ **MATURED INSTALLMENT**

FOR COURT USE ONLY

1. Satisfaction of the judgment is acknowledged as follows:
   a. ☐ Full satisfaction
      (1) ☐ Judgment is satisfied in full.
      (2) ☐ The judgment creditor has accepted payment or performance other than that specified in the judgment in full satisfaction of the judgment.
   b. ☐ Partial satisfaction
      The amount received in partial satisfaction of the judgment is $
   c. ☐ Matured installment
      All matured installments under the installment judgment have been satisfied as of *(date):*

2. Full name and address of judgment creditor:*

3. Full name and address of assignee of record, if any:

4. Full name and address of judgment debtor being fully or partially released:*

5. a. Judgment entered on *(date):*
   b. ☐ Renewal entered on *(date):*

6. ☐ An ☐ abstract of judgment ☐ certified copy of the judgment has been recorded as follows *(complete all information for each county where recorded):*

   COUNTY   **DATE OF RECORDING**   **INSTRUMENT NUMBER**

7. ☐ A notice of judgment lien has been filed in the office of the Secretary of State as file number *(specify):*

NOTICE TO JUDGMENT DEBTOR: If this is an acknowledgment of full satisfaction of judgment, it will have to be recorded in each county shown in item 6 above, if any, in order to release the judgment lien, and will have to be filed in the office of the Secretary of State to terminate any judgment lien on personal property.

Date:

▶ _____
*(SIGNATURE OF JUDGMENT CREDITOR OR ASSIGNEE OF CREDITOR OR ATTORNEY**)*

Page 1 of 1

*The names of the judgment creditor and judgment debtor must be stated as shown in any Abstract of Judgment which was recorded and is being released by this satisfaction. ** **A separate notary acknowledgment must be attached for each signature.**

Form Approved for Optional Use
Judicial Council of California
EJ-100 [Rev. January 1, 2005]

ACKNOWLEDGMENT OF SATISFACTION OF JUDGMENT

American LegalNet, Inc.
www.USCourtForms.com

Code of Civil Procedure, §§ 724.060, 724.120, 724.250

CHAPTER 14

When You Have to File for Bankruptcy

Small to medium-sized businesses make up a substantial portion of the United States' economy. Many businesses will experience financial difficulties at one time or another. These forms focus on bankruptcy relief for small to medium-sized businesses in financial distress, providing the forms required to complete the steps. In some cases, where the core business plan is sound, the business may be salvageable with the assistance of bankruptcy. Where the core business plan is not sound and the business needs to be wound down, bankruptcy may provide an orderly way to liquidate the business's assets. There are various bankruptcy provisions available to assist businesses with either restructuring their finances or liquidating their assets. In addition, there are some non-bankruptcy alternatives that may be available to provide aid.

When reviewing the bankruptcy forms included in this chapter, keep in mind that bankruptcy law is complex and technical. In addition to the bankruptcy code, which is a set of federal statutes, and national bankruptcy rules, the courts around the country have published decisions and enacted local rules that vary the substance and procedures of the bankruptcy practice from one part of the country to another. Bankruptcy law also looks to state law for certain determinations, which varies the substance of bankruptcy practices around the country.

The bankruptcy case commences with the filing of either a *voluntary bankruptcy petition* form or an *involuntary petition* form. Either way, the bankruptcy petition is the document that starts the process. All assets owned by the debtor on the date the bankruptcy is filed (the petition date), including real and personal property, and tangible and intangible property, become property of the bankruptcy estate and are commonly referred to as "property of the estate." The estate itself is commonly referred to as the "bankruptcy estate." On the petition date, the automatic stay is imposed to prevent creditors from seizing property of the estate or continuing to sue the debtor.

Although debtors file approximately 99% of all bankruptcy cases voluntarily, an involuntary bankruptcy petition filed by one or more creditors of a debtor is sometimes an effective collection tool. If a business isn't prepared for it, an involuntary bankruptcy petition can cause havoc on business operations. Usually the management of a business knows of outstanding debt. An involuntary bankruptcy is filed only after other collection demands have failed.

An involuntary bankruptcy petition is prosecuted like a lawsuit. An involuntary petition must be filed in the district where the debtor's principal place of business, residence, domicile, or principal assets were located for 180 days before the involuntary bankruptcy petition is filed. After the filing of an involuntary bankruptcy petition, the bankruptcy court may hold a trial to determine whether the petition was proper. Until that determination is made, the debtor, with some limitations, may continue to operate the business and dispose of property as if the involuntary petition had not been filed.

The first step in an involuntary bankruptcy proceeding is the filing of a petition. *The Summons to Debtor in Involuntary Case* is the notice that accompanies the petition, advising of the names of the debtor and the attorney for the petitioning creditor(s), the court in which the proceeding was filed, and the time limits for responding to the petition.

When completing a voluntary petition, the debtor must include form *Exhibit A* should the debtor be required to file periodic reports (e.g., forms 10K and 10Q) with the Securities and Exchange Commission pursuant to Section 13 or 15(d) of the Securities Exchange Act of 1934 and is requesting relief under chapter 11 of the Bankruptcy Code. In addition, the debtor must attach a completed *Exhibit C* form if, to the best of the debtor's knowledge, the debtor owns or has possession of property that may pose harm to the public health or safety.

Creditors whose claims are not secured by liens are referred to as "unsecured creditors." Creditors whose claims are secured by liens are referred to as "secured creditors." There are different classes of unsecured creditors. The class to which a particular unsecured creditor belongs determines the priority in which that creditor will receive payment. Rule 1007(d) of the Federal Rules of Bankruptcy Procedure (referred to as "Bankruptcy Rule" requires chapter 11 and chapter 9 debtors to file, with the petition, a list containing the name, address, and claim of the creditors holding the 20 largest unsecured claims. Refer to the sample form that should contain the *List of Creditors Holding 20 Largest Unsecured Claims.* Keep in mind for all petitions, the *Statement of Social Security Number* and the *Under Penalty of Perjury* form for corporate or partnership debtors must be submitted, as well.

Within 10 days after the date of the filing of a petition, the company filing the petition must file a declaration under penalty of perjury any fee received from or on behalf of the debtor within 12 months immediately prior to the filing of the case, and any unpaid fee charged to the debtor using the *Disclosure of Compensation* form.

In a bankruptcy case, the financial affairs of the business will become an open book. The bankruptcy code requires the debtor to file a detailed and itemized list of all of its assets and debts after a petition is filed. The *Statement of Financial Affairs* (on the Web) requires the business to disclose its income over the past few years, all payments made to creditors in the 90 days preceding the case, all payments made to insiders of the business (e.g., shareholders, officers, directors, partners) within two years prior to the bankruptcy case, the name and address of anyone who has kept the books and records of the business, a list of bank accounts, even if the accounts are closed, a list of anyone who has been provided with a financial statement of the business within one year preceding the bankruptcy case, and the amount of money paid to the debtor's attorney for insolvency-related advice, among other information.

The debtor must file the required lists of assets and liabilities to commence a bankruptcy case, collectively called the "schedules." The lists of assets and debts are referred to as the "bankruptcy schedules." The list of assets is required to be itemized and to contain a detailed description of each asset and its location and fair market value. The list of debts (or creditors) is required to identify the name and address of and amount owing to each creditor. This chapter includes the following schedules:

- Schedule A. Real Property
- Schedule B. Personal Property
- Schedule C. Property Claimed as Exempt
- Schedule D. Creditors Holding Secured Claims
- Schedule E. Creditors Holding Unsecured Priority Claims
- Schedule F. Creditors Holding Unsecured Nonpriority Claims
- Schedule G. Executory Contracts and Unexpired Leases
- Schedule H. Codebtors
- Schedule I. Current Income of Individual Debtor(s)
- Schedule J. Current Expenditures of Individual Debtor(s)

The Declaration Concerning Debtor's Schedules is filed separately from the petition and schedules at the case opening. After completing all the schedules and the *Summary of Schedules*, debtors should complete the *Declaration Concerning Debtor's Schedules*. The schedules are a document for filing that may be prepared by a bankruptcy petition preparer. If multiple people sign the prepared the document, additional signed sheets conforming to the certification on the Official Form must be attached for each person.

A chapter 11 case is intended to reorganize either an individual's or a business entity's financial affairs. An example of the *Notice of Chapter 11 Bankruptcy Case, Meeting of Creditors, and Deadlines* is included in this chapter for reference. The goal of a chapter 11 bankruptcy is to propose a plan that will pay creditors some amount over time and obtain sufficient votes to confirm the plan. In essence, a plan of reorganization is a promise to repay the pre-petition debts over time or an involuntary refinance. Although somewhat contrary to its stated goal, a chapter 11 can be used for an orderly liquidation of a debtor's assets.

Before a chapter 11 plan can be given to creditors and other interested parties for voting, a disclosure statement or reorganization plan, which is sent with the chapter 11 plan, usually has to be approved by the bankruptcy court. A disclosure statement must contain enough detailed information about the plan and the debtor so that a hypothetical creditor will have enough information to make an informed decision about whether to vote for or against the debtor's proposed plan. Typically, the disclosure statement will contain information regarding the debtor's historical and present financial performance, solutions or proposals to address the debtor's financial problems, the debtor's financial projections, a description of the debtor's assets and liabilities, a description of the plan, future management of the debtor, potential risks and tax liabilities associated with the plan, and what creditors can expect to receive if the debtor's assets were to be liquidated in a chapter 7.

The Legal Department will request that a hearing date be assigned by the Office of Administrative Hearings and will mail an *Order and Notice of Hearing* drafted to advise parties of the date and time of the hearing as well as the location and pertinent legal stipulations.

Once the disclosure statement is approved, it is sent to creditors with the plan and a ballot for voting for or against the plan. Official Form14, or the *Class Ballot for Accepting of Reorganization* is used as a ballot for accepting or rejecting the plan(s) of reorganization. The ballot is to be used by general creditors (including secured, priority unsecured, and non-priority unsecured creditors), bondholders, debenture holders, other debt security holders, and equity security holders who are entitled to vote on the plan(s).

Debtors can use the *Order for Relief in an Involuntary Case* 180 days after the petition date or entry of the order for relief to obtain acceptances of its plan.

Creditors can file a *Proof of Claim* in a bankruptcy proceeding, which is necessary if the creditor desires to be paid. The procedure for filing a proof of claim depends on the chapter of the U.S. Bankruptcy Code under which the bankruptcy case is filed.

Certain categories of relief may be granted in a bankruptcy court only through an adversary proceeding. The usual focus of the adversary proceeding is a trial of the allegations made by the plaintiff against the defendant. The first step in an adversary proceeding is filing a complaint, the *Summons in an Adversary Proceeding*, setting forth the facts and allegations that the plaintiff believes justify the granting of relief against the defendant and stating the relief that the plaintiff seeks.

The *Order Approving Disclosure Statement and Fixing Time for Filing Acceptances or Rejections of Plan, Combined with Notice Thereof* is used in conjunction with Official Form 13 used in chapter 11 reorganization cases to provide parties with notice of the court's approval of the disclosure statement, their opportunity to file acceptances or rejections of the plan, and an order and notice of a hearing to consider the approval of the plan of reorganization. The *Order Finally Approving Disclosure Statement and Fixing Time for Filing Acceptances or Rejections of Plan, Combined with Notice Thereof* form must be filed and copies mailed to those parties specified in Bankruptcy Rule 3017(d), discussed above when, in a small business case, the court conditionally approves a disclosure statement subject to final approval after notice and a combined disclosure statement/plan confirmation hearing.

136. Voluntary Bankruptcy Petition

Official Form 1 (10/06)

United States Bankruptcy Court _____ **DISTRICT OF** _____	**Voluntary Petition**

Name of Debtor (if individual, enter Last, First, Middle):	Name of Joint Debtor (Spouse) (Last, First, Middle):
All Other Names used by the Debtor in the last 8 years (include married, maiden, and trade names):	All Other Names used by the Joint Debtor in the last 8 years (include married, maiden, and trade names):
Last four digits of Soc. Sec./Complete EIN or other Tax I.D. No. (if more than one, state all):	Last four digits of Soc. Sec./Complete EIN or other Tax I.D. No. (if more than one, state all):
Street Address of Debtor (No. and Street, City, and State): ZIP CODE	Street Address of Joint Debtor (No. and Street, City, and State): ZIP CODE
County of Residence or of the Principal Place of Business:	County of Residence or of the Principal Place of Business:
Mailing Address of Debtor (if different from street address): ZIP CODE	Mailing Address of Joint Debtor (if different from street address): ZIP CODE
Location of Principal Assets of Business Debtor (if different from street address above): ZIP CODE	

Type of Debtor
(Form of Organization)
(Check **one** box.)

☐ Individual (includes Joint Debtors)
  See Exhibit D on page 2 of this form.
☐ Corporation (includes LLC and LLP)
☐ Partnership
☐ Other (If debtor is not one of the above entities, check this box and state type of entity below.)

_____

Nature of Business
(Check **one** box.)

☐ Health Care Business
☐ Single Asset Real Estate as defined in 11 U.S.C. § 101(51B)
☐ Railroad
☐ Stockbroker
☐ Commodity Broker
☐ Clearing Bank
☐ Other

Tax-Exempt Entity
(Check box, if applicable.)

☐ Debtor is a tax-exempt organization under Title 26 of the United States Code (the Internal Revenue Code).

Chapter of Bankruptcy Code Under Which the Petition is Filed (Check **one** box.)

☐ Chapter 7
☐ Chapter 9
☐ Chapter 11
☐ Chapter 12
☐ Chapter 13

☐ Chapter 15 Petition for Recognition of a Foreign Main Proceeding
☐ Chapter 15 Petition for Recognition of a Foreign Nonmain Proceeding

Nature of Debts
(Check one box.)

☐ Debts are primarily consumer debts, defined in 11 U.S.C. § 101(8) as "incurred by an individual primarily for a personal, family, or house-hold purpose."
☐ Debts are primarily business debts.

Filing Fee (Check one box.)

☐ Full Filing Fee attached.

☐ Filing Fee to be paid in installments (applicable to individuals only). Must attach signed application for the court's consideration certifying that the debtor is unable to pay fee except in installments. Rule 1006(b). See Official Form 3A.

☐ Filing Fee waiver requested (applicable to chapter 7 individuals only). Must attach signed application for the court's consideration. See Official Form 3B.

Chapter 11 Debtors

Check one box:
☐ Debtor is a small business debtor as defined in 11 U.S.C. § 101(51D).

☐ Debtor is not a small business debtor as defined in 11 U.S.C. § 101(51D).

Check if:
☐ Debtor's aggregate noncontingent liquidated debts (excluding debts owed to insiders or affiliates) are less than $2 million.
- -
Check all applicable boxes:
☐ A plan is being filed with this petition.
☐ Acceptances of the plan were solicited prepetition from one or more classes of creditors, in accordance with 11 U.S.C. § 1126(b).

Statistical/Administrative Information

☐ Debtor estimates that funds will be available for distribution to unsecured creditors.
☐ Debtor estimates that, after any exempt property is excluded and administrative expenses paid, there will be no funds available for distribution to unsecured creditors.

THIS SPACE IS FOR COURT USE ONLY

Estimated Number of Creditors

1-49	50-99	100-199	200-999	1,000-5,000	5,001-10,000	10,001-25,000	25,001-50,000	50,001-100,000	Over 100,000
☐	☐	☐	☐	☐	☐	☐	☐	☐	☐

Estimated Assets

☐ $0 to $10,000	☐ $10,000 to $100,000	☐ $100,000 to $1 million	☐ $1 million to $100 million	☐ More than $100 million

Estimated Liabilities

☐ $0 to $50,000	☐ $50,000 to $100,000	☐ $100,000 to $1 million	☐ $1 million to $100 million	☐ More than $100 million

Official Form 1 (10/06) | Form B1, Page 2

Voluntary Petition	Name of Debtor(s):
(This page must be completed and filed in every case.)	

All Prior Bankruptcy Cases Filed Within Last 8 Years (If more than two, attach additional sheet.)

Location Where Filed:	Case Number:	Date Filed:
Location Where Filed:	Case Number:	Date Filed:

Pending Bankruptcy Case Filed by any Spouse, Partner, or Affiliate of this Debtor (If more than one, attach additional sheet.)

Name of Debtor:	Case Number:	Date Filed:
District:	Relationship:	Judge:

Exhibit A	Exhibit B
(To be completed if debtor is required to file periodic reports (e.g., forms 10K and 10Q) with the Securities and Exchange Commission pursuant to Section 13 or 15(d) of the Securities Exchange Act of 1934 and is requesting relief under chapter 11.)	(To be completed if debtor is an individual whose debts are primarily consumer debts.) I, the attorney for the petitioner named in the foregoing petition, declare that I have informed the petitioner that [he or she] may proceed under chapter 7, 11, 12, or 13 of title 11, United States Code, and have explained the relief available under each such chapter. I further certify that I have delivered to the debtor the notice required by 11 U.S.C. § 342(b).
☐ Exhibit A is attached and made a part of this petition.	X _____ Signature of Attorney for Debtor(s) (Date)

Exhibit C

Does the debtor own or have possession of any property that poses or is alleged to pose a threat of imminent and identifiable harm to public health or safety?

☐   Yes, and Exhibit C is attached and made a part of this petition.

☐   No.

Exhibit D

(To be completed by every individual debtor. If a joint petition is filed, each spouse must complete and attach a separate Exhibit D.)

☐   Exhibit D completed and signed by the debtor is attached and made a part of this petition.

If this is a joint petition:

☐   Exhibit D also completed and signed by the joint debtor is attached and made a part of this petition.

Information Regarding the Debtor - Venue
(Check any applicable box.)

☐   Debtor has been domiciled or has had a residence, principal place of business, or principal assets in this District for 180 days immediately preceding the date of this petition or for a longer part of such 180 days than in any other District.

☐   There is a bankruptcy case concerning debtor's affiliate, general partner, or partnership pending in this District.

☐   Debtor is a debtor in a foreign proceeding and has its principal place of business or principal assets in the United States in this District, or has no principal place of business or assets in the United States but is a defendant in an action or proceeding [in a federal or state court] in this District, or the interests of the parties will be served in regard to the relief sought in this District.

Statement by a Debtor Who Resides as a Tenant of Residential Property
(Check all applicable boxes.)

☐   Landlord has a judgment against the debtor for possession of debtor's residence. (If box checked, complete the following.)

_____
(Name of landlord that obtained judgment)

_____
(Address of landlord)

☐   Debtor claims that under applicable nonbankruptcy law, there are circumstances under which the debtor would be permitted to cure the entire monetary default that gave rise to the judgment for possession, after the judgment for possession was entered, and

☐   Debtor has included with this petition the deposit with the court of any rent that would become due during the 30-day period after the filing of the petition.

Official Form 1 (10/06)	Form B1, Page 3
Voluntary Petition *(This page must be completed and filed in every case.)*	Name of Debtor(s):

Signatures

Signature(s) of Debtor(s) (Individual/Joint)	Signature of a Foreign Representative

Signature(s) of Debtor(s) (Individual/Joint)

I declare under penalty of perjury that the information provided in this petition is true and correct.

[If petitioner is an individual whose debts are primarily consumer debts and has chosen to file under chapter 7] I am aware that I may proceed under chapter 7, 11, 12 or 13 of title 11, United States Code, understand the relief available under each such chapter, and choose to proceed under chapter 7.

[If no attorney represents me and no bankruptcy petition preparer signs the petition] I have obtained and read the notice required by 11 U.S.C. § 342(b).

I request relief in accordance with the chapter of title 11, United States Code, specified in this petition.

X _____
   Signature of Debtor

X _____
   Signature of Joint Debtor

_____
Telephone Number (if not represented by attorney)

_____
Date

Signature of a Foreign Representative

I declare under penalty of perjury that the information provided in this petition is true and correct, that I am the foreign representative of a debtor in a foreign proceeding, and that I am authorized to file this petition.

(Check only **one** box.)

☐ I request relief in accordance with chapter 15 of title 11, United States Code. Certified copies of the documents required by 11 U.S.C. § 1515 are attached.

☐ Pursuant to 11 U.S.C. § 1511, I request relief in accordance with the chapter of title 11 specified in this petition. A certified copy of the order granting recognition of the foreign main proceeding is attached.

X _____
   (Signature of Foreign Representative)

_____
(Printed Name of Foreign Representative)

_____
Date

Signature of Attorney

X _____
   Signature of Attorney for Debtor(s)

_____
Printed Name of Attorney for Debtor(s)

_____
Firm Name

_____
Address

_____
_____

_____
Telephone Number

_____
Date

Signature of Non-Attorney Bankruptcy Petition Preparer

I declare under penalty of perjury that: (1) I am a bankruptcy petition preparer as defined in 11 U.S.C. § 110; (2) I prepared this document for compensation and have provided the debtor with a copy of this document and the notices and information required under 11 U.S.C. §§ 110(b), 110(h), and 342(b); and, (3) if rules or guidelines have been promulgated pursuant to 11 U.S.C. § 110(h) setting a maximum fee for services chargeable by bankruptcy petition preparers, I have given the debtor notice of the maximum amount before preparing any document for filing for a debtor or accepting any fee from the debtor, as required in that section. Official Form 19B is attached.

_____
Printed Name and title, if any, of Bankruptcy Petition Preparer

_____
Social Security number (If the bankruptcy petition preparer is not an individual, state the Social Security number of the officer, principal, responsible person or partner of the bankruptcy petition preparer.) (Required by 11 U.S.C. § 110.)

_____
Address

X _____

_____
Date

Signature of Debtor (Corporation/Partnership)

I declare under penalty of perjury that the information provided in this petition is true and correct, and that I have been authorized to file this petition on behalf of the debtor.

The debtor requests the relief in accordance with the chapter of title 11, United States Code, specified in this petition.

X _____
   Signature of Authorized Individual

_____
Printed Name of Authorized Individual

_____
Title of Authorized Individual

_____
Date

Signature of bankruptcy petition preparer or officer, principal, responsible person, or partner whose Social Security number is provided above.

Names and Social Security numbers of all other individuals who prepared or assisted in preparing this document unless the bankruptcy petition preparer is not an individual.

If more than one person prepared this document, attach additional sheets conforming to the appropriate official form for each person.

A bankruptcy petition preparer's failure to comply with the provisions of title 11 and the Federal Rules of Bankruptcy Procedure may result in fines or imprisonment or both. 11 U.S.C. § 110; 18 U.S.C. § 156.

137. Involuntary Petition for Bankruptcy

Official Form 5 (10/06)

United States Bankruptcy Court _____District of_____	INVOLUNTARY PETITION

IN RE (Name of Debtor – If Individual: Last, First, Middle)	ALL OTHER NAMES used by debtor in the last 8 years (Include married, maiden, and trade names.)
Last four digits of Soc. Sec. No./Complete EIN or other Tax I.D. No. (If more than one, state all.):	
STREET ADDRESS OF DEBTOR (No. and street, city, state, and zip code) COUNTY OF RESIDENCE OR PRINCIPAL PLACE OF BUSINESS ZIP CODE	MAILING ADDRESS OF DEBTOR (If different from street address) ZIP CODE

LOCATION OF PRINCIPAL ASSETS OF BUSINESS DEBTOR (If different from previously listed addresses)

CHAPTER OF BANKRUPTCY CODE UNDER WHICH PETITION IS FILED

☐ Chapter 7   ☐ Chapter 11

INFORMATION REGARDING DEBTOR (Check applicable boxes)

Nature of Debts (Check **one** box.) Petitioners believe: ☐ Debts are primarily consumer debts ☐ Debts are primarily business debts	Type of Debtor (Form of Organization) ☐ Individual (Includes Joint Debtor) ☐ Corporation (Includes LLC and LLP) ☐ Partnership ☐ Other (If debtor is not one of the above entities, check this box and state type of entity below.) _____	Nature of Business (Check **one** box.) ☐ Health Care Business ☐ Single Asset Real Estate as defined in 11 U.S.C. § 101(51)(B) ☐ Railroad ☐ Stockbroker ☐ Commodity Broker ☐ Clearing Bank ☐ Other

VENUE ☐ Debtor has been domiciled or has had a residence, principal place of business, or principal assets in the District for 180 days immediately preceding the date of this petition or for a longer part of such 180 days than in any other District. ☐ A bankruptcy case concerning debtor's affiliate, general partner or partnership is pending in this District.	**FILING FEE** (Check one box) ☐ Full Filing Fee attached ☐ Petitioner is a child support creditor or its representative, and the form specified in § 304(g) of the Bankruptcy Reform Act of 1994 is attached. *[If a child support creditor or its representative is a petitioner, and if the petitioner files the form specified in § 304(g) of the Bankruptcy Reform Act of 1994, no fee is required.]*

**PENDING BANKRUPTCY CASE FILED BY OR AGAINST ANY PARTNER
OR AFFILIATE OF THIS DEBTOR** (Report information for any additional cases on attached sheets.)

Name of Debtor	Case Number	Date
Relationship	District	Judge

ALLEGATIONS (Check applicable boxes)	COURT USE ONLY

1.   ☐ Petitioner (s) are eligible to file this petition pursuant to 11 U.S. C. § 303 (b).
2.   ☐ The debtor is a person against whom an order for relief may be entered under title 11 of the United
 States Code.
3.a. ☐ The debtor is generally not paying such debtor's debts as they become due, unless such debts are the
 subject of a bona fide dispute as to liability or amount;
      or
  b. ☐ Within 120 days preceding the filing of this petition, a custodian, other than a trustee receiver, or
 agent appointed or authorized to take charge of less than substantially all of the property of the
 debtor for the purpose of enforcing a lien against such property, was appointed or took possession.	

Official Form 5 (10/06) – Cont.

Name of Debtor

Case No._____

TRANSFER OF CLAIM	

☐ Check this box if there has been a transfer of any claim against the debtor or to any petitioner. Attach all documents that evidence the transfer and any statements that are required under Bankruptcy Rule 1003(a).

REQUEST FOR RELIEF

Petitioner(s) request that an order for relief be entered against the debtor under the chapter of title 11, United States Code, specified in this petition. If any petitioner is a foreign representative appointed in a foreign proceeding, a certified copy of the order of the court granting recognition is attached.

Petitioner(s) declare under penalty of perjury that the foregoing is true and correct according to the best of their knowledge, information, and belief.

x_____
Signature of Petitioner or Representative (State title)

Name of Petitioner   Date Signed

Name & Mailing
Address of Individual   _____
Signing in Representative
Capacity   _____

x_____
Signature of Attorney   Date

Name of Attorney Firm (If any)

Address

Telephone No.

x_____
Signature of Petitioner or Representative (State title)

Name of Petitioner   Date Signed

Name & Mailing
Address of Individual   _____
Signing in Representative
Capacity   _____

x_____
Signature of Attorney   Date

Name of Attorney Firm (If any)

Address

Telephone No.

x_____
Signature of Petitioner or Representative (State title)

Name of Petitioner   Date Signed

Name & Mailing
Address of Individual   _____
Signing in Representative
Capacity   _____

x_____
Signature of Attorney   Date

Name of Attorney Firm (If any)

Address

Telephone No.

PETITIONING CREDITORS

Name and Address of Petitioner	Nature of Claim	Amount of Claim
Name and Address of Petitioner	Nature of Claim	Amount of Claim
Name and Address of Petitioner	Nature of Claim	Amount of Claim
Note: If there are more than three petitioners, attach additional sheets with the statement under penalty of perjury, each petitioner's signature under the statement and the name of attorney and petitioning creditor information in the format above.		Total Amount of Petitioners' Claims

_____continuation sheets attached

138. Summons to Debtor in Response to Involuntary Petition

B 250E
(6/91)

United States Bankruptcy Court

_____ District Of _____

In re _____

Debtor

Case No. _____

Chapter _____

SUMMONS TO DEBTOR IN INVOLUNTARY CASE

To the above named debtor:

A petition under title 11, United States Code was filed against you on _____

(date)

in this bankruptcy court, requesting an order for relief under chapter _____ of the Bankruptcy Code

(title 11 of the United States Code).

YOU ARE SUMMONED and required to file with the clerk of the bankruptcy court a motion or answer to the petition within 20 days after the service of this summons. A copy of the petition is attached.

Address of Clerk

At the same time, you must also serve a copy of your motion or answer on petitioner's attorney.

Name and Address of Petitioner's Attorney

If you make a motion, your time to serve an answer is governed by Federal Rule of Bankruptcy Procedure 1011(c).

If you fail to respond to this summons, the order for relief will be entered.

_____

Clerk of the Bankruptcy Court

_____   By:_____

Date   Deputy Clerk

*Set forth all names, including trade names, used by the debtor within the last 6 years. (Fed. R .Bankr. P. 1005).

Case No._____

CERTIFICATE OF SERVICE

I
of**
certify:

       That I am, and at all times hereinafter mentioned was more than 18 years of age;
       That on the   day of   , 19
I served a copy of the within summons, together with the petition filed in this case, on

the debtor in this case, by [describe here the mode of service]

the said debtor at

I certify under penalty of perjury that the foregoing is true and correct.

Executed on _____   _____
                [Date]   [Signature]

**State mailing address.

139. Exhibit A to Voluntary Petition

Form B1, Exh.A (9/97)

Exhibit "A"

[If debtor is required to file periodic reports (*e.g.*, forms 10K and 10Q) with the Securities and Exchange Commission pursuant to Section 13 or 15(d) of the Securities Exchange Act of 1934 and is requesting relief under chapter 11 of the Bankruptcy Code, this Exhibit "A" shall be completed and attached to the petition.]

[Caption as in Form 16B]

Exhibit "A" to Voluntary Petition

1.   If any of the debtor's securities are registered under Section 12 of the Securities Exchange Act of 1934, the SEC file number is _____.

2.   The following financial data is the latest available information and refers to the debtor's condition on _____.

a.   Total assets $ _____

b.   Total debts (including debts listed in 2.c., below) $ _____

Approximate
number of
holders

c.   Debt securities held by more than 500 holders.

secured / /   unsecured / /   subordinated / / $ _____   _____

secured / /   unsecured / /   subordinated / / $ _____   _____

secured / /   unsecured / /   subordinated / / $ _____   _____

secured / /   unsecured / /   subordinated / / $ _____   _____

secured / /   unsecured / /   subordinated / / $ _____   _____

d.   Number of shares of preferred stock   _____   _____

e.   Number of shares common stock   _____   _____

Comments, if any: _____
_____
_____

3.   Brief description of debtor's business: _____
_____
_____

4.   List the names of any person who directly or indirectly owns, controls, or holds, with power to vote, 5% or more of the voting securities of debtor:
_____
_____
_____

140. Exhibit C to Voluntary Petition

Form B1, Exhibit C
(9/01)

Exhibit "C"

[If, to the best of the debtor's knowledge, the debtor owns or has possession of property that poses or is alleged to pose a threat of imminent and identifiable harm to the public health or safety, attach this Exhibit "C" to the petition.]

[Caption as in Form 16B]

Exhibit "C" to Voluntary Petition

1. Identify and briefly describe all real or personal property owned by or in possession of the debtor that, to the best of the debtor's knowledge, poses or is alleged to pose a threat of imminent and identifiable harm to the public health or safety (attach additional sheets if necessary):

....
....
....
....

2. With respect to each parcel of real property or item of personal property identified in question 1, describe the nature and location of the dangerous condition, whether environmental or otherwise, that poses or is alleged to pose a threat of imminent and identifiable harm to the public health or safety (attach additional sheets if necessary):

....
....
....
....

141. List of Creditors for Voluntary Petition

Form 4
(10/05)

United States Bankruptcy Court

_____ District Of _____

In re _____,

Debtor

Case No. _____

Chapter _____

LIST OF CREDITORS HOLDING 20 LARGEST UNSECURED CLAIMS

Following is the list of the debtor's creditors holding the 20 largest unsecured claims. The list is prepared in accordance with Fed. R. Bankr. P. 1007(d) for filing in this chapter 11 [*or* chapter 9] case. The list does not include (1) persons who come within the definition of "insider" set forth in 11 U.S.C. § 101, or (2) secured creditors unless the value of the collateral is such that the unsecured deficiency places the creditor among the holders of the 20 largest unsecured claims. If a minor child is one of the creditors holding the 20 largest unsecured claims, indicate that by stating "a minor child" and do not disclose the child's name. See 11 U.S.C. § 112: Fed. R. Bankr. P. 1007(m).

(1)	(2)	(3)	(4)	(5)
Name of creditor and complete mailing address including zip code	*Name, telephone number and complete mailing address, including zip code, of employee, agent, or department of creditor familiar with claim who may be contacted*	*Nature of claim (trade debt, bank loan, government contract, etc.)*	*Indicate if claim is contingent, unliquidated, disputed or subject to setoff*	*Amount of claim [if secured also state value of security]*

Date: _____

_____
Debtor

[Declaration as in Form 2]

142. Statement of Social Security Number for Volunary Petition

Form B 21 Official Form 21
(12/03)

FORM 21. STATEMENT OF SOCIAL SECURITY NUMBER

[*Caption as in Form 16A.*]

STATEMENT OF SOCIAL SECURITY NUMBER(S)

1.Name of Debtor (enter Last, First, Middle):_____
(Check the appropriate box and, if applicable, provide the required information.)

/ /Debtor has a Social Security Number and it is: _ _ _-_ _-_ _ _ _
(If more than one, state all.)
/ /Debtor does not have a Social Security Number.

2.Name of Joint Debtor (enter Last, First, Middle):_____
(Check the appropriate box and, if applicable, provide the required information.)

/ /Joint Debtor has a Social Security Number and it is: _ _ _-_ _-_ _ _ _
(If more than one, state all.)
/ /Joint Debtor does not have a Social Security Number.

I declare under penalty of perjury that the foregoing is true and correct.

X _____
       Signature of Debtor   Date

X _____
       Signature of Joint Debtor   Date

_____

**Joint debtors must provide information for both spouses.*
Penalty for making a false statement: Fine of up to $250,000 or up to 5 years imprisonment or both. 18 U.S.C. §§ 152 and 3571.

143. Declaration Under Penalty of Perjury for Voluntary Petition

Official Form 2
6/90

DECLARATION UNDER PENALTY OF PERJURY
ON BEHALF OF A CORPORATION OR PARTNERSHIP

I, [the president or other officer or an authorized agent of the corporation] [or a member or an authorized agent of the partnership] named as the debtor in this case, declare under penalty of perjury that I have read the foregoing [list or schedule or amendment or other document (describe)] and that it is true and correct to the best of my information and belief.

Date _____

Signature _____

_____
(Print Name and Title)

144. Disclosure of Compensation of Attorney for Debtor

B 203
(12/94)

United States Bankruptcy Court

_____ District of _____

In re

Case No. _____

Debtor

Chapter _____

DISCLOSURE OF COMPENSATION OF ATTORNEY FOR DEBTOR

1. Pursuant to 11 U.S.C. § 329(a) and Fed. Bankr. P. 2016(b), I certify that I am the attorney for the above-named debtor(s) and that compensation paid to me within one year before the filing of the petition in bankruptcy, or agreed to be paid to me, for services rendered or to be rendered on behalf of the debtor(s) in contemplation of or in connection with the bankruptcy case is as follows:

   For legal services, I have agreed to accept . . . . $_____

   Prior to the filing of this statement I have received . . . . $_____

   Balance Due . . . . $_____

2. The source of the compensation paid to me was:

   ☐ Debtor   ☐ Other (specify)

3. The source of compensation to be paid to me is:

   ☐ Debtor   ☐ Other (specify)

4. ☐ I have not agreed to share the above-disclosed compensation with any other person unless they are members and associates of my law firm.

   ☐ I have agreed to share the above-disclosed compensation with a other person or persons who are not members or associates of my law firm. A copy of the agreement, together with a list of the names of the people sharing in the compensation, is attached.

5. In return for the above-disclosed fee, I have agreed to render legal service for all aspects of the bankruptcy case, including:

   a. Analysis of the debtor's financial situation, and rendering advice to the debtor in determining whether to file a petition in bankruptcy;

   b. Preparation and filing of any petition, schedules, statements of affairs and plan which may be required;

   c. Representation of the debtor at the meeting of creditors and confirmation hearing, and any adjourned hearings thereof;

DISCLOSURE OF COMPENSATION OF ATTORNEY FOR DEBTOR (Continued)

d. Representation of the debtor in adversary proceedings and other contested bankruptcy matters;

e. [Other provisions as needed]

6. By agreement with the debtor(s), the above-disclosed fee does not include the following services:

CERTIFICATION

I certify that the foregoing is a complete statement of any agreement or arrangement for payment to me for representation of the debtor(s) in this bankruptcy proceedings.

_____   _____
Date   *Signature of Attorney*

                                                      _____
                                                      Name of law firm

145. Schedule A—Real Property for Voluntary Petition

Form B6A
(10/05)

In re _____,   Case No. _____
                    Debtor   **(If known)**

SCHEDULE A - REAL PROPERTY

Except as directed below, list all real property in which the debtor has any legal, equitable, or future interest, including all property owned as a co-tenant, community property, or in which the debtor has a life estate. Include any property in which the debtor holds rights and powers exercisable for the debtor's own benefit. If the debtor is married, state whether husband, wife, or both own the property by placing an "H," "W," "J," or "C" in the column labeled "Husband, Wife, Joint, or Community." If the debtor holds no interest in real property, write "None" under "Description and Location of Property."

Do not include interests in executory contracts and unexpired leases on this schedule. List them in Schedule G - Executory Contracts and Unexpired Leases.

If an entity claims to have a lien or hold a secured interest in any property, state the amount of the secured claim. See Schedule D. If no entity claims to hold a secured interest in the property, write "None" in the column labeled "Amount of Secured Claim."

If the debtor is an individual or if a joint petition is filed, state the amount of any exemption claimed in the property only in Schedule C - Property Claimed as Exempt.

DESCRIPTION AND LOCATION OF PROPERTY	NATURE OF DEBTOR'S INTEREST IN PROPERTY	HUSBAND, WIFE, JOINT, OR COMMUNITY	CURRENT VALUE OF DEBTOR'S INTEREST IN PROPERTY, WITHOUT DEDUCTING ANY SECURED CLAIM OR EXEMPTION	AMOUNT OF SECURED CLAIM
		Total		

(Report also on Summary of Schedules.)

146. Schedule B—Personal Property for Voluntary Petition

Form B6B
(10/05)

In re _____,   Case No. _____
            Debtor   **(If known)**

SCHEDULE B - PERSONAL PROPERTY

Except as directed below, list all personal property of the debtor of whatever kind. If the debtor has no property in one or more of the categories, place an "x" in the appropriate position in the column labeled "None." If additional space is needed in any category, attach a separate sheet properly identified with the case name, case number, and the number of the category. If the debtor is married, state whether husband, wife, or both own the property by placing an "H," "W," "J," or "C" in the column labeled "Husband, Wife, Joint, or Community." If the debtor is an individual or a joint petition is filed, state the amount of any exemptions claimed only in Schedule C - Property Claimed as Exempt.

Do not list interests in executory contracts and unexpired leases on this schedule. List them in Schedule G - Executory Contracts and Unexpired Leases.

If the property is being held for the debtor by someone else, state that person's name and address under "Description and Location of Property." In providing the information requested in this schedule, do not include the name or address of a minor child. Simply state "a minor child."

TYPE OF PROPERTY	NONE	DESCRIPTION AND LOCATION OF PROPERTY	HUSBAND, WIFE, JOINT, OR COMMUNITY	CURRENT VALUE OF DEBTOR'S INTEREST IN PROPERTY, WITH-OUT DEDUCTING ANY SECURED CLAIM OR EXEMPTION
1. Cash on hand.				
2. Checking, savings or other financial accounts, certificates of deposit, or shares in banks, savings and loan, thrift, building and loan, and homestead associations, or credit unions, brokerage houses, or cooperatives.				
3. Security deposits with public utilities, telephone companies, landlords, and others.				
4. Household goods and furnishings, including audio, video, and computer equipment.				
5. Books; pictures and other art objects; antiques; stamp, coin, record, tape, compact disc, and other collections or collectibles.				
6. Wearing apparel.				
7. Furs and jewelry.				
8. Firearms and sports, photographic, and other hobby equipment.				
9. Interests in insurance policies. Name insurance company of each policy and itemize surrender or refund value of each.				
10. Annuities. Itemize and name each issuer.				
11. Interests in an education IRA as defined in 26 U.S.C. § 530(b)(1) or under a qualified State tuition plan as defined in 26 U.S.C. § 529(b)(1). Give particulars. (File separately the record(s) of any such interest(s). 11 U.S.C. § 521(c); Rule 1007(b)).				

Official Form 6E (10/06) - Cont.

In re _____ ,   Case No._____
                    Debtor   **(if known)**

☐ **Certain farmers and fishermen**

   Claims of certain farmers and fishermen, up to $4,925* per farmer or fisherman, against the debtor, as provided in 11 U.S.C. § 507(a)(6).

☐ **Deposits by individuals**

   Claims of individuals up to $2,225* for deposits for the purchase, lease, or rental of property or services for personal, family, or household use, that were not delivered or provided. 11 U.S.C. § 507(a)(7).

☐ **Taxes and Certain Other Debts Owed to Governmental Units**

   Taxes, customs duties, and penalties owing to federal, state, and local governmental units as set forth in 11 U.S.C. § 507(a)(8).

☐ **Commitments to Maintain the Capital of an Insured Depository Institution**

   Claims based on commitments to the FDIC, RTC, Director of the Office of Thrift Supervision, Comptroller of the Currency, or Board of Governors of the Federal Reserve System, or their predecessors or successors, to maintain the capital of an insured depository institution. 11 U.S.C. § 507 (a)(9).

☐ **Claims for Death or Personal Injury While Debtor Was Intoxicated**

   Claims for death or personal injury resulting from the operation of a motor vehicle or vessel while the debtor was intoxicated from using alcohol, a drug, or another substance. 11 U.S.C. § 507(a)(10).

* Amounts are subject to adjustment on April 1, 2007, and every three years thereafter with respect to cases commenced on or after the date of adjustment.

_____ **continuation sheets attached**

Form B6B-cont.
(10/05)

In re _____, Case No. _____
　　　　Debtor　　　　　　　　　　　　　　　　　　　　　(If known)

SCHEDULE B -PERSONAL PROPERTY
(Continuation Sheet)

TYPE OF PROPERTY	N O N E	DESCRIPTION AND LOCATION OF PROPERTY	HUSBAND, WIFE, JOINT, OR COMMUNITY	CURRENT VALUE OF DEBTOR'S INTEREST IN PROPERTY, WITHOUT DEDUCTING ANY SECURED CLAIM OR EXEMPTION
22. Patents, copyrights, and other intellectual property. Give particulars.				
23. Licenses, franchises, and other general intangibles. Give particulars.				
24. Customer lists or other compilations containing personally identifiable information (as defined in 11 U.S.C. § 101(41A)) provided to the debtor by individuals in connection with obtaining a product or service from the debtor primarily for personal, family, or household purposes.				
25. Automobiles, trucks, trailers, and other vehicles and accessories.				
26. Boats, motors, and accessories.				
27. Aircraft and accessories.				
28. Office equipment, furnishings, and supplies.				
29. Machinery, fixtures, equipment, and supplies used in business.				
30. Inventory.				
31. Animals.				
32. Crops - growing or harvested. Give particulars.				
33. Farming equipment and implements.				
34. Farm supplies, chemicals, and feed.				
35. Other personal property of any kind not already listed. Itemize.				

_____continuation sheets attached　　Total $ _____

(Include amounts from any continuation sheets attached. Report total also on Summary of Schedules.)

147. Schedule C–Exempt Property for Voluntary Petition

Form B6C
(10/05)

In re _____, Case No. _____
                    Debtor   **(If known)**

SCHEDULE C - PROPERTY CLAIMED AS EXEMPT

Debtor claims the exemptions to which debtor is entitled under:
(Check one box)
- ☐ 11 U.S.C. § 522(b)(2)
- ☐ 11 U.S.C. § 522(b)(3)

☐ Check if debtor claims a homestead exemption that exceeds $125,000.

DESCRIPTION OF PROPERTY	SPECIFY LAW PROVIDING EACH EXEMPTION	VALUE OF CLAIMED EXEMPTION	CURRENT VALUE OF PROPERTY WITHOUT DEDUCTING EXEMPTION

148. Schedule D–Creditors Holding Secured Claims

Official Form 6D (10/06)

In re _____ ,   Case No. _____
              Debtor   **(if known)**

SCHEDULE D - CREDITORS HOLDING SECURED CLAIMS

State the name, mailing address, including zip code, and last four digits of any account number of all entities holding claims secured by property of the debtor as of the date of filing of the petition. The complete account number of any account the debtor has with the creditor is useful to the trustee and the creditor and may be provided if the debtor chooses to do so. List creditors holding all types of secured interests such as judgment liens, garnishments, statutory liens, mortgages, deeds of trust, and other security interests.

List creditors in alphabetical order to the extent practicable. If a minor child is a creditor, indicate that by stating "a minor child" and do not disclose the child's name. See 11 U.S.C. § 112. If "a minor child" is stated, also include the name, address, and legal relationship to the minor child of a person described in Fed. R. Bankr. P. 1007(m). If all secured creditors will not fit on this page, use the continuation sheet provided.

If any entity other than a spouse in a joint case may be jointly liable on a claim, place an "X" in the column labeled "Codebtor," include the entity on the appropriate schedule of creditors, and complete Schedule H – Codebtors. If a joint petition is filed, state whether the husband, wife, both of them, or the marital community may be liable on each claim by placing an "H," "W," "J," or "C" in the column labeled "Husband, Wife, Joint, or Community."

If the claim is contingent, place an "X" in the column labeled "Contingent." If the claim is unliquidated, place an "X" in the column labeled "Unliquidated." If the claim is disputed, place an "X" in the column labeled "Disputed." (You may need to place an "X" in more than one of these three columns.)

Total the columns labeled "Amount of Claim Without Deducting Value of Collateral" and "Unsecured Portion, if Any" in the boxes labeled "Total(s)" on the last sheet of the completed schedule. Report the total from the column labeled "Amount of Claim Without Deducting Value of Collateral" also on the Summary of Schedules and, if the debtor is an individual with primarily consumer debts, report the total from the column labeled "Unsecured Portion, if Any" on the Statistical Summary of Certain Liabilities and Related Data.

☐   Check this box if debtor has no creditors holding secured claims to report on this Schedule D.

CREDITOR'S NAME AND MAILING ADDRESS INCLUDING ZIP CODE AND AN ACCOUNT NUMBER (*See Instructions Above.*)	CODEBTOR	HUSBAND, WIFE, JOINT, OR COMMUNITY	DATE CLAIM WAS INCURRED, NATURE OF LIEN , AND DESCRIPTION AND VALUE OF PROPERTY SUBJECT TO LIEN	CONTINGENT	UNLIQUIDATED	DISPUTED	AMOUNT OF CLAIM WITHOUT DEDUCTING VALUE OF COLLATERAL	UNSECURED PORTION, IF ANY
ACCOUNT NO.								
			VALUE $					
ACCOUNT NO.								
			VALUE $					
ACCOUNT NO.								
			VALUE $					
_____ continuation sheets attached			Subtotal ▶ (Total of this page)				$	$
			Total ▶ (Use only on last page)				$	$
							(Report also on Summary of Schedules.)	(If applicable, report also on Statistical Summary of Certain Liabilities and Related Data.)

Official Form 6D (10/06) – Cont.

In re _____ ,   Case No. _____

    Debtor   **(if known)**

SCHEDULE D - CREDITORS HOLDING SECURED CLAIMS
(Continuation Sheet)

CREDITOR'S NAME AND MAILING ADDRESS INCLUDING ZIP CODE AND AN ACCOUNT NUMBER (*See Instructions Above.*)	CODEBTOR	HUSBAND, WIFE, JOINT, OR COMMUNITY	DATE CLAIM WAS INCURRED, NATURE OF LIEN , AND DESCRIPTION AND VALUE OF PROPERTY SUBJECT TO LIEN	CONTINGENT	UNLIQUIDATED	DISPUTED	AMOUNT OF CLAIM WITHOUT DEDUCTING VALUE OF COLLATERAL	UNSECURED PORTION, IF ANY
ACCOUNT NO.								
			VALUE $					
ACCOUNT NO.								
			VALUE $					
ACCOUNT NO.								
			VALUE $					
ACCOUNT NO.								
			VALUE $					
ACCOUNT NO.								
			VALUE $					

Sheet no. ___ of ___ continuation sheets attached to Schedule of Creditors Holding Secured Claims

Subtotal (s) ▶
(Total(s) of this page) $ $

Total(s) ▶
(Use only on last page) $ $

(Report also on Summary of Schedules.)

(If applicable, report also on Statistical Summary of Certain Liabilities and Related Data.)

149. Schedule E–Creditors Holding Unsecured Priority Claims

Official Form 6E (10/06)

In re _____,   Case No._____
                    Debtor   (if known)

SCHEDULE E - CREDITORS HOLDING UNSECURED PRIORITY CLAIMS

A complete list of claims entitled to priority, listed separately by type of priority, is to be set forth on the sheets provided. Only holders of unsecured claims entitled to priority should be listed in this schedule. In the boxes provided on the attached sheets, state the name, mailing address, including zip code, and last four digits of the account number, if any, of all entities holding priority claims against the debtor or the property of the debtor, as of the date of the filing of the petition. Use a separate continuation sheet for each type of priority and label each with the type of priority.

The complete account number of any account the debtor has with the creditor is useful to the trustee and the creditor and may be provided if the debtor chooses to do so. If a minor child is a creditor, indicate that by stating "a minor child" and do not disclose the child's name. See 11 U.S.C. § 112. If "a minor child" is stated, also include the name, address, and legal relationship to the minor child of a person described in Fed. R. Bankr. P. 1007(m).

If any entity other than a spouse in a joint case may be jointly liable on a claim, place an "X" in the column labeled "Codebtor," include the entity on the appropriate schedule of creditors, and complete Schedule H-Codebtors. If a joint petition is filed, state whether the husband, wife, both of them, or the marital community may be liable on each claim by placing an "H," "W," "J," or "C" in the column labeled "Husband, Wife, Joint, or Community." If the claim is contingent, place an "X" in the column labeled "Contingent." If the claim is unliquidated, place an "X" in the column labeled "Unliquidated." If the claim is disputed, place an "X" in the column labeled "Disputed." (You may need to place an "X" in more than one of these three columns.)

Report the total of claims listed on each sheet in the box labeled "Subtotals" on each sheet. Report the total of all claims listed on this Schedule E in the box labeled "Total" on the last sheet of the completed schedule. Report this total also on the Summary of Schedules.

Report the total of amounts entitled to priority listed on each sheet in the box labeled "Subtotals" on each sheet. Report the total of all amounts entitled to priority listed on this Schedule E in the box labeled "Totals" on the last sheet of the completed schedule. Individual debtors with primarily consumer debts who file a case under chapter 7 or 13 report this total also on the Statistical Summary of Certain Liabilities and Related Data.

Report the total of amounts <u>not</u> entitled to priority listed on each sheet in the box labeled "Subtotals" on each sheet. Report the total of all amounts not entitled to priority listed on this Schedule E in the box labeled "Totals" on the last sheet of the completed schedule. Individual debtors with primarily consumer debts who file a case under chapter 7 report this total also on the Statistical Summary of Certain Liabilities and Related Data.

☐ Check this box if debtor has no creditors holding unsecured priority claims to report on this Schedule E.

TYPES OF PRIORITY CLAIMS (Check the appropriate box(es) below if claims in that category are listed on the attached sheets)

☐ **Domestic Support Obligations**

Claims for domestic support that are owed to or recoverable by a spouse, former spouse, or child of the debtor, or the parent, legal guardian, or responsible relative of such a child, or a governmental unit to whom such a domestic support claim has been assigned to the extent provided in 11 U.S.C. § 507(a)(1).

☐ **Extensions of credit in an involuntary case**

Claims arising in the ordinary course of the debtor's business or financial affairs after the commencement of the case but before the earlier of the appointment of a trustee or the order for relief. 11 U.S.C. § 507(a)(3).

☐ **Wages, salaries, and commissions**

Wages, salaries, and commissions, including vacation, severance, and sick leave pay owing to employees and commissions owing to qualifying independent sales representatives up to $10,000* per person earned within 180 days immediately preceding the filing of the original petition, or the cessation of business, whichever occurred first, to the extent provided in 11 U.S.C. § 507(a)(4).

☐ **Contributions to employee benefit plans**

Money owed to employee benefit plans for services rendered within 180 days immediately preceding the filing of the original petition, or the cessation of business, whichever occurred first, to the extent provided in 11 U.S.C. § 507(a)(5).

Official Form 6E (10/06) - Cont.

In re _____ ,   Case No._____
                     Debtor   **(if known)**

☐ **Certain farmers and fishermen**

Claims of certain farmers and fishermen, up to $4,925* per farmer or fisherman, against the debtor, as provided in 11 U.S.C. § 507(a)(6).

☐ **Deposits by individuals**

Claims of individuals up to $2,225* for deposits for the purchase, lease, or rental of property or services for personal, family, or household use, that were not delivered or provided. 11 U.S.C. § 507(a)(7).

☐ **Taxes and Certain Other Debts Owed to Governmental Units**

Taxes, customs duties, and penalties owing to federal, state, and local governmental units as set forth in 11 U.S.C. § 507(a)(8).

☐ **Commitments to Maintain the Capital of an Insured Depository Institution**

Claims based on commitments to the FDIC, RTC, Director of the Office of Thrift Supervision, Comptroller of the Currency, or Board of Governors of the Federal Reserve System, or their predecessors or successors, to maintain the capital of an insured depository institution. 11 U.S.C. § 507 (a)(9).

☐ **Claims for Death or Personal Injury While Debtor Was Intoxicated**

Claims for death or personal injury resulting from the operation of a motor vehicle or vessel while the debtor was intoxicated from using alcohol, a drug, or another substance. 11 U.S.C. § 507(a)(10).

* Amounts are subject to adjustment on April 1, 2007, and every three years thereafter with respect to cases commenced on or after the date of adjustment.

_____ **continuation sheets attached**

Official Form 6E (10/06) - Cont.

In re _____,   Case No. _____
                    Debtor   **(If known)**

SCHEDULE E - CREDITORS HOLDING UNSECURED PRIORITY CLAIMS
(Continuation Sheet)

Type of Priority for Claims Listed on This Sheet _____

CREDITOR'S NAME, MAILING ADDRESS INCLUDING ZIP CODE, AND ACCOUNT NUMBER (See instructions above.)	CODEBTOR	HUSBAND, WIFE, JOINT, OR COMMUNITY	DATE CLAIM WAS INCURRED AND CONSIDERATION FOR CLAIM	CONTINGENT	UNLIQUIDATED	DISPUTED	AMOUNT OF CLAIM	AMOUNT ENTITLED TO PRIORITY	AMOUNT NOT ENTITLED TO PRIORITY, IF ANY
Account No.									
Account No.									
Account No.									
Account No.									
Sheet no. ___ of ___ continuation sheets attached to Schedule of Creditors Holding Priority Claims			Subtotals (Totals of this page)				$	$	
			Total (Use only on last page of the completed Schedule E. Report also on the Summary of Schedules.)				$		
			Totals (Use only on last page of the completed Schedule E. If applicable, report also on the Statistical Summary of Certain Liabilities and Related Data.)					$	$

150. Schedule F–Creditors Holding Unsecured Nonpriority Claims

Official Form 6F (10/06)

In re _____,   Case No. _____
                    Debtor   **(if known)**

SCHEDULE F - CREDITORS HOLDING UNSECURED NONPRIORITY CLAIMS

State the name, mailing address, including zip code, and last four digits of any account number, of all entities holding unsecured claims without priority against the debtor or the property of the debtor, as of the date of filing of the petition. The complete account number of any account the debtor has with the creditor is useful to the trustee and the creditor and may be provided if the debtor chooses to do so. If a minor child is a creditor, indicate that by stating "a minor child" and do not disclose the child's name. See 11 U.S.C. § 112. If "a minor child" is stated, also include the name, address, and legal relationship to the minor child of a person described in Fed. R. Bankr. P. 1007(m). Do not include claims listed in Schedules D and E. If all creditors will not fit on this page, use the continuation sheet provided.

If any entity other than a spouse in a joint case may be jointly liable on a claim, place an "X" in the column labeled "Codebtor," include the entity on the appropriate schedule of creditors, and complete Schedule H - Codebtors. If a joint petition is filed, state whether the husband, wife, both of them, or the marital community may be liable on each claim by placing an "H," "W," "J," or "C" in the column labeled "Husband, Wife, Joint, or Community."

If the claim is contingent, place an "X" in the column labeled "Contingent." If the claim is unliquidated, place an "X" in the column labeled "Unliquidated." If the claim is disputed, place an "X" in the column labeled "Disputed." (You may need to place an "X" in more than one of these three columns.)

Report the total of all claims listed on this schedule in the box labeled "Total" on the last sheet of the completed schedule. Report this total also on the Summary of Schedules and, if the debtor is an individual with primarily consumer debts filing a case under chapter 7, report this total also on the Statistical Summary of Certain Liabilities and Related Data..

☐ Check this box if debtor has no creditors holding unsecured claims to report on this Schedule F.

CREDITOR'S NAME, MAILING ADDRESS INCLUDING ZIP CODE, AND ACCOUNT NUMBER *(See instructions above.)*	CODEBTOR	HUSBAND, WIFE, JOINT, OR COMMUNITY	DATE CLAIM WAS INCURRED AND CONSIDERATION FOR CLAIM. IF CLAIM IS SUBJECT TO SETOFF, SO STATE.	CONTINGENT	UNLIQUIDATED	DISPUTED	AMOUNT OF CLAIM
ACCOUNT NO.							
ACCOUNT NO.							
ACCOUNT NO.							
ACCOUNT NO.							
						Subtotal	$

_____ continuation sheets attached

Total $

(Use only on last page of the completed Schedule F.)
(Report also on Summary of Schedules and, if applicable, on the Statistical Summary of Certain Liabilities and Related Data.)

Official Form 6F (10/06) - Cont.

In re _____,   Case No. _____
          Debtor   **(if known)**

SCHEDULE F - CREDITORS HOLDING UNSECURED NONPRIORITY CLAIMS
(Continuation Sheet)

CREDITOR'S NAME, MAILING ADDRESS INCLUDING ZIP CODE, AND ACCOUNT NUMBER (See instructions above.)	CODEBTOR	HUSBAND, WIFE, JOINT, OR COMMUNITY	DATE CLAIM WAS INCURRED AND CONSIDERATION FOR CLAIM. IF CLAIM IS SUBJECT TO SETOFF, SO STATE.	CONTINGENT	UNLIQUIDATED	DISPUTED	AMOUNT OF CLAIM
ACCOUNT NO.							
ACCOUNT NO.							
ACCOUNT NO.							
ACCOUNT NO.							
ACCOUNT NO.							

Sheet no.___of___continuation sheets attached to Schedule of Creditors Holding Unsecured Nonpriority Claims   Subtotal $

Total $
(Use only on last page of the completed Schedule F.)
(Report also on Summary of Schedules and, if applicable on the Statistical Summary of Certain Liabilities and Related Data.)

151. Schedule G–Executory Contracts and Unexpired Leases

Form B6G
(10/05)

In re _____,   Case No._____
             Debtor　　　　　　　　　　　　　　　　　　　　　　　　　**(if known)**

SCHEDULE G - EXECUTORY CONTRACTS AND UNEXPIRED LEASES

Describe all executory contracts of any nature and all unexpired leases of real or personal property. Include any timeshare interests. State nature of debtor's interest in contract, i.e., "Purchaser," "Agent," etc. State whether debtor is the lessor or lessee of a lease. Provide the names and complete mailing addresses of all other parties to each lease or contract described. If a minor child is a party to one of the leases or contracts, indicate that by stating "a minor child" and do not disclose the child's name. See 11 U.S.C. § 112; Fed.R. Bankr. P. 1007(m).

☐ Check this box if debtor has no executory contracts or unexpired leases.

NAME AND MAILING ADDRESS, INCLUDING ZIP CODE, OF OTHER PARTIES TO LEASE OR CONTRACT.	DESCRIPTION OF CONTRACT OR LEASE AND NATURE OF DEBTOR'S INTEREST. STATE WHETHER LEASE IS FOR NONRESIDENTIAL REAL PROPERTY. STATE CONTRACT NUMBER OF ANY GOVERNMENT CONTRACT.

152. Schedule H—Codebtors

Form B6H
(10/05)

In re _____ ,   Case No. _____
                    Debtor   **(if known)**

SCHEDULE H - CODEBTORS

Provide the information requested concerning any person or entity, other than a spouse in a joint case, that is also liable on any debts listed by debtor in the schedules of creditors. Include all guarantors and co-signers. If the debtor resides or resided in a community property state, commonwealth, or territory (including Alaska, Arizona, California, Idaho, Louisiana, Nevada, New Mexico, Puerto Rico, Texas, Washington, or Wisconsin) within the eight year period immediately preceding the commencement of the case, identify the name of the debtor's spouse and of any former spouse who resides or resided with the debtor in the community property state, commonwealth, or territory. Include all names used by the nondebtor spouse during the eight years immediately preceding the commencement of this case. If a minor child is a codebtor or a creditor, indicate that by stating "a minor child" and do not disclose the child's name. See 11 U.S.C. § 112; Fed. Bankr. P. 1007(m).

☐ Check this box if debtor has no codebtors.

NAME AND ADDRESS OF CODEBTOR	NAME AND ADDRESS OF CREDITOR

153. Schedule I—Current Income of Individual Debtor(s)

Official Form 6I (10/06)

In re _____ ,   Case No. _____
                    Debtor   **(if known)**

SCHEDULE I - CURRENT INCOME OF INDIVIDUAL DEBTOR(S)

The column labeled "Spouse" must be completed in all cases filed by joint debtors and by every married debtor, whether or not a joint petition is filed, unless the spouses are separated and a joint petition is not filed. Do not state the name of any minor child.

Debtor's Marital Status:	DEPENDENTS OF DEBTOR AND SPOUSE	
	RELATIONSHIP(S):	AGE(S):

Employment: Occupation	DEBTOR	SPOUSE
Name of Employer		
How long employed		
Address of Employer		

INCOME: (Estimate of average or projected monthly income at time case filed)	DEBTOR	SPOUSE
1. Monthly gross wages, salary, and commissions (Prorate if not paid monthly)	$_____	$_____
2. Estimate monthly overtime	$_____	$_____
3. SUBTOTAL	$_____	$_____
4. LESS PAYROLL DEDUCTIONS		
a. Payroll taxes and social security	$_____	$_____
b. Insurance	$_____	$_____
c. Union dues	$_____	$_____
d. Other (Specify): _____	$_____	$_____
5. SUBTOTAL OF PAYROLL DEDUCTIONS	$_____	$_____
6. TOTAL NET MONTHLY TAKE HOME PAY	$_____	$_____
7. Regular income from operation of business or profession or farm (Attach detailed statement)	$_____	$_____
8. Income from real property	$_____	$_____
9. Interest and dividends	$_____	$_____
10. Alimony, maintenance or support payments payable to the debtor for the debtor's use or that of dependents listed above	$_____	$_____
11. Social security or government assistance (Specify):_____	$_____	$_____
12. Pension or retirement income	$_____	$_____
13. Other monthly income (Specify):_____	$_____	$_____
14. SUBTOTAL OF LINES 7 THROUGH 13	$_____	$_____
15. AVERAGE MONTHLY INCOME (Add amounts shown on lines 6 and 14)	$_____	$_____
16. COMBINED AVERAGE MONTHLY INCOME: (Combine column totals from line 15; if there is only one debtor repeat total reported on line 15)	$_____	

(Report also on Summary of Schedules and, if applicable, on Statistical Summary of Certain Liabilities and Related Data)

17. Describe any increase or decrease in income reasonably anticipated to occur within the year following the filing of this document:

_____

_____

154. Schedule J–Current Expenditures of Individual Debtor(s)

Official Form 6J (10/06)

In re _____ ,   Case No._____
        Debtor   **(if known)**

SCHEDULE J - CURRENT EXPENDITURES OF INDIVIDUAL DEBTOR(S)

Complete this schedule by estimating the average or projected monthly expenses of the debtor and the debtor's family at time case filed. Prorate any payments made bi-weekly, quarterly, semi-annually, or annually to show monthly rate.

☐   Check this box if a joint petition is filed and debtor's spouse maintains a separate household. Complete a separate schedule of expenditures labeled "Spouse."

1. Rent or home mortgage payment (include lot rented for mobile home) $ _____
    a. Are real estate taxes included?   Yes _____   No _____
    b. Is property insurance included?   Yes _____   No _____
2. Utilities: a. Electricity and heating fuel $ _____
          b. Water and sewer $ _____
          c. Telephone $ _____
          d. Other _____ $ _____
3. Home maintenance (repairs and upkeep) $ _____
4. Food $ _____
5. Clothing $ _____
6. Laundry and dry cleaning $ _____
7. Medical and dental expenses $ _____
8. Transportation (not including car payments) $ _____
9. Recreation, clubs and entertainment, newspapers, magazines, etc. $ _____
10. Charitable contributions $ _____
11. Insurance (not deducted from wages or included in home mortgage payments)
        a. Homeowner's or renter's $ _____
        b. Life $ _____
        c. Health $ _____
        d. Auto $ _____
        e. Other _____ $ _____
12. Taxes (not deducted from wages or included in home mortgage payments)
(Specify) _____ $ _____
13. Installment payments: (In chapter 11, 12, and 13 cases, do not list payments to be included in the plan)
        a. Auto $ _____
        b. Other _____ $ _____
        c. Other _____ , $ _____
14. Alimony, maintenance, and support paid to others $ _____
15. Payments for support of additional dependents not living at your home $ _____
16. Regular expenses from operation of business, profession, or farm (attach detailed statement) $ _____
17. Other _____ $ _____
18. AVERAGE MONTHLY EXPENSES (Total lines 1-17. Report also on Summary of Schedules and, $ _____
    if applicable, on the Statistical Summary of Certain Liabilities and Related Data.)
19. Describe any increase or decrease in expenditures reasonably anticipated to occur within the year following the filing of this document:
_____
_____

20. STATEMENT OF MONTHLY NET INCOME
    a. Average monthly income from Line 15 of Schedule I $ _____
    b. Average monthly expenses from Line 18 above $ _____
    c. Monthly net income (a. minus b.) $ _____

155. Declaration Concerning Debtor's Schedules

Official Form 6 - Declaration (10/06)

In re _____ ,   Case No. _____
        Debtor   **(if known)**

DECLARATION CONCERNING DEBTOR'S SCHEDULES

DECLARATION UNDER PENALTY OF PERJURY BY INDIVIDUAL DEBTOR

I declare under penalty of perjury that I have read the foregoing summary and schedules, consisting of ____ sheets (*total shown on summary page plus 2*), and that they are true and correct to the best of my knowledge, information, and belief.

Date _____   Signature: _____
                                           Debtor

Date _____   Signature: _____
                                      (Joint Debtor, if any)

[If joint case, both spouses must sign.]

DECLARATION AND SIGNATURE OF NON-ATTORNEY BANKRUPTCY PETITION PREPARER (See 11 U.S.C. § 110)

I declare under penalty of perjury that: (1) I am a bankruptcy petition preparer as defined in 11 U.S.C. § 110; (2) I prepared this document for compensation and have provided the debtor with a copy of this document and the notices and information required under 11 U.S.C. §§ 110(b), 110(h) and 342(b); and, (3) if rules or guidelines have been promulgated pursuant to 11 U.S.C. § 110(h) setting a maximum fee for services chargeable by bankruptcy petition preparers, I have given the debtor notice of the maximum amount before preparing any document for filing for a debtor or accepting any fee from the debtor, as required by that section.

_____   _____
Printed or Typed Name and Title, if any,   Social Security No.
of Bankruptcy Petition Preparer   *(Required by 11 U.S.C. § 110.)*

If the bankruptcy petition preparer is not an individual, state the name, title (if any), address, and social security number of the officer, principal, responsible person, or partner who signs this document.

_____
_____
_____
Address

X _____   _____
  Signature of Bankruptcy Petition Preparer   Date

Names and Social Security numbers of all other individuals who prepared or assisted in preparing this document, unless the bankruptcy petition preparer is not an individual:

If more than one person prepared this document, attach additional signed sheets conforming to the appropriate Official Form for each person.

A bankruptcy petition preparer's failure to comply with the provisions of title 11 and the Federal Rules of Bankruptcy Procedure may result in fines or imprisonment or both. 11 U.S.C. § 110; 18 U.S.C. § 156.

DECLARATION UNDER PENALTY OF PERJURY ON BEHALF OF A CORPORATION OR PARTNERSHIP

I, the _____ [the president or other officer or an authorized agent of the corporation or a member or an authorized agent of the partnership] of the _____ [corporation or partnership] named as debtor in this case, declare under penalty of perjury that I have read the foregoing summary and schedules, consisting of ____ sheets (*total shown on summary page plus 1*), and that they are true and correct to the best of my knowledge, information, and belief.

Date _____

        Signature: _____

                     _____
                     [Print or type name of individual signing on behalf of debtor.]

[An individual signing on behalf of a partnership or corporation must indicate position or relationship to debtor.]

Penalty for making a false statement or concealing property: Fine of up to $500,000 or imprisonment for up to 5 years or both. 18 U.S.C. §§ 152 and 3571.

156. Notice of Chapter 11 Bankruptcy Case, Meeting of Creditors and Debtors

FORM B9F (Chapter 11 Corporation/Partnership Case (10/05))

UNITED STATES BANKRUPTCY COURT_____ **District of**_____

<table>
<tr><td colspan="2" align="center">**Notice of**
Chapter 11 Bankruptcy Case, Meeting of Creditors, & Deadlines</td></tr>
<tr><td colspan="2">[A chapter 11 bankruptcy case concerning the debtor(s) listed below was filed on _____ (date).]
or [A bankruptcy case concerning the debtor(s) listed below was originally filed under chapter_____ on _____ (date) and was converted to a case under chapter 11 on_____ .]

You may be a creditor of the debtor. **This notice lists important deadlines.** You may want to consult an attorney to protect your rights. All documents filed in the case may be inspected at the bankruptcy clerk's office at the address listed below.
NOTE: The staff of the bankruptcy clerk's office cannot give legal advice.</td></tr>
<tr><td colspan="2" align="center">See Reverse Side for Important Explanations</td></tr>
<tr><td>Debtor(s) (name(s) and address):</td><td>Case Number:</td></tr>
<tr><td></td><td>Last four digits of Social Security No./Complete EIN or other Taxpayer ID No.:</td></tr>
<tr><td>All other names used by the Debtor(s) in the last 8 years (include trade names):</td><td>Attorney for Debtor(s) (name and address):</td></tr>
<tr><td>Telephone number:</td><td>Telephone number:</td></tr>
</table>

Meeting of Creditors

Date: / /   Time: ( ) A. M.   Location:
                                    ( ) P. M.

Deadline to File a Proof of Claim

Proof of Claim must be *received* by the bankruptcy clerk's office by the following deadline:

Notice of deadline will be sent at a later time.

Foreign Creditors

A creditor to whom this notice is sent at a foreign address should read the information under "Claims" on the reverse side.

Deadline to File a Complaint to Determine Dischargeability of Certain Debts:

Creditors May Not Take Certain Actions:

In most instances, the filing of the bankruptcy case automatically stays certain collection and other actions against the debtor and the debtor's property. Under certain circumstances, the stay may be limited to 30 days or not exist at all, although the debtor can request the court to extend or impose a stay. If you attempt to collect a debt or take other action in violation of the Bankruptcy Code, you may be penalized. Consult a lawyer to determine your rights in this case.

<table>
<tr><td>**Address of the Bankruptcy Clerk's Office:**</td><td colspan="2" align="center">**For the Court:**</td></tr>
<tr><td></td><td colspan="2">Clerk of the Bankruptcy Court:</td></tr>
<tr><td>**Telephone number:**</td><td></td></tr>
<tr><td>Hours Open:</td><td>Date:</td></tr>
</table>

157. Order and Notice for Hearing on Disclosure Statement

Official Form 12
(12/03)

Form 12. ORDER AND NOTICE FOR HEARING
ON DISCLOSURE STATEMENT

[Caption as in Form 16A]

ORDER AND NOTICE FOR HEARING
ON DISCLOSURE STATEMENT

To the debtor, its creditors, and other parties in interest:

A disclosure statement and a plan under chapter 11 [*or* chapter 9] of the Bankruptcy Code having been filed by
_____ on _____ ,

IT IS ORDERED and notice is hereby given, that:

1. The hearing to consider the approval of the disclosure statement shall be held at:
_____ , on _____ , at _____ o'clock ___.m.

2. _____ is fixed as the last day for filing and serving in accordance with Fed.
R. Bankr. P. 3017(a) written objections to the disclosure statement.

3. Within _____ days after entry of this order, the disclosure statement and plan shall be distributed
in accordance with Fed. R. Bankr. P. 3017(a).

4. Requests for copies of the disclosure statement and plan shall be mailed to the debtor in possession [*or*
trustee *or* debtor *or* _____] at * _____ .

Dated: _____

BY THE COURT

_____
United States Bankruptcy Judge

* State mailing address

158. Ballot for Accepting or Rejecting Plan of Reorganization

Official Form 14
(12/03)

Form 14. CLASS [ ] BALLOT FOR ACCEPTING OR REJECTING PLAN OF REORGANIZATION

[Caption as in Form 16A]

CLASS [ ] BALLOT FOR ACCEPTING OR REJECTING PLAN OF REORGANIZATION

[Proponent] filed a plan of reorganization dated *[Date]* (the "Plan") for the Debtor in this case. The Court has *[conditionally]* approved a disclosure statement with respect to the Plan (the "Disclosure Statement"). The Disclosure Statement provides information to assist you in deciding how to vote your ballot. If you do not have a Disclosure Statement, you may obtain a copy from *[name, address, telephone number and telecopy number of proponent/proponent's attorney.]* Court approval of the disclosure statement does not indicate approval of the Plan by the Court.

You should review the Disclosure Statement and the Plan before you vote. You may wish to seek legal advice concerning the Plan and your classification and treatment under the Plan. Your *[claim] [equity interest]* has been placed in class [ ] under the Plan. If you hold claims or equity interests in more than one class, you will receive a ballot for each class in which you are entitled to vote.

If your ballot is not received by *[name and address of proponent's attorney or other appropriate address]* on or before *[date]*, and such deadline is not extended, your vote will not count as either an acceptance or rejection of the Plan.

If the Plan is confirmed by the Bankruptcy Court it will be binding on you whether or not you vote.

ACCEPTANCE OR REJECTION OF THE PLAN

[At this point the ballot should provide for voting by the particular class of creditors or equity holders receiving the ballot using one of the following alternatives;]

[If the voter is the holder of a secured, priority, or unsecured nonpriority claim:]

The undersigned, the holder of a Class [ ] claim against the Debtor in the unpaid amount of Dollars ($)

[or, if the voter is the holder of a bond, debenture, or other debt security:]

The undersigned, the holder of a Class [ ] claim against the Debtor, consisting of Dollars ($) principal amount of *[describe bond, debenture, or other debt security]* of the Debtor (For purposes of this Ballot, it is not necessary and you should not adjust the principal amount for any accrued or unmatured interest.)

[or, if the voter is the holder of an equity interest:]

The undersigned, the holder of Class [ ] equity interest in the Debtor, consisting of _____ shares or other interests of *[describe equity interest]* in the Debtor

Official Form 14 continued
(12/03)

[In each case, the following language should be included:]

(Check one box only)

[ ] ACCEPTS THE PLAN   [ ] REJECTS THE PLAN

Dated: _____

Print or type name: _____

Signature: _____

Title (if corporation or partnership) _____

Address: _____

_____

RETURN THIS BALLOT TO:

[Name and address of proponent's attorney or other appropriate address]

159. Order for Relief in an Involuntary Bankruptcy Case

B 253
(8/96)

United States Bankruptcy Court

_____ District of _____

In re

Case No. _____

Debtor
Address:
Social Security No.:
Employer Tax I.D. No.:

Chapter _____

ORDER FOR RELIEF IN
AN INVOLUNTARY CASE

On consideration of the petition filed on _____ against
(date)
the above-named debtor, an order for relief under chapter _____ of the Bankruptcy Code (title 11
of the United States Code) is granted.

_____   _____
Date   Bankruptcy Judge

160. Proof of Claim Form

FORM 10 (Official Form 10) (10/05)

UNITED STATES BANKRUPTCY COURT _____ DISTRICT OF _____	PROOF OF CLAIM

Name of Debtor	Case Number	

NOTE: This form should not be used to make a claim for an administrative expense arising after the commencement of the case. A "request" for payment of an administrative expense may be filed pursuant to 11 U.S.C. § 503.

Name of Creditor (The person or other entity to whom the debtor owes money or property):	□ Check box if you are aware that anyone else has filed a proof of claim relating to your claim. Attach copy of statement giving particulars.	
Name and address where notices should be sent:	□ Check box if you have never received any notices from the bankruptcy court in this case.	
	□ Check box if the address differs from the address on the envelope sent to you by the court.	THIS SPACE IS FOR COURT USE ONLY
Telephone number:		

Last four digits of account or other number by which creditor identifies debtor:	Check here □ replaces if this claim □ amends a previously filed claim, dated:_____

1. Basis for Claim
- □ Goods sold
- □ Services performed
- □ Money loaned
- □ Personal injury/wrongful death
- □ Taxes
- □ Other_____

- □ Retiree benefits as defined in 11 U.S.C. § 1114(a)
- □ Wages, salaries, and compensation (fill out below)
  Last four digits of your SS #:____
  Unpaid compensation for services performed
  from _____ to _____
        (date)   (date)

2. Date debt was incurred:	**3. If court judgment, date obtained:**

4. Classification of Claim. Check the appropriate box or boxes that best describe your claim and state the amount of the claim at the time the case was filed. See reverse side for important explanations.

Unsecured Nonpriority Claim $_____

□ Check this box if: a) there is no collateral or lien securing your claim, or b) your claim exceeds the value of the property securing it, or c) none or only part of your claim is entitled to priority.

Unsecured Priority Claim

□ Check this box if you have an unsecured claim, all or part of which is entitled to priority.

Amount entitled to priority $_____

Specify the priority of the claim:

□ Domestic support obligations under 11 U.S.C. § 507(a)(1)(A) or (a)(1)(B).

□ Wages, salaries, or commissions (up to $10,000),* earned within 180 days before filing of the bankruptcy petition or cessation of the debtor's business, whichever is earlier - 11 U.S.C. § 507(a)(4).

□ Contributions to an employee benefit plan - 11 U.S.C. § 507(a)(5).

Secured Claim

□ Check this box if your claim is secured by collateral (including a right of setoff).

    Brief Description of Collateral:
    □ Real Estate   □ Motor Vehicle   □ Other_____

    Value of Collateral: $_____

Amount of arrearage and other charges <u>at time case filed</u> included in secured claim, if any: $_____

□ Up to $2,225* of deposits toward purchase, lease, or rental of property or services for personal, family, or household use - 11 U.S.C. § 507(a)(7).

□ Taxes or penalties owed to governmental units - 11 U.S.C. § 507(a)(8).

□ Other – Specify applicable paragraph of 11 U.S.C. § 507(a)(___).

Amounts are subject to adjustment on 4/1/07 and every 3 years thereafter with respect to cases commenced on or after the date of adjustment.

5. Total Amount of Claim at Time Case Filed: $_____ _____ _____ _____
                   (unsecured)   (secured)   (priority)   (total)
□ Check this box if claim includes interest or other charges in addition to the principal amount of the claim. Attach itemized statement of all interest or additional charges.

6. Credits: The amount of all payments on this claim has been credited and deducted for the purpose of making this proof of claim.

7. Supporting Documents: *Attach copies of supporting documents,* such as promissory notes, purchase orders, invoices, itemized statements of running accounts, contracts, court judgments, mortgages, security agreements, and evidence of perfection of lien. DO NOT SEND ORIGINAL DOCUMENTS. If the documents are not available, explain. If the documents are voluminous, attach a summary.

8. Date-Stamped Copy: To receive an acknowledgment of the filing of your claim, enclose a stamped, self-addressed envelope and copy of this proof of claim.

THIS SPACE IS FOR COURT USE ONLY

Date	Sign and print the name and title, if any, of the creditor or other person authorized to file this claim (attach copy of power of attorney, if any):

Penalty for presenting fraudulent claim: Fine of up to $500,000 or imprisonment for up to 5 years, or both. 18 U.S.C. §§ 152 and 3571.

FORM 10 (Official Form 10) (10/05)

INSTRUCTIONS FOR PROOF OF CLAIM FORM

The instructions and definitions below are general explanations of the law. In particular types of cases or circumstances, such as bankruptcy cases that are not filed voluntarily by a debtor, there may be exceptions to these general rules.

------ DEFINITIONS ------

Debtor

The person, corporation, or other entity that has filed a bankruptcy case is called the debtor.

Creditor

A creditor is any person, corporation, or other entity to whom the debtor owed a debt on the date that the bankruptcy case was filed.

Proof of Claim

A form telling the bankruptcy court how much the debtor owed a creditor at the time the bankruptcy case was filed (the amount of the creditor's claim). This form must be filed with the clerk of the bankruptcy court where the bankruptcy case was filed.

Secured Claim

A claim is a secured claim to the extent that the creditor has a lien on property of the debtor (collateral) that gives the creditor the right to be paid from that property before creditors who do not have liens on the property.

Examples of liens are a mortgage on real estate and a security interest in a car, truck, boat, television set, or other item of property. A lien may have been obtained through a court proceeding before the bankruptcy case began; in some states a court judgment is a lien. In addition, to the extent a creditor also owes money to the debtor (has a right of setoff), the creditor's claim may be a secured claim. (See also *Unsecured Claim.*)

Unsecured Claim

If a claim is not a secured claim it is an unsecured claim. A claim may be partly secured and partly unsecured if the property on which a creditor has a lien is not worth enough to pay the creditor in full.

Unsecured Priority Claim

Certain types of unsecured claims are given priority, so they are to be paid in bankruptcy cases before most other unsecured claims (if there is sufficient money or property available to pay these claims). The most common types of priority claims are listed on the proof of claim form. Unsecured claims that are not specifically given priority status by the bankruptcy laws are classified as *Unsecured Nonpriority Claims.*

Items to be completed in Proof of Claim form (if not already filled in)

Court, Name of Debtor, and Case Number:
Fill in the name of the federal judicial district where the bankruptcy case was filed (for example, Central District of California), the name of the debtor in the bankruptcy case, and the bankruptcy case number. If you received a notice of the case from the court, all of this information is near the top of the notice.

Information about Creditor:
Complete the section giving the name, address, and telephone number of the creditor to whom the debtor owes money or property, and the debtor's account number, if any. If anyone else has already filed a proof of claim relating to this debt, if you never received notices from the bankruptcy court about this case, if your address differs from that to which the court sent notice, or if this proof of claim replaces or changes a proof of claim that was already filed, check the appropriate box on the form.

1. **Basis for Claim:**
   Check the type of debt for which the proof of claim is being filed. If the type of debt is not listed, check "Other" and briefly describe the type of debt. If you were an employee of the debtor, fill in the last four digits of your social security number and the dates of work for which you were not paid.

2. **Date Debt Incurred:**
   Fill in the date when the debt first was owed by the debtor.

3. **Court Judgments:**
   If you have a court judgment for this debt, state the date the court entered the judgment.

4. **Classification of Claim:**
   Secured Claim:
   Check the appropriate place if the claim is a secured claim. You must state the type and value of property that is collateral for the claim, attach copies of the documentation of your lien, and state the amount past due on the claim as of the date the bankruptcy case was

filed. A claim may be partly secured and partly unsecured. (See DEFINITIONS, above).

   Unsecured Priority Claim:
   Check the appropriate place if you have an unsecured priority claim, and state the amount entitled to priority. (See DEFINITIONS, above). A claim may be partly priority and partly nonpriority if, for example, the claim is for more than the amount given priority by the law. Check the appropriate place to specify the type of priority claim.

   Unsecured Nonpriority Claim:
   Check the appropriate place if you have an unsecured nonpriority claim, sometimes referred to as a "general unsecured claim." (See DEFINITIONS, above.) If your claim is partly secured and partly unsecured, state here the amount that is unsecured. If part of your claim is entitled to priority, state here the amount **not** entitled to priority.

5. **Total Amount of Claim at Time Case Filed:**
   Fill in the total amount of the entire claim. If interest or other charges in addition to the principal amount of the claim are included, check the appropriate place on the form and attach an itemization of the interest and charges.

6. **Credits:**
   By signing this proof of claim, you are stating under oath that in calculating the amount of your claim you have given the debtor credit for all payments received from the debtor.

7. **Supporting Documents:**
   You must attach to this proof of claim form copies of documents that show the debtor owes the debt claimed or, if the documents are too lengthy, a summary of those documents. If documents are not available, you must attach an explanation of why they are not available.

161. Summons in an Adversary Proceeding

B 250A
(8/96)

United States Bankruptcy Court

_____ District of_____

In re _____,)
                        Debtor   )   Case No. _____
)
)   Chapter _____
)
     _____,   )
                        Plaintiff   )
)
          v.   )
)
     _____,   )   Adv. Proc. No. _____
                        Defendant   )

SUMMONS IN AN ADVERSARY PROCEEDING

YOU ARE SUMMONED and required to file a motion or answer to the complaint which is attached to this summons with the clerk of the bankruptcy court within 30 days after the date of issuance of this summons, except that the United States and its offices and agencies shall file a motion or answer to the complaint within 35 days.

```
Address of Clerk




```

At the same time, you must also serve a copy of the motion or answer upon the plaintiff's attorney.

```
Name and Address of Plaintiff's Attorney




```

If you make a motion, your time to answer is governed by Fed. R. Bankr. P. 7012.

IF YOU FAIL TO RESPOND TO THIS SUMMONS, YOUR FAILURE WILL BE DEEMED TO BE YOUR CONSENT TO ENTRY OF A JUDGMENT BY THE BANKRUPTCY COURT AND JUDGMENT BY DEFAULT MAY BE TAKEN AGAINST YOU FOR THE RELIEF DEMANDED IN THE COMPLAINT.

_____
Clerk of the Bankruptcy Court

_____   By: _____
        Date   Deputy Clerk

CERTIFICATE OF SERVICE

I, _____, certify that I am, and at all times during the
(name)

service of process was, not less than 18 years of age and not a party to the matter concerning which service of process was made. I further certify that the service of this summons and a copy of the complaint was made
_____ by:
(date)

☐ Mail Service: Regular, first class United States mail, postage fully pre-paid, addressed to:

☐ Personal Service: By leaving the process with defendant or with an officer or agent of defendant at:

☐ Residence Service: By leaving the process with the following adult at:

☐ Certified Mail Service on an Insured Depository Institution: By sending the process by certified mail addressed to the following officer of the defendant at:

☐ Publication: The defendant was served as follows: [Describe briefly]

☐ State Law: The defendant was served pursuant to the laws of the State of _____,
as follows: [Describe briefly]   (name of state)

Under penalty of perjury, I declare that the foregoing is true and correct.

_____   _____
Date   Signature

Print Name		
Business Address		
City	State	Zip

162. Order Conditionally Approving Disclosure Statement

Form B 13S
12/94

United States Bankruptcy Court

_____ District of _____

In re

Case No. _____

Debtor*
Address:
Social Security No(s).:
Employer's Tax Identification No(s). [if any]:

Chapter 11
(Small Business)

ORDER CONDITIONALLY APPROVING DISCLOSURE STATEMENT, FIXING TIME FOR FILING ACCEPTANCES OR REJECTIONS OF PLAN, AND FIXING THE TIME FOR FILING OBJECTIONS TO THE DISCLOSURE STATEMENT AND TO THE CONFIRMATION OF THE PLAN, COMBINED WITH NOTICE THEREOF AND OF THE HEARING ON FINAL APPROVAL OF THE DISCLOSURE STATEMENT AND THE HEARING ON CONFIRMATION OF THE PLAN

A disclosure statement under chapter 11 of the Bankruptcy Code having been filed by _____-
_____, on _____ with respect to a plan under chapter 11 of the
Code filed by _____, on _____; and the debtor being, and having
elected to be considered, a small business:

IT IS ORDERED, and notice is hereby given, that:

A. The disclosure statement filed by _____ is conditionally approved.

B. _____ is fixed as the last day for filing written acceptances or rejections of
the plan referred to above.

C. Within _____ days after the entry of this order, the plan, the disclosure statement and a ballot
conforming to Official Form 14 shall be mailed to creditors, equity security holders, and other parties in interest, and shall
be transmitted to the United States trustee.

D. _____ is fixed for the hearing
on final approval of the disclosure statement (if a written objection has been timely filed) and for the hearing on
confirmation of the plan.

E. _____ is fixed as the last day for filing and serving written objections to
the disclosure statement and confirmation of the plan.

Dated: _____

BY THE COURT

_____
United States Bankruptcy Judge

_____
**Set forth all names, including trade names, used by the debtor within the last 6 years. (Fed. R. Bankr. P. 1005). For joint debtors, set forth
both social security numbers.*

163. Order Finally Approving Disclosure Statement and Confirming Plan

Form B 15S
12/94

United States Bankruptcy Court
_____ District Of _____

In re

Debtor*
Address:
Social Security No(s).:
Employer's Tax I.D. No(s). [if any]:

Case No. _____

Chapter 11
(Small Business)

ORDER FINALLY APPROVING DISCLOSURE STATEMENT AND CONFIRMING PLAN

The plan under chapter 11 of the Bankruptcy Code filed by _____, on _____ having been transmitted to creditors and equity security holders together with a copy of the disclosure statement conditionally approved by court on _____; and

It having been determined after notice and a hearing that the requirements for final approval of the disclosure statement have been satisfied, and it having been determined after a hearing on notice that the requirements for confirmation of the plan under 11 U.S.C. § 1129 have been satisfied;

IT IS ORDERED that:

The disclosure statement filed by _____ on _____ is finally approved, and

The plan filed by _____, on _____, *[If appropriate, include dates and any other pertinent details of modifications to the plan] is confirmed.* A copy of the confirmed plan is attached.

Dated: _____

BY THE COURT

_____
United States Bankruptcy Judge.

*Set forth all names, including trade names, used by the debtor within the last 6 years. (Fed. R. Bankr. P. 1005). For joint debtors, set forth both social security numbers.